HISTORY
as an ART of
MEMORY

HISTORY
as an ART of
MEMORY

Patrick H. Hutton

University Press of New England

HANOVER AND LONDON

University of Vermont

Published by University Press of New England, Hanover, NH 03755

© 1993 by Trustees of University of Vermont

Printed in the United States of America   5   4   3   2

CIP data appear at the end of the book

Portions of this book have earlier appeared in the learned journals, among them *Historical Reflections / Réflexions Historiques, History and Memory, History and Theory,* and the *Journal of the History of Ideas.* I have also borrowed a short passage from my essay in *The Technologies of the Self: A Seminar with Michel Foucault,* published by the University of Massachusetts Press. I am grateful to the editors of these publications for permission to republish this material here.

For my mother Virginia,

in memory of my father John

CONTENTS

A JOURNEY OUT OF
LOCAL MEMORY

I have always cherished local memories for the way they lead into a larger past. I grew up in what remains for me an enchanted landscape. Princeton, New Jersey, where I was raised, was saturated with commemorative places, to which a wonderful, old teacher, Lilian Wakefield, led me and my third-grade classmates on her last walking tour of the historic houses of old Princeton. Then there is my Irish heritage, with its sentimental lore, though this past is more obscure. On my mother's side we had a famous ancestor, Thomas Francis Meagher, of Young Ireland fame in 1848 and who later played a less distinguished role as a Union general in the War Between the States. He was handsome and dashing, and, from the many images we have of him, one might presume that he liked to be photographed. But most of the family history beyond three generations of genealogical tracing was forever lost. My father would occasionally mention a paternal grandfather he had never known, Tom Hutton, remembered fondly by a family friend, old Pete Yates, who had admired him when he himself was a young man. The Huttons, it seems, were horse people—blacksmiths and trainers. It was difficult to know much about them, my father observed. They were humble people, not given to memorable accomplishments.

I prided myself on the strength of my memory when I was young, a gift nurtured by a love of history, a fascination with geography, and, with a certain apprehension, the training of my rote memory in catechismal classes. My memory served me well through school and college, and it must have played a role in my eventual choice of history as a vocation. But in middle age, I recognized that my memory was changing. My powers of recall were not as quick as they had once been. As Sigmund Freud observed, memory becomes less efficient with age. At the same time, I found that I could place what I was learning in surer contexts. If there was a history to the changes in my own memory, I wondered, was it not analogous in some way to that of the changes in the collective memory of societies at large?

The phenomenon about which I puzzled concerned the dynamics of tradition, though I identified it as such only by a circuitous route. My path into the memory problem was by way of the history of collective mentalities, a subject I discovered during a year in France while directing a junior year abroad program in the late 1970s. The field considers the mores with which we live and the attitudes we bring to life's major passages—interests I identified with recollections of my own upbringing. I had little time for research that year, but I made time to read the pioneering works by Lucien Febvre, Marc Bloch, Philippe Ariès, Emmanuel Le Roy Ladurie, and Norbert Elias who set forth guidelines to its domains. I quickly saw the significance of their investigations for understanding the nature of tradition, a realm of history spurned by the professional historians of the 1960s, but that roused my curiosity for my own lingering attachments to a religious tradition from which I sensed myself to be intellectually emancipated and a family one from which I was geographically separated. Later, I tried to reestablish connections with these traditions of my youth through personal pilgrimages. Retreats to a Trappist monastery put me in touch with the medieval sources of the living tradition from which my faith had sprung, and visits to the places of my memory around Princeton quickened nostalgia, together with a recognition of how small was the scale of the landscape I had loved as a wide-eyed child.

My interest in tradition, of course, related to scholarly projects as well. At the University of Wisconsin, I was trained in the positivist ways of French historiography as they had filtered through American Ph.D. programs during the 1960s—specialized research overlaid with a vaguely Marxist mystique. Training in techniques of quantification as a preparation for research in economic and social history was then in vogue. As the venerable dean of French Revolutionary studies Georges Lefebvre admonished our generation, "if you want to become an historian, you must learn to count." But even within this genre of French history, I found that the topics that interested me the most were those with attachments to traditionalist perspectives on the past. I couldn't deny this interest, even in the studies of the French Left to which I was directed by my mentors. As a student of the French Revolution, my interests eventually gravitated to the revolutionary tradition through which its political ambitions were continued into the nineteenth century. That is how I became interested in the Blanquists, a quixotic band of insurrectionists who harassed the officials of the Second Empire, fought for the Commune of Paris, and eventually became the guardians of the revolutionary tradition for a socialist movement that no longer considered popular insurrection a political alternative to be encouraged. I wrote a book on their role in French politics, published over a decade ago. From my present vantage point, it was the right topic for my development as a scholar—but the wrong time for its reception by the world of scholarship. The problem of tradition, with its vital claims on collective memory, was not yet one on which the academy was ready to focus its attention.

But the time of the memory topic was about to come, as scholars began to see its relationship to the history of collective mentalities. By the early 1980s, I was teaching a seminar on recent studies in this field. Although the course was broadly conceived, a colleague, Janet Whatley, suggested to me that memory was its missing dimension and referred me to the book by Michel Beaujour, *Miroirs d'encre,* a study of the mnemonic underpinnings of autobiography. Beaujour's book raised interesting issues about the role of memory in the developing notion of the self from the eighteenth century. But his sensitivity to the cultural implications of the topic was an exception; moreover, his was a literary study apart from the historiographical field I was investigating. Therein the notion of memory rarely surfaced. As theoretical discussions of mentalities as a genre of history got underway, many of the critics presented it as something other than what it appeared to be at face value or as described in the autobiographical memoirs of its pioneering practitioners—a study of the workings of tradition. Some were determined to reconcile its insights and methods with positivist practice and so to crowd memory out of its history. Its research problems were formidable, some argued, characterizing it not as a topic of interest but as a stage of initiation into more sophisticated research techniques—"*recherches au troisième niveau.*"

As I launched my inquiry into the topic of memory, I discovered that it was the quintessential interdisciplinary interest. It was a topic for everyone over which no one was able to exercise a preemptive claim. I began with the book by Frances Yates on the revival of the art of memory during the Renaissance. The art had long been proffered as a practical technique to aid the rhetoricians' systematic recall. But in their mnemonic schemes, Yates noted especially the cosmological speculations they were designed not only to preserve but also to hide. In its Renaissance applications, she argued, the art of memory provides testimony of a sixteenth-century counterculture whose history has gone unrecognized, comprising such forgotten fields as alchemy, astrology, cabalism, and magic. The art, once a key to their workings, became in Yates's splendid studies a key to their history, opening a prospect on an unseen land of hermetic knowledge. Yates showed the wider horizons of the high culture of the Renaissance by following paths that generally led its philosophers nowhere, or elsewhere in roundabout ways.

Using Yates as a point of departure, I began my inquiry into the hidden mnemonic techniques in modern cultural practices—autobiography, psychoanalysis, commemoration. In one of my early essays on the subject, a charitable critic pointed out the significance of the orality/literacy problem as an essential context for any consideration of the properties of memory. The suggestion led me to the wonderful books by Eric Havelock and Walter Ong that enabled me to see how memory was conceived in oral tradition and how the uses of memory had been transformed historically by innovations in the technologies of communication. I immediately saw the connections between this approach to the refashioning of mnemonic capabilities and my earlier work on Giambattista Vico's ideas on the modification of the human mind. Vico was a philosopher to whom I was particularly drawn and in whose ideas I had been immersed since graduate school. He was certain to be a key figure in the larger study of memory and mentalities that I was beginning to sketch.

There were other authors who helped me to block out the dimensions of the memory topic. Philippe Ariès's traditionalist histories particularly interested me and led me to his historiographical and autobiographical writings with their many insights into the memory/history problem. These writings had been overlooked in the critics' assessments of his well-known studies of childhood and family. I also looked into the work on collective memory by Maurice Halbwachs, a sociologist whose circuitous style beclouded my first efforts to appreciate his insight into this topic. My work on memory also gave me a perspective on the philosophical and historiographical ideas of Michel Foucault, in whose faculty seminar at the University of Vermont in 1982 on the "technologies of the self" I was privileged to participate. I had read his early work in my explorations of the historiographical dimensions of the history of mentalities and had taught several of his texts in my own seminar. His topic for his seminar at the University of Vermont, the techniques of self-care that had contributed to the rhetorical constitution of the self in antiquity, had more obvious implications for memory's significance in postmodern thinking. It was a problem I began to explore in a Freud/Foucault comparison I wrote for a volume I published with my colleagues Huck Gutman and Luther Martin on the seminar's work.

A comprehensive grasp of the memory problem nonetheless eluded me. To approach the topic of memory by the standard bibliographical route is to encounter the scientific literature straightaway. I discovered the psychologists' studies of the role of memory in cognition but found more fascinating those of the neurologists on memory and brain, which is a frontier of scientific research. I had thought at first of trying to incorporate the scientific with the cultural in my own book. I was fascinated by the classic studies of brain and memory by the Russian psychologist Alexander Luria and the more recent ones by the American neurologist Gerald Edelman. Having read Yates's book, I found Luria's famous psychological profile of a modern-day mnemonist valuable for the striking connections it enabled me to see between the techniques of recall that he intuitively employed and the studied methods of the Renaissance rhetorician. Equally instructive was his study of the differences in the cognitive skills displayed by people living in traditional and in modern societies, which suggested a pattern to the modification of the uses of memory in the transition between the two. I appreciated how easily his study in collective psychology correlated with the historical one that I had in mind, particularly for its affinities with Vico's theory of the historical modification of the mind. In Edelman's study, too, I was struck by the connection with classical mnemonics. His thesis about the genetic formation of primary and secondary repertoires of synaptic connections in cell networks suggested an analogy with the emplotment of places and images in the art of memory as primary and secondary schemes of classification. But it also confirmed my suspicion that penetrating the recesses of the brain is like penetrating the deep time of the human past. All of our research notwithstanding, we know little about either. Chastened by such reflections, I was prepared to persevere in my historical research. But to draw conclusions about memory derived from recent brain research, I had to concede that I could not proceed very far in a field in which I had no laboratory training. It was the first part of the project that I realized I would have to give away.

By this time I possessed disparate materials, though I was excited by the many interconnections I recognized among them. I had already traced the theme of mnemonics into the modern age in an article that I published in 1987. One of my original ideas was to build the entire project around the uses of mnemonic schemes in the modern world. As an exaggeration of memory's ordinary capacities for recollection, the art of memory presented itself tacitly in the thoughts of all of the authors to whom I turned. But classical mnemonics, a theory of displacement, had never been specifically associated with historical ends. Moreover, for some memory problems, the fixation on mnemonics was obviously contrived. Even within this more limited framework toward which I had found my way, the examples that I might choose to illustrate my argument could easily be dismissed as arbitrary. And what of all that I would have to ignore? In the end, I decided to give mnemonics an important but lesser place in an inquiry turned toward the problem of memory's relationship to historical understanding. Historical thinking, after all, was what I knew best by virtue of more than twenty-five years of study and teaching.

Raising memory in the midst of history created another set of problems. By the late 1980s, historians were increasingly giving attention to problems of rhetoric. One critic called it history's "return to literature." But the interest was in fact more narrowly focused on the power of language to form ideas, and, in turn, on the way in which such rhetorical forms could be turned to political ends. It was the direction in which the literary critics had gone a few years before and the philosophers a generation earlier still. The historians' first studies were of the history of commemoration. Their interest was in showing how memorialists use commemorative rites and monuments disingenuously. For that reason their work was closely tied to the postmodern perspective of the contemporary age. Postmodern historians were interested in memory as a resource in the mobilization of political power, and they were dismissive of the intrinsic value of tradition itself. Their work reflected the urgent need in the contemporary age to understand the rhetoric of propaganda. Accordingly, they concluded that commemoration was a form of mnemonics for the modern age, self-consciously designed by leaders of the nation-state to prompt the desired recall, and so to rouse latent emotional energies. Historical studies of such commemorative practices pointed out the exaggeration in which memorialists had once engaged. But ironically they themselves exaggerated the commemorative aspect of memory's resources by focusing almost exclusively on self-conscious techniques of recall. Such studies of commemorative representation suggested why Foucault, with his provocative notion of counter-memory, was receiving such critical acclaim throughout academia. His discussion of the "archaeology of knowledge" provided the philosophical groundwork for the project on which the historians of commemoration had already embarked. It helped them to see their evidence in a different way, and it addressed the problem of the manipulation of commemorative practices to serve political ends.

Considered philosophically, the approach seemed to me to be one-sided in its studied detachment from the traditions these practices were designed to honor. The historians of commemoration tended to bracket the question of what might be authentic in tradition, or what power of influence the past possesses in its own right, apart from our conscious efforts to reconstruct it. My first insight, therefore, was that such studies denied memory's claims on our attention. These historians seemed to propose the disassembling and critical analysis of traditions to which they had no genuine attachment. As Pierre Nora remarked with bemused irony of the phenomenon of commemoration in France: "We no longer celebrate the nation. Instead we study its celebrations."

But common sense suggests that we need the past and must maintain our living connections with it. What had shown through all of the reflections on the nature of memory by poets and philosophers across the ages was the interplay between repetition and recollection. The tension between the two was as old as the Greek myth of Mnemosyne, at once the goddess of imagination and of memory, and it was one that bestowed on memory its particular ambiguity. It draws the past into the present but colors it with its particular hues and reflections.

At the same time, the attention the topic was beginning to receive suggested to me why the memory/history puzzle was becoming a preoccupation of contemporary historiography. The fragmentation of so many of the traditions of modern culture (notably those identified with the making of the modern state) evoked curiosity about how they had originally been elaborated, and it opened the way for an appreciation of alternative visions of the past. On second insight, therefore, I construed this historiographical trend more positively. I concluded that the postmodern archaeology of memory identified with Foucault actually facilitated the historians' efforts to recover the past by making them more aware of their many options. For too long they had entered the past by too few routes. Alternate pathways into history revealed unsuspected worlds, complicating the appreciation of our heritage. The problem for the historian, then, is how to proceed in the quest to recover lost traditions and how to reconcile them with long-standing historiographical positions.

It was here that I returned to the art of memory as it was appreciated by Frances Yates in her study of the hermetic philosophers of the Renaissance.

As Yates had shown, the art of memory was not just a technique. It was also a resource for recovering lost worlds. In that sense, I wondered, was not history the art of memory for the modern age? Was it not a way of codifying and lending substance to valued traditions, notably those that incorporated notions of development or progress? That proposition gave me the title for my book, for it speaks to our current predicament. We know that we need to connect with the past. But it is a proposition about which we have grown more reflective. Our heritage in the postmodern world is multifold, as the traditions in which we have been formed, some old and some new, compete for our allegiances.

On this note, I might say a few words about how I have organized this book. To do so, let me set forth my own mnemonic scheme of its structure. I mix chapters of broad synthesis with those of concentrated focus on specific thinkers. Chapters 1 (Placing Memory in Contemporary Historiography) and 8 (History at the Crossroads of Memory) explore a broad range of issues concerning the relationship between memory and history. The former is a survey of contemporary historical interest in the memory topic. The latter is a meditation on the eternal paradox of repetition and recollection as moments of memory, presented as a prelude to my perspective on its role in historical studies today. Chapters 2 (The Art of Memory Reconceived) and 7 (Memory and the Historiography of the French Revolution) are also matched as explorations of broad themes. The former shows how the art of memory was refashioned to serve the needs of the modern age and so was integrated into historical thinking. The latter applies insights learned from the major theorists under investigation to a study of the historians' changing attitudes toward a particular historiographical tradition, that of scholarship on the French Revolution. The core of the book, Chapters 3 (Wordsworth and Freud), 4 (Halbwachs), 5 (Ariès), and 6 (Foucault), explores the thoughts of five authors who reflected profoundly on the way in which memory was historicized in the modern age, each from a different vantage point in the historical elaboration of the process between the early eighteenth and the late twentieth century.

As for getting there, I remember the beginnings well. Late in 1984, I presented a free-ranging paper on the culture of memory to John Hellman's seminar in collective mentalities at McGill University. On the drive from Burlington to Montreal, I placed the major points of my talk in my memory, in imitation of the rhetorician's placing of *topoi* by means of the classical art. Some fifty professors and graduate students gathered for my talk at Hellman's home, and it led to a lively discussion. In a postmortem on my lecture a few days later, Hellman's graduate students took me to task for too much brainstorming. But I recall that following my presentation Hellman's wife Odile had expressed admiration for my ability to commit so long a paper on so erudite a subject to memory. I was not then, nor am I now, the equal of the Renaissance mnemonist. But clearly I was learning something about this useful rhetorical skill.

In my first article on memory, a study of modern uses of mnemonics in autobiography and psychoanalysis, everything fell into place with such ease that it was subsequently difficult to figure out how to integrate new perspectives for a book-length project of greater complexity. For the moment, I continued to pursue discrete issues, notably those that concerned the dynamics of collective memory from an historical perspective. Presentations at the University of California and the Western Society for French History in 1987, for example, helped me to explore Ariès's thoughts on the relationship between collective memory and historical understanding. At Berkeley, Lucette Valensi urged me to try Halbwachs again, noting that his historical study of the shrines of the Holy Land was the key to his thinking.

Meanwhile I outlined a vast project in anticipation of my forthcoming sabbatical in 1988–89 and prepared to spend the year writing. But when the moment came to concentrate on it all day everyday I had to admit to myself that it was blithely conceived. It was a difficult, sometimes isolating year in which I felt thrown back on my own resources in pursuing a project that many of my colleagues in history considered odd. I wrote what I thought was good copy, but at the same time sensed that it was superficial. I was venturing further into philosophy than I had before in my scholarly writing. More troubling, I was not sure how to put it together. I read widely but found myself moving too quickly from topic to topic in an effort to get a comprehensive grasp of the project.

I settled down as the Vermont winter set in, sustained by my work on William Wordsworth's beautiful autobiography and Freud's profound insights into the secrets of the psyche. Ariès's work in which I was already well grounded and with which I felt a special affinity provided a sure point of reference, and I was beginning to deepen my understanding of the understated purposes of Halbwachs's methodical survey of the commemorative shrines of the Holy Land as well as his more theoretical works on collective memory. His work prefigured today's studies of commemoration in its concentration on the recollective perspective of modern historiography. For a long time, therefore, I brainstormed on its counterpoint—the perspective of repetition, or as we say more commonly, of habit. I was intrigued by the thesis of the English botanist Rupert Sheldrake about morphic resonances, which he presented in a controversial book in 1988 and explicated in a visit to the University of Vermont later that same year. His work and our conversation prompted me to read the work of the late-nineteenth-century English essayist Samuel Butler on habit and collective memory. Preoccupied with Charles Darwin's paradigm of evolutionary processes, Butler ruminated on the sure but silent influences of biological memory, images and impulses working their way across generations as a genetic inheritance. But habit unglued from the problem of change, as it was in Butler's considerations, struck me as an intellectual dead end for historical inquiry.

My rebound from habit as an instinct of collective memory (Butler, Sheldrake) to habit as a trait of tradition (Halbwachs, Ariès) freed me to return to history, and I began to think harder about practical applications of the theories that I had been considering. I turned therefore to a reconsideration of the French revolutionary tradition, a topic to which I had devoted so much attention as a young scholar. I used an invitation to visit St. John's College, Cambridge (coincidentally, the alma mater of Wordsworth and Butler), in the spring of 1989 for a conference on nationalism to test my ideas on memory and French historiography. It turned out not to have been the most suitable forum, because the discussion centered on a rather conventional exposé of the politics of French nationalism and several participants were puzzled by my theoretical musings on memory's role in its historiography. But Robert Tombs, the conference director, made the constructive suggestion that I rework my material to focus more directly on the historiographical foundations of the politics of memory. I remodeled my essay through presentations at the bicentennial meeting of the Society for French Historical Studies at Georgetown and the Eighteenth-Century Studies conference at Worcester later in the year. A later version appeared in *History and Theory* in 1991, and an augmented version is published herein as Chapter 7.

Teaching has always helped me to set my ideas straight. My book began to take form in an interdisciplinary seminar that I arranged for graduate students in the humanities on my return from sabbatical in the fall of 1989. I entitled the course "Cultural Contexts of Memory" and used what was a very rough draft of my book in typescript as a working text. Putting the text together, and teaching the course, obliged me to think much harder about audience. As for writing, I tried a different tactic. I realized that the book was too inchoate to be completed soon. I therefore reworked a number of chapters into scholarly articles. Luther Martin, my colleague at the University of Vermont, and Stuart Campbell, the editor of *Historical Reflections,* were an enormous support at this stage. Both encouraged me to write an overview of the significance of Foucault's work for French historiography, and both gave me the benefit of their editorial insight. For the next few summers I concentrated on individual articles. Stuart asked me to consider writing an overview of the memory/history problem, and I originally drafted the introductory chapter, "Placing Memory in Contemporary Historiography," in article format with *Historical Reflections* in mind.

I also returned to Vico, a favorite resource throughout my scholarly career, nurtured by my friendship with the American dean of Vichian studies, Giorgio Tagliacozzo. This time I addressed the orality/literacy problem more directly. Presented as Chapter 3 in this book, the essay was originally published in the *Journal of the History of Ideas* in 1992. Gathering momentum, I wrote a fuller study of Ariès that same winter, included herein as Chapter 5 and recently published in *History and Memory.* Preparing this essay for publication was a pleasant task, facilitated by a useful exchange of correspondence with Gulie Arad, the editor of that journal, concerning the relationship between Ariès's life and work. In the spring of 1992, I prepared diligently for a conference on Halbwachs sponsored by Harold Abramson and Gaye Tuchman of the Sociology Department at the University of Connecticut. The conference provided a wonderful exchange of ideas among scholars from several fields.

By the summer of 1992 I had been working on the memory project, off and on, for nearly eight years. Jeanne West, acquisitions editor at the University Press of New England, had expressed interest in my book two years earlier and I had signed a contract then. Now she encouraged me to bring it to a conclusion. It was the incentive I needed. I spent the summer writing, most days all day, and before summer's end I had finished a draft with which I could live.

My book is broadly conceived. It considers the memory/history problem as a crossroads for assessing modern and postmodern thinking about a number of current historiographical issues: the uses of mnemonic schemes in historical interpretation; the significance of tradition as a foundation of the historians' curiosity about the past; the historical impact of changing technologies of communication (orality, literacy, print culture, electronic media) upon conceptions of memory; the politics of commemoration in modern times; the relationship between collective memory and social power; and the theoretical problems recently raised about the role of rhetoric in the representation of the past. Individual chapters focus on philosophers, poets, and historians who have addressed these issues, among them: Giambattista Vico (the poetics of memory in oral tradition); William Wordsworth (the role of memory in autobiography); Sigmund Freud (the mnemonics of the unconscious mind); Maurice Halbwachs (the dynamics of collective memory); Philippe Ariès (tradition as the foundation of historical inquiry); Michel Foucault (the repudiation of tradition in postmodern thought); Søren Kierkegaard (repetition and recollection as the moments of memory); and Hans-Georg Gadamer (memory and hermeneutics). The book also includes a chapter on the historiography of the French Revolution as an application of my thinking about the memory/history problem.

Though the topic of memory's relationship to history is a frontier of historiographical research, my own presentation is in some ways an old-fashioned narrative in the history of ideas as it has been practiced since the days of Arthur Lovejoy. Given the range of ideas under review and the array of philosophers and historians with whom I deal, I thought it would be helpful if I were to set forth in bold outline the larger thesis at which I have arrived. I build my argument around four major themes whose interrelationships emerged with clarity as I deepened my appreciation of this topic:

1. *the interplay between repetition and recollection as the foundation of any consideration of the memory/history problem.* I argue that history is an art of memory because it mediates the encounter between two moments of memory: repetition and recollection. Repetition concerns the presence of the past. It is the moment of memory through which we bear forward images of the past that continue to shape our present understanding in unreflective ways.

One might call them habits of mind; they are the stuff of the collective memories that we associate with living traditions. Recollection concerns our present efforts to evoke the past. It is the moment of memory with which we consciously reconstruct images of the past in the selective way that suits the needs of our present situation. It is the opening between these two moments that makes historical thinking possible.

Historical thinking mimics the operations of memory in its consideration of these moments, though typically they are characterized as an exchange between received tradition and critical historical interpretation. What has changed in the history of Western historiography is the historians' understanding of the relationship between the two. Historiography in its ancient beginnings was heavily dependent on repetition. Historical understanding was literally immersed in collective memory, which continuously invoked the presence of the past. Since then, history has always in some measure been concerned with that presence, for it is mementos issuing from the living traditions of the past that inspire the historians' curiosity. Generally speaking, though, the trend of modern (and more emphatically postmodern) historiography has been away from reliance on the authority of received tradition. Modern historical understanding reflects the values of modern culture, which displays less reverence for the past, and invests greater hope in innovations for the future. Though we know more about the past than did our ancestors, the weight of its authority on us is not as heavy, and its appeal is more easily manipulated. In our own time, we have come to speak of the uses rather than the influences of the past, and its mementos are often little more than signatures employed to underscore our present concerns.

2. *the orality/literacy problem and historically changing conceptions of the meaning of memory.* My study pays considerable attention to scholarship dealing with changing technologies of communication (oral, chirographic, typographic, electronic), for it is an essential background to the rise and transformation of historical understanding. It would be an exaggeration to say that the possibility of history is tied to the rise of literacy. One could argue, as does Vico, that literacy was present from the beginnings of civilization in hieroglyphics and other symbolic markings. Still, before the emergence of manuscript culture, knowledge of the past was largely conveyed through oral traditions that continually updated the past to reflect present circumstances. Change, although real, often passed unperceived or was integrated into the cycles of mythological time. Correspondingly, particular events were conflated into the archetypes of legend. Manuscript literacy, therefore, contributed powerfully to the exteriorization of collective memory. Memory transposed into script seemingly made time stand still, permitting a specificity in recollection that had not been possible in oral culture. Memories—fluid, dynamic, and ever-changing in the repetitions

of oral tradition—could thenceforth be framed in more enduring representations of the past. In this way, accounts about the past rendered in script became places of memory, static simulacra that could nonetheless inspire the particular recollections that we have come to call history.

The trend in modern print culture was to democratize access to the historians' representations of the past. The literacy of manuscript culture, after all, did little to make exteriorized memory available to anyone outside a tiny intellectual elite. One could make a practical case for the proposition that the distinguishing feature of the historiography that we characterize as modern was its capacity to make available printed explications of less accessible manuscripts housed in archives and libraries. Our present-day electronic culture has intensified and deepened this trend toward easier access to representations of the past. In the computer, for example, not only can memory be exteriorized but it may also be instantaneously retrieved. In these circumstances, the imagery of representation is more easily manipulated. Factual information ironically becomes more malleable, for the contexts in which it may be located have grown exponentially, dissolving the once close relationship between specific places and particular memories. Historians today speak less of invoking the past, and more of using it. The point is that history as a memory problem concerns not only the recollection of images but also the modes of their representation. Changing technologies of communication, therefore, present an historical problem in understanding how over time the relationship between memory and history has been reconceived.

3. *the historicizing of collective memory in the eighteenth and nineteenth centuries as the foundation of modern historical scholarship.* The heart of my argument turns on the proposition that the art, one might say the beauty, of modern historical scholarship lay in its striving to capture memory and history in equipoise—as an interplay between tradition's repetitions and history's recollections. The work of nineteenth-century historians was continually marked by their sympathetic understanding of the traditions they wished to explicate. Much of this scholarship concerned the recollection of particular traditions, notably those identified with the rise of the modern nation-state or the advancement of the conception of progress derived from the culture of the Enlightenment. From our postmodern historiographical perspective, historians used such scholarship to confirm these traditions as official memories for the modern world.

The grounding of modern historiography in memory was often hidden beneath a facade of scientific objectivity, although its scholarship did display discerning standards for gathering, verifying, and discriminating among evidentiary sources, not to mention meticulous documentation in appendices to historical narratives. Still, modern historical scholarship was presented as a "new science" (a term coined by Vico), different in its methods and purposes from the natural sciences whose authority it strove to emulate. Modern historiography found its philosophical justification in the doctrine of historicism. Historicism was based upon the proposition that humankind, having created its own experience, can re-create it. The historians' task, the doctrine proposed, is to reenter the mind-set of the historical actors they would examine, however strange and alien that mind-set might be, with a view to understanding the challenges of their particular circumstances and even to thinking through their problems as they would have themselves. In effect, the historicists called on the historians to re-create the historical imagination. Recollecting the world as it was once perceived became the goal of their endeavor.

As a theory of history, therefore, historicism was in fact a problem of memory, for imagination and memory deal in images that are interchangeable. The historiographical issue was how images derived from the past might be invoked for the present age. The modern historians adopted a range of positions on what the relationship between repetition (images received from living tradition) and recollection (images retrieved from a forgotten past) ought to be (which I explore in depth in my chapter on memory and the historiography of the French Revolution). There were some (particularly among the romantic historians of the early nineteenth century) who put their emphasis on the moment of repetition. They believed that the historians' task is to resurrect the mentality of the past, literally to reaffirm tradition by making its images live again. But most historians (particularly as the century wore on) acknowledged that this is an impossible task and accordingly shifted their emphasis to the moment of recollection. What historians can do, they contended, is to reconstruct images as they must once have existed, beyond the bounds of their own living memories. Thereby they maintain connections with the past by integrating its imagination into their own.

4. *the fading of the collective memories bequeathed by the traditions of modern culture to our own postmodern age as the source of the current historiographical interest in the memory/history problem.* Having rejected or lost touch with the nineteenth-century traditions in which modern historiography was formed, historians today have become interested in a more detached and reflective way in how these now-fragmenting traditions took shape. The critique of the traditions of modern historiography has surfaced across the spectrum of present-day historical inquiry. To that end, postmodern historians examine old traditions not to reconstruct their imaginary conceptions but rather to de-construct their modes of publicity and their strategies for exercising power. In doing so, they have exposed the weakness of modern historiography in its naïveté about its own conceptual foundations. In place of the search to enliven memories that once sustained political ideals, they study the forms of the politics of commemoration.

One could argue that postmodern historians are not rejecting the traditions of modern history but are only appealing to others that have been too long neglected or forgotten. In opposition to the official memories enshrined in modern historiography, they contend, postmodern historiography poses new lines of historical inquiry in the guise of countermemories: social history as an alternative to political history; the history of collective mentalities (attitudes toward everyday life) to that of the history of ideas (elite culture); women's history to that of men's history; non-Western history to that of European history; global history to that of national history. But the difficulty lies deeper, for the tendency of postmodern historiography is to see memory and history as sharply opposed in their purposes. In this view, memory is not the hidden ground of history, as it was in the historicist conceptions of modern historiography, but rather an internal activity of the living mind that can never be recovered. The imagery of the past establishes barriers beyond which we cannot go. Historians cannot hope to return to the sources of the protean images of living memory, the postmodern argument goes. But they can describe the way in which the remembered past has been inscribed over time in memorial forms. The recovery of memory in its material representations ("words and things," as Foucault characterized them) has therefore become a project over which postmodern historians believe they can exercise some mastery, even if they must set aside the historicists' more ambitious claims. They may not be able to bring alive the thoughts of the actors of history, as the historicists proposed they could. But they can write histories of the changing ways in which the past has been portrayed in commemorative forms over time. If the modern historicists saw their task as using the recollective techniques of history to recover the repetitive truths of tradition, their postmodern counterparts focus almost exclusively on the material leavings once designed to inspire recollection. Historical memory, in their view, is a function of the power to determine the way in which the past is to be presented. Ultimately the problem of history is a problem of the politics of commemoration, that is, of identifying and inventorying those events, ideas, or personalities chosen by the power brokers of an earlier age for remembrance.

A fair portion of this book consists of my reconstruction of the emergence and articulation of this postmodern perspective, especially as exemplified in the work of Halbwachs and Foucault. But the postmodern perspective has its limitations, for no culture can sustain itself with autopsies of the institutional forms and modes of discourse of its discarded past. In the end, therefore, I want to reaffirm my conviction that even these days history is best appreciated as an art of memory. It is not enough to describe the past through its representations, for such an approach presupposes a detachment alien to the lived experiences that memory bears into the present. Historians neglect the moment of repetition at their peril, for living memory ultimately remains the ground of their interest in the past, just as it was once the foundation of the identity of the historical actors they seek to understand. Memory prompts our inquiries as historians, just as the search for that which has been forgotten focuses them. The past as it was experienced, not just the past as it has subsequently been used, is a moment of memory we should strive to recover.

The manner in which I have dealt with these themes reflects my particular interests, not to mention my idiosyncrasies. It contains most of what I know about this subject. Certainly there is more that I might have done. There are major thinkers that I have ignored (Marcel Proust), or about whom I have not said nearly enough (Henri Bergson). But as the philosopher George Allan, who has himself written a fine study on the nature of tradition, has noted, memory is a source of meaning whose depths may be plumbed forever. As one colleague pointed out to me, memory is a nearly impossible topic because the range of its considerations encompasses the entire field of epistemology. But one could make a like complaint of history. Its endless possibilities have not constrained me. Nor should those of memory deter others from venturing into this elusive field. With memory, as with history, we look for interesting conjunctures. Here I have called them crossroads, an image that Wordsworth once employed. That is what I have attempted to locate in this book—interesting crossroads at which particular themes illustrate the memory/history problem well. History draws on both sides of the memory puzzle. It seeks to reconstruct the past through an act of recollection. But the past that prompts the historian's consideration is borne into the present by oft-repeated habits of mind.

Research on the nature and uses of memory today is being pursued with newfound interest and intensity. The study of the representations of the past (the past as it was once imagined) promises to reconstruct patterns in the use of rhetoric in the past that parallel those devised earlier to place its events (the past as it actually transpired). It has added a new dimension to historiography by revealing the myriad ways in which memory inspires and directs the course of historical inquiry. In this respect, I do not see the study of memory's relationship to history as a cumulative enterprise, as do some of its practitioners. The positivist quest for certainty in our collective memory of the past is likely to remain an unrealized goal, just as memory itself is likely to remain an elusive topic. Interest in it crops up when we need to reflect on its power, as we do these days when so many historical certainties are being called into question. For us as historians, thinking about memory in a critical way confirms the power of the past and the depth of our attachments to it. It teaches us humility about what we may know of a past that forms us in countless ways still hidden, while providing us with the imaginative resources to speculate on what the future may hold. Such notions are worth remembering as one proceeds into this book.

PLACING MEMORY IN CONTEMPORARY HISTORIOGRAPHY

From Collective Mentalities to Collective Memory in Contemporary Historiography

The topic of memory today elicits widespread scholarly interest across the humanities. It serves as a crossroads of learning on which cultural anthropologists, psychologists, literary theorists, and students of oral tradition have recently converged in their efforts to make sense of its puzzles. Terms such as habit, recollection, commemoration, image-making, representation, and tradition, once considered separately within particular disciplines, have become the currency of an interdisciplinary discourse. Historians have come late to such discussions, but their participation is becoming more prominent.[1] The problem of the historical status of memory, therefore, is at last an issue, and the question recently posed by the French scholar Nathan Wachtel is whether it is possible today to write a history of memory.[2] This book is an inquiry into the historiographical conditions under which that question is beginning to be addressed.

The historians' interest in the problem of memory has in large measure been inspired by French scholarship. It is derived from work in the history of collective mentalities, which since the 1960s has enlivened French historiography. The historians of mentalities dealt in topical issues about popular culture. Attitudes toward family life and local communities, social manners and mores, and popular religious devotions figured prominently in their repertoire of interests. Focusing on the structures of thought rather than on particular ideas, they cited habits of mind, conventions of speech, customary practices, and folk traditions as the unifying themes of their inquiry.[3] But all such topics, by virtue of their identification with the inertial power of the past, led in one way or another to the underlying issue of the nature and resources of collective memory, which was rarely examined directly in their studies.[4] The question that has come to mind for some current practitioners in the field, therefore, is whether the problem of collective memory may not contain the hidden agenda of the interest in collective mentalities. As the historian Pierre Nora, a pioneer in the field, has remarked, the problem of memory today raises the kind of historiographical issues identified with mentalities a generation ago.[5] Once passed over without reflection, the problem of memory provides this generation of historians with the more interesting critical questions.

In this inquiry into the history of memory, commemoration was the first topic to draw the historians' attention. The work of Philippe Ariès prepared the way. Ariès was a pioneering scholar in the history of mentalities, who first gained wide recognition for his study of changing attitudes toward the role of children in family life.[6] His last major book, *L'Homme devant la mort* (1977), was a sweeping study of attitudes toward death and dying in Western culture, and among the most significant of his findings was the unprecedented interest in commemoration in the nineteenth century.[7] Commemorative practices, he observed, multiplied and took on more intense meaning within the culture of that day. The passing of loved ones acquired a poignancy never known before. On one level, memorializing the deceased reflected the deepening bonds of personal affection that characterized the sensibilities of late-eighteenth- and early-nineteenth-century culture. But on another it signified a new awareness that the lived experience of the past can never be directly retrieved. What had been lost was the presence of the past, felt with immediacy by societies that sensed themselves to be more completely immersed in living traditions. In an age of political revolution, emerging into a fuller awareness of the realities of change, the past came to be held at a critical distance. The passion for commemoration, therefore, was in some measure tied to the need to reaffirm ties to a world that was passing.[8]

Ariès himself was especially interested in the practices of personal commemoration. But he also pointed out the role that memorial monuments and rituals came to play in the public sphere over the course of the nineteenth century, as the leading political personalities of the age became objects of commemorative veneration. The cult of personality, in turn, flowed into the more general commemoration of major historical events, as memorial imagery lent definition to official conceptions of the significance of the emerging nation-state. In these ways, commemorative practices became an essential mode of modern political representation.[9]

Following the suggestive route opened by Ariès, a new genre of historical scholarship emerged by the 1980s. It might best be characterized as a history of the politics of commemoration. Leading the way in this venture was Maurice Agulhon, who offered a pioneering study of the way in which a commemorative image may be used to give concrete form to political identity. In his *Marianne au combat* (1979), he charted the fortunes of a century of efforts to fashion such an image of the French republic (1789–1879).[10] Agulhon focused on the image of Marianne, a symbol of republican virtue, employed to idealize the tenuous activities of republican secret societies in the 1830s and carried forward into the triumphal accomplishments of the republican party in the 1870s, when the republic was at last securely established. Turned to reflect the light of its varied causes over nearly a century of political struggle, the image of Marianne mirrored the fortunes of the republican movement along the way. Agulhon recounted the manner in which the image was constructed, displayed, and modified. From her early image as an effigy on little statues struck to publicize the republican cause to her mature representation on grand monuments fixed in important public places to celebrate republican triumphs, Marianne gave symbolic form to the rising power of the movement.[11]

Agulhon's study signified a shift of historiographical interest from ideology to imagery, from the history of politics to the politics of culture. Images, not ideas or events, served as his principal data. He characterized his study as a history of political symbolism, and as such "a useful counterpoint to the history of ideological alternatives."[12] Agulhon focused on the way in which symbolic images serve the purposes of political propaganda. To discuss republican ideas might be edifying, he allowed. But only concrete imagery could give such an abstract notion the emotional appeal needed to acquire a following. To personify the republic was to make it a memento with which citizens might more readily identify.[13] The image of Marianne, therefore, played a commemorative role from the moment of its invention. In legend, Agulhon explained, it was a "name given in memory of the early secret societies," and it was remembered as "the dream in which the image was first coined."[14] To remember Marianne was to fire the popular imagination.

Agulhon provided an absorbing case study of the way in which the modification of an image reveals the changing nature of a political cause. In the process, he tacitly offered insight into the workings of collective memory. He showed how an image, once invented, tends to proliferate into myriad reconfigurations.[15] But if the image is identified with a powerful cause, it will eventually coalesce into an ideal type. So it was that the idiosyncratic edges of the image of Marianne were gradually worn away as the republican movement extended its political power. In the early days, competing images of Marianne provide evidence of tensions within the republican camp. But as republican solidarity within France grew strong by the late 1870s, the demand was raised for a "lasting effigy" of the republican ideal, a single stately image that would serve as a foundation for its place in the collective imagination. In this way, the image of Marianne passed from the republican cause into the larger national memory.[16]

To underscore the particular, historical nature of his study, Agulhon pointed out that the female image of the republic was a "peculiarly French" characterization without wider application. The Americans, after all, remembered their republic in terms of icons of the founding fathers, just as the English identified their nation in the emblem of John Bull.[17] But one might also contend that Agulhon's study of this icon of the French republican movement

highlights the general significance of rhetorical issues in historical investigation by laying open the divide between image and idea in the politics of commemoration. By tracking the fortunes of an image rather than an idea,
Agulhon showed how it might be deployed to convey variations on an ideological theme, or even redeployed to further unrelated causes. In this way, the
image itself acquired an historical identity.[18] Herein lies the originality of
Agulhon's study. It provides a methodological alternative to the history of
ideas, as practiced in the historiographical tradition inaugurated by Arthur
Lovejoy some fifty years before.

Given the power of publicity makers in our own time, Agulhon's mode of
investigation was certain to inspire imitators. The phenomenon of image-
making that he traced through the nineteenth century has become even more
prominent in twentieth-century political practice; thus it made sense to many
of his colleagues to see the memorialists of nineteenth-century traditions as
their forerunners. Politicians in the contemporary age, after all, rely on images
more often than ideas to persuade others of the merits of their causes, so that
form takes precedence over substance in the communication of political messages. Within only a few years, therefore, the topic of memory's politics
moved to the center of historiographical interest, this time more obviously
focused on image-making in commemorative practice.

It would be impossible to survey the interests of this new history of commemorative imagery in any detail. Suffice it to say that studies of cemetery
statuary, war memorials, the pageantry of patriotic festivals, state funerals,
anniversary celebrations of notable events or political leaders, and national
holidays, particularly as they were represented during the Third Republic,
have carved out the particular directions that this emerging genre of historical
research has taken.[19] Implicit in nearly all of these studies was a tendency to
desacralize tradition by reducing it to the images in which it was represented.
Tradition, construed by a more reverent age as the expression of an interior
impulse to perpetuate values and mores, was for these historians to be un-
masked as the exterior form of the bias of those who would appropriate the
past for their present political purposes. The habits of mind in which traditions
were purported to have been conceived, they explained, were often carefully
constructed images, calculated to glamorize commemorative practices. Modern politicians who took seriously the task of making tradition appealing, they
argued, were in fact image-makers intent on furthering a more current agenda.

Particularly provocative in this respect were the essays by Eric Hobsbawm
and his colleagues in the anthology *The Invention of Tradition* (1983).[20] Hobsbawm, too, was impressed with the scope and intensity of commemorative
practices in western Europe in the late nineteenth century. He referred to them
as "mass-produced traditions," manifestations in the cultural sphere of parallel trends in the political and economic. To explain the passion for political
commemoration in that era, he pointed to new realities—an industrialized
economy, an urbanized society, and emerging nation-states, all guided by the

newly powerful bourgeoisie. Ironically, this society, self-conscious about the new culture that it was creating, also needed a new past with which it might identify. People felt the need for stability in such a rapidly changing world, where customs were being abandoned or marginalized. That is why tradition had to be invented for this modern world. Tradition provided imaginary places immune to the process of change, even if its images of stability were themselves little more than representations of present-minded notions about the past.[21]

Like Agulhon, Hobsbawm laid emphasis on the constructed nature of the commemorative traditions of the modern age. In doing so, he took pains to distinguish custom from tradition. He characterized customs as practices bequeathed by the past to which a society naturally has recourse for practical ends. The traditions of the nineteenth century were more contrived. They displaced historical realities with factitious images that created the illusion of continuity with the past when in fact such ties were being loosened.[22] Hobsbawm conceded that there may be limits to the uses of invented traditions to foster popular attachment to a sentimental past. They must in some measure be attuned to the felt needs of the communities to which they are addressed.[23] The imposition of state-sponsored traditions with which people have no genuine attachment has, by contrast, become blatant in totalitarian politics in the twentieth century. Even the contrived traditions of the nineteenth century may be distinguished from what is today characterized as kitsch.[24] In Hobsbawm's interpretation, though, the line between genuine customs and make-believe traditions was not so obviously drawn in late-nineteenth-century Europe. Drawing that line, therefore, is much of what this genre of scholarship has come to be about.

The history of the politics of commemoration showed the visible influence of the methods of Michel Foucault (1926–84), the French philosopher who turned to historical scholarship to explore the significance of the formalities of language and institutions in the making of human culture.[25] Foucault helped historians to understand the rhetorical context in which the politics of memory was being considered. He did not write on the phenomenon of commemoration himself. But he dealt with historiographical issues that set the stage for this reconsideration of commemoration within a rhetorical mode. He cast the aforementioned distinction between ideas and images as one between the history of ideas and that of discourse. The former, he explained, seeks continuity between past and present by showing the way in which founding ideas reappear in new historical contexts. The latter, by contrast, reveals historical discontinuities, as images are continually being appropriated and redeployed to convey unrelated thoughts.[26]

To the memory of the historian of ideas, Foucault juxtaposed what he characterized as the counter-memory of the historian of discourse.[27] The history of discourse inventories and describes the images in which ideas are represented, as each age refashions its discourse to serve new causes. In such historical analysis, tradition, with its pretense to sustaining a continuous thread of the past remembered, is revealed to be a fabrication. Beneath the memories enshrined in officially sanctioned traditions, counter-memories abound. Foucault's point is that the past is continually being remolded in our present discourse. What is remembered about the past depends on the way it is represented, which has more to do with the present power of groups to fashion its image than with the ability of historians to evoke its memory.[28] Rather than culling the past for residual memories, each age reconstructs the past with images that suit its present needs. Given interchangeable connections with ideas in modern discourse, images may appear to be devoid of substance. They nonetheless provide a reliable record of humankind's efforts to give form to its creativity. In Foucault's rendering, what had once been conceived as the past transmitted was reconceived as the past reconstructed. The reality of the past, he maintained, resides in the artifacts of its representation.[29] The history of discourse, therefore, enables the historian to discriminate among the many forms in which the past may be remembered. Rhetoric, Foucault argued, is more than a vehicle of discourse; in fact, it constitutes a cultural reality.[30] Discourse itself serves as historical evidence that historians can describe with greater certainty than they can the meaning of ideas, which are always open to subjective interpretation. One cannot re-create the thought processes of historical actors, but one can ascertain what they said, insofar as it has been encoded in commemorative form. The task of creating images in which ideas may be persuasively conveyed is an essential ingredient of cultural practice—and for the historian a sure index to the configurations of power in the society that invented them.

Even more significant for the theoretical formulation of this genre of historiography was a new appreciation of the work of Maurice Halbwachs (1877–1945), a sociologist who wrote with insight on the nature of collective memory well before the topic had begun to receive the historians' attention. In the years between the world wars, he wrote a series of studies on the dynamics of collective memory.[31] His work, long neglected, is currently receiving critical acclaim from historians who find his theory a useful guide for their own work. Frequently cited by the new historians of the politics of memory, he is more fully appreciated today than he was in the age in which he wrote.[32] Not only was his interpretation highly original; it also anticipated the postmodern thinking on the topic displayed in the theory of Foucault and the practice of the historians of the politics of commemoration.

Halbwachs's main point was that memory is only able to endure within sustaining social contexts. Individual images of the past are provisional. They are "remembered" only when they are located within conceptual structures that are defined by communities at large. Without the life-support system of group confirmation, individual memories wither away.[33] For that matter, he taught, even individual memories have their social dimension, for they are in fact composite images in which personal reminiscences are woven into an understanding of the past that is socially acquired.[34] Halbwachs's theory was particularly appealing to the historians of the politics of commemoration because of his insistence on the way in which collective memory is continually revised to suit present purposes. Because we continually reinvent the past in our living memories, they are highly unreliable as a guide to what actually transpired, and their imagery must be interpreted for hidden agendas. Halbwachs's work on the social foundations of collective memory, therefore, has provided an important theoretical groundwork for the study of the politics of memory in which contemporary historians are currently engaged.[35]

Halbwachs accepted the long-standing philosophical proposition that living memory involves an interplay between repetition and recollection. Two of his notions about that proposition, however, distinguish his research. First, he taught that in repetition memories are not transmitted intact. Rather they are conflated as they are continually being revised. Over time, the diverse expressions of individual memories gradually coalesce into the stereotypical images that give form to collective memories. In each repetition, the particular idiosyncrasies of individual memories are worn away. That which is remembered of oft-repeated experience is a reduction of particular memories into an idealized image, or imago. Such composite memories provide the conceptual schemes, or as Halbwachs put it, the "social frameworks" (*cadres sociaux*) in which individual memories come to be located. The structure of collective memory, in turn, provides the model to which individual memory is bound to conform.[36] Second, Halbwachs contended that the capacity of a collective memory to endure depends on the social power of the group that holds it. In recollection, we do not retrieve images of the past as they were originally perceived but rather as they fit into our present conceptions, which are shaped by the social forces that act on us. The prominence of a collective memory, therefore, is a reflection of the social role of a particular group, and accordingly the study of the phenomenology of social representation provides an important cultural perspective on social history.[37]

Halbwachs's work directly challenged the teachings of Sigmund Freud and the psychoanalytic school, which believed that memories are preserved whole within the unconscious of the individual psyche. In remembering, Freud taught, one resurrects or reimagines the past.[38] Halbwachs took issue with this view, for he believed that Freud's approach showed little insight into the way in which collective memory is remodeled through its winnowing over time into an ideal type. Halbwachs contended that individual memories are fleeting, passing elusively in and out of the minds of historical actors. They cannot be documented with any accuracy, and the subjective interpretation of their meaning is a problematic task.[39]

Halbwachs's argument had important implications for historical understanding that prefigured the agenda of postmodern historiography. Because the past is continually being revised in our living memories, he argued, what historians can know of the remembered past depends entirely on its commemorative leavings. Only as memories have been enshrined in material form can historians know them. These fixed representations provide a barrier beyond which they cannot go. From these hollow forms, they cannot rethink what people once thought, or reenter their minds to recover their intentions. Still, they can write histories of the changing ways in which particular images of the past were represented in commemorative forms over time. As particular representations fixed in iconography and discourse, memory's images acquire stasis, providing concrete evidence of society's efforts to give form to its imagination. Halbwachs's theory of memory, therefore, revealed how a history of commemoration might be possible. In locating the images with which the historical actors of the past represented their world, historians can see the structure of their collective imagination and the relative power of the social groups to which they belonged.[40] The historians' task, therefore, is not to resurrect the past by restoring an idea to living memory, as Freud believed but rather to describe the images in which collective memory once lived.

What Halbwachs set forth as method, Pierre Nora has set out as project. His *Lieux de mémoire* (1984–92), a history of the collective memory of France as revealed through its representations, is the most ambitious project within the new history of the politics of memory and the crowning achievement of the genre to date. Aided in his venture by some forty-five of France's best known historians, Nora traces the commemorative record of France retrospectively through the widening circles of its imaginary representations: nineteenth-century images of the republic, seventeenth- and eighteenth-century images of the French nation, and (in a volume recently published) medieval images of France as a popular culture.[41] If the nineteenth century was an age given to commemoration, Nora contends, ours is one that is beginning to sense the limitations of a viewpoint that sees history as a studied way to perpetuate particular traditions.[42] In the nineteenth century, historians sought to explicate traditions that, even when they were beginning to disappear from living memory, continued to provide a sense of continuity, sympathy, and identity with the past. Although they established a critical distance from the events and personalities that they examined, these historians still regarded them as the places of their memory. Collective memory continued to serve as a backdrop to their historical investigations, providing the reference points that gave them an orientation from which to proceed. Places of memory provided the framework, vocabulary, and cultural conventions in which the meaning of their work was carried out and communicated to a larger community.[43]

But for the contemporary age, Nora points out, the traditions to which French historians have long had recourse are losing their power of appeal.[44] They no longer see their destiny so closely tied to the revolutionary tradition, whose major goals have long since been realized. As the prospects for European community intrude on traditional French conceptions of their identity, their statesmen consider their European as well as their Jacobin heritage. Anticipating a different kind of future, French historians have come to consider a different past, hidden beneath the dominant trends of nineteenth- and twentieth-century historiography. The consolation of historians in such an age, Nora suggests, lies in their opportunity to locate and describe these places with which living memory was once identified. "We no longer celebrate the nation," he comments. "Instead we study its celebrations."[45] Nora and his colleagues, therefore, have sought to unlayer French commemorative traditions to see how they were originally constructed.

Sensing the waning of emotional attachments to those places of memory that have traditionally given French historians their bearings, Nora and his colleagues survey the places where living traditions were once situated. In this sense, their project might be said to concern the waning of the French national memory, for which their anthology is a testament. The historical identity of France resides in the representations through which it has been remembered. Today historians consult "places of memory because there are no longer milieux of memory," Nora remarks.[46] But in another sense, his critical stance enables us to see that collective memory is lodged in more places than historians have previously imagined. What is called history is no more than the official memory a society chooses to honor. During the modern era, that memory was closely identified with the political history of the modern state, particularly as it was fashioned in the era of the French Revolution.[47] The historians' task in our postmodern age, however, is to identify and classify the imaginary schemes in which the nation's past has been conceived according to an assortment of places of memory. In his distinction between republic, nation, and France as categories of remembrance, Nora shows how the national identity is appreciated differently in each. To sever history from the memory of the particular political tradition in which it has been studied frees historians to search for counter-memories, and counter-traditions derived from them.[48]

Nora relates the interest in memory in the contemporary age to our sense of the accelerating pace of time. Hobsbawm, it will be recalled, linked the rising interest in commemoration a century ago to the rapid changes that accompanied industrialization in the Western world. In the nineteenth century, change was of a pace to evoke a nostalgic sense of the traditional world that was being lost. Places of memory still anchored the present in the past. But changes in the contemporary world, Nora contends, are so precipitous that recourse to collective memory has diminishing importance. The wisdom of the past in which communities once trusted is immaterial to a culture in which today's improvisations pass quickly into tomorrow's obsolescence. In a world of future shock, places of memory disappear, and history surrenders its mediating role between past and future.[49] At the crossroads of history, Nora contends, places of memory are no longer visited to reconfirm the meanings that an earlier generation of historians would have expected to find there.[50] The commemorative practices of ages past, therefore, may be disassembled today with a detachment that would have been impossible a century ago.

But in detaching themselves from direct contact with places of memory, what knowledge can historians hope to uncover there? Like Foucault, Nora suggests that their current enterprise is an archaeology of memory. The leavings of memory provide a record of the efforts of historical actors to describe their cultural values.[51] Places of memory, viewed as wellsprings by the memorialists of the nineteenth century, are regarded by historians today as mirrors in which people once tried to see themselves. In other words, the places of memory were self-referential for those who had recourse to them. In their attempts to reckon with their own heritage, they invented them in order to assign a meaning to the past that accorded with their contemporary concerns. Yesterday's places of memory, therefore, are today's place markers for historians mapping the many ways in which the past was once imagined. In inventorying the images found there, historians come to recognize that the same ones may represent many, sometimes unrelated traditions, for they may be used and reused in profoundly different ways.[52] The insistence on the radical separation between image and idea, noted in both Agulhon and Foucault, herein becomes programmatic. As images in imaginary frameworks designed to evoke feelings for the past, these places of the memory of France seem surprisingly akin to those that once adorned the imaginary memory palaces designed by the rhetoricians of the Renaissance.

Rediscovering the Art of Memory

Nora's use of the phrase places of memory as a title for his book may be more than a rhetorical gesture, for there are links between the methods of the modern politics of commemoration and those of the ancient art of memory. For the rhetoricians of Greece and Rome in antiquity, the art was a mnemonic technique. Its method of recall was based on a principle of displacement. Rhetoricians constructed easily remembered paradigms in which to place ideas so that they might be recalled at will in the appropriate sequence. To do so they utilized a dual repertoire of places and images. They conjured up striking images, to which they attached the ideas they wished to remember, and then located them within imaginary frameworks that served as paths for their narrative walks through the past. The connection between the art and modern-day commemorative practice might seem remote. But one could argue that the highly visible, geographical landscapes of memory identified with nineteenth-century commemorative practice corresponded closely to the imaginary schemes of the classical mnemonists. Both relied on concrete places of memory, adorned with images that symbolized a larger cause. Modern commemoration only turned mnemonic technique to more obvious political ends. But images displace ideas in the modern politics of memory much as they did in this ancient art, whereas commemorative monuments and museums play the role of the mnemonists' memory palaces in highlighting the conceptual design of the remembered past.[53] Nora is in effect suggesting that the historians' task today is to decode the mnemonic schemes unwittingly employed by those who gave France its identity.

It is worth noting, therefore, that the ancient art of memory, of peripheral interest since the sixteenth century, has also recently recaptured the historians' attention. The historical interest in this topic dates from the early 1960s and is best known through the work of Frances Yates.[54] Yates was an English scholar, affiliated with the Warburg Institute, an archive of Renaissance manuscripts and memorabilia assembled by the German collector Aby Warburg and moved from Germany to Britain shortly before the Second World War.[55] Yates may be said to have rescued this archaic skill from oblivion by explaining the nature of its intellectual resources for an earlier age. As a student of the intellectual underworld of the Renaissance, she revealed the diversity of a cultural movement identified by an earlier generation of historians with the preoccupations of a tiny elite of artists and savants. She showed the more panoramic dimensions of Renaissance scholarship—its arcane domains of learning, its false starts and intellectual impasses, its exotic and occult philosophies in what was a vastly more pluralistic cultural milieu than historians had previously imagined. For Yates, the art of memory was among the most intriguing of these intellectual endeavors. Superficially, it may appear to have been no more than a technical skill. But Yates showed how some Renaissance philosophers used it as a magical method with which to uncover hidden harmonies between earthly and transcendental spheres.[56] Yates was particularly fascinated with the mnemonic schemes devised by the Neapolitan philosopher Giordano Bruno to further his search for ancient sources of hermetic knowledge. Through Bruno, she was introduced to a tradition of gnostic philosophy that harked back to the obscure intellectual recesses of antiquity. Steeped in gnostic thought, Bruno sought access to lost knowledge of an ideal universe with which he believed the phenomenal world to be magically connected. The art of memory was his key for unlocking the mystery of this connection.[57]

Yates's rediscovery of the hermetic philosophers' belief in the magical powers of memory explains why the art was able to assume new life in an age in which the printing press might otherwise have rendered memory systems obsolete. Mnemonic schemes for their Renaissance designers were in fact paradigms of the structure of cosmic forces. Yates reviewed the accomplishments of a number of mnemonists who constructed imaginary memory palaces of ornate design to contain their intricate cosmological conceptions: Bruno and Giulio Camillo in Italy, John Dee and Robert Fludd in Britain. For these sixteenth-century magi, the mnemonic scheme was like a mirror—it reflected images of a transcendental world. One can see why the hermetic philosophers taught that the art possessed magical powers, for they believed that there were correspondences between their imaginary paradigms and the ideal forms of the cosmos. The images in their schemes were empowered by their magical connections with eternal ideas.[58]

In Yates's rendering of its role, the art of memory was portrayed as an arcane method in an errant search for divine wisdom. Such an interpretation, however, marginalized the topic by characterizing it as a line of intellectual inquiry without an enduring legacy. In its penchant for the systematic orga- nization of knowledge, she suggested, the art may have trained scholars in the kind of systematic thinking that made possible the scientific revolution.[59] But the art of displacing ideas with images was itself displaced once that revolution arrived, because it returned speculations about the nature of the cosmos from a metaphysics lodged in transcendental idealism to a physics grounded in earthly empiricism.

Yates may have traced the history of the art through its varied formulations for a period of some 2,000 years. But the timeline of her considerations was not lengthy enough to reveal the historical relationship between mnemonics and the larger problem of collective memory. For all the fascination of the exotic schemes of the mnemonists, they were tied to a relatively circumscribed domain of high culture. Just as the art was employed in the service of exotic philosophies, so it functioned in the service of a particular kind of commu- nication. Yates's history of the classical art of memory parallels the rise and fall of manuscript culture. The art was a technique devised in antiquity to meet the needs of an emerging literacy that relied heavily on the protocols of orality for the organization of knowledge. It employed in a studied way tech- niques of recall expressed intuitively in oral cultures.

It was only the classical form of the art, therefore, that was moving toward obsolescence. The appeal of the art had always been in its image-making as well as its knowledge-bearing capacities. If the uses of the art for an accurate reiteration of knowledge had clearly diminished for the modern age, the need to create images that could convey knowledge persuasively remained vital to intellectual inquiry. Modern science may have dispelled magic from human understanding of the workings of nature. But the magic of memory itself hardly disappeared with the obsolescence of classical mnemonic schemes. From our vantage point, the genius of the hermetic philosophers' art lay not in their discovery of cosmological congruences between human images and eternal ideas but in their insight into the inspiring effect of memory on the imagination. Teachers of rhetoric had always pointed out the connection, and the poets of the modern age would insist as fervently as did their predecessors on the magic of memory's inspiring powers. The mirrors they saw in their mnemonic schemes reflected not a transcendent cosmos but the imaginative powers of their own minds. The mnemonist was, in effect, the image-maker of the sixteenth century, giving rhetorical form to a kind of imaginative spec- ulation that was not about to disappear. The question was how the project of image-making would change as the technologies of communication were transformed. Historical investigation of that issue would reveal that the clas- sical art of memory had in fact been situated in the midst of a long-term trans- formation of the relationship between orality and literacy. In that wider context, the assessment of its significance moves to issues beyond those that Yates had identified.

Memory and Changing Modes of Communication

Not only does the topic of the technologies of communication reveal the limits of the continuum within which Yates situated the art of memory; it provides as well a context for considering the history of memory apart from that being sketched by the historians of the politics of commemoration. It shifts the focus from politics to culture. This topic, too, was first presented to the scholarly world in the early 1960s, notably by the Canadian scholar Marshall McLuhan, who speculated about the cultural implications of the proliferation of the media that was by then well under way.[60] McLuhan's intellectual virtuosity won him a wide following in that era, even if his ideas were appreciated only belatedly within the academy.[61] His theory is epitomized in his famous dictum "the medium is the message."[62] McLuhan wanted to show how the move to an electronic culture dissolved the framework in which typographic culture had been conceived. Typographic culture, he pointed out, possessed historically distinctive ways of organizing knowledge. Knowledge once held to be objective was in fact relative to the properties of the print medium.[63]

McLuhan's work was a manifesto for the electronic revolution in communication. But it also had larger implications for the history of changing modes of communication. He developed his argument by pointing out a corresponding reordering of the frameworks of knowledge in the move from manuscript to print culture two centuries before, and from orality into literacy a millennium earlier still. The contemporary revolution in the media therefore raised fundamental questions about the relationship between ways of thinking and modes of communication across the pageant of the past. Specialized studies on each of these topics were already in progress. But McLuhan's work highlighted their interrelationship and showed the degree to which they were aspects of a larger process of historical change.[64] As modes of communication were modified, so too were the uses of memory, and with them the historians' perceptions of the past.

The American literary scholar and cultural historian Walter J. Ong has provided what many regard as the best overview of the way in which these long-range changes in modes of communication transformed culture. Ong became acquainted with McLuhan while a student at St. Louis University shortly before the Second World War, and it was at McLuhan's suggestion that he embarked on his intellectual biography of Peter Ramus, a rhetorician and mnemonist of the Renaissance.[65] Ramus had a more abstract bent than did the hermetic philosophers that so fascinated Yates, and his move toward a visual mode of learning set Ong in search of the nature of the oral traditions from which this new rhetorical practice departed.[66] His several studies of the relationship between oral and literate traditions, culminating in his *Orality and Literacy* (1982), analyzed the process of cultural change that accompanied the transition from one form of communication to another.[67]

Ong built his argument around his perception of the formative power of orality in human communication. Oral expression, he contended, is a matrix from which all communication proceeds, and it continued to envelop human culture long after artificial technologies of communication had been super-imposed. Its traits are easily distinguished from those of literacy, bespeak-ing the differences in mind-set between the two. In this respect, he stressed the existential character of the spoken word. With its recourse to meta-phor and its poetical mimicking of the rhythms of nature, oral expression is immersed in the life world. Ong spoke of the "presence of the word," which binds past and future to present perceptions. Oral expression tends to be co-pious; it relies heavily on preset formulaic phrasing. Literate expression, by contrast, tends to be spare; its facile use of words lends itself more easily to abstract thought. More important for our purposes, it makes possible a critical awareness of the differences between past and present, and so of the uses of memory.[68]

In Ong's view, the rise of literacy by no means displaced the power of orality. Until the eighteenth century, he explained, literate culture was still primarily a manuscript culture, with limited power to shape the way in which the word was transmitted. It is true, he conceded, that the invention of script in antiquity permitted more abstract ways of thinking. But oral modes of expression continued to exercise a tenacious hold over the organization and transmission of knowledge well into the modern era.[69] The world of manu-script literacy of late antiquity and the Middle Ages was for the most part a sphere of elite culture apart. Literacy until the seventeenth century was in-sufficiently pervasive to provide a textual frame of reference for society at large. Few scholars had ready access to the written word, and those who did thought of literacy as a personal rather than a public resource. Literacy en-hanced the rhetorician's spoken skills; it provided a foundation for dialogue within the community of scholars. But such erudition was usually removed from society at large. The refinements of the intellectual accomplishments of this elite notwithstanding, traditional European culture remained grounded in habits of everyday life, customs of popular mores, values of popular piety, and respect for unwritten law, all of which remained indebted to oral modes of communication.[70] The boundary between orality and literacy, therefore, served as an open frontier for much of Western history.

The more profound changes attending the impact of literacy, Ong therefore argued, arrived only with the advent of print culture, whose influence was becoming pervasive by the eighteenth century. Print culture intensified and publicized changes inaugurated within manuscript literacy. It enhanced the possibilities of abstract thought by removing communication further from the life world. It recast phonetic utterances as typographic symbols. To receive such a message required a shift from ear to eye as the primary means of per-ception. Messages, as they were detached from the personal signature of script, became more impersonal and more uniform in their potential for lim-itless reproduction. Most impressive of all was the power of the printed word to reach a wider readership. What had been a mode of privacy in manuscript culture became one of publicity in that of print. Print quickened the spread of mass literacy. It made manifest its power in its capacity to publicize messages in unprecedented ways.[71]

The primary effect of the print revolution, Ong explained, was to textualize culture. Common sense, once construed as the wisdom of unwritten tradition, was recast as the common knowledge stored in textbooks. As the primary frame of reference for public communication, the printed text had profound implications for the learning process. On the one hand, it exteriorized knowledge. Knowledge might be stored with unparalled accuracy outside the human mind in books and newspapers, and these in turn in libraries and archives. It provided a common frame of reference for encoding knowledge; it stimulated a need for clear and precise formulation of ideas. Knowledge was henceforth to be indexed according to an alphabetic sequence, displacing the mnemonic loci to which rhetoricians had once looked for their cues.[72] On the other hand, the printed text internalized the quest for knowledge. Reading encouraged introspection.[73] The search for the identity of the self as a unique personality, therefore, became a prominent theme from the late eighteenth century.[74]

For Ong, the electronic revolution of our own time is once more transforming our mode of communication in elemental ways. The intrusion of the radio, film, the computer screen, and especially television has led once again to the reorganization of the canons of knowledge. Ong referred to the present age as one of a secondary orality.[75] The soundbyte is displacing typeset as the basic unit for the organization of knowledge, transforming and vastly expanding the speed and scope of communication. Accelerating the pace of communication beyond anything that humans can comprehend through their sense experience, the electronic media have reinforced a trend toward abstraction dating from the beginnings of literacy. The avenues opened by the electronic revolution for organizing and presenting knowledge have made possible a more reflective stance toward the resources of print culture, analogous to the stance of manuscript literacy toward orality. Media culture has made the contemporary age aware of the limits of print culture, indeed of the relativity of knowledge generally to the medium through which it is conveyed. Ong suggested, therefore, that the coming of an electronic culture has returned rhetoric to the prominence it once held in manuscript culture, this time presenting it not simply as a repertoire of techniques for conveying messages but as a constituent element of culture itself.[76]

One might argue that Ong groups modes of communication as stages in a long-range pattern of historical change: from orality, to manuscript literacy, to print culture, to media culture. The pattern may be interpreted diachronically, in that the properties of communication in each stage are different from those in the preceding one. But the stages may also be appreciated synchronically, because each new stage coexists with those already extant in interchanges of gathering complexity. In the most refined reaches of media culture, orality continues to exercise at least a limited authority. Ong does not address the problem of memory in a systematic way. But his argument has important implications for its changing uses in the long-range shift from oral to literate modes of communication. The expressive, collective memory of oral tradition gives way to the introspective, personal memory of literate culture. Memory, first conceived as a repetition, is eventually reconceived as a recollection. Over the long run, the appreciation of memory as a habit is displaced by one of memory as a representation. For this reason, Ong's work provides a broader framework for conceptualizing the history of memory than any previously conceived.[77]

McLuhan, Ong, and those who have followed them in treating the orality/ literacy question in this vein have their critics, who claim that in privileging the role of technology in cultural change they overlook the way in which such technologies were themselves molded by social and cultural forces. The impact of technology, they contend, cannot be divorced from its particular uses in concrete historical settings. When communication is considered within the complex web of the civilizing process, these scholars argue, Ong's broad pattern of historical development from orality into refined stages of literacy disintegrates into a maze of particular situations. They also chide Ong for presenting orality as a pristine foundation of human communication, vitiated by the introduction of artificial technologies that enhance the efficiency of communication at the expense of expressive utterance. They suggest that Ong considers the move from naive orality into ever more sophisticated literacy to be a degenerative process.[78]

Ong's argument, it is true, does have a reductionist character. But one need not interpret it as an unfolding teleological scheme, or to view advances in the technologies of communication as the primary causal force in cultural history. Whatever its limitations, Ong's conceptual framework provides a practical guide to the places to which historians have actually turned in their research into the orality/literacy problem, which accounts in some measure for his book's popularity. In that perspective, the pattern Ong has discerned is itself not unlike a mnemonic scheme. Each stage in the history of changing modes of communication might be linked to a different historical perspective on memory: orality with the reiteration of living memory; manuscript literacy with the recovery of lost wisdom; print literacy with the reconstruction of a distinct past; and media literacy with the deconstruction of the forms with which images of the past are composed. Not only does such a scheme provide an outline for a history of memory; it also makes it possible for us to see how historical understanding originally issued from memory, which in turn became hidden in the historians' abstractions. The inquiry into the history of memory requires consideration of the historiographical relationship between memory and history, for memory is integral to historical understanding itself. The historians' task is to figure out how that relationship changes. That is a project that is only beginning to get under way and whose directions my book is intended to chart.

Stages on Memory's Way to History

Two broad areas of scholarship emerge within the McLuhan/Ong framework for the historians' consideration: (1) the formulation of an historical perspective on the orality/literacy problem; and (2) the consideration of the relationship between the print revolution and the commemorative cast of modern historiography. The orality/literacy problem is today a sprawling topic of historical investigation. It takes its beginnings from the inquiry by classicists of the early twentieth century into the relationship between the Homeric epics and oral tradition. The focus has since shifted to the comparative study of oral traditions, especially in non-Western cultures. It has become a fertile field for interdisciplinary research and provides the foundation for a thriving scholarship in oral history.[79] Historians have borrowed insights from such anthropologists as Edward Evans-Prichard, Mary Douglas, and Jack Goody, who have worked on contemporary African cultures.[80] Studies by clinical psychologists dating from the 1930s, such as those by the English scholar Frederic Bartlett or the Russians Lev Vygotsky and Alexander Luria, have also continued to provide insight for historians of oral culture.[81] All emphasize the special properties of memory in oral tradition. Oral culture provides a milieu of living memory. Therein one speaks of a memory of the past that is bound to the present for its survival. The past exists only insofar as it continues to be held in living memory, and it is so remembered only as long as it serves present need.[82] In such a milieu, imagination and memory are virtually interchangeable, because each is defined by its capacity to form images in which past, present, and future are intimately joined. In oral tradition, memory is presumed to be the archetypal form in which imagination is vested.[83]

This conception of memory as a repetition of archetypal events is based on a profound respect for custom. Memory in oral tradition is identified primarily with habit; its authority is derived from the felt need to reiterate the wisdom bequeathed by the past. Custom gives testimony to the enduring power of the past without revealing the specific nature of its heritage. The paradox is that the past is continually being updated as new realities present themselves. But improvisation is slow enough to be incorporated into custom imperceptibly, accommodating change under the guise of changelessness.[84] In oral tradition, collective memory is the only frame of reference by which to judge the past, which recedes into oblivion at the edge of living memory.[85] The problem of origins, therefore, does not enter its considerations. For the ancients, time immemorial was a past beyond memory but one that continued to live in the present insofar as it was identified with customs and traditions in use.[86] Epic was the first and most enduring subject to attract the oral historians' attention because it was the quintessential form for remembering the past within oral tradition. It was a celebration of the presence of the past, reborn each time it was told. The storyline of epic moved in cycles. No tale was told in exactly the same way. But each telling was based on a story drawn from the living resources of collective memory.[87]

Scholarly work on the impact of literacy on oral cultures permits us to see how the coming of script made possible a critical perspective on the past. But the memory of manuscript culture represented less an opening into history (conceived as an appreciation of the reality of change) than an attempt to hold onto the wisdom of time immemorial derived from oral tradition. The past as it was examined within this context was appreciated not as a different reality but rather as a lost mentality. Thus the notion of memory as a repetition, carried over from oral culture, was gradually replaced by one of memory as a resurrection. Memory was reconceived as a capacity to make the experiences of the past live again.[88] A manuscript culture respects the authority of the past but longs to overcome a newfound disquiet about its remove. The wisdom inherited from the past is acknowledged to be lodged in sources that cannot be completely retrieved, for script provides mementos of the past that stand apart from the living memories identified with time immemorial.[89] Origins take on more authority in this kind of memory, as they are recognized to be distant, even if they cannot be fixed with precision. This reverence for the past is evinced in epic and in law, as they pass from oral tradition into script. Beginnings become important in a way they had not before. Epics come to be identified with authors of surpassing wisdom, and laws with lawgivers at the founding of nations.[90] Such traits are revealed as well in historical writing, in which the past is presented as being exemplary of human practice. The need to reaffirm the identity between past and present outweighs the need to remark upon their differences. It was not until the Renaissance that scholars became interested in verifying the authenticity of their manuscript sources.[91]

An appreciation of the uses of memory within manuscript culture also permits a modern perspective on the purpose of the art of memory. Mnemonic schemes employ techniques of displacement, involving studied recourse to the eidetic imagery that had evoked memory spontaneously in oral culture. One might therefore contend that the art of memory employs evocative images to resuscitate fading habits of mind. Mnemonics is a skill, but like the technology of script itself, it is limited in its applications. Those initiated into its methods hope to use it to resurrect a living past for a present that senses its loss. Yates surveyed the most grandiose of these mnemonic designs. But the art found more ready expression in the easily memorized maxims with which rhetoricians displayed their erudition or the oral formulae to which jurists had recourse to ensure accuracy in their interpretation of the law.[92]

In retrospect, we can see that the art of memory had a legacy for historical understanding, its spatial formulations notwithstanding. The mnemonist claimed not only to have recovered the secret wisdom of the ancients but also to have resurrected their state of mind. For the hermetic philosophers especially, the art of memory was a way toward initiation into a state of spiritual enlightenment in which the past was not merely revisited but actually restored. Eventually, this conception of the art would find its way directly into certain kinds of modern historical thinking. Autobiography, psychoanalysis, and its offshoot, psychohistory, are all in a way modern arts of memory. Though they lodge memories in temporal rather than spatial schemes, all work with the same principle of displacement as did the classical art, and all seek to evoke a forgotten mind-set. Images continue to mark significant, hidden ideas, and they in turn are placed on a timeline of remembrance that shows the route into the past to be followed in the search for a lost truth.[93]

Despite its obvious significance in the making of modern historical consciousness, the problem of the relationship between the rise of print culture between the sixteenth and the eighteenth centuries and the commemorative cast of modern historiography has yet to receive scholarly attention.[94] The authority of modern historiography has been closely bound to the power to publish. Since the early nineteenth century, professional historical scholarship has been a project of producing printed books based on research in manuscript collections.[95] The mnemonist of the sixteenth century professed to resurrect the wisdom of an earlier age with techniques borrowed from oral tradition; the historian of the nineteenth century, by contrast, endeavored to reconstruct traditions that could no longer be culled from living memory. With the coming of print culture, memory was historicized in more concrete ways. Print culture textualized the past. By removing ideas, personalities, and events from the milieu of oral tradition and giving them a specific time and place in collective memory, texts enabled readers to comprehend the historicity of the past in a more profound way. The textualizing of collective memory deepened the readers' awareness of temporality, and this in turn led to the recasting of mnemonic schemes, previously conceived spatially, onto timelines on which historical events served as places of memory.[96]

In the new thinking about memory there was much sensitivity to the interchange between its habits and its images. Scholars of the late eighteenth and early nineteenth centuries began to reflect on the meaning of the distinction between repetition and recollection, thenceforth viewed as antinomies within an ongoing, dialectical interchange.[97] Within this new text-based culture, the meaning of memory at once diminished and expanded. Although one might remember the past, its meaning for the present age could never be wrested from the historical context in which it was embedded. One acknowledged the reality of change, and the critical distance from which the past had to be surveyed. The past could be neither repeated (as in oral culture) nor resurrected (as in manuscript culture) but only reconstructed. But at the same time, one might reach back farther into the past and with greater certainty than ever before. For this reason, the fixing of specific dates for events in the past became an issue in a way that it had not before.[98]

The stress of poets, philosophers, and historians on recollective memory,

so much in evidence by the early nineteenth century, suggests why commemoration acquired rising prominence during this era. The pathos of nineteenth-
century commemoration that Ariès identified was derived from an awareness
that the past could not be recovered as a living experience. In acknowledging
the loss of the presence of the past, historical memory carried traces of sentimentality. Commemoration acknowledged the limits of memory's restor-
ative powers. But in appreciating the reality of a discrete past, what one
wanted to remember were connections with it. The present might be different
from the past, yet remained linked to it through developmental lines of continuity. In remembering, one could locate beginnings and trace developments.
The growing awareness that recollection was a distinct moment of memory,
therefore, marked the emergence of an historical perspective that distinguished present understanding from that of earlier traditions. The past of living memory, conceived as a continuum that recedes from the present toward
vague horizons in the past, yielded place to an historical memory that places
events of past and present within invented chronologies. In this way, historical
understanding began to take possession of memory, and in the process transformed its meaning. Historical memory depended less on inherited wisdom,
more on reconstructive interpretation. One revisited the past by traveling over
time to visit unfamiliar places that one had to learn how to comprehend. The
task was to reconstruct its mind-set as best one could imagine. In this way,
the historians' recollections reached back toward distant horizons in order to
reconstruct the imagination of an earlier age.[99]

This new self-consciousness about the historicity of the past led to new
reflections on the nature of historical understanding, which by the end of the
century had come to be termed historicism. Historicism taught that historians
must judge the past on its own terms, but with a view to widening the horizons of their present understanding. Much was made of the need to re-create
the imagination of the historical actors of the past. One might judge the past
but always within its own context.[100] Unacknowledged, however, was the way
in which collective memory continued to provide the larger framework for the
historical linking of past to present.[101] The historical context being considered
was assimilated into a conception of the past ultimately derived from the unexamined assumptions of the historiographical tradition in which historians
themselves were situated. Some historians were more committed to explicating grand schemes of history than were others. But all made use of timelines on which images of salient events or notable personalities served as places
of their memory. The most grandiose versions of such schemes came to be
identified with the philosophy of history, and by the early twentieth century
they were regarded by most professional historians with suspicion.[102] But in
the nineteenth century, the line between history and the philosophy of history
was not so easily drawn, for few historians wrote without an open profession
of the direction in which they believed the past to be tending. Essentially these
historians were explicating traditions with which they personally identified.

Typically these were political traditions that underpinned the rise of the modern state. Often camouflaged in the guise of science, such histories established the official framework in which the past was to be considered.[103]

In light of such observations on the historicizing of memory within a print-based culture, one may better understand why historians writing within today's media culture have become more self-conscious about the relationship between memory and history. The exteriorization of memory in its textualized representations in print culture has itself come to be viewed as an historical phenomenon. Print is recognized as but one context of communication. The imagination it inscribes crowds out alternative representations of the past. Historians in media culture, therefore, have become more readily disposed to analyze the images through which the past is remembered. They contend that history is no more than an official memory, one among many possible ways in which to imagine the past.[104]

One may therefore better understand why Nora presented his search for the "places of memory" of the French national identity as an exercise in archaeology. The text, viewed in print culture as a source of a past imagination to be revealed, is reviewed in media culture as an artifact to be excavated, akin in its commemorative function to monuments and rituals. As artifacts, texts surrender their claim to evoke substantive meanings out of the past and settle for the more modest one of displaying the way in which meanings were once represented. The historian no longer aspires to recollect the ideas of the authors or the intentions of the actors under consideration but rather to inventory their imagery. One may appreciate as well the insistence of Agulhon and Hobsbawm on the divide between images and ideas. As the presence of the past is no longer felt, the commemorative stance, with all of its sentimental attachments, is abandoned.

The appreciation of memory within the context of media also enables one to see more clearly the connection that Nora made between classical mnemonics and history reconceived as a modern art of memory. In contemporary postmodern historiography, access to knowledge of the past as a living experience is considered to be beyond our powers of comprehension. The inner life of those who fashioned culture in the past remains hidden and inaccessible. One cannot recollect the authors' intentions, for the images they have left behind are impossible to penetrate. An image is not a conduit to the inner workings of the imagination of those who created it but rather a mirror reflecting present concerns. In this way, the past itself for the historians of the media age becomes completely absorbed in its representations. Through them, historians describe the forms in which the past was once imagined.[105]

It is no surprise, therefore, that historians sensitive to the politics of commemorative practices should view with suspicion historians who identify closely with the traditions they study. The English scholar Herbert Butterfield's critique of Whig historians was an early expression of this stance.[106] On the eve of the bicentennial of the French Revolution, the position was restated more polemically by the French historian François Furet. Furet repudiated the commemorative character of modern historical scholarship on the Revolution. In an essay entitled "The Revolution Is Over," he challenged the interpretation of the dominant school of historiography, launched by Jules Michelet in the early nineteenth century and perpetuated into the twentieth by such renowned historians as Albert Mathiez, Georges Lefebvre, and Albert Soboul. Committed to a political tradition inaugurated by parties in the Revolution itself, they confirmed in their reading of the past what the revolutionaries had once envisioned for their future.[107] There are other ways in which the past might be remembered, Furet cautions. Much depends on the images in which the event has been represented. In this respect, he contends, the Revolution had less to do with social upheaval (as these historians argued) than with rhetorical claims about the Revolution's meaning. The real revolution at the end of the eighteenth century was in political discourse, which created a new vocabulary for discussing advanced republican (Jacobin) goals and expectations. In inventing a discourse, the revolutionaries created a memory, for the imagery in which political discussions were cast established the linguistic code in which the event would thenceforth be remembered. It framed not only the future of political discourse but also that of historical writing. Rather than perpetuate political traditions, Furet suggests, historians today would do better to describe the ways in which the Revolution has been represented. What is left of the imagination of the Revolution resides not in a reconstruction of its direction of intention (as Georges Lefebvre believed) but in an inventory of the images invented by its participants and enshrined by its historians.[108] In this way, Furet may be said to have prepared the way for the deconstruction of the places of the French national memory undertaken a few years thereafter by Nora.

Habit and the Horizons of Tradition

To the historians' fascination with the commemorative practices of the past, therefore, we must juxtapose their reluctance to bear the taint of being identified with commemorative historical writing. As I have shown, the historians' recent interest in memory is tied to the postmodern emphasis on the images and forms of its representation. The problem with such an approach, however, is that it reduces the memory of the past to the history of its images. It makes of rhetorical practice itself a level of reality that intervenes between historians and the events, personalities, and ideas of the past that they would study.

But is there not a way to appreciate the reality of the past that is incommensurable with the record of its imaginative description? The question raises the problem of the nature of tradition, which provides our closing perspective on the history/memory topic.[109] The efforts of the historians of the politics of memory to deconstruct the frameworks through which the past has been represented provide the groundwork for reconstructing the history of memory. But in their historiographical methods, they tend to emphasize tangible icons in order to hold onto a claim to objectivity. These historians trace the way in which the archaeology of the places of memory displaces an historicism grounded in memory conceived as imagination. But none is sufficiently attentive to the ways in which the imagination implicit in hidden habits of mind remain crucial to the historians' enterprise.[110] That may explain why historicism has recently begun to inspire renewed interest among literary historians and among historians addressing the problem of the limits of representation.[111]

Such practical scholarship is related to the reconsideration of historicism as a theoretical problem in the hermeneutics of history. Herein lies the significance of Hans-Georg Gadamer's work in *Truth and Method* (1960). Gadamer reviews the making of the historicist tradition from Giambattista Vico to Wilhelm Dilthey, with its attention to the developmental character of history. He accepts their argument that historical understanding is based on an imaginative reconstruction of the past.[112] Historicism, he explains, has taught us to recognize the historicity of events and to widen our horizons to grasp the realities of change within particular historical traditions. But he also points out the limitations of the historicist enterprise, for he is interested as well in the power of the past that is encountered in historical study—that past that prompts the historians' inquiry as it is carried forward by tradition for their consideration.[113] Historians too, he contends, are immersed in tradition and ought to acknowledge its authority.[114] The problem of history, he maintains, involves not just the reconstruction of the past, but also an openness to the encounter with it. It is at the edge of memory that the past recedes into strangeness and historians must become accustomed to its alien character. After all, they share with the historical actors of the past the temporality of the human condition. Their task, therefore, is not only to explore the mental horizons of a given historical milieu but also to recognize its relationship to the widening of their own.[115] Gadamer speaks of this encounter as a "fusion of horizons," through which historians come to recognize that their capacity to interpret the past proceeds from the understanding they have acquired through participation in traditions of their own.[116] It is the historians' experience of memory that serves as the basis of their ability to engage in historical inquiry. Memory joins anticipation and recollection and so imbues thought with an awareness of temporality. As Gadamer concludes, "It is time to rescue the phenomenon of memory from being regarded merely as a psychological faculty and to see it as an essential element of the finite historical being of man."[117]

To deal with Gadamer's insights in terms of French historiography, we might return to the author with whom we began. In our understanding of the rise of historiography as a memory problem we are indebted to an early and largely forgotten work of Philippe Ariès, whom we mentioned above in connection with the history of nineteenth-century commemorations. Having been drawn to the study of history through personal memories of the traditionalist lore of his own family, Ariès was sensitive to memory's power to inspire interest in the past. His own efforts to reach back from the living memories of the deep traditions of his family's heritage (bequeathed to him by his parents and relatives) became the working model for his larger conception of historical inquiry.[118] His *Le Temps de l'histoire* (1954), therefore, is particularly worth revisiting for its direct insights into the history/memory problem from a hermeneutical perspective. In this study, Ariès considers how French historiography came into being in the late Middle Ages in those places where history began to be distinguished from collective memory. He contends that in the script culture of the Middle Ages, historical writing was but a marginal extension of traditions of living memory. Fathoming the past in that milieu was a pluralistic enterprise, in which history and memory were in constant interchange. Therein historical understanding continued to bear many of the traits of collective memory. Rival groups presented discordant conceptions of the past in a collage of local and regional histories of religious groups and feudal causes, often against a backdrop of universal history borrowed from such early chronologists as Eusebius. Ariès argues that the rise of French historiography in the early modern era was essentially a project of consolidating this mix of collective memory and local history into a single chronological scheme that framed the ascent of the French monarchy. Herein lay the importance of the royal historiographers of the seventeenth century. In writing a history of France, they either bent local histories to conform to its design or discarded them altogether. Royal historiography was a counterpart to political absolutism, for it cast the identity of France into a pattern that mirrored the aspirations of its absolutist kings.[119]

Ariès's point was that the pageant of the French past as it was transmitted through local histories and oral traditions was obscured by the interests of this emerging historiography, intent on accommodating the vanities of its kings in its accounts of their lives and accomplishments. Official history, in effect, surrendered its capacity to acknowledge its beginnings in collective memory. The French Revolution may have toppled the king, but the historical accounts of the event only hardened the political framework in which French historiography had already been conceived. Factional rivalries among the politicians displaced the contest between nobles and kings as subjects of topical interest, and much was made of ideological differences among modern historians. But the political focus remained, and the customs and mores of traditional French society, situated in a past that lay closer to the stuff of life, were either ignored or fitted to the political framework.[120]

One might not warm to Ariès's conservative views on the nature and significance of the French Revolution. But he did anticipate the work of the historians of the politics of commemoration in his insight into memory's power to shape historical conceptions. He prepared the way for their deconstruction of the French national memory by explaining why French historiography assumed its particular rhetorical guise. Ariès, on the other hand, never wrote with their detachment, for he was sympathetic to the traditions that were being obscured.[121] His interest was less in the power of historians in the present to mold images of the past than in the power of the past to inspire the historians' curiosity. Images freshly conceived, he suggested, obscured the ongoing significance of inveterate habits of mind. If the official political history represented an advance out of parochial traditions into a wider consciousness of the past, he contended, it was nonetheless diminished by its forgetfulness of its origins in collective memory. Historical understanding is selective, but collective memory is sustaining. If popular mores and manners were ignored by an official historiography, they remained alive in the oral traditions that have recently recaptured the historians' attention. Curiosity, Ariès believed, prompted the historians of collective mentalities to search for the deep sources of this past that lie close to memory.[122] For the renaissance of interest in this field since the 1960s, Ariès's vision of the past betokened a new approach to history.[123]

For the historians of the politics of commemoration, history begins where memory ends. But for Ariès, the essential task is not to distinguish history from memory, but to recognize their interchange. That is why he characterizes his love of history as an encounter with a beckoning horizon. The horizon marks the present limits of the historians' efforts to imagine the past. It is the boundary between what is known and unknown, or more precisely, the past that historians have interpreted and that which awaits their consideration. History for Ariès is therefore something more than the aggregate of the images in which historians have chosen to represent the past. His approach reaffirms the reality of what lies beyond the historians' vision. Its effect is to restore to the past the power to prompt the present. For Ariès, history is an art of memory because it is situated at the crossroads between tradition and historiography. Such an approach restores to historical inquiry its mediating role. It rescues the unrecollected past from oblivion. It underscores the significance of tradition, which carries into the present the unexamined past.[124]

It is significant, I think, that in *Le Temps* Ariès labeled his approach to history existential.[125] He later discarded the term in favor of the one then in vogue—collective mentalities.[126] But the notion of existential history is suggestive of what he was trying to convey about the task of the historian, especially when compared to the postmodern orientation of most of those who have recently pursued the project of the politics of memory. Existential history affirms the reality of the past that rhetorical history would limit to its imaginative representations. Ariès's point is that historians do not simply reconstruct the past. They encounter its enduring power as they endeavor to describe it in imaginative ways.[127]

Ariès's observations bring us to a reckoning with the many interchanges in which memory may be recognized, and which we have noted over the course of this essay: memory and imagination; habit and image; repetition and recollection; collective and individual memory; tradition and history. All are ways of expressing the relationship between the two moments in which the past is continually perceived. Memory, as we suggested at the outset, is like a crossroads. What we see at this juncture depends on the direction in which we are traveling. Looking back on an earlier phase of the journey, we recollect our experiences on the particular road that we have taken. But looking forward, we repeat what first inspired us to undertake the journey. In setting forth, we find that many roads are open to our imagination and that in anticipation itself each becomes a moment of our memory.

THE ART OF MEMORY RECONCEIVED

From Renaissance Rhetoric to
Giambattista Vico's Historicism

The Art of Memory Revisited

Mnemonics, or the art of memory, is today regarded as an arcane intellectual interest. It functions on the periphery of popular culture, largely through a literature of self-help designed to bolster the confidence of people insecure about their powers of recollection. If it is a useful skill, it is not an essential one in a civilization whose collective memory is stored securely in the printed word. Today's archive for reliable reference is the library or the computer, not the depths of a well-ordered mind. Yet there was a time in the not-too-distant past when the art of memory held pride of place in the councils of learning, for it enhanced one's power to lecture or preach in a world that trusted in the authority of the spoken word. From the wandering rhapsodes of ancient Greece who enthralled listeners with the epic tales of Homer to the philosophers of the Renaissance who constructed imaginary memory palaces to present their intricate designs of the cosmos, the development of the powers of memory was perceived to be an essential intellectual skill.

The art of memory as it was traditionally conceived was based upon associations between a structure of images easily remembered and a body of knowledge in need of organization. The mnemonist's task was to attach the facts that he wished to recall to images that were so visually striking or emotionally evocative that they could be recalled at will. He then classified these images in an architectural design of places with which he was readily familiar. The landscape of memory so constructed was an imaginary tableau in which a world of knowledge might be contained for ready reference. It was in effect a borrowed paradigm, the logic of whose imaginary structure gave shape to the otherwise formless knowledge he wished to retain.[1]

Legend has it that the art of memory was invented by the Greek poet Simonides of Ceos (ca. 556–468 B.C.), who provides the first recorded reflection on the emotional power of a system of images as an aid to memory. Simonides claims to have discovered the power of pictorial images when he, as a guest at a palace banquet, fortuitously exited just before the palace collapsed. Awestruck by his good fortune, he found that his emotional reaction to the experience enabled him to conjure up a vivid and detailed picture of the banquet's participants in their assigned places just before the crash. Thus he discovered that ideas difficult to remember can be systematically committed to memory by associating them with unforgettable images.[2]

The mnemonic technique that Simonides recognized, of course, must have been derived from powers of memory employed naturally and spontaneously in a still earlier age. Interestingly, Simonides' reflections coincide roughly with the rise of literacy in ancient Greece, and were soon to be incorporated into the mnemonic schemes of classical rhetoric. These expressions of a felt need to enhance the powers of memory through artificial techniques in the classical age of Greece hint at a sense of lost innate mnemonic powers. They raise the question of whether humankind deep in its primordial history may have possessed greater natural powers of memory, of the sort that would have been useful in an oral culture heavily dependent on received wisdom, but that were bound to atrophy in a literate one beginning to pride itself on its capacity for abstract reflection.

Examples of humans with this type of prodigious memory continue to appear occasionally in modern times. The study of the mind of an unusually gifted twentieth-century mnemonist by the distinguished Russian neuropsychologist Alexander Luria is a case in point.[3] The subject of his study, S. V. Sherashevsky, entertained audiences across Russia during the 1930s with his capacity to commit to memory any data with which they wished to test his talent, including long lists of random monosyllables or the elements of complex, sometimes incorrect, mathematical equations. He could still recall such information without prompting a decade later. Sherashevsky possessed what Luria characterized as a "marked degree of synesthesia," that is, acute sensory perception that heightened his capacity to remember ideas by virtue of the vivid imagery that he could attach to them.[4] Yet he lacked the capacity for abstraction and the agility of mind essential for success in the modern world. Tormented by a clutter of facts that he could forget only through an enormous effort of will, he found his gift a burden. Unable to hold an ordinary job, he plied the trade of a showman for want of something better to do.[5]

In the modern world, one might admire the mnemonist's genius while recognizing its obsolescence.[6] It is as if Sherashevsky had been for Luria a clinical psychological find, in its significance akin to an anthropologist's discovery of a Stone-Age tribe in some forgotten corner of the world. For this reason, most professional psychologists today dismiss mnemonics as irrelevant to the concerns of their discipline. Some are puzzled by the elaborate and seemingly cumbersome systems of recall employed by mnemonists through the ages and question whether the systems themselves might not be more difficult to remember than the facts to be committed to memory. Others, while conceding the efficacy of schemes that help us to retrieve facts in serial order, regard mnemonics as a skill with relatively few contemporary applications.[7] If the art of memory was an essential technique of learning for yesterday's rhetoricians, it has become for today's psychologists the stuff of sideshows.

In focusing on the practical techniques of mnemonics, however, the psychologists have overlooked its historical ties to the conceptual schemes in which humans have always organized knowledge. The art of memory as it was understood in its classical formulation provided not only a useful skill but also a way of understanding the world. For some mnemonists the design of the structure of their mnemonic system corresponded to their conception of the structure of knowledge and so implied a vision of the world. The power of the mnemonist lay in his ability to interpret the world through a paradigm that would provide its initiates with a *clavis universalis,* a master key to the workings of the universe.[8] From this perspective the art of memory was not only a pedagogical device but also a method of interpretation. It is this link between the art of memory and the formulation of paradigms of cultural understanding that suggests the larger significance of this topic and its enduring applications in the modern world. If the art of memory as it was employed from classical antiquity until the Renaissance seems cumbersome in comparison with our present mental operations and remote from our current needs, we may ask whether the art's intimate association with model building has not enabled it to survive in the modern world in a different guise.

In this and the following chapter, I shall consider the transformation of the art of memory into an art of history since the eighteenth century. I shall point out the correspondences between the art of memory as it was practiced in the rhetorical tradition of the Renaissance and its hidden presence in the temporal paradigms of some modern modes of inquiry into the past: as a "new science" of history since characterized as historicism; as a technique of soul-searching identified with modern autobiography; and finally as a substructure of psychoanalysis. Three figures especially are prominent in explaining this transition from memory into history: the eighteenth-century Neapolitan historian Giambattista Vico, who developed a method for decoding the poetic consciousness of ancient civilizations for the hidden memories it contained; the nineteenth-century English poet William Wordsworth, who searched for the sources of his poetical inspiration in memories of his childhood; and the Austrian physician Sigmund Freud, who pressed the search for memory's sources into the recesses of the unconscious mind. Just as the mnemonists of the Renaissance sought to convey to their initiates a hidden knowledge of the world, so I shall seek in this chapter to show how the art of memory itself is hidden in the rhetoric of more recent forms of historical discourse and how in the process mnemonic schemes were adapted to the needs of modern historical understanding.

Frances Yates and the History of the Art of Memory

For an understanding of what the art of memory was in the distant past, the work of the English historian Frances Yates (1899–1981) is an essential point of departure. Yates was a student of the intellectual underground of the Renaissance and her study of mnemonics was an offshoot of her inquiry into the thought of Giordano Bruno, a sixteenth-century Neapolitan philosopher whose fascination with systems of memory had roots in the ancient hermetic tradition of gnostic thought.[9] Yates was intrigued with the Renaissance revival of the art of memory at a time when one might suppose the advent of printing would have rendered it obsolete. In the course of her investigations she traced mnemonics as a system of artificial memory to its origins in Greece in the fifth century B.C. From its simple beginnings in the rhetoric of sophistry to its sophisticated refinement in the hermetic cosmology of the Renaissance, Yates explains, the art of memory was employed in the service of diverse philosophies. In Greco-Roman times it enhanced the rhetorician's eloquence. During the High Middle Ages it was used to classify an increasingly complex scheme of ethics. By the Renaissance it had become intertwined with Neoplatonic metaphysics. Yet through all of these cultural transformations, Yates stresses, the techniques of the art of memory remained essentially the same.[10] Indeed, across these 2,000 years a sense of a classical mnemonic tradition developed, as each restatement of the art alluded to earlier formulations, notably the *Rhetorica ad Herennium,* an anonymous Roman tract written about 82 B.C., and even to that of its legendary Greek founder, the poet Simonides.

The technique of artificial memory that Yates identifies with the classical tradition of mnemonics consisted of arrangements of places and images. The places provided an architectonic design in which the knowledge to be remembered was to be situated. These were places deeply embedded in the mind of the mnemonist that could not be forgotten. The architecture of place, often conceived as a palace or a theater, might be likened to a sacred space with which the mnemonist possessed intuitive familiarity. This deep structure of memory, in turn, was given its particular character by the images with which it was adorned. A good memory was a function of a resilient imagination, and images were chosen for their aesthetic appeal. Vivid pictorial imagery that inspired awe was judged to be the most effective.[11]

If the techniques of the art of memory remained essentially the same, change was visible in the purposes for which the art was used. Yates explains that these oscillated between two theories of knowledge, one derived from Aristotle and the other from Plato. In the Aristotelian tradition, the art of memory was merely instrumental. Aristotle taught that knowledge is derived from sense experience and that a mnemonic system is to be judged by its practical capacity to fix knowledge in images that heighten sense perception. Whether mnemonic images possessed any correspondence of meaning to the ideas to be conveyed was irrelevant. This conception was especially popular during the High Middle Ages, when scholastic philosophers valued memory systems for their utility in communicating moral lessons, yet held them in suspicion because of their derivation from the pagan learning of classical civilization. Mnemonics was a profane art, always subordinate to the sacred message it carried.[12] In the Platonic tradition, however, the powers of memory were judged to be more substantive. Plato taught that mnemic images were directly expressive of a transcendental reality. For the mnemonist who shared these views, the value of a mnemic image was directly tied to the ideal reality that it was empowered to represent. The art of memory, therefore, was a way of establishing correspondences between the microcosm of the mind's images and the macrocosm of the ideal universe, which were believed to be congruent structures. In such a conception, the role of the mnemonist took on added importance. Not only did he practice a skill but he also assumed a priestly status as an interpreter of the nature of reality.[13]

This Platonic conception of the art of memory, Yates explains, received its fullest expression during the Italian Renaissance of the sixteenth century. In that era, Neoplatonic philosophers employed the art of memory in an ambitious quest for a unified paradigm of knowledge. Among many ingenious designs, Yates singles out for special attention the mnemonic systems of Giulio Camillo and of Giordano Bruno, both of whom were in search of the key to the hidden structure of the universe in the hermetic teachings of the ancient Egyptian divine, Hermes Trismegistus. Camillo designed a memory theater in which the drama of all human experience was played out on an imaginary stage.[14] Bruno's model was more intricate still. Devising a memory wheel that incorporated geometrical designs borrowed from the most inventive mnemonic systems of the day, he conceived of himself as the architect of a synthetic paradigm of the universe that would provide its practitioners with insight into the deep structural unity of all knowledge of heaven and earth.[15]

It is not surprising that these Neoplatonic paradigms were presented in images of wheels, palaces, theaters, and other geometrical configurations. The structure of knowledge envisioned by the Neoplatonic philosophers was spatial. It was based on an unchanging reality, as all of these mnemonic images implied. Journeys into the memory moved along fixed trajectories to be traveled again and again. The wheel, the palace, and the theater were mementos of repetition. Working from a conception of a timeless cosmos, the Neoplatonic mnemonists possessed no sense of development. They were in search of knowledge that was eternal yet presently hidden. Discovered by the gnostic philosophers of antiquity yet forgotten in the intervening millennium, this hermetic knowledge was waiting to be revealed once more. As the purveyors of secrets at once ancient and powerful, the mnemonists viewed themselves as magi, dealing in an esoteric knowledge that made them privy to the workings of the universe, with all of the powers that such omniscience implied.[16]

As a paradigmatic expression of the worldview of the idealist philosophers of the Renaissance, Yates contends, mnemonics survived into the seventeenth

century because it served a line of intellectual inquiry that continued to display
vitality. Mnemonics would begin to lose its honored status only as Neoplatonic idealism was successfully challenged by scientific empiricism in the
course of that century. The new science, she suggests, would continue to employ the art of memory but in a less exalted role. In a world in which reliable
knowledge was identified with a systematic understanding of sense experience, mnemonics was destined to return to an Aristotelian formulation.
Herein lies the importance of the English philosopher Francis Bacon. Rejecting
the notion of magical correspondences between mnemic images and the powers governing the heavens, Bacon spurned the prideful role of magus for the
more modest one of scientific investigator.[17] Having contributed to the rise of
science in its stress on systematic classification, Yates concludes, mnemonics
lost this distinguishing characteristic as the scientific method acquired an autonomous identity.[18] Having outlived its usefulness, the art of memory as a
recognizable intellectual tradition came to an end.[19]

Giambattista Vico and the Poetics of Memory

Yates persuasively explains the eclipse of the art of memory by the seventeenth century. But if the art had contributed so powerfully to the paradigmatic expression of such a variety of worldviews popular in earlier periods of
Western civilization, would not its imaging resources be appropriated to advance new schemes of knowledge in the modern age? The science into which
the classical art of memory was absorbed was a science of nature. By the
eighteenth century, however, a new science of history was in the making, and
it was in this context that the art of memory was to be reconceived. The
central figure in this revisioning of the role of memory in modern culture was
the Neapolitan scholar Giambattista Vico (1670–1744). In his own day, Vico
was admired as a teacher of rhetoric.[20] But today he is remembered primarily
for his "new science" of history, devised late in life through his search for the
deep sources of the discipline that he had practiced. Rhetoric was the mainstay
of a manuscript culture dating from antiquity, preserving and adapting techniques of oral tradition to serve its needs. For more than a millennium, rhetoricians had founded their reputation on their verbal skill in expounding on
written texts for an audience still heavily dependent on oral communication.
As a late exemplar of this rhetorical tradition of teaching, Vico, too, was engaged in such exegesis. But as a scholar aware that interest in his field of study
was flagging, he inquired into the nature of the mind-set from which it was
derived. Vico's originality lies in his analysis of ancient texts for what they
reveal about a still earlier, preliterate culture. It was in these investigations that
he uncovered the workings of collective memory in oral tradition. If Vico was
a teacher of rhetoric of modest reputation in his own day, he has come to be
honored by ours as a pioneering historian in this field.

Vico's conception of memory, as it had been for the Renaissance Neoplatonists, was tied to a search for deep structures of knowledge hidden from contemporary humankind.[21] But for Vico such knowledge was hidden in the origins of civilization, a lost history of human creation, not in the heavens as an expression of God's design. The Renaissance Neoplatonists had taught that the magi of antiquity were in possession of an occult wisdom that put them in touch with the divine plan. The ancients, Vico explained, did possess wisdom, but it was a wisdom of poetry not philosophy. The ancient poets were magi of sorts, seeking to divine the mysteries of the universe. What they discovered in the process were their own human powers of understanding and acting. In his *New Science* (1744) he provided what he characterized as the "master key" to this poetic knowledge in his interpretation of the dynamics of collective memory.[22]

Vico's vision of the world was historical rather than cosmological, and his work is significant for this study because he was the first scholar to explain the historical conditions out of which the techniques of the ancient art of memory had emerged. If the art dealt in spatial imagery, he would show its place in his own temporal scheme of the historical unfolding of human consciousness. From Vico's perspective, the art of memory may have been a technique invented by Simonides. But Simonides and the classical rhetoricians who embellished his teachings were only restating principles about the dynamics of memory that had been understood intuitively from the dawn of civilization. The artificial memory systems employed by rhetoricians since the classical age were but studied variations on the poetic structure of language employed spontaneously by primitive people. Mnemonics, therefore, is no more than a refinement of the poetic logic of memory, grounded in the primordial structures of poetic expression.[23]

The key to understanding the nature of memory, Vico contended, is derived from the direct correspondence between image and idea in primitive poetic language. In the beginnings of civilization, image and idea were one. Primitive people possessed robust memories because of the inseparable association they made between images and ideas in their comprehension of the world. They thought metaphorically, and the metaphors that they uttered were easily mimicked and remembered because they were richly expressive, grandiose, and full of wonder at the world. The link between human imagination and the universe that the Renaissance Neoplatonists had sought to discover magically, Vico revealed to have been born historically in the development of human consciousness.[24]

The source of the mnemonist's method is visible in the poetic logic of Vico's theory of the emergence of human consciousness. That theory, too, involves the relationship between places and images, which Vico labeled topics and tropes. Topics were the poetic formulae through which primitive people identified the phenomena of the world.[25] As imaginative representations of particular aspects of reality, they provided commonplaces or fixed points of reference amidst the flux of sense experience. As topics multiplied, they came to constitute a structure of the perception of reality. Topics were in effect the groundwork of an emerging field of knowledge. For Vico consciousness developed out of the formulation of topics in imaginary expressions known as tropes. Originally, all topics were interpreted metaphorically. But the use of metaphor was itself a selection of a particular image in which to represent a topic, and the human capacity to be selective was gradually refined. As their knowledge of topics became more extensive, humans learned to express themselves in an imaginative shorthand that modified metaphor: first in terms of metonymy (an eidetic image of a detail that stands for a complete metaphorical topic); then of synecdoche (an image that conveys the character or quality of a topic); and finally of irony (an image that has acquired a generalized meaning of its own, without reference to the particular topic to which it originally had been attached).[26] The development of consciousness, therefore, is for Vico a process of abstraction in which the distance between topics (places) and tropes (images) widens until the metaphorical origins of a topic are forgotten in the ironical imagery of modern discourse. The process of abstraction that inheres in the development of consciousness, therefore, is one of forgetting the connection between our present vocabularies and the poetic process through which they were originally formed. As Vico expressed it in a poetic image of his own, "metonymy draws a cloak of learning over the prevailing ignorance of these origins of human institutions, which have remained buried until now."[27]

Considered in this context, Vico's new science of history involved a retrospective search for the connection between our present conceptions and the lost poetic images out of which they were born. In the logic of Vichian poetics, the new art of memory is an historical reconstruction of the imaginative process by which the poets of antiquity gave shape to their perception of the world. Therein the imaginative sources of our present ideas are to be found. The original topic might be likened to a palimpsest, repeatedly covered over with more abstract imagery as the human mind historically ascended the tropological gradient of linguistic expression. Vico's art of memory was to decipher each tropological layer along the way until the original metaphorical topic, long forgotten, was recalled to mind.[28]

We might say that what Vico offered is an historical model of the life cycle of collective memory. Memory originates in the ontological act of creating images in order to give form and meaning to the phenomena of the world. But as civilization advances, memory comes to be identified with mimesis, that is, it mimics or repeats the creative act in order to discover its original meaning.[29] Such meanings elude the modern philosopher, who does not understand the historical circumstances in which topics originated or the way in which the mind has been altered in the interim.[30]

Vico's theory of memory as an act of interpretation that enables us to establish connections between the familiar images of the present and the unfamiliar ones of the past anticipates the modern science of hermeneutics.[31] Vico described the hermeneutical process as it was understood metaphorically by the ancient Greeks in their image of the god Hermes. Hermes was the messenger of the gods, and he taught humankind the art of communication. He did so by traveling from familiar into strange places and back again. Hermes taught humans to understand the unfamiliar by relating it to the familiar. The ancient poet interpreted the world creatively by explaining strange phenomena in terms of images that he knew well, initially images of his own body. He created new images to explain new experiences but always related these to his extant structure of knowledge. The contemporary philosopher, Vico argued, must use his memory to reverse the process. He must return from the rational discourse in which he is presently at home into the alien poetic idiom of the past whose meaning he will rediscover as he establishes connections with its imagery. In descending the tropological gradient of linguistic expression, the new art of memory completes the hermeneutical circle, the circle of Hermes' flight and his return.[32]

Implicitly, Vico explained why the art of memory as practiced from classical antiquity until the Renaissance worked. In its association of a mnemonic image and an unrelated idea, it borrowed primordial poetic techniques to convey modern prosaic knowledge. Amidst the flux of abstractions of modern discourse, it reached back to poetic forms of an earlier age to aid in the classification of modern knowledge and to provide the emotional power needed to evoke that knowledge at will.[33] So wide had the distance between image and idea become for mnemonists who practiced the classical art in the modern age that they had lost touch with the structure of the poetic code. This structure was important because it provided a coherence that the ideas to be remembered did not in themselves symbolically convey. In other words, mnemonics as a skill to be acquired was a response to the loss of a linguistic frame of reference. It was the need for such a frame of reference that prompted the search for a mnemonic model that might serve as a practical substitute. By the age of the Renaissance this need had set Neoplatonic mnemonists on a course of seeking to uncover such connections in the past.

Vico's *New Science* pointed toward a fundamental reorientation of thought about the uses of memory. Thenceforth memory would be employed as a technique to uncover forgotten origins understood as lost poetic powers. The quest to touch the original, imaginative powers that make us creative would become the primary quest of the Romantic poets and philosophers of the early nineteenth century. It pointed as well toward the new interest in autobiography, in which the notion of continuous development from infancy to adulthood would provide the sense of unity that could no longer be discovered in the heavens. As metaphysics yielded to psychology, memory as a key to magic was displaced by memory as a key to soul-searching. The distance that the art of memory had traveled in the journey from sixteenth-century rhetoric to nineteenth-century psychology is revealed in the revisioning of the image of

memory itself. The image of memory as a brightly lit theater of the world
was replaced by one better attuned to the kind of inquiry with which the art
of memory was thenceforth to be allied—that of memory as a mirror of the
dark abyss of the mind.[34] Equally profound were the effects of this revisioning
of the uses of memory on historical thinking itself. To this new science of
history with which historians would seek to reimagine the past—"historicism" as it would later be called—Vico is our initial guide.

Vico's *New Science* as a History of Oral Tradition

Some sense of Vico's crossing from rhetoric into history and back again
may be immediately surmised from the diagrams that embellish his preface
to the third edition of the *New Science,* the masterpiece in which his studies
culminated.[35] He begins with a frontispiece, presenting in pictorial design a
mnemonic scheme of the argument he propounds in the body of the work.
Employing vivid imagery within an imposing landscape, it sets forth the organization of the study. A stock-in-trade of the rhetorician, the design permits
an imaginative appreciation of the argument that is to follow.[36] But to the
frontispiece he juxtaposes a chronological chart. Plotting the significant events
of seven ancient civilizations in parallel track, it transforms imaginative conceptions of the past into places on an abstract timeline. A methodological device of the historian, it frames the critical interpretation at which he finally
arrived.[37]

Like the age of antiquity that Vico studied, that in which he lived was one
of constant crossings between old and new techniques of communication. The
printing press was invented in the fifteenth century, but the relationship between written and oral communication continued to be dynamic and varied.
Only by the eighteenth century were the influences of print culture on pedagogical practice becoming pervasive, obviating the rhetorical methods on
which manuscript culture had thrived.[38] As the practitioner of a discipline
tailored to the needs of a way of learning that was passing, Vico expressed
some reservations about the change. From his vantage point, the exponential
growth of the printed word might easily lead to a profusion of unworthy publications, for the tedious labor of copying by hand had ensured that only the
most meritorious studies were to be bequeathed to posterity. He worried, too,
that ready access to books might lead to a neglect of the training of memory,
an exercise he judged indispensable for the development of imagination.[39] Still,
his self-conscious witness to this crossing may have contributed to his insights
into the historical relationship between the meaning of ideas and their mode
of expression in a corresponding crossing in the ancient world.

Vico's meditation on the implications of transcending a threshold in the
technology of communication is not unlike our own. Our age is witnessing
a transition from a typographic to an electronic culture, and we have become

increasingly reflective about its implications. As the printed page yields primacy of place to the computer screen, communication is vastly accelerated. As the alphabet is supplanted by the soundbyte, the index of knowledge is reordered in profound ways. The electronic revolution has involved us in a more complex interplay of sound and sight and has made us more aware of the relativity of the organization of knowledge to the medium in which it is conveyed.[40] Such an awareness has inspired interest in the science of semiotics, which functions in the present age much as did the art of memory in the chirographic culture of which Vico was a late representative. As the Italian scholar Umberto Eco has recently pointed out, mnemonics is a semiotics because it presupposes that language is a system of symbolic references that may convey more than one level of meaning.[41]

This observation suggests the basis of our appreciation of Vico's work today. His admirers have long praised him for his insights into the pattern and meaning of history.[42] If he is renowned as a philosopher of history, however, his importance as an historian of oral tradition has generally been overlooked. Modern historiography has been painstaking in its attention to the written record but sometimes naive in reading it as transparent testimony of the past.[43] Vico, by contrast, analyzed documentary evidence for the hidden meanings about an earlier oral tradition that it continued to bear. His inquiry focused on the displacement of understanding that transpired in the historical move from the poetic mentality of oral tradition to the more prosaic mentality of literate culture. He looked across the divide between orality and literacy in order to understand the interchanges between them. Thereby he anticipated our recent entry into new domains of historiography that analyze written documents for what they reveal about the customs and traditions of preliterate societies. His method prepared the way for historical inquiry into collective mentalities, collective memory, historical psychology, and oral tradition, which since the 1960s has set historical scholarship on a new course.[44] It is the affinities between this work and his own that accounts for what the Italian scholar Andrea Battistini has recently characterized as the Vico phenomenon in our times.[45]

Although Vico established the groundwork for a new historiography dedicated to uncovering the forgotten mentalities of an earlier oral tradition, he did not formulate the project in quite these terms. The vocabulary employed by today's scholars (orality, oral tradition, collective mentalities) had yet to be coined. But the basic techniques of the field—the etymological analysis of language and the interpolation of written texts for the tacit meanings they carried from earlier oral tradition—were essential to his method.[46] Like today's students of semiotics, Vico devoted considerable attention to the relationship between language and its multiple modes of expression.[47] He argued that "language and letters" had evolved together, and he ridiculed the grammarians of his day for separating them in their scholarly considerations. The grammarians believed that the creation of language predated the invention of letters. But that is only true, Vico countered, if letters are narrowly construed as manifestations of alphabetic literacy. Rather speaking and writing were coextensive in their historical development, for they drew on a mental "dictionary" common to all humanity.[48]

To illustrate his argument about the deep antecedents of alphabetic literacy, Vico pointed out distortions in the modern interpretation of the myth of Cadmus. The grammarians, he claimed, erroneously taught that the myth signified the way in which the ancient Greeks received literacy from the Phoenicians. The Greeks may have appropriated the Phoenician alphabet, he conceded. But their writings in this new mode drew on a mental language already embodied in their own earlier script and developed within their own indigenous traditions of learning.[49] The age that preceded that of facile alphabetic literacy was literate in another way. At the dawn of civilization, he explained, people engaged in mute communication. They "spoke" in physical gestures and wrote in hieroglyphs before they ever uttered sounds. What we might properly call an age of oral tradition followed, though it too had its script in the heraldic emblems emblazoned on the shields of its noble warriors. Following at last was an age of "vulgar letters"—that identified with alphabetic literacy. Thus understanding was refined as it evolved out of the poetic language of oral tradition and, more remotely, the sign language of mute gesture. But along the way, the correspondences between verbal and written expression were continually maintained.[50]

As an historian of the ancient world, Vico sought to strike down the historical barrier that alphabetic literacy had erected before the grammarians in their efforts to make sense of this primordial past. These modern philosophers imagined the deep past to be similar to the more recent one that lived in their memories. They believed the poets of antiquity to be sages and lawgivers of "matchless wisdom," and they presented them as they wished to see themselves: serene and reflective.[51] But the wisdom of the ancients, Vico proposed, had been conceived in fear and wonder at a world they struggled to understand. They used their minds in a different way and their wisdom contained a different order of meaning. As poets of an oral tradition, they expressed themselves in a metaphorical language that philosophers of a literate one were unable to decipher. Hence the modern philosopher misconstrued the nature of ancient poetry. Between the mentalities of the poets of antiquity and the philosophers of the present, the horizons of living memory intervene, encapsulating the understanding of each age within its own imagination. Living memory evolves continuously in ways that its bearers fail to grasp. It introduces distortions into the interpretation of the past.[52] The historian's task, Vico therefore contended, is not to construe ancient wisdom as it is presently remembered but rather to decipher its poetic code for the original meaning it contained.[53]

To crack the code Vico turned to the writers of antiquity, although it was to their texts rather than to their teachings that he repaired. As interpreters of their preliterate past, the literate philosophers of late antiquity were no more insightful than their modern counterparts, for present-minded memories like-wise stood in their way. Thus they bequeathed to posterity a misinterpretation of the wisdom of earlier oral traditions. Their texts were nonetheless useful, for their phrasing often bore vestiges of the poetic code and hence unwittingly enshrined its wisdom. It is important to note that Vico's primary sources for his history of the origins of civilization are these texts of the manuscript cul-ture of Greece and Rome, particularly the early texts that stood just beyond the threshold of literacy. In the *New Science,* he interpolated them for what they encoded of the mentality of the preliterate culture out of which they had emerged and of which they continued to provide indirect testimony.

In his exploration of the poetic sources of knowledge, Vico engaged in a wide range of text criticism.[54] But two in particular held his attention as he sought to span the gap between the mentalities of literate and preliterate peo-ple: the Law of the Twelve Tables of ancient Rome and the Homeric epics of ancient Greece. Both emerged out of oral tradition yet stood for the historian as signposts on the threshold of literacy in the ancient world. They adduce the two sides of Vico's project: his inquiries into law and literature. These might seem to be quite different topics. But Vico showed how closely they were allied in antiquity, and he argued for their common foundations. Ancient Ro-man law, he explained, was in its origins "a serious poem, and ancient juris-prudence a severe kind of poetry."[55] Just as the Homeric epics were sung by wandering rhapsodes across several centuries, so Roman law was once chanted by its guardians. Long after the epics had been entered into script and the law enshrined on tablets, they continued to be told through traditions of living memory. Vico's point is that Roman law, like Greek epic, has a deep history in oral tradition and cannot be understood apart from this grounding.[56] Ven-erated by the ancients as the sources of their wisdom, these works are espe-cially important because they stand at the crossroads between oral tradition and manuscript culture. The crossroads define not a point of transition but an ongoing exchange, a circulation between living memory and literate com-munication. They serve as the most important examples of Vico's pioneering contribution to our understanding of the way in which oral tradition was in-corporated into literate culture while continuing to influence it. Neglected for two centuries, Vico's method captures our attention once more as the problem of crossings between technologies of communication rises to the surface of our modern-day scholarly preoccupations.

Decoding the Legends of Roman Law

Vico's formulation of a new science of history emerged out of his lifelong study of Roman law.[57] In his own day, legal history centered on the search for its universal principles in natural law. For Hugo Grotius, Samuel von Pufendorf, and John Selden, leading seventeenth-century authorities on questions of jurisprudence, Roman law was of particular interest as an early statement of such principles, and its lawgivers were acclaimed as sages for their wisdom in formulating them.[58] But through his own investigations, Vico came to recognize that this interpretation raised more questions than it answered about the origins of Roman law and he gradually repudiated much of what these scholars argued, not to mention some of his own early musings on the subject.[59] The error of the modern scholar of jurisprudence, he concluded, lay not in searching for universal principles of law but in locating their enunciation at the beginning of history.[60] Ancient law, he concluded, was in fact born of rough custom, devised by people seeking rudimentary rules for civic life. Under such conditions, law was narrowly conceived to confirm the particular privileges of the ruling elite.[61] Only gradually did commoners gain access to these rights, and it was only at a relatively advanced stage in the evolution of the law that they were written down. The principle of universal law was an ideal toward which the Roman legal tradition tended over the course of its development, not one from which it sprang. In a tentative way in his *Universal Law* and more assertively in his *New Science,* Vico explained how unwritten customs served as the humble beginnings for the well-defined legal code of the late Roman Republic that posterity would praise.[62]

In Vico's efforts to plot the development of the Roman legal tradition from rights enjoyed exclusively by nobles toward rights broadly shared with plebeians, his attention focused on the Law of the Twelve Tables, the first written statement of the law in the early Roman Republic. Reputedly set forth on twelve wooden tablets in 451 B.C., the Law was recognized by ancient and modern scholars alike as a landmark in Roman jurisprudence.[63] It dealt with a variety of issues concerning legal proceedings, public and private rights and obligations, personal contracts, and property ownership.[64] Vico refers to it as the second agrarian law because the "quiritary " rights that it granted to the plebeians entitled them to a greater measure of autonomy over their land than had the "bonitary" rights the nobles had earlier obliged them to accept.[65] But more important than its specific provisions, Vico argued, was the deeper, ongoing social struggle over civil rights that it revealed. If for the jurists the Law was important as a statement of founding principles, for the historian it provided insight into the process by which a Roman legal tradition had come into being.[66]

Not the least of the significance of the Law, Vico argued, were the conditions under which it was written. Contrary to the teachings of the scholars of Roman jurisprudence, it was drafted centuries after the republic was founded as a negotiated settlement over rights, not at its beginnings as a statement of first principles.[67] The plebeians' demand for access to rights was also a demand for their public disclosure, because the nobles had previously maintained their privileges by enshrouding the customary law in secrecy.[68] Vico, therefore, set out to uncover the lost oral tradition out of which the codified written law had actually emerged. Considering the text of the Law of the Twelve Tables within the context of oral tradition, he showed how its interpolation revealed the nature of the earlier, private legal tradition of the nobles that the plebeians challenged, and even glimmerings of the customs of the poet-fathers of the families around which Roman society had first been formed.[69]

In this respect, Vico identified the Law of the Twelve Tables as one of a series of laws that punctuate an emerging tradition of jurisprudence during the early republic.[70] Considered in their ensemble, they denote not the formulation of universal principles but the extension of particular rights originally enjoyed by a tiny elite of nobles to a widening circle of commoners through their hardwon struggle for a place in public life.[71] By the late republic, the praetors had lessened the earlier severity of the law, and by the late Empire they had recast it "in all the openness and generosity appropriate to the gentleness to which the nations had become accustomed."[72] In this way what had been a specific code of rights gradually took on a more benign tenor and with it a more universal allure.

The history of the legal tradition that Vico decoded, moreover, reveals an ongoing interplay between orality and literacy in its transmission. Casting the Law of the Twelve Tables in public tablets, he pointed out, did not ensure that it would thenceforth be immune to revision. As a written document, it survived only in fragments. The tablets on which its provisions were originally struck were destroyed within a century. Although facsimiles were reproduced, its protocols, Vico concluded, were certainly modified to reflect the legal practices of a later age. Such modifications were facilitated by the fact that the Law continued to be chanted by its official bearers, the decemvirs, as it had been from time immemorial.[73] If the Law was a charter of the rights of the Romans, it nonetheless remained deeply embedded in oral tradition and hence was subject to all of the revisions that such tradition allows.

As the Law of the Twelve Tables was modified, so too was the story of how it had come to be written. The actual historical tradition out of which the Law had emerged was obscured by the legendary one with which it was remembered. Legend had it that the Law had been given to the Romans by the Athenian sage Solon, who received a Roman embassy sent for that purpose.[74] The legend further taught that Hermadorus of Ephesus, a Greek exile living in Rome, helped Roman jurists to formulate its provisions. In legend, therefore, the Law was remembered as an integral text, a document given for all time through the wisdom of its author. Even in Vico's day, the teachers of jurisprudence still conceived of the ancient constitution of the Romans as a founding document drafted by founding fathers.[75]

Vico took issue with the legend by reading the text of the Law for archaic survivals in its phrasing and the hidden meanings that these concealed. He showed the underlying severity of the law, its tacit exclusions, the unstated privileges it protected, and the ongoing authority it ascribed to oral contracts.[76] All of these revealed the Law as a particular settlement within a dynamic legal tradition, one that secretly withheld some rights while it publicly accorded others.[77] The legend of Solon as Roman lawgiver and Hermadorus as his surrogate, Vico concluded, was apocryphal. Far from being a set of Greek juridical principles appropriated by the Romans, the Law of the Twelve Tables was a Roman invention fashioned over several centuries to deal with indigenous conditions.[78] Even the number twelve, he suggested, connoted not a specific number of provisions but a number too great for the Romans to calculate.[79]

The Law of the Twelve Tables, Vico argued, was a written monument to a long-standing oral tradition. It was a place of memory in an ongoing search for civic wisdom. The wisdom that the ancient Romans would have enshrined in the Law in fact resided in the tradition itself, slowly elaborated through custom and only tardily set forth in writing. To trace its history was to witness the growth of Rome from a tiny city-state dominated by feudal warlords to a vast and prosperous empire bound together by a system of law that tended toward civic equality.[80] This system of law became the pride and strength of Rome the empire. But its greatness, Vico suggested, lay in the steady and sustained way in which it had come into being over hundreds of years.[81] The universality of Roman law was revealed in its historical elaboration.

Vico's theory of the emergence of Roman law out of unwritten custom was well-known in eighteenth-century Europe, though it was never fully appreciated.[82] The intellectual tenor of the times continued to favor the natural law doctrine that Vico had disputed, and the coming of a print culture reinforced the imperative for clear and precise legal formulations. Everywhere in the eighteenth century, the task of codifying the law proceeded apace, culminating in the drafting of the Civil Code of Napoleon at the outset of the nineteenth century. This and like codes may have drawn heavily on customary law. But in incorporating such customs into codes that proclaimed to set forth the foundations of the law in definitive texts that all might read, they operated as points of departure for future judicial interpretation.[83] To employ Vico's metaphor, the Napoleonic Code "drew a cloak of learning" over earlier traditions and, so, obscured the deep history of the law. It is not surprising, therefore, that the legal scholars of the Enlightenment continued to view the Law of the Twelve Tables as a founding document, even though they came to doubt that it had been borrowed from the Greeks.[84]

There was, of course, a nineteenth-century romantic tradition of historiography in which Vico's interpretation of Roman law was warmly received. The German jurist Frederick von Savigny was familiar with Vico's thesis, and the French historian Jules Michelet expounded at length on Vico's insights into the deep sources of Roman law in popular custom.[85] But Michelet was preoccupied with the destiny of a national culture in which he himself took great pride. Tracking the unfolding of this culture in a grand teleological design, he naturally emphasized Vico's importance as a philosopher of history and paid comparatively little attention to the method he had devised to explore the nature of customary law.[86] He read the historical record for its clues to the future, whereas Vico read it backward for what it might reveal about an obscure past. For this reason, Vico's early excursions into the oral sources of legal tradition were during the nineteenth and even the better part of the twentieth century overshadowed by the interest in his philosophy of history.[87] The problem of the grounding of the legal tradition in oral tradition remains a frontier of research that is only beginning to be explored today.[88]

Discovering the "True Homer"

Vico's work on the nature of Roman law was a lifelong labor. But he used the lessons learned to inquire into the nature of ancient literature and in the process made a discovery that reveals more clearly his links with the work of contemporary historians of oral tradition: namely, the nature of the "true Homer."[89] Following the method he had employed in interpreting the nature of the Law of the Twelve Tables, Vico disputed the notion that the Homeric epics were integral texts drafted by a single author of surpassing wisdom. Just as the Law of the Twelve Tables was a reference point for an emerging tradition of law, so Homer was an image of an evolving tradition of storytelling.[90]

In Vico's own day, there was still a scholarly tradition dating from antiquity that taught that Homer was the wisest of men, an ancient sage who set down his esoteric wisdom in epic narratives that defined the values of Greek culture over the following 400 years.[91] Vico sought to refute this argument by examining the cultural context out of which the Homeric epics had emerged. Homer, he contended, was not a "rare and consummate poet" but a popular one who sang the folk tales that his society honored.[92] As such, he did not compose his epics to instruct his age with his learned wisdom but rather to give passionate voice to the popular culture of his day.[93] Homer, Vico believed, could not possibly have been literate, and his tales were told for centuries before being set down in writing.[94] The name Homer, Vico pointed out, was derived from the term "Homeros," the blind seers renowned for their prodigious memories as storytellers.[95] Homer, therefore, was better appreciated not as an individual author but as an emblem of the collective authorship of the epic poetry that bears the name.[96] The Homeric epics were a popular art form, recited by countless rhapsodes who for centuries wandered among the cities of ancient Greece. Each Greek city claimed Homer as its own.[97] In a way each did possess him, for he gave expression to the collective memory of the Greek people, bequeathed generation after generation by these tellers of tales. The Homeric epics, Vico pointed out, had to be understood within the context of a continually evolving tradition of storytelling. He hypothesized that the episodes of the Homeric epics had originally been told as separate fables. Having recounted them for centuries as scattered stories of legendary valor and traditional lore, the rhapsodes gradually wove them together into grand designs.[98] Rhapsode, he explained, literally meant "stitcher-together of songs," and Homer was such a "binder of fables."[99] By the time the original stories had been gathered into the Homeric epics, moreover, they had been substantially modified and divested of much of their original meaning.[100] The rhapsode's gift, therefore, was not the creation of myth but the invention of epic, and each rhapsode told his tale in a slightly different way. So different is the *Odyssey* from the *Iliad,* he proclaimed, that it must have been composed in a later age.[101] Not until the time of the Pisistratids some two centuries thereafter (mid-sixth century B.C.), Vico surmised, were the epics actually arranged in more lasting textual form.[102] Until then, they were a dynamic repository of oral tradition, bequeathing the folk wisdom of a primordial civilization to an increasingly refined and intellectually sophisticated one.

Vico's pioneering work on the way in which epic verse was composed and transmitted in preliterate Greek culture was not immediately recognized. The age into which he was born was one that was busy emancipating itself from the surviving cultural vestiges of oral tradition. The Enlightenment was an intellectual renaissance that owed its renown at least in part to the ever more pervasive influence of the printed word. Scholars in the eighteenth and nineteenth centuries were more interested in discrediting the inherited teachings of oral tradition than in exploring their hidden wisdom. When Vico concluded that Homer was an emblem of collective authorship for the ancient Greeks, his argument ran against the intellectual grain of his own culture, which was increasingly preoccupied with personal identity and hence the autonomy of the individual author.[103] In nineteenth-century scholarship, the classicists' search for the identity of the poet Homer reflected this bias: artistic creation was a highly personal enterprise; collective authorship was not authorship at all.[104] Not until the early twentieth century would the Homeric question be considered in light of the properties of language and the modes of communication of oral tradition.[105] This more recent breakthrough in the interpretation of the Homeric epics returns to the problem of the poetics of oral tradition into which Vico had such early insight.

In the 1920s, Milman Parry, a Berkeley-trained classicist, sought to shed light on the composition of the Homeric epics by comparing them with a living oral tradition of storytelling that survived among Serbo-Croatian rhapsodes.[106] The line of argument that Vico had sketched through his interpretation of ancient texts Parry confirmed in his comparative study of living practitioners of the rhapsodic art.[107] Epic poetry, Parry explained, is formulaic, rhythmical, and repetitious, traits of composition shunned by modern prose authors but nonetheless essential for an art form that was to be preserved through a living, oral tradition. Of the Homeric rhapsode he gave a more elaborate profile. He portrayed a poet who possessed a well-defined sense of both the larger narrative structure of his story and the formulaic phrasing with which the story was to be told. His creativity was displayed in the ingenuity with which he wove the story's episodes into the plot of the larger narrative, as well as the skill with which he adapted preset phrasing to the rhythms of his recitation. His gift, Parry explained, lay in his capacity for invention, not the highly individualized, more personal forms of creative expression we have come to expect in modern literate culture. The rhapsode did not recite a fixed text, but rather evoked an archetypal story.[108]

Parry died young, but his fieldwork in Yugoslavia was carried on by Albert Lord, who shared his interests.[109] Lord, too, studied living rhapsodes, and he cast the comparatist net more broadly by considering literacy's impact on the epics of their oral tradition. In the passage of an epic from orality into literacy, he discovered, its function and meaning were transformed. What had been a dramatic act affirming present values in oral tradition increasingly became a commemorative one enshrining older virtues for the manuscript culture that supervened. To the degree that literacy displaced orality, Lord concluded, the rhapsode lost his function as the essential bearer of the collective memory of his community. He might still recite epics, but as memorized texts not as living memories. Lord's study of literacy's impact on contemporary Serbo-Croatian rhapsodes shed light on the fortunes of the Homeric epics in antiquity. As literacy encroached on orality between the eighth and the fifth centuries B.C., the image of Homer as dramatist gradually yielded to one of Homer as memorialist. His epics became fixed references, monuments to traditions of the Archaic Age that still inspired reverence, but that were divorced from living traditions in the making.[110]

In the studies by Parry and Lord, we note so many affinities with Vico's analysis of the mentality of preliterate people: the nature of epic recitation, the properties of language in oral communication, and the emblematic nature of authorship in a culture in which creativity was a collective enterprise. The importance of Vico's work on Homer lies in his formulation of a method for exploring the relationship between language and mentality in the interchange between oral and literate traditions.[111]

That is why the parallels between Vico's work on the poetic language of the Homeric epics and recent studies by the classicist Eric Havelock are so illuminating. Writing in the wake of the investigations of Parry and Lord, Havelock focused squarely on the cultural context of the Homeric epics. In his *Preface to Plato* (1963), he traced the cultural transition from the orality of Homer to the literacy of Plato.[112] Although formulating the problem in a different terminology, Havelock worked with a method of analysis pioneered by Vico more than 200 years before. In constructing his argument, he studied texts that stood just beyond the threshold of literacy and interpolated them for what they revealed about the oral tradition out of which they had emerged. Like Vico, he was interested in the changes in the mind-set of the Greeks during that era. Havelock was struck by the vehemence with which the philosopher Plato in his famous essay *The Republic* banished the poet Homer from his projected ideal society for the "crippling effect" his poetry might have on the mind.[113] Although scholars had long construed Plato's judgment as a philosophical position in a quarrel between ancients and moderns, Havelock pointed out that the quarrel was better appreciated as a clashing of incompatible mentalities, not merely of opposing ideas. The Homeric epics, he explained, were encyclopedias of the poetic mind of the Archaic Age, whereas Plato's philosophical treatise was a product of the more reflective mentality of the Classical Age some 400 years later. Plato scorned Homer because he formed his thoughts in an altogether different way. In his rational analysis, he was incapable of appreciating the ideas contained in Homer's poetical mode of discourse and hence of grasping the meaning of his thought.[114]

What Vico had earlier explained as the historical evolution of poetical thought into ever more abstract modes of expression, Havelock characterized as the transformation of mentalities in the passage from orality into literacy.[115] Either way, their discussion of the process by which the human mind is modified is essentially the same: between the time of Homer and that of Plato, they argue, the Greeks acquired a capacity for abstract thought that transformed their poets into philosophers. There is nothing in Havelock's documentation to suggest that he was in any way influenced by Vico. Nor did Vico, writing in the eighteenth century, work within an intellectual context in which it would have been possible for him to formulate the orality/literacy problem in the same way. Still, the topical issues to which they allude are virtually the same.[116] For both, the concept of mimesis holds the key to the meaning of creativity for the epic poet of oral tradition. Creativity in the age of Homer, they agree, was conceived as mimicry.[117] The poet's forms of speech mimicked the archetypal forms of nature, as if in creating language he were imitating the creative act of God.[118] Ultimately, it is these forms of nature that inspire imagination, so that creativity in the present always harks back to the precedent of the past. From this perspective, imagination is grounded in memory, which, reiterated and preserved in its epic poetry, sustains the cultural values of the community.[119] Both Vico and Havelock base their argument about the historical significance of the Homeric epics on the proposition that they were the sustaining sources of the collective memory of the Greeks of the Archaic Age.[120] For Vico, they are the "treasure houses" of ancient wisdom.[121] Havelock refers to them as "encyclopedias" of the culture of that age.[122]

The Certain and the True as Modes of Memory

One purpose of our discussion of Vico has been to provide examples of his practical criticism of early written documents for the insights they offer into the workings of oral tradition. But another is to show how his pioneering work on oral tradition was tied to his formulation of a method by which historians might see beyond the horizons of their living memories. Vico's work as an historian of oral tradition was from a theoretical standpoint a reckoning with the unreliability of collective memory as a way of understanding the past. The scholars of his own highly literate age, Vico claimed, still clung to a way of remembering the past derived from oral tradition and therefore were unable to acquire a critical perspective on the events and people that they studied. He characterized the past as it is remembered in terms of two conceits: that of nations and that of scholars. A nation believes that "its remembered history goes back to the very beginning of the world."[123] The scholars believe that "whatever they know is as old as the world."[124] Both construe the past from the vantage point of collective memory. The nation commemorates the past, and so emphasizes its similarities with the present rather than its differences. The scholars ascribe their way of thinking to the poets of an ancient world and so misconstrue the meaning of their creations. The nation loses sight of the parallels between its course and that of others, the scholars of the differences between the mode of thought of ancient people and their own.[125]

Vico was therefore determined to write a history that would provide a critical perspective on collective memory, while incorporating its insights into his formulations.[126] He characterized his method as a blending of philology and philosophy, uncovered at the crossroads where knowledge of the "certain" meets knowledge of the "true."[127] The search for the certain, for Vico, is the province of philology. It is a quest to recover and inventory the written literature, legal maxims, and other tangible artifacts bequeathed to the present by the past as evidence of what was once said and done. These are the documentary forms through which the mythological stories and social customs of preliterate people have been preserved.[128] They are useful because they arrest the past at a moment in time so that its mores may be studied and deciphered. In the texts of the Homeric epics, set down with the advent of literacy, the wisdom of oral tradition was sealed, as in a time capsule destined for posterity. Epics inscribed into a literate culture are no longer dynamic in the way their prototypes were in oral tradition. But the rhapsode's loss, Vico suggests, is the philologist's gain. The elusive forms of a living oral tradition are enshrined in the more enduring forms of a manuscript culture. Even though the traditions of such a culture continue to evolve, their writings become reference points in a fixed chronology. Epics that are continually being revised in an oral culture are left behind as commemorative places in a literate one. They pay homage to an age that is passing and so make possible an awareness of change.

But the more durable forms of written literature are not without their shortcomings. They cannot carry forward a tradition with the same passion. An author such as Homer no longer lives in his legend. He becomes enshrined in a text into which later-day scholars project passions of their own. Herein, Vico claims, the preconditions for the conceits of modern culture are established. For modern civilization, the Homeric epics are remembered as landmarks along the path of its own presumed destiny. Their meaning is reconceived in light of present-day preoccupations.

The philologist's search for certain knowledge of what transpired in antiquity was, therefore, only half of the equation of Vico's new science of history.[129] It was completed only by grasping what the philosophers sought to uncover as the truth of these ancient traditions. The texts had to be understood in the contexts in which they were written. Vico saw that literary artifacts, whose origins might be documented with certainty, presented the modern scholar not with transparent representations of ideas out of the past but rather with images that concealed their true meaning. The images of the poetic language of preliterate people contained secrets of their inspired imagination. If the province of the certain lay in verifying the language of texts that commemorate oral tradition, the province of the true lay in grasping the meaning of the imagination that had once informed them.[130] Ancient poetry, Vico argued, even if fanciful from our vantage point, must have contained "some public ground of truth."[131] For contemporaries, it was understood as a "true narrative" of their condition.[132] It was Vico's interest in the truth of what the ancients said, not just the certain knowledge of how they said it, that constitutes the full dimensions of his new science. The search for the true, Vico concluded, is the search for the eternal in the human condition, that element of thought that remains constant through successive metamorphoses of figurative expression. "Truth," Vico explained, "exists under masks."[133] Whatever the figure of speech through which it is expressed, thought issues from the common ground of humankind's imaginative efforts to make sense of its lived experience. The historian discovers the constancy of this human capacity for creativity in the face of changing realities.

Vico's explanation of the relationship between the certain and the true might be characterized as an interchange between two kinds of memory that his new science of history joins: recollection and repetition. The search for the certain is an act of recollection. By plotting texts in a chronological pattern, recollection reconstructs the outward forms of the modification of the human mind as it ascends a gradient of abstraction, one germinating in a crude poetic metaphysics and growing into a branching tree of increasingly refined philosophical knowledge.[134] But the search for the true is an act of repetition, or, as the ancients would have said, mimesis. In repetition, we imitate the past by empathizing with its creativity. That is what inspires our interest in the past and confirms our ties with our heritage. Recollection reveals the differences in mind-set between past and present. It forms the basis of a history of ideas, or, as we might say today, of collective mentalities. But repetition reveals that all people are endowed with the same mental capacities and that over the long run all will follow the same course in exploring their potential. In the repetition of such cycles of history everywhere in the world, the pattern of an ideal eternal history is revealed.[135] For Vico, the pattern of history revolved as it did because of the way in which collective memory was created, preserved, and eventually lost within oral tradition.

The Life Cycle of Collective Memory and the Orality/Literacy Problem

Just as Vico sought to show how the modification of the human mind proceeded in the same way everywhere in antiquity, so modern students comparing oral traditions have launched a far-reaching inquiry into the way cultures change as they move from orality into literacy. Most of this work is practical and deals with specialized problems in individual cultures.[136] But the inquiry itself has led to speculation about the impact of literacy on the civilizing process that is reminiscent of the theorizing in which Vico once engaged. It is therefore not such a long step from Vico's discussion of the pattern of history's cycle to Walter J. Ong's panoramic formulation of the stages by which orality passes into literacy. Ong, a contemporary American scholar, identifies innovation in the technologies of communication as the moving force for change across the broad sweep of Western culture. For him, the shift from orality to literacy in antiquity was only the beginning of the process. He plots the further development of literacy into print culture between the fifteenth and the eighteenth century and eventually into what he characterizes as the secondary orality of our own day. In this move through four stages of cultural communication (oral, chirographic, typographic, and electronic), he discerns corresponding stages in the modification of the human mind. Ong is sensitive to the complexity of the process. He describes it as being synchronic in that earlier modes of communication exercise an ongoing cultural influence long after they have been superseded by new innovations. The organization of knowledge in script culture, for example, was orally based and shaped learning in significant ways at least until the eighteenth century. But the process is also dialectical in that a new technology of communication leads logically to the creation of a qualitatively different mind-set.[137] The move from orality to literacy represents a shift from ear to eye as the dominant mode of perception, and in the succeeding stages the power of the eye is accentuated further still.[138] Each stage represents a further interiorization of thought, whereby cultural exchange becomes at once more abstract, more personalized, and more self-conscious.[139]

It would be tempting to suggest that Ong returns to Vico's model of the civilizing process.[140] Both plot modifications in collective mentalities across four broad stages of civilization. Both argue that each stage represents a further modification of mind made possible by a new mode of communication. Both stress the residual power of earlier cultural forms on present modes of conceptualization. Ong's notion of a secondary orality, moreover, is reminiscent of Vico's notion of the "recourse" to poetic origins.[141] But Ong's explanation of the way in which print culture has intensified abstract thinking since the eighteenth century concerns a process beyond any on which Vico might have been able to offer a critical perspective. Ong in fact sketches a linear pattern of cultural change tied to advances in the technologies of communication. For Vico, by contrast, the course of history follows a pattern of repetition because it operates within the ambit of oral tradition.[142] His "new science" provides an historical perspective on oral tradition as it enters into a literate culture still heavily influenced by the canons of orality. Beyond that context it cannot go. Vico's method of comprehending the nature of thought in preliterate societies worked because of the direct correspondence between knowing and doing in their use of language, a correspondence that does not necessarily hold in our own, with its more complex modes of communication. Vico therefore might have been baffled by Jacques Derrida and the grammarians of our own time, who have reestablished the barrier between text and author that Vico worked so hard to strike down.[143]

The appeal of Vico's theory of the civilizing process, therefore, is bound up in his explanation of the dynamics of oral tradition. He began with a description of the formative powers of the primordial poets, lawgivers at the founding of nations. In a poetic metaphor of his own, he likened their passion to that of "a great rushing torrent (that) cannot fail to carry turbid waters and roll stones and trunks along in the violence of its course."[144] Over the long run the inertial power of their epics sustains tradition "much as great and rapid rivers continue far into the sea, keeping sweet the waters borne on by the force of their flow."[145] But Vico made the further point that there are limits to the power of the collective memories carried forward by tradition. For its inspiration, a society returns continually to its epics as the remembered sources of its cultural traditions. But eventually these, too, will be forgotten, just as the river's waters are absorbed by the sea, and the creative process through which a culture is fashioned must then repeat itself. This is "the course the nations run" and then rerun, as he explained in his interpretation of the history of medieval Europe (also a largely oral culture) as a "recourse" of the path traveled by the nations of antiquity.[146]

That course, Vico explained, turns on the inverse relationship between imagination and reflection within the context of oral tradition. The modification of mind that leads toward reflective thinking effects a corresponding weakening of the powers of memory. Eroded in the process are those mnemic faculties that draw on inspired imagination, with its sublime emotions, eidetic metaphorical imagery, and mythic narratives.[147] The course a nation runs in Vico's scheme might be likened to the process of entropy. Its energy levels run down and must be replaced with new sources of inspiration. What Vico called an "ideal eternal history" is close to what Mircea Eliade has referred to as the myth of the eternal return.[148] Vico's theory of history, therefore, is based not on a pattern of rise and fall of civilizations (a formulation employed to compare him with the speculative philosophers of history of the nineteenth and twentieth centuries) but rather on one of the waning and renewal of collective memory.[149] His model of the dynamics of history is more like a wave that breaks on the shore, then recedes to gather force once more. It describes the waning of oral tradition as it moves away over time from the sources of its imagination.

Vico used his new science of history to restore to us a world that had been lost, but one that we can still understand because it was made by our ancestors with poetic powers that continue to move us. In light of the degree to which recent scholarship on the history of oral tradition has confirmed his findings, his accomplishment seems all the more imposing. He prepared the groundwork for a theory of history that would guide historians in the modern age. Vico might be called the first historicist, for he was the first to argue that historical interpretation is a task of reconstructing the collective mentalities of the past. Nor was he unaware of the significance of his accomplishment, particularly for the depths his method enabled the historian to plumb. "To discover the way in which this first human thinking arose in the gentile world," he complained, "we encountered exasperating difficulties which have cost us the research of a good twenty years."[150] But of the meaning of the discovery itself there was no equivocation. As he wrote in the *New Science*:

> But in the night of thick darkness enveloping the earliest antiquity, so remote from ourselves, there shines the eternal and never failing light of a truth beyond all question: that the world of civil society has certainly been made by men, and that its principles are therefore to be found within the modifications of our own human mind. Whoever reflects on this cannot but marvel that the philosophers should have bent all their energies to the study of the world of nature, which, since God made it, He alone knows; and that they should have neglected the study of the world of nations, or civil world, which, since men had made it, men could come to know.[151]

If Vico's method was a new science, it was also a new art of memory, for it enabled historians in the modern age to unlock memories hidden in the recesses of a distant past in which ideas and images were directly connected.

3

WILLIAM WORDSWORTH AND SIGMUND FREUD

The Search for the Self Historicized

William Wordsworth and the Mnemonics of Autobiography

In his autobiographical poem, *The Prelude,* the English poet William Wordsworth (1770–1850) recalls an arresting memory of his vigil as a child of thirteen high on a bluff overlooking a crossroads near his boarding school. There on a morning shortly before Christmas he and his brothers searched the horizon for a glimpse of their father's horses, which they hoped were already en route to speed them home for the holidays. The juncture of highways was such that the horses might have arrived from either direction, rousing in young William's mind an uncertainty about what the routes of their arrival and departure might be. That day no one came for them, a disappointment immeasurably deepened ten days later when their father died unexpectedly in the midst of their vacation. Thenceforth, the tableau of his wait at the crossroads remained indelibly fixed in William's memory, and he reflected profoundly on the mixed feelings it evoked as he wrote and revised his poetical autobiography over the course of his lifetime. At the time of his vigil at the crossroads, he recalled, his childlike thoughts had been outward bound, full of happy anticipation of his journey home. But afterward his recollection of that place was also filled with somber images of the sorrow that would await him on his arrival home, marking the intrusion of death into his childhood innocence. Mediating the crossing paths of his initial expectation and his following regret, his image of that crossroads became a place marker in his memory for a crossroads in his life. He called it a "spot of time."[1]

Wordsworth's "spot of time" is a metaphor for the places of memory that would punctuate his inquiry into his own life history. To that project he brought the same historicist vision that had earlier inspired Vico. Vico had uncovered the historical origins of the imaginative powers of the poets of antiquity. Wordsworth was a modern poet who sought to recover those powers for his own age. He revisited the memories of his childhood as if they summoned a wondrous, primordial past hidden within his own psyche. Childhood had been for him a time of spiritual depth with which he wished never to lose touch, for he believed that it was the source of his creativity. As a poet, Wordsworth celebrated the sublime powers of nature, and he remembered his childhood as a time when his imagination was perfectly attuned to nature's forms. Vico had described the powers of the poets of antiquity in much the same way. It is in the imaginative forms of poetic expression inspired by nature, he explained, that we discover the sources of our collective consciousness. The poetical mentality of the ancients that Vico had identified was as old as the myth and fables in which their collective memory was stored. But the self-consciousness that Wordsworth revealed in his poetry was of relatively recent origin. There was in his understanding of memory a perspective that was new and distinctly modern. If Vico's poets extolled a collective imagination, Wordsworth praised one that was individually unique. To that end, he wrote an autobiography as a means of analyzing his personal development. "Each man is a memory to himself," he remarked in explaining his endeavor.[2] By this he meant that it is through soul-searching that each of us forms an understanding of personal identity. Through his inquiry into the growth of the powers of his own imagination, he refashioned the genre of autobiography as a modern art of memory. There was, of course, an autobiographical literature of ancient lineage, and some famous examples come readily to mind. St. Augustine's *Confessions* (400), a meditation on his quest for religious salvation, has made edifying reading since late antiquity. Benvenuto Cellini's *Autobiography* (1562) is valued as a celebration of the Renaissance artist's quest for undying fame. Even Vico's *Autobiography* (1731) records the scholar's claim for recognition by posterity.[3] All were monuments to ways of life that readers might find exemplary without being drawn to self-analysis. Modern autobiography was different.[4] As a search for the meaning of their interior lives, modern autobiographers invited their readers to engage in a similar kind of introspection.[5]

The French philosopher Jean-Jacques Rousseau (1712–78) is generally credited with having invented this new form of autobiography. His *Confessions* (1781) is a saga of emotional discovery, and he was very much aware of the originality of his enterprise.[6] His purpose was to search out the hidden feelings of the child within his soul. In much the same way that Vico had associated emotional expression with the poetic perceptions of primitive people, so Rousseau culled his memory for images of the experiences that had shaped his feelings about himself.[7] We might have made Rousseau's self-portrait the focus of our study of the uses of memory in autobiography. He can claim with good reason to have written a powerful and evocative work that drew his generation into the project of soul-searching.[8] But he is insufficiently critical of the implications of his own uses of memory in the construction of this work. Indeed, his ingenuousness is part of his appeal. Wordsworth, by contrast, was more reflective about the process of imaginative reconstruction in which he was engaged. He lays a better claim to our attention, therefore, in our consideration of the way in which modern autobiography is an art of memory reconceived.

By comparison with Rousseau's adventurous and often precarious life, that of Wordsworth, England's best known Romantic poet, was tame. The leading events of his life history are easily plotted.[9] He was born into comfortable circumstances in a remote region of northern England. His parents died when he was young, but he was well provided for. A solitary child, he felt most at home among the lakes and mountains of the surrounding countryside. Early on, he sensed his gifts as a poet and wrote verse from age ten. As a young man, he attended St. John's College, Cambridge, although he was an indifferent student. There, as in childhood, he found solace in his excursions into the country, although he now sought wider horizons. It was during his college years that he first journeyed into France en route to an ascent of the high passes of the Swiss Alps. Such travels continued to be a sustaining passion throughout his life. Following college, he resided briefly in London, which he enjoyed but about which he did not deeply care. Then he sojourned for three years in France. His stay coincided with the heyday of the French Revolution, and he was soon caught up in its passions. A republican by sympathy, he considered his personal witness of that upheaval to have been among his greatest privileges in life. "Bliss was it in that dawn to be alive," he later exalted over the experience. "But to be young was very heaven!"[10] Living in Blois in the Loire valley, he mixed in the social circles of the Girondins, a leading republican faction. While in France, he had a love affair and fathered a child. Disappointed in his hope for marriage and despondent over the Revolution's turn toward a repressive terror, he returned to England in 1796 in a state of depression. He took up residence in a rural cottage in the south, where his sister Dorothy aided him in his psychological recovery. She remained his amanuensis and closest intellectual companion through his later years. His marriage to Mary Hutchinson in 1805 was a happy one. All the while he had been writing poetry, and by the turn of the century he had acquired a certain reputation for his work. During these years, he met the eminent poet and critic Samuel Coleridge, and they became lifelong friends and mutually admiring correspondents.

These public events of Wordsworth's life journey, however, tell us little about the design, or even the subject matter, of his autobiography, *The Prelude,* which he characterized as an inquiry into the growth of his imagination.[11] A recollective search for the sources of his powers as a poet, it also reveals an historian's discrimination of the critical distance between past and present states of mind. He recalls the images of the world that he formed in his childhood, especially those of nature, but he also meditates upon the differences between these images as he had perceived them as a child and as he remembered them as an adult. "The vacancy between me and those days," he remarked, "which yet have such self-presence in my mind that sometimes when I think of them I seem two consciousnesses—conscious of myself and of some other being."[12] His autobiography, therefore, is not merely a recollection of his past states of mind but of his pilgrimage through recollection to earlier stages in the development of his imagination and back again. It is a studied inquiry into the use of memory as a form of soul-searching in the reconstruction of one's own life history. Rousseau may have succeeded equally well in conveying the depth of his hidden feelings, especially as a child. But Wordsworth offered more insight into the way in which memory enlivens the imagination that sustains us.[13]

For Wordsworth, the writing of his autobiography was a lifelong project. It was neither named nor published until after his death. *The Prelude,* so entitled by his wife, was a series of manuscript drafts, written in blank verse, that he periodically augmented and revised. As a young man he sketched a short version (two books; 1798). In his prime, he embarked on an expanded design (five books; 1804), which he then turned into a still more substantial self-portrait (thirteen book; 1805). Shortly before his death, he edited and slightly modified this text (fourteen books; 1850).[14] It is not surprising that Wordsworth should have revised *The Prelude* so many times along the way. His active memory was continually revising the past, reframing it to fit his present needs and conceptions. To have given his autobiography a final form would have thwarted the purpose for which it was undertaken: to deepen his understanding of his own soul. In this sense, it was a work of ongoing self-care.

The key to the organization of *The Prelude* lies not in the salient events that mark the flow of Wordsworth's life history on the surface of his narrative but, rather, in the arresting moments of self-illumination that reveal its psychological substructure. These were the unforgettable memories that he called "spots of time."[15] Had Wordsworth not chosen to immortalize these moments, it is unlikely that his biographers would have mentioned them, for they do not mark visible turning points in his life. They serve rather as clues to crises in his interior life, to passages in the formation of his imagination. He referred to them as "the hiding places of my power," as if they were points of entry into the subterranean recesses of his soul.[16] Seemingly inconsequential in their imagery, they were for Wordsworth all-important, for they were the keys to his search for the deep structures of his personal identity. The spots evoked vivid images of troubling psychological intrusions into otherwise ordinary days: his discovery of the ruins of a gibbet in a hollow in the countryside at age five;[17] his sighting across a lake of a dead man in the midst of a beautiful landscape at age eight;[18] his disappointing vigil near a crossroads awaiting a coach when he was age thirteen;[19] his chance encounter on a country road with a destitute war veteran when he was seventeen.[20] All of these images were mementos of mortality suddenly and magically interjected into the course of his everyday life and, as such, laden with wonder and fear. Each image, moreover, was juxtaposed to a more benign one that distracted him from morbid thoughts. It is as if the benign image shadowed, or screened, the more troubling one.

Wordsworth's spots of time lie scattered across his autobiography, showing up in different places in the different versions. Through all the reorderings, displacements, and conflations of his recollections that may be noted in his many versions of *The Prelude,* these remained fixed points in his memory. Each time he described them in exactly the same way. Just as the Homeric rhapsodes stitched together invariable poetic formulae in different patterns with each recitation of their epics, so Wordsworth wove the various sketches of his self-portrait around these indelible moments in his memory. Like time capsules retrieved from the past, they provided the elements of his mnemonic powers, the concrete materials with which he as a poet fashioned the imaginative structure of his life history. [21]

Wordsworth's spots of time have obvious associations with mnemonic schemes, for they evoke the past through a juxtaposition of images and places. The imagery of the spots are emotionally attached to his deepest memories of past states of mind, and these images in turn are situated within landscapes that are unforgettable in their awe or enchantment. All his life he had been a traveler, and his excursions into his own past were shaped by his memories of these travels. He thought of himself as a wanderer, and his journeys enriched the spatial dimension of his imagination, for he internalized the landscapes that he saw as places in his memory. As in the classical art of memory, the association of concrete images with particular places was essential to his method. [22]

Although the spots of time marked places in Wordsworth's memory, they also served as channels into his soul. In his depiction of spots, he frequently located images of caves. [23] These were reminders of the underground routes into the recesses of his mind, places that were frightening to enter, but enticing in their invitation to explore deeper mysteries. Wordsworth's caves, in turn, sometimes contained springs. The critic Geoffrey Hartman has likened these to the "genius loci," the places that in popular legend were inhabited by spirits and hence points of contact with the supernatural. [24] To visit such places was to immerse oneself in a world of imagination that transcends time. Wordsworth's spots of time, therefore, conjoined the imagery of the phenomenal world with the ideal forms of a transcendental one, much as had the Neoplatonic mnemonists of the Renaissance. His deepest memories opened on the prospect of an eternal order.

Wordsworth believed that the deep structures of his imagination had been formed in childhood through his contact with nature, whose divine powers mediate phenomenal and transcendental levels of reality. [25] Nature presses its forms on the mind of the child in such a way that they become habits of his imaginative expression. Repeated contact with nature nurtures the child's imagination and encourages his or her propensity for introspection. It is in this sense that Wordsworth understood imagination and memory to be moments of the same kind of mental activity. Imagination becomes a remembrance of the forms that nature has written on the mind. To remember, therefore, is to see with what Wordsworth characterized as an inward eye.[26] Nature's forms, however, are of such sublimity as to be ineffable. As a child, he perceived them only on the level of intuition. But as his mental faculties developed, he began to acquire independence of mind and with it the capacity to describe nature's forms by reducing them to human proportions. In this way, imagination, nature's gift to the child, is displaced by fancy, the consolation of the mature poet who must form his images on a human scale.[27] With such images Wordsworth gave concrete expression to the feelings with which he continued to experience the natural order, while indirectly conveying an intimation of the archetypal natural forms that had inspired him. For Wordsworth, the interchange between imagination and fancy never completely disappears. The latter leads back to the former, just as the cave is the route to the underground spring. Therein the world of perception grasped with the outward eye is transfigured by the inward eye, which leads the mind into deeper contact with the forms of nature. The deep structures of memory, the places where time meets eternity, can only be perceived with this inward eye. The spots of time, resting on the surface of the imagination, mark their hiding places.

All of this is reminiscent of the correspondences between microcosm and macrocosm postulated by the hermetic philosophers of the Renaissance. Wordsworth's notion of imagination implies hidden connections between a phenomenal and a transcendental reality for which the spot of time is the place of memory. His interest in memory, therefore, may be likened to that of his Renaissance forbearers. At the same time, his introspective use of memory anticipates modern historical thinking. Wordsworth's microcosm is a private world of particular landscapes in which he located personal recollections unique to his own experience. In his self-conscious reformulation of the art of memory, he sought private places for recollection, even if he was no less confident about their transcendental connections. Though Wordsworth's conception of memory harks back to Renaissance magic, it also displays an awareness of time that is distinctly modern. In *The Prelude,* memory as habit is counterbalanced by memory as recollection. As his spots of time brought him back into contact with the habits of mind of his childhood, they did so from the vantage point of a mature reflectiveness. Recollection made Wordsworth aware of the differences between imagination and memory, whereas his habits of mind as a child had enabled him only to see their correspondences. The images that he recalled acquired a clarity of outline that he as a child had not been able to grasp, but at the same time they were "wearied" of their emotions.[28] He could remember not "what he felt but only how he felt."[29] In looking back in memory, Wordsworth claimed, our understanding of our lives takes on a coherence never achieved in our immediate experiences, which are full of expectations about the future. Recollection unearths hidden connections between past and present and gives a sustaining meaning to our lives.

If spots of time were images in landscapes, they sometimes conveyed the notion of a timeline emanating from the past. This is exemplified in his repeated recourse to the metaphor of islands in a stream.[30] The image of the flowing waters suggests the ongoing movement of the imagination; the islands, significant moments of its expression. In a closely related metaphor, he characterizes spots of time as oases ("green spots") visited in the course of a desert trek.[31] His capacity to cast his places of memory in an imagery of time as well as space suggests his historical perspective on his search for his personal identity. He distanced his past even as he endeavored to reaffirm his links with it. His spots of time marked the essential moments in the growth of his imagination. They lent structure to psychological transformations that might otherwise have passed unnoticed. By fixing the places of his memory in a temporal pattern he conveyed an historical sense of what his journey of becoming a poet had been like. By integrating images out of his past into his present imagination he salvaged the only past he believed to be worth knowing: one that restored connections with the time when his imaginative powers had been formed.[32]

Such a conception of the spots of time is closely linked to the therapeutic purposes to which Wordsworth turned his journey of self-discovery. As he explained, recollecting spots of time "renovates" the soul.[33] Our personalities develop over time, and to grow we must sacrifice something of our former identity. Wordsworth's art of memory, a technique of recollection through poetic soul-searching, sustained his sense of the line of continuity within his developing self. His early life had been a time when his aspirations matched his growing powers of mind. But in hurrying toward the future, he sensed that he had lost his way and had ceased to feel the inspiration of nature's sustaining forms. The project of writing an autobiography was conceived in the midst of such a crisis of identity.[34] He wrote the first version of The Prelude at age twenty-eight, a time when he was trying to come to terms with the frustrations of his early adulthood. He had been disappointed with his experience at St. John's College. College years he recalled as "an eddy" in the stream of the development of his imagination.[35] He had enjoyed the sociability of his peers, but remembered these years as a time when his "imagination slept."[36] He loved the following years in London, but its distractions drew him away from his calling as a poet. Even his stay in France produced its disillusionments. His love affair with Annette Vallon failed, and the Terror of 1792–93 dispelled his vision of the French Revolution as the best hope for the future of humankind. Cambridge, London, and Paris had once been places of his residence, but they were never to become places of his memory. In pursuing his worldly aspirations, he had lost touch with the wellsprings of his imagination. In his disappointment he sought solace in his memories of childhood. Recollection restored his balance of mind by casting psychological anchors to stay the forward rush of the currents of his poetic imagination.[37] The spots of time served as reference points in his retrospective reconstruction of the growth of his mind because they provided moments of illumination about the ways in which life's losses are intermixed with its gains. As such, they deepened his powers of understanding, bringing him closer to his mind's grounding as a child in nature's forms. In this sense, his writing of *The Prelude* may be said to have been an act of recollection intended to recover his power of repetition—those habits of mind that had nurtured his poetic gifts. Such a sentiment he conveyed in an imaginary tableau that elaborated on his metaphor of islands in the stream. A shepherd boy leaps to an island in the stream to retrieve a lost sheep and in the process becomes separated from his father. Unable to ford the stream, he is stranded there until his father returns later in the day to rescue him. Wordsworth fathered memories of the lost child within himself in much the same way.[38]

Wordsworth's spots of time, therefore, center on those crossing perspectives where the retreat of the adult into recollection encounters the advance of the child into greater powers of mind. They convey Wordsworth's understanding of the ambiguity that lies at the heart of memory's power to mix recollection with anticipation. This notion, too, he conveyed poetically by transposing himself into a medieval tale of an errant knight who, approaching and returning on the same road, saw both sides of a signpost along the way. Traveling out, he saw its golden side; it signified his expectations. Traveling back, he saw its silver reverse image; it evoked his recollections.[39] In his *Prelude*, Wordsworth celebrated the golden side, but he appreciated the silver side even more. Anticipation, he believed, too often ended in disappointment, whereas retrospection provided a surer hold on reality. All his life he had expected too much of his visions of the future. He recalls his disappointment even in the heights of the Alps on learning that he had already traversed the summit pass without having realized it.[40] While acknowledging the poet's foresight, he came to trust his recollective judgment more.

"I would enshrine the spirit of the past for future restoration," Wordsworth remarked of his spots of time.[41] In this wish he succeeded beyond his own expectations. Few nineteenth-century autobiographers tried to emulate his poetic style. But all accepted his conception of autobiography as a reconstruction of life history through the recollective search for the self in its first imaginative promptings. Wordsworth had established the framework for autobiography as a modern art of memory. He epitomized a new way of thinking about the meaning of memory, one that Sigmund Freud would seek to turn into a science of psychoanalysis.

Sigmund Freud and the Mnemonics of the Unconscious Mind

Among the last of the collected writings of Sigmund Freud (1856–1939) is a letter he wrote to the French novelist Romain Rolland honoring his seventieth birthday. Freud himself was then eighty years old. Freud's gift to his colleague was a meditation on memory, more precisely a particular memory over which he had puzzled inconclusively for many years. His reminiscence was of his visit to the Acropolis in Athens during a summer vacation when he was forty-eight and in the prime of life. The journey to Greece was itself impromptu, and Freud recalled a feeling of unreality—or as he put it "derealization"—as he surveyed the city from the heights of that shrine. Freud sensed himself to have been of two minds. Consciously, he was certain of the reality of the setting. But simultaneously he experienced the sentiment, issuing from some-where in his unconscious mind, that the shrine did not really exist.

Now, in his reflection on this reminiscence that had stayed with him all of these years, Freud concluded that the experience of unreality was a substitute for a memory, buried deep in his unconscious mind, of his longing as a child to travel to the intriguing places about which he had read, but in the face of his awareness that he would probably never be able to do so. Growing up in a family of modest means in late-nineteenth-century Vienna, he had only modest hopes for his future. His visit to the Acropolis at mid-life, therefore, revealed his ambiguous feelings about the positive turn in his fortunes during his life as an adult. That he should have the opportunity to visit this place that had so captivated his imagination as a child, just as he should have traveled so far in wealth and fame, seemed too good to be true. To this place in his memory of mid-life, therefore, he had projected a sensation of unreality to cover over his painful memory of his frustration as a child about what he then perceived to be his limited prospects in life. In the parlance of the theory of psychoanalysis for which he is famous, this "Disturbance of Memory on the Acropolis" was a defense mechanism of his unconscious mind to conceal a memory that could not be consciously tolerated in undisguised form.[42]

Freud's letter to Rolland analyzed the ambiguity of this memory. But there was also an ambiguity about the letter itself. Freud had prefaced his account of the incident with a lament that he would travel no more; his most important intellectual labors were behind him. But in this modest interpretation of a seemingly inconsequential episode, he had traveled in memory across his entire life in order to show the hidden connection between his expectations as a child and his recollections as an old man. Standing midway in his life, the incident on the Acropolis marked a crossroads in his memory. The letter also reveals something of Freud's technique of psychoanalysis and helps us to understand the importance of memory in its use. As the historian Carlo Ginzburg has pointed out, Freud's method of seeking the truth is not unlike that of the famous fictional detective Sherlock Holmes created by his contemporary Arthur Conan Doyle: he was always looking for the unsuspected clue that would open the way to some hidden reality of far-reaching importance.[43]

In this respect, we might say that Freud's account of his experience on the Acropolis serves as such a clue to his theory of memory. Appended as a minor memoir in the penultimate volume of his collected works by his editor, the letter to Rolland contains in miniature the essence of Freud's theory of the repression of memory: the mind puts away memories it cannot easily tolerate by consigning them to the unconscious but always leaves clues as to how they may be retrieved. Freud's theory of the psyche underscores how little we consciously remember of our past experience. But it also affirms the power of the mind trained for critical introspection to recover that lost heritage. The more we know of our lives in the past, Freud believed, the better equipped we shall be to deal with our lives in the future. The unconscious contains secrets to our identity that we would do well to recover. To explain how that task might be accomplished, Freud described psychological disturbances as if they were features on a mnemonic map that mark places of memory in the unconscious mind. His invention of psychoanalysis as a technique with which to read that map is a modern art of memory.

Freud thought of research on the workings of the psyche as a new frontier of science. But psychoanalysis, for all of its originality as a paradigm for understanding the psyche and its efficacy in curing troubled souls, was essentially a technique for retrieving lost memories. One cannot help but notice the affinities between his interests and those of the students of memory that we have considered thus far. Though Freud was a scientist, there was something in his method akin to that of the magi of the Renaissance.[44] Like Giordano Bruno, he was in search of a *clavis universalis* to a secret universe. In place of Bruno's map of the powers of the heavens, Freud may have substituted one of the dynamics of the mind. But Freud's depiction of the psyche conjures up the same vision of a hidden realm of reality accessible only through the proper interpretation of the images that mark its points of contact with the phenomenal world.

Despite the seemingly ahistorical character of his model, Freud believed that humans have molded the psyche through their efforts to deal with life's challenges since prehistoric times. Like Vico, therefore, he attached enormous importance to the formative influence of origins. They shared a fascination with the proposition that the mental development of the individual (ontogeny) recapitulates that of the entire species (phylogeny). Indeed, Freud's interest in the possibility of a phylogenetic inheritance lured him in his later years into speculation about the shaping of the psyche in some distant, primordial past.[45] Like Vico, he analyzed the myths of antiquity for their hidden meanings. Vico had studied these for what they reveal about the times in which they were created. He contended that they were transparent representations of the poetic mind and hence keys to the collective memory of the people who created them. But for Freud, myths and legends were of interest for what they might reveal about an even more remote past; they displaced repressed memories of even earlier human experience of which we have no conscious record. Freud was inspired to travel into a realm of which Vico could not have conceived—that of the unconscious mind.[46] For Vico, this would have been like traversing the mythological river Lethe into a realm of oblivion beyond forgetfulness. But

what Freud believed he had discovered by making the passage was the deep
structure of human memory. In his view, images of memory contain mnemonic codes for recalling the deeper secrets of the unconscious mind.

Finally, there are far-reaching analogies between Freud's conceptions of
memory and those of Wordsworth. In many ways, Freud brings to the techniques of introspection employed by early nineteenth-century poets the authority of late-nineteenth-century science.[47] With Wordsworth, he shared the
notion that there is a deep unconscious structure of the mind that shapes the
workings of consciousness. What Freud calls the unconscious Wordsworth
had previously called nature. However they defined their terms, both conceived of the dynamics of the psyche in terms of the interplay between a hidden
structure that was the source of human energy and imagination and a visible
one that revealed only derivative powers of intellectual invention. Both believed that memory constitutes the essential link between these realms of
mind, and both developed techniques for enhancing memory's power to do
so. Both thought of memory in terms of its therapeutic capacity to repair
severed connections between these realms of mind. Last, they shared an
awareness of the impact of historical understanding on memory's uses and
brought that understanding to bear in the task of reconstructing life history.
In this respect, both adopted an historical perspective on memory by distinguishing the conscious task of recollection from the unconscious one of
repetition.

Yet for all the similarities with which they described the structure of the
mind and approached the task of introspection, they worked within cultural
settings that were far removed from one another and hence viewed life with
differing sentiments about its meaning and possibilities. Despite his own self-
doubts and psychological crises, Wordsworth envisioned the human condition
with the romantic's optimism. Freud, in contrast, viewed it from a more
somber perspective. One can see the differences in the way in which they
presented themselves in their autobiographies. Wordsworth focused on his
inner life, revealed his weaknesses and failings, and openly disclosed the psychological dilemmas with which he wrestled. For all his sufferings, his autobiography is sustained by the continuity of his search for harmony within
himself and with his surroundings.

Freud is not nearly so forthcoming. His autobiography is rather a record
of his public accomplishments.[48] Elsewhere, scattered amidst his clinical studies, he offered vignettes of his personal experience with doubt and fear. But
on the whole, he presents himself as he wished to be recognized by the world,
not as he struggled in his interior life with his personal dilemmas. Probity for
the individual, like constraint for the civilization, was a necessary strategy for
self-preservation in middle-class Viennese culture at the turn of the century.[49]
The romantic might have openly pursued his quest for happiness. But in the
positivistic milieu of late-nineteenth-century science in which Freud practiced
his craft, flights of imagination were regarded as dangerous illusions. Freud

was typical of the positivist savant who believed that the pursuit of happiness is the most dangerous illusion of all. For him, there are no happy endings to life's strivings. One is wiser to try to mitigate unhappiness, for life's struggles are unending.[50] One's consolation is in coping with life more effectively. Herein Freud extolled the power of reason as a tool for critical self-analysis. Greater self-awareness can enhance one's capacity to deal with life situations more effectively and courageously. Rigorous self-analysis provides the insight and the strength of mind needed to meet life's challenges and to endure its sufferings.[51]

This stoical perspective on the human condition became the primary orientation of Freud's psychology: the need to face reality with a greater measure of rational self-understanding. Not that this challenge was easily met. Freud believed that the human psyche is continually tempted to flee from reality, and when it succumbs to that temptation, to raise all of its defenses in order to ward off conscious awareness of the dilemmas that such flight entails. The dreams, myths, and memories which for the romantics had been expressions of deep psychological truths were for Freud only symptoms of unresolved conflicts within the unconscious psyche. They were illusions to be clinically analyzed for what they indirectly revealed about psychical disturbances, not realities into which one wanted to become absorbed. The task was to view them from a critical perspective. For Freud, therefore, the problem of the workings of the psyche is primarily one of its pathology. In his view, psychical life is inherently flawed, for the conscious and the unconsicous domains of the psyche often work at cross-purposes. Consciousness is far too often clouded by its illusions. Only the unconscious domain of the psyche comprehends reality without distortions, even if its dynamics are hidden from view.[52]

Above all else, Freud wished to emphasize the determining influence of the unconscious on psychical life. He characterized the psyche as an arena of perpetual conflict between instinctual impulses pressing for expression (id) and the no less insistent demands of conscience (superego) for their repression. Mediating the conflict is the self (ego), beleaguered by the task of determining the mix of acquiescence and constraint through which it defines personal identity.[53] Even the healthiest ego, Freud taught, has difficulty resolving some of these conflicts, to such a degree that the most ordinary life history is a saga of ongoing psychological crisis. Memories of the most painful of these experiences are repressed and hence forgotten by the conscious mind. But repressed desires remain unrequited and continue to press the ego for expression. Some are turned toward different ends; they are sublimated as the creative drives that sustain civilization's most noble causes. But others can impair, and in extreme cases, paralyze the ego's capacity to sort out the conflicting claims of psychical need. In a spectrum of possibilities from the anarchic free rein of impulses to their total repression, the ego resolves these conflicts through a series of compromises. It is these compromises that are the stuff of memory, a complex weave of fantasy and reality. Freud's point was that memories, however accurate they might seem to be as a record of the past, are always revised by the time they find conscious expression. Memories are bent to conform to the struggles within the unconscious psyche. They must be read as signs of these hidden conflicts rather than at face value. Let everyone be aware, Freud asserted, that memories as they surface in the conscious mind are full of such distortions.[54]

In the transactions between the conscious and unconscious domains of the psyche, Freud believed, the latter is the more important in shaping the course of life. It lies closer to the life world and is far more powerful as a determinant of psychical life. Herein a complete record of life's experiences is inscribed. It is as if the unconscious were a hidden archive in which all of life's memories are stored intact.[55] Such a view ascribed to the unconscious a coherence denied the conscious mind. From the vantage point of consciousness, the past is only a discontinuous series of memory fragments, punctuated by countless gaps as it recedes toward the amnesia of life's earliest stages. In its unconscious domain, the psyche hordes its impressions of life's realities, while offering to the conscious mind only glimpses of its efforts to cope with these. The memory fragments transmitted to the conscious mind, moreover, are not transparent representations of past realities. They always surface in disguise. Revised and distorted by the psyche's conflicting needs, they are consciously rendered as a composite of truth and fiction. What is offered to consciousness is an interpretation based not on what is accurate in the psyche's unconscious perceptions but rather on what is tolerable in its conscious recollections. Consciously we experience the need to reconstruct our life histories. But the lives that we re-create are always in some measure fictionalized accounts.[56]

When too caught up in such illusions, Freud explained, the conscious mind is ill-equipped to cope with life's realities. The health of the ego, therefore, turns on altering the transactions between the conscious and the unconscious domains of the psyche. In Freud's view, the ego could become stronger if it could become more aware of the tensions within the unconscious. The key to mental health lies in the recollection of those internal struggles through which the psyche has been formed in the course of its development. The therapeutic task is to raise the repressed struggle to the level of consciousness. By becoming aware of the reality of those experiences that have contributed to its formation, the ego is better equipped to cope with its problems.[57] In this way, Freud returns to the maxim of Socrates: know thyself. To know oneself, Freud believed, is to possess the capacity to recall the true record of life history through which one's identity has actually been formed. To the degree that such knowledge can be acquired, one's power to act effectively in the world is enhanced.

The interpretation of memory, Freud believed, held the key to understanding the interactions between the conscious and the unconscious sides of the psyche. Psychoanalysis was the science that he devised to accomplish that task.[58] As a method, it uses the conscious mind's critical capacity for recollection to understand the unconscious mind's compulsion to repeat its unresolved dilemmas. In effect, it employs one kind of memory (conscious recollection) to discern another (unconscious repetition). Divided against itself, the psyche possesses two versions of the past: the real record of the continuity of the events of the past, permanently inscribed in an unconscious that is largely inaccessible; an imaginary record of discontinuous memories of the past, fleeting in and out of consciousness in images that are continually being revised.[59] The recollection of life history reconstructed by the conscious psyche, therefore, might be likened to a topographical map, whose surface is dotted by prominent mnemic images. Although these images do not themselves reveal the past accurately, they mark places in the life of the psyche that remain hidden from view. At these junctures, one might say, the conscious self in its recollections is meeting the unconscious psyche in its repetitions halfway. For this reason, these places provide channels into the unconscious. Psychoanalysis, then, is a method for retrieving deep, forgotten memories at these remembered places.[60] In decoding the images located there, the analyst seeks to disassemble the chain of associations originally constructed by the unconscious mind to sequester the memory of the original experience.[61]

Freud contended that the individual must learn to read this map of the places of his memory. He must use what he remembers to uncover what he has forgotten. In this way, he can break through the screen of fantasies with which his unconscious psyche has revised his life history in order to recover those memories that will enable him to reconstruct the actual record of his experiences. The task is to treat the interpretation conjured up in conscious memory not as a true presentation of the past but, rather, as a mnemonic scheme. Memories are to be analyzed for their associations, not their direct representations. That is why an essential technique of psychoanalysis is free association. In self-analysis, one seeks to disassemble the chain of associations originally constructed by the unconscious mind.[62] In this way, one can locate the places of memory through which access to the real record of the past may be uncovered. These places of memory are marked in many ways: among them, parapraxes (slips of the tongue); jokes; dreams; screen memories; and even compulsive behavior. In an ascending order of insistence, these psychical phenomena displace memories of the real events.

Although psychoanalysis can be a technique of self-analysis, its efficacy is enhanced by a professional analyst who becomes a participant in the individual's search for a hidden self. The analyst provides a frame of reference against which the patient can see the process of self-exploration. Freud likened the analyst's role to that of a substitute father in whom the patient trusts enough to be willing to recount to him his recollections of his inner life. Essentially, he projects this map of his memories upon the mind of the analyst, who in effect reflects them as if his own mind were a mirror. The analyst does not so much explain the meaning of the images he reflects as clarify the patient's process of self-interpretation by helping him to see the connections among the images of the past that he has recovered from his unconscious mind.[63]

This topographical map of the places of one's memory along life's way displays a variety of features, each of which can provide access to thoughts repressed in the unconscious mind. The problem turns on the level at which the memory of a past experience is buried. Some are more thoroughly repressed than others, and those that are the furthest removed from consciousness surface in the fullest disguise. There is, then, a relationship between the degree of conscious distortion of a memory and the level at which it has been unconsciously repressed. But all memories are in some measure worked over by the unconscious mind and represent some form of revision. One might say that they are not really memories at all but fictive images marking places where genuine memories remain hidden.[64]

Among these place markers, parapraxes and jokes mask the memories that lie closest to the surface of consciousness, and the unconscious conflicts that they hide are the easiest to discern. Screen memories and dreams occupy a middle ground. They are deciphered through their imagery rather than through their manifest content. Most obscure are those memories that display themselves only as behavioral patterns: compulsive obsessions and other forms of neurotic behavior such as paranoia and schizophrenia. These places of memory on the map of the conscious mind signal what Freud characterized as "the return of the repressed."[65] From the vantage point of memory, each is a camouflaged repetition of some unresolved psychical conflict borne forward out of the past. What guides the analyst in his efforts to break through the artifice with which the unconscious mind clothes its memories is his understanding that all of them are revised reconstructions of unresolved conflicts. Whatever the psychical material he considers, the analyst is predisposed to look for clues to underlying conflicts.

If psychoanalysis is an art of memory, it is an infinitely more complex one than that practiced by the classical mnemonists.[66] The mnemonist was able to scan a complete array of images housed in the brightly lit rooms of his memory palace, whereas the analyst is obliged to scrutinize the haphazard images cast up in distorted memories and shadowy dreams. The mnemonist worked from a clearly delineated architectural design, whereas the analyst must decode memory fragments as pieces in the mosaic of unconscious psychical intent. The analyst must skillfully lead his patient along the path of recollection. He must encourage him to draw forth as many memory images as he can, and he must then interpret the pattern of remembrances in a way that will raise the patient's awareness of others that remain hidden. The goal of this reconstruction is to find the way to the hidden motive, the repressed desire. As an art of memory, then, psychoanalysis is akin to the historicist's reconstruction of the historical imagination. It is a method of interpretation that seeks to grasp the meaning of psychical life as it is revealed at the crossroads between the repetitions of the unconscious and the recollections of the conscious mind.

Given the nature of the technique, therefore, it is not surprising that Freud worked most effectively with those places of memory that occupied the middle ground on the map of conscious recollection: dreams and screen memories. Both deal in mnemic images whose deeper connections are more easily established than are those of obsessive behavioral patterns. Dreams were for Freud the most fascinating expression of unconscious psychical life, and they are the phenomena that have most interested his readers over the years. He characterized them as "the royal road to the unconscious mind," for they contain the deepest level of memory capable of interpretation through the reconstruction of a pattern of mnemic associations.[67] Dreams are full of memories that the psyche more willingly gives up as it relaxes its watch during sleep. But the memories of dreams surface in random fragments and so, even if they are successfully interpreted, only provide clues to the code of unconscious psychical intent. These memory fragments must still be decoded to discover their connection to forgotten experiences yet to be disclosed.[68] On his way to formulating his theory, Freud found that dreams provided him with some of his most profound insights into the workings of the psyche, and he spent a considerable amount of time analyzing his own dreams. But it is his theory of screen memories that best illustrates how psychoanalysis as an art of memory works.

The substitution of an image for an idea, the key to the method of the classical mnemonist, is also the central proposition of Freud's theory of screen memories.[69] Screen memories are mnemic images that displace deeper, hidden memories. By comparison with the memories that they shield, they are of lesser consequence, arouse fewer emotions, and relate to more recent experience. They are projected backward in time to fill the gaps created by the repression of memories of actual experience and thereby fulfill the ego's need for a coherent sense of life's development. As in the associations prescribed in classical mnemonic technique, the link between the screen memory and the repressed one is an attachment of place rather than of content. The screen memory fits the pattern of the past envisioned in our conscious reminiscences, yet marks the place where the repressed memory of our actual experience may be retrieved.[70] As Freud explained, screen memories "are not made of gold themselves but have lain beside something that *is* made of gold."[71] Elsewhere he likens the connection to that of the hermit crab with its shell.[72]

We might note that the purpose of the screen memory, in contrast with that of the classical art of memory, is to enable us to forget. Screen memories are defenses employed by the unconscious psyche to ward off recollections of intense, painful, or traumatic experiences, especially those of childhood. Whereas the mnemonist employed vivid images to stimulate his recall of ideas, the unconscious psyche uses inconsequential ones to spare the conscious psyche exposure to distressing memories.[73] Freud's description of the workings of the unconscious psyche, therefore, reveals a reverse mnemonics. Forgetting rather than remembering is what we wish to do because it is easier to live with a screen of fantasies about what our lives have been than with the reality. In his theory of screen memories Freud asserts the constructive power of the unconscious mind to shape recollection. To use his terminology, memory is tendentious in that it reflects unconscious psychical intent.[74] In this respect the unconscious mind is the guardian of memory. It legislates the selection of what is to be remembered and hides the rest away. As an art of memory, therefore, Freud's psychoanalysis employs a technique for deciphering the unconscious intentions encoded in screen memories and like psychical displacements.

Freud's psychobiography of Leonardo da Vinci is his most famous case study of the analysis of a screen memory. It is based on da Vinci's account of his recollection as an adult of a childhood memory of a vulture placing its tail in his mouth. Freud concluded that it was a fantasy transposed on his early childhood from adolescence. This screen memory shielded him from the painful memory of his separation from his father during infancy, when he lived alone with his mother. During latency, when he had repressed his feelings of erotic love for his mother, he took himself as a model for emulation to fill the void left by his absent father, and so came to love his own childish self. The screen memory of the vulture, Freud explained, was a homosexual fantasy of this narcissistic self-love, projected into infancy to displace the painful memory of his lost father. But this repressed memory continued to work its power on his unconscious mind. Da Vinci's repressed memory of his love for his mother, therefore, was eventually transfigured in the creative images that he painted in his adult years, notably that of the beguiling smile of Mona Lisa.[75]

Although Freud never analyzed the memories of William Wordsworth, the parallel between his conception of a screen memory and Wordsworth's notion of a spot of time is striking. Spots of time, like screen memories, are recollections from childhood of benign, relatively inconsequential experiences. They retain an inexplicable vividness in later years, and, as in the case of Wordsworth's recovery from depression, they can serve a therapeutic purpose. Wordsworth recognized that, although they may have been inconsequential in themselves, they were associated with insights of profound importance. The poetic imagery with which he described the spots pointed toward deep levels of psychical reality that lay at the source of his imagination.[76]

From Psychoanalysis to Psychohistory

Freud's work on the psychological development of individuals eventually led him to inquire into that of the species. His faith that all human memories are recoverable disposed him to believe that psychoanalytic technique could be enlisted in the service of history in a way that transcends the limits of individual memory. It could take the historian into the collective memory of the past and so reveal its hidden sources. It could do so by virtue of its capacity as a technique of recollection to uncover those unconscious habits of mind that prompted the historical actors' responses to life. The deep source of memory as repetition is in effect the "historical truth" that Freud the psychohistorian sought to discover beneath the representations bequeathed by historical actors to posterity.[77]

To deal with this problem of collective memory Freud returned to the approach first suggested by Vico—the analysis of representations of memories in the mythologies of early civilizations. In light of his hypothesis that ontogeny recapitulates phylogeny, Freud reasoned that if the analysis of a screen memory can disclose the lost experiences of childhood, then the analysis of the myths of primitive people should enable us to recover lost memories of human origins.[78] But Freud sought to extract from these myths memories of experiences prior to the conscious beginnings of civilization that Vico had identified with mythopoetic creation. For Freud, these myths were not transparent representations of the age in which they were created, as Vico believed them to be, but screen memories covering earlier events from which humankind wished to shield itself. The memory of civilization's beginnings was reconstructed after an historical period of latency, whereas the actual beginnings remained hidden in repressed memories that we collectively retain in our unconscious minds.[79]

To unblock these memories Freud turned to the analysis of religious myths of origins. Struck by the ongoing power of religion to mold people's minds from antiquity to the present, Freud sought to demythologize religious imagery to uncover the secrets about human origins that he believed they contained. Through his analysis of the myths of totemic religions, regarded as the earliest faiths of civilized people, he concluded that they screened acts of tribal parricide in which warrior sons murdered the omnipotent tribal father and reluctantly apportioned his power among themselves in a collective covenant. The totem was an emblem of worship. Usually an animal, it symbolized the displaced father even as it obliterated him from conscious memory. The totem feast, in turn, was a symbolic act of worshipping while devouring this father whom they had once held in awe yet had been willing to destroy.[80] The father and son imagery of monotheistic religions such as Judaism and Christianity merely reiterated the screening of this primal truth.[81] Religious myth transfigured the primordial conflict of love and aggression into a sacred memory that rendered tolerable a profane truth that remained repressed. The power of religious myth in the present age, Freud concluded, testifies to the power of the repressed memory it screens. Born historically in the first social contract, the religious myth of origins has become timeless as it is unconsciously recapitulated by each generation in the psychological revolt of sons against their fathers.[82]

Late in life, Freud turned to one last project in history as a means of explicating his theory of the relationship between collective memory and historical understanding. His history of the origins of the Hebrews, *Moses and Monotheism* (1939), is likewise based on the proposition that a legend that displaces a reality nonetheless contains the key to its recovery. In this respect he argued that the legend of Moses served as a screen memory covering over the true historical circumstances of his fate. He therefore interpolated the imago of Moses bequeathed by Jewish tradition for what it might reveal about the deep structure of an unconscious memory of Hebrew origins.[83]

In Freud's interpretation, the legend of Moses reflects the deep-seated human ambivalence about the authority of leadership. He speculated that Moses was an Egyptian nobleman, who fell from favor for his enduring faith in a monotheistic religion spurned by the pharaoh. Moses found consolation in proselytizing his beliefs among a tribe of Hebrew slaves that he then led out of bondage. Although it was Moses who gave them the law that became the cornerstone of their faith, his followers resented his authority and eventually murdered him. They abandoned his faith and repressed the memory of the event. In time, however, their descendants merged with a desert people of western Arabia, whose leader, also named Moses, taught them to worship the volcano god Yahweh. This Midian Moses also met a violent end. But the blending of the cultures permitted the return of the repressed memory of the Egyptian Moses and his teachings. Eventually the memories of the two Moses were amalgamated and transfigured into a single legend. The religion of Yahweh, too, was gradually transformed so as to give expression to the tenets and the spirituality of the Egyptian monotheism.[84]

But how could the repressed memory be transmitted as a collective inheritance? Herein Freud flirted with the notion of a phylogenetic inheritance. It was not that he had in mind a free-floating collective memory. Rather he argued that the re-creation of similar conditions historically calls the same psychical predispositions to come into play.[85] Any human experience, he believed, remains a part of our psychical makeup. The psyche is an historical creation, a truth lost on many people in the modern age because its making dates from primordial beginnings. Accordingly, the problem of the history of the psyche is one of deep time. The legend of Moses could be made to evoke a hidden content because it was only a place marker for the "deep memory" of the original experience. Because that imago marks an important episode in the shaping of the human psyche, Freud believed, historians can recover the conditions under which it was created. To remember the past is to reimagine it.[86] As Freud explained, the truth that he sought to recover is an "historical, not a material truth."[87] In the story of Moses, it is not the particular circumstances but the general human response to like conditions that he sought to uncover, a "repetition" with affinities to the earlier legend of the father in the totemic religions of the primal horde and the later one of the son in Christianity.[88]

Whatever the limitations of Freud's scholarship, the model of historical understanding at which he arrived provided the consolation of a coherent conception of the human condition. Freud is one of the last exemplars of a historicist tradition inaugurated by Vico that was based on the faith that humans have the capacity to recover the memory of all human experiences and thereby can make the record of human history whole. In this respect, Freud's distinction between "material" and "historical" truth is close to that made by

Vico between the "certain" and the "true." The classical art of memory, with its spatial paradigms, might appear to have been eclipsed by the rise of this modern historical scholarship. But in the historicism of Vico, Wordsworth, and Freud, the art was rather reformulated in temporal schemes. All three employed places of memory to emplot the emergence of an historical understanding of human identity.[89] In their conceptions, memory and history became indissolubly united.

Since Freud's death the historicist tradition has come under more frequent criticism. Our postmodern age possesses considerably less faith in the proposition that the development of civilization, or for that matter the development of the individual psyche, possesses a continuous thread of meaning. In this respect, recent work by cultural historians has tended to place the accent on the discontinuities between historical epochs, and even among the mentalities of different social groups living beside one another in the same historical era.[90] Michel Foucault's notion of "counter-memory," which denies the ability of collective memory to bind meanings across dissimilar historical epochs, is a provocative statement of this point of view.[91] Foucault's questioning of the intrinsic value of remembering the past for its intellectual or moral authority suggests why our present perception of the problem of memory has shifted from the problem of forgetfulness to that of amnesia. Mementos that for Freud were signposts to a past we might hope to revisit become for Foucault all that remains of one otherwise lost in oblivion. The current popular obsession with maladies of amnesia certainly derives from a legitimate medical worry. But it is also a metaphor for the cultural malaise of our time. As Oliver Sacks, a neurologist with a philosopher's bent, suggests in his description of the consciousness of a victim of Korsakov's syndrome, amnesia is especially terrifying in our culture because it severs connections with memories of specific experiences in the past that we once believed to be essential for maintaining our identity.[92] To some degree, memory is a problem in the postmodern age because of our anxieties about the implications of our loosening attachments to the collective memories that once sustained us.

Among historians interested in the memory/history problem today, most of the work deals with the way in which the past has been represented. In method it follows Foucault's deconstructionist bent, with its genealogical inventories and descriptions of commemorative forms. There is nonetheless a return in some quarters to an historicism that draws on Freud's insights. One notes it especially among historians concerned with the history of the Holocaust. They present the problem of its history in terms of the limits of representation. Herein the Freudian method and model of history continue to have an appeal. Such historians want to gather the testimony of survivors of the Nazi atrocities, for whom the past is not a problem of working back but of "working through." They must consider their evidence not only from the vantage point of history but also from that of living memory, no longer construed ingenuously but now informed by an awareness of the issues the postmodern historians have raised. What is at issue here is not how history can recover memory but, rather, what memory will bequeath to history. These historians worry about maintaining the integrity of memory as it passes into historical scholarship. They are concerned with memories that are vitally important to them in a way they never were for the postmodernists. But they are also aware of how selective recollection is, dependent as it is on those who would fashion its representation. Their question is: how will the past be remembered as it passes from living memory into history? In light of this question, the problem of history is revealed to be vitally tied to that of the integrity of memory. It is the problem of historicism self-consciously reconceived.[93]

Here the work of Saul Friedländer is important. He was himself a victim of the Holocaust but in a way that made him particularly reflective about his identity. A Jewish refugee in France as an adolescent, he was given a Catholic identity and so escaped detection until war's end. His moving autobiographical memoir, *When Memory Comes,* explores the way in which he "worked through" his memories of his experiences in the Freudian manner.[94] Although not a disciple of Freud, he is sympathetic to his method because it contributed to his recovery of the layered identities of his own past.[95]

Like Freud, Friedländer is particularly interested in the power of that past that cannot be represented. He calls it "deep memory," as does Lawrence Langer in his study of the testimonials of other Holocaust survivors.[96] To what degree can "deep memory" be recovered? It is the Freudian proposition, and Friedländer's conclusion follows that of Freud: a great deal if one can work the problem through.[97] Friedländer raises the question of memory's role in history from the vantage point of repetition: what representation can I make of the painful experiences of my past that is capable of being recollected by future generations? If all history is that of representation, as the postmodernists teach, what are the terms and the limits of my attempts to represent my own experiences? It is, in effect, the problem of commemoration considered with an eye to the future. How shall we represent the past in a way that the truth of its "deep memory" will not be forgotten by posterity?

Freud believed that the historians' mission is to reach for that truth. It is not enough to describe the past through its representations, for that presupposes a detachment that is alien to the lived experiences that memory bears into the present. Living memory is ultimately the ground of the historians' interest in the past, just as it was once the foundation of the identity of the historical actors that they now seek to understand. It inspires the historians' inquiry, just as the search for that which has been forgotten serves as their goal. Freud's own inquiries as an historian may be dated and his conclusions dubious. But the purpose with which he pursued his task remains vital to that of today's historians, a testimony to the limits of the stance of the postmodernists on the archaeology of memory's representations. Freud's quest continues to sustain those historians who maintain faith in the proposition that the past as it was experienced, not just the past as it has since been used, is the "historical truth" that historians should strive to recover.

4

MAURICE HALBWACHS AS HISTORIAN
OF COLLECTIVE MEMORY

Halbwachs among the Historians

Among the many evocative tableaux to which the French sociologist
Maurice Halbwachs had recourse in his efforts to convey his understanding
of the workings of collective memory, one of the most illustrative is that of
sea waves breaking on a rocky shore. As the tide rises, the rocks are immersed
in the advancing sea. But with its retreat, what remains of the sea's presence
are only "miniature lakes nestled amidst the rocky formations." In Halbwachs's analogy, the advancing sea is the tide of living memory. Its waves pulse
forward, bearing toward the future the turbulent presence of the past. With
the ebbing of the tide, only tranquil pools of recollection are left behind. In
them, the past remains alive, but with a diminished presence. More conspicuous now are the rocks, the places of memory that shape as well as contain
our recollections. Vis-à-vis the sea tide of past perceptions, they provide in
their ensemble what Halbwachs characterized as the social frameworks of our
memory.[1] Like the rocky shore in Halbwachs's tableau, the social side of memory always figured most prominently in his discussion of the subject. It was
his highly original argument about the social contexts of collective memory
that historians have recently found to be such a useful guide to their reconsideration of the connections between memory and history. Long neglected,
his work today serves as a theoretical groundwork in the emerging project of
the history of memory.

Halbwachs was an eclectic scholar with wide-ranging interests. A disciple
of Emile Durkheim, he was a leading member of a coterie of French scholars
that introduced a more theoretical cast to sociological research in the era between the world wars, and he has continued to enjoy the respect of his colleagues in that discipline.[2] His early reputation in academic circles was based
on his studies of social class. He was an admirer of the socialist tribune Jean

Jaurès and himself a committed socialist. His writings display his thorough grounding in economics, not to mention a passion for statistical analysis seemingly at odds with the focus on imagery and imagination that the topic of memory requires. Just after the First World War, he was appointed to a professorship at the University of Strasbourg, a new university that became a center of intellectual ferment in the interwar years.[3] It was there in the prime of his academic career that his interest in memory was kindled. The topic of collective memory, therefore, was one into which he was drawn in his middle and later years, a line of inquiry that he might otherwise have neglected but for the stimulating milieu of intellectual innovation and interdisciplinary exchange at Strasbourg.

Halbwachs's reflections on the workings of collective memory are currently enjoying a renaissance of interest among his colleagues in the social sciences.[4] The English scholar Mary Douglas has underscored the importance of his work on collective memory by editing his last book on the subject, *La Mémoire collective,* prefaced by an insightful essay of her own about the meaning of his work.[5] Douglas related Halbwachs's theory of the dynamics of collective memory to that of the anthropologist Edward Evans-Pritchard, who had done fieldwork on the remodeling of collective memory in the living oral tradition of the Nuer tribe in Africa.[6] Other scholars have noted the affinities between Halbwachs's study and that of the English psychologist Frederic Bartlett, whose *Remembering,* published a few years before, parallels Halbwachs's exploration of the role of contextual frameworks in prompting recollection.[7] Recently, sociologists such as Barry Schwartz and Yael Zerubavel have begun to use his theory as a foundation for their own studies of the uses of commemorative practice.[8] Their work displays a new sensitivity toward the historical dimension of collective memory and points toward a convergence of interests on the part of sociologists and historians investigating this topic.[9]

The problem of memory's relationship to historical understanding was one that Halbwachs considered only in his last writings. His most comprehensive and best known work, *Les Cadres sociaux de la mémoire,* published in 1925, never touches directly on the memory/history relationship. In those days, his attention was directed toward the problem of the dynamics of memory itself, and the intellectual issues with which he wrestled were those posed by the philosopher Henri Bergson and the psychologist Sigmund Freud. Only subsequently, in his posthumously published *La Mémoire collective* (1950), did he consider the problem of memory from an historical perspective. One senses, too, that his thoughts on the subject were still provisional at the time of his death in 1945 in a concentration camp at Buchenwald, a victim of Nazi persecution.[10] Some contemporary historians commented on the originality of his work, but Philippe Ariès was the only one to use Halbwachs's theoretical model as a guide for his own fieldwork on the traditions of Old Regime France.[11] Over the past fifteen years, however, the historians' acclaim for his insight into the workings of collective memory has become a chorus, and new voices are continually being added.[12]

As in the case of the sociologists, the problem of memory in oral tradition was the topic that first turned the attention of historians to Halbwachs's work. The French scholar, Nathan Wachtel, in an important essay on the relationship between memory and history, pointed out how Halbwachs's study of the workings of collective memory offers a method for analyzing forms of oral communication once considered to be beyond the historian's ken.[13] Today, however, it is less the dynamics of oral tradition than the politics of representation that heralds his reputation as a pioneer in the history of memory. In this postmodern age, scholars have become particularly sensitive to the images through which the themes of contemporary culture are presented to the world at large.[14] Alongside the search for substantive facts, the decoding of rhetorical images has become a major project of historical inquiry.[15] Historians today are preoccupied with the problem of the power of forms of representation, as current work in the history of commemoration attests. Fifty years ago, Halbwachs published what is today regarded as the inaugural study in this genre of historical research. Not only has his *La Topographie légendaire des évangiles en Terre Sainte* (1941), a history of the making of the commemorative landscape of the Holy Land, been rediscovered by historians, it has also come to be regarded as something of a model in the field.[16] Halbwachs showed historians how to write a history of the politics of memory, and it is especially for this accomplishment that they pay him homage today.

Halbwachs's gravitation toward problems of historical interpretation was certainly encouraged by his professional association with Marc Bloch and Lucien Febvre in the 1920s at the University of Strasbourg, where they first published their now-famous scholarly journal, *Les Annales*.[17] Indeed, Halbwachs was a member of its first editorial board, and he contributed a number of articles and reviews as well.[18] Bloch and Febvre, celebrated as the founders of a new kind of history, took an expansive view of the historians' realm. They reached out across disciplinary lines into economics, geography, ethnology, and social psychology. Febvre especially was interested in the last topic, and in an indirect way he touched on the problem of memory. He pointed to the need for an understanding of habits of mind as the building blocks of thought, and he encouraged his colleagues to investigate the inertial power of such habits in the shaping of culture.[19] Febvre's agenda for exploring new directions in cultural history prepared the way for today's flourishing studies in the history of collective mentalities, but the topic of collective memory, which in many ways underpins the entire enterprise, owes far more to Halbwachs's preliminary endeavors.

It is therefore surprising to learn that Halbwachs, despite this association with the illustrious founders of *Annales* historiography, should have offered such a narrow and old-fashioned definition of history as a field of study, one close to the positivist-inspired narrative historiography of the nineteenth century that Bloch and Febvre wished to move beyond. In this respect, Halbwachs remained faithful to Durkheim's claim for the surpassing role of sociology among the human sciences. If Strasbourg was a center of interdisciplinary collaboration, it was also one of rivalry, in which each discipline was intent on staking out its claim on the academic terrain. A respected scholar active in intellectual discussions with his colleagues, Halbwachs was appointed to the editorial board of *Les Annales* to provide the sociologist's viewpoint, but he was always viewed as an outsider. His debates with the historians, therefore, were vigorous and combative, for there were only so many concessions he was willing to make to these ardent apostles of a new, more ambitious historiography.[20] That is why an appreciation of his contribution to history is complex. Despite his foresight into historiographical issues that would claim the historians' attention two generations thereafter, his own perceptions of the historian's method remained grounded in the anachronistic theory of Auguste Comte.

Halbwachs's theoretical position on the memory/history problem is most readily grasped from the summary assessment that he offered in his *La Mémoire collective*. Therein he referred to "the ultimate opposition between memory and history."[21] By this formulation he meant to underscore the differences between the kind of past that each restores. Memory confirms similarities between past and present. There is a magic about memory that is appealing because it conveys a sense of the past coming alive once more. It touches the emotions. History, by contrast, establishes the differences between past and present. It reconstructs the past from a critical distance and strives to convey the sense that its connections with the present are devoid of emotional commitment. Memory deals in customary events that recur all the time. History identifies singular events that happen once and for all time. The images retrieved by memory are protean and elusive, whereas the data of history are durable and verifiable. To Halbwachs's way of thinking, history considers a past from which living memory has been distilled, one that may be reconstructed from its evidentiary leavings but whose mentality or subjective state of mind cannot be resurrected. As he remarked in a telling simile: "History is like a crowded graveyard to which new tombstones are continually being added."[22] "How could history ever be a memory," he asked, "since there is a break in continuity between the society reading this history and the group in the past who acted in or witnessed the event?"[23]

In assessing Halbwachs's analysis of the relationship between memory and history, one should keep in mind that he was caught up in the promise of positivist science for early-twentieth-century scholarship.[24] That he should have ignored the interconnections of mnemonic and historical perspectives on the past is perhaps understandable. He wrote at a time when the boundaries around history as a field of scholarly inquiry were still sharply drawn, and he clung to the positivist conception of the historian as an authenticator of documented facts.[25] His main purpose as an historian was to show how unreliable memory is as a guide to the realities of the past. Certainly, he possessed some sense of the interpenetration of memory and history; indeed he used this very phrase to characterize the relationship between autobiographical and historical memory for time periods in which they overlap.[26] But he believed that the historian's first task is to keep memory honest, to remedy its distortions of the past by comparing its suspect claims to those based on documented historical evidence. Recourse to memory is but an art, he suggested, fabricated around a few salient personalities and events whose role is exaggerated. Not only does memory invent a skewed pattern of the past; it clings tenaciously to its invention in the face of changing realities. By contrast, the writing of history is a science, whose evidentiary record as it is aggregated over time bodies forth a more objective pattern of the past. Its outlines become ever more finely delineated as more factual details are filled in.[27]

Because he believed that history begins where living memory ends, Halbwachs never reflected sufficiently on their interconnections.[28] He confined historical understanding to a range of considerations too narrow to encompass his fascinating findings about the dynamics of collective memory within evolving traditions. To put it another way, he never looked at history as a kind of official memory, a representation of the past that happens to enjoy the sanction of scholarly authority.[29] Hence he failed to recognize the full implications of what he himself had discovered about the history/memory relationship, circumspect as he was about what historians might consider as their field of scholarly endeavor. History in the older, conventional definition searched for certainties about substantive realities. But the new history of mentalities, inspired by *Annales* historiography and reconceived to encompass the analysis of collective memories, considers human hopes and dreams, that realm of the human imagination that deals in possibilities as well. To take cognizance of the rhetorical and iconographic forms in which humans had couched their visions of the world—their conceptions of the past and their expectations for the future—permits the historian to entertain a far wider range of considerations.

Halbwachs's circumscribed definition of history may be one that few historians would today accept. At the same time, his profound insight into the nature of tradition now enables them to appreciate collective memory at once as the foundation of historical inquiry and as a province for historical study. For this reason, we might say that Halbwachs was an historian despite himself. To understand how, we must consider the way in which his theory of the workings of collective memory served as a foundation for his subsequent, more practical work as an historian. In other words, we must consider how Halbwachs the sociologist of collective memory in *Les Cadres sociaux* in the 1920s becomes Halbwachs the historian of commemoration in *La Topographie* by the 1940s.

How Collective Memory Works chez Halbwachs

Halbwachs set forth his theory of collective memory in a programmatic way in *Les Cadres sociaux*. For him, the key to decoding the workings of collective memory turns on the problem of localization. In remembering, we locate, or localize, images of the past in specific places. In and of themselves, the images of memory are always fragmentary and provisional. They have no whole or coherent meaning until we project them into concrete settings. Such settings provide us with our places of memory. Remembering, therefore, might be characterized as a process of imaginative reconstruction, in which we integrate specific images formulated in the present into particular contexts identified with the past. The images recollected are not evocations of a real past but only representations of it. In that sense, they give expression to a present-minded imagination of what the past was like. The contexts, in turn, contribute to the shaping of these representations by highlighting the habits of mind of the social groups with which they are associated. As the essential reference points for any consideration of memory's workings, they reveal its essentially social nature. Collective memory is an elaborate network of social mores, values, and ideals that marks out the dimensions of our imaginations according to the attitudes of the social groups to which we relate. It is through the interconnections among these shared images that the social frameworks (*cadres sociaux*) of our collective memory are formed, and it is within such settings that individual memories must be situated if they are to survive.[30]

In this respect, Halbwachs specifically repudiated Sigmund Freud's contention that the entire record of an individual's memory is preserved whole in the psyche.[31] He believed that memories are conscious fragments of integral ones that lie buried in the unconscious mind. In developing his argument, Freud paid particular attention to the significance of screen memories and the memory-images that surface in dreams. Memories for Freud either displace forgotten ones that remain hidden in the unconscious or are retrieved in distorted forms that obscure deeper memories. Memories from the Freudian perspective are clues to experiences out of the past that we hide from ourselves, but which, with the patient technique of psychoanalysis, we may eventually recover. It is as if the psyche were an encyclopedic archive to which human recollection had complete, if hardwon, access.[32] Halbwachs challenged this view. In reflecting on the memories associated with his own dreams, he noted that dream-images are perpetually elusive and unstable because the social frameworks that lend them stability in wakeful life have been removed. We may remember the images of our dreams, he argued, but remembering while dreaming is beyond our capabilities. In convincing himself, he noted that in analyzing his dreams, he could not, despite all attempts, recall a single act of remembering.[33]

What Freud characterized as individualized images stored deep in the human mind was for Halbwachs the collective imagery of social discourse, espoused openly in our everyday lives. Places of memory are not repositories of individual images waiting to be retrieved but points of convergence where individual reminiscences are reconstructed by virtue of their relationship to a framework of social memory that sustains them. Recollection is always an act of reconstruction, and the way in which we recall an individual memory depends on the social context to which we appeal. We participate in many social groups, which compete for our allegiances. For Halbwachs, therefore, the problem of memory is also one of social power. What we remember depends on the contexts in which we find ourselves and the groups to which we happen to relate. The depth and shape of our collective memory reflect this configuration of social forces that vie for our attention.[34]

These conceptual structures of the social imagination, moreover, are fashioned out of the interplay between two moments of memory: our habits of mind and our recollections.[35] Habits of mind are the myriad images to which we have such frequent recourse that they elide to form the composite images of our collective memory. Recollections concern more distinctive experiences. They are images that we continue to identify with particular persons or events. Both moments of memory concern imagination or image-making. But the images of habit are intuitively repeated, whereas those of recollection are consciously reconstructed. In habit, we bear memories forward unreflectively as commonplaces. In recollection, we reconstruct the past retrospectively by localizing specific images in relationship to these well-formed places of memory. The reciprocity between these two moments of memory is dynamic and ongoing. Places of memory, therefore, are like crossroads where habits of mind and particular recollections encounter and reshape one another. If our recourse to a specific recollection is frequent enough, its particular imagery eventually gets worn away. It too is reduced to an ideal type and as such finds an habitual place within the structures of our collective imagination. For this reason, collective memory distorts the past in that with the passage of time a few personalities and events stand out in our recollections, and the rest are forgotten. In this way, "distant frameworks" become distinguished from "nearby milieux." In other words, collective memory factors the past into structured patterns by mapping its most memorable features. That is why it appears to form its imagery around spatial reference points that emerge prominently from the surrounding milieux of perception.[36]

Halbwachs identified the process by which individual recollections are integrated into the structures of collective memory as tradition. Tradition preserves but also modifies the social frameworks of memory over time. It is a process that transpires so slowly that its incremental changes are imperceptible to those who have ongoing recourse to them. Only an historian scanning particular representations of a tradition at intervals over a long period of time is in a position to observe the change.[37] There is, moreover, considerable resistance on the part of those immersed within a tradition to accepting the reality of this inevitable transformation.[38] The defenders of a tradition, therefore, are likely to buttress its places of memory through acts of commemoration.

Commemoration, Halbwachs argued, is a self-conscious effort on the part of memorialists to stay or at least to disguise the process by which traditions slowly evolve. Commemorative places of memory reinforce our habits of mind by prompting our specific recollections of the past. That is why commemoration is so politically significant. As an activity it seeks to strengthen places of memory, enabling fading habits of mind to be reaffirmed and specific images to be retrieved more easily. For this reason, it provides historians with a frame of reference by which they can measure the way in which the representations of collective memory change over time.[39] There is in the project of commemoration, then, a contrived structuring of time and space that deepens and accentuates the natural tendency of collective memory to select a limited number of events and places for recollection. Time is a problem of memory in that there is no common frame of time to which all humans continually relate. Human time is defined by chronological frameworks on which social groups agree, and its possibilities are infinite.[40] As Halbwachs remarked, "each group immobilizes time in its own way."[41]

Space factoring is even more obviously tied to commemoration. Herein one notes striking connections between Halbwachs's description of the techniques of commemoration and those of the classical art of memory. Like the practitioners of that ancient art, Halbwachs described the materials of commemoration in terms of images and places.[42] Although he never made this association with the mnemonic technique of classical rhetoric, it nonetheless lies at the heart of the process that he describes. Like the mnemonists of old, Halbwachs suggested that memory is a problem of mental geography in which the past is mapped in our minds according to its most unforgettable places.[43] Indeed, it is Halbwachs's investigation of the way in which this mnemonic process is turned to political ends that serves as his point of entry into history.

Halbwachs as Historian of Memory despite Himself

Halbwachs's *La Topographie* is a study of how the memorialist transposes a mental map onto a topographical plane, where it becomes a visible landscape of memory.[44] In this work, he studied the use of geographical places as the foundation for a tradition of commemoration. It is a history of how the project of localization of the collective memory of the life of Jesus proceeded over time through the construction, elaboration, modification, and remodeling of the places of memory of the New Testament. By studying the images and places of the commemoration of the Holy Land rather than the teachings that they signified, he set aside the issue of the intellectual content of Christian tradition and focused instead on the decoding of its forms of commemorative representation.[45]

Halbwachs's thesis is that the biblical Holy Land was an imaginary landscape conjured up during the Middle Ages in Europe and superimposed on the actual terrain of Palestine. Beginning in the fourth century, he explained, European pilgrims constructed a Holy Land of religious shrines that faithfully reflected their imagined conceptions of Jesus' sojourn on earth. The Holy

Land, therefore, was not a discovery but a localization of a mind-set they carried with them on their journeys. By the time they had begun to arrive, Christianity as a religious tradition had already undergone many modifications. The actual physical architecture extant in the epoch of the historical Jesus had long since disappeared through environmental erosion. For that matter, the gospels of the New Testament contained virtually no specific references to the geography of Palestine. The collective memory of the life of Jesus bequeathed by tradition, therefore, was derived solely from imaginative conceptions, not from actual physical locations. It was on such images that the pilgrims relied. Portrayed as discoveries, the places of Christian memory that they identified were in fact projections of these notions, derived from a tradition that may have dated from a time when the life of Jesus was still a living memory but that had been remodeled in substantive ways over the intervening centuries.[46]

If *La Topographie* is a study of the cultural uses of commemoration, it is also an investigation of its politics. The making of the Holy Land, Halbwachs contended, was a colonization of the culture as well as the terrain. He never spoke openly of the politics of memory, but the concept is implicit in his argument. Mnemonic props to a creed, the shrines erected by the pilgrims were also monuments to the rising power of Christianity to impose its tradition on the space of an alien culture. The success of the project fluctuated according to the vicissitudes of political fortune, for Palestine was a contested area throughout the Middle Ages. Not until Christianity had received the official favor of the Roman emperor in the fourth century did the plotting of this landscape of memory begin. The project was halted by the Muslim invasion of the seventh century; many shrines were dismantled or rededicated as sacred places of Islam. Only with the military conquests of the twelfth-century crusaders were the topographical features of the Christian Holy Land further elaborated, though the landscape of memory was often remapped in new and arbitrary ways. In the process, the older shrines of indigenous Christians and Jews, built on less powerful local traditions, were reidentified and in some measure reshaped to conform to the dominant European Christian conception. In this sense, commemoration was an important political technique of colonization.[47]

The invention of the Holy Land, Halbwachs contended, also played a role within the politics of Christianity itself. In the early days of Christianity, religious interpretations of the meaning of the life and teachings of Jesus abounded. Not the least of these were the gnostic conceptions that dismissed the story of his bodily resurrection and emphasized his role as a purveyor of spiritual enlightenment. With the conversion of the Roman emperor Constantine to Christianity (311) and the consolidation of Christian teaching at the Council of Nicea (325), Christian tradition took on an official form. Alternative traditions of the life and teachings of Jesus were suppressed or revised to conform to the Church's interpretation. That official tradition was confirmed by the shrines of the Holy Land. With its focus on the bodily resurrection of Jesus, the Church took advantage of the Roman Empire's sway over Palestine to locate places that would render the memory of his suffering, death, and resurrection concrete and visible. The shrines, therefore, were part of a practical strategy for retarding change within Christianity itself. These places of memory acted as a brake upon its modification as an oral tradition. Fixed in stone, the mnemonic landscape that enshrined the life of Jesus for popular religious devotions held fast the religious beliefs for which it was an emblem. In this way, Halbwachs concluded, these shrines exercised an inertial power on Christian piety. In a world in which the wisdom of the past took precedence over improvisation for the future, commemoration contributed not only to the continuity but also to the stability of an official religious tradition.[48]

By the end of the Middle Ages, Halbwachs explained, places of Christian memory dotted the Holy Land. Typically, the shrines that identified them were churches, dedicated to the events in the gospels that were to be commemorated there. The pilgrim Theodosius counted no less than twenty-four on the Mount of Olives alone. Effectively, they were memory palaces on location, revealing in an imposing way the connection we have noted between commemoration and the ancient art of memory.[49] Over the centuries, the shrines themselves were remodeled, fell into ruin, and were reconstructed, so that the identification and classification of the commemorative edifices themselves became preliminary archaeological tasks for historians of Christian tradition.[50] Halbwachs organized his study around the history of the localization of seven of the most salient of these places of memory: Bethlehem; the "upper room" (cenacle); the praetorium of Pontius Pilate; the way of the cross (via dolorosa); the Mount of Olives; Nazareth; the lake of Tiberius. Because the physical evidence of these biblical places had long since disappeared, the pilgrims located them on what appeared to be propitious sites. Not an insignificant factor in their selection was the natural terrain itself. Imposing or distinctive geographical landmarks—grottoes, springs, and mountains—conveniently suited commemorative needs, especially if they were to be found along the routes traveled by the pilgrims.[51]

Some places were like magnets. The "upper room," for example, grouped a host of memories: the last supper, the pentecost, the dormition of the Virgin.[52] The Mount of Olives served as the commemorative place for even more: the teaching of the disciples; the sermon on the mount; the recitation of the Lord's prayer; the transfiguration; the last supper; Gethsemene; the ascension; and the tomb of the Virgin.[53] For particularly significant places, such as those marking the passion and death of Christ, places within places multiplied as the stages of the events being venerated were defined in detail.[54] Other events were located in more than one place because of competing conceptions derived from local traditions. The Bethlehem of the nativity, for example, was commemorated in two far removed places. The praetorium of Pontius Pilate was identified with both Herod's royal palace and the fortress of Antonia. Modern scholars favor the former. But the latter had a tenacious popular appeal, linked as it was to Jewish tradition. Thus the place of one memory dictated the localization of another, even though the memories were of different events. Then, too, places of memory were sometimes chosen to serve the needs of the pilgrims. Such was the case of Cana, site of the miracle of Jesus' conversion of water into wine, which was conveniently situated on the route they traveled from the lake of Tiberius.[55] The investiture of the landscape with such places often proceeded slowly, and some were very late additions. The way of the cross, for example, was not "located" until the sixteenth century, when the Franciscans made a spiritual exercise of following the route. As an ideal type of place, it was subsequently internalized in religious devotions throughout the Christian world as the stations of the cross.[56] In its making over the course of a millennium, the Holy Land conceived as a landscape of memory gradually acquired a mnemonic logic of its own.

Correspondingly, Halbwachs remarked, the geographical centering on Jerusalem in the landscape of commemoration signifies the way in which a basic quarrel over the meaning of the life of Jesus was resolved in the early politics of Christianity. The places of memory of Jerusalem, marking Christ's last days, are more conspicuous in the topography of the Holy Land than are those attesting to his far longer ministry in Galilee.[57] As Halbwachs observed, "It is an odd paradox that in the very place where Jesus must have lived the greater part of his life, his traces have completely vanished."[58] This neglect of the ministry of Jesus reflects the bending of memory to the purposes of the orthodox Christian message, which stressed the "good news" of the death and resurrection of Jesus. The wisdom tradition of gnostic Christianity was unable to survive because it was given no official place in Christian commemoration.[59]

Most important of all, the shaping of Christian tradition through its places of memory involved the remaking of an older tradition, now absorbed into its mnemonic landscape. The physical places of memory that Christian pilgrims identified with the life of Jesus, Halbwachs pointed out, were nearly all sacred to Jewish memory.[60] This was the hidden history of collective memory that he considered his most important finding. The birthplace of Jesus was fixed at Bethlehem because it was the city of David, even though it is more likely that he was born elsewhere.[61] The upper room, where the last supper was held and where the pilgrims gathered after the resurrection, was situated over the tomb of David, a spot sacred in Jewish tradition as Mount Zion.[62] As noted above, the praetorium where Pontius Pilate turned Jesus over for execution was placed over the well of Jeremiah.[63] In some ways, such localization was a matter of displacement. The shrines of Judaism were reidentified and in some measure reshaped to conform to Christian conceptions. Recommemoration was a reworking of memory, or as it has more recently been characterized, an act of *bricolage* in that old places were adorned with new images.[64] But in others, it underscored the degree to which the life and death of Jesus in the minds of these early Christian pilgrims marked the fulfillment of Jewish prophecy and, so, bore close links to Jewish tradition.[65] In either case, the essential point that Halbwachs wished to convey was that the *cadre social* of Jewish tradition constituted the deep structure that dictated the choice of the places of Christian memory.

Halbwachs's Methods and Sources: Navigators and Pilots

Halbwachs's guiding principle in composing his study was that, although there were sharp limits to what one might be able to reconstruct of the milieu in which Jesus lived, one could more easily deconstruct the images through which his life had been memorialized over the centuries. This proposition gives us a perspective on his method and sources, not to mention his appeal to the postmodern temper of contemporary historiography. Halbwachs is interested in the history of images rather than of ideas, of Christian tradition rather than the events associated with the life of Christ. He provided a hint of what he had in mind about method in an analogy he offered in his *Mémoire collective*. Herein he presented a tableau of a passenger on a riverboat wending its way downstream. The passenger takes note of landmarks along the shore. His observations are not continuous, for now and then he gets distracted. Only at journey's end, when he tries to reconstruct his voyage with the aid of a map, is he able to put the landmarks in their proper place along the route.[66] His recollection of the past is a composite of personal experience and acquired learning.

As an historian, Halbwachs seems to have had both perspectives in mind as he approached the task of describing the construction of the Holy Land as a commemorative landscape. Extrapolating from Halbwachs's tableau, one might extend his analogy this way. Think of the river as the river of time, and its waters as a living tradition. The landmarks signify memorable events marking changes in the course of history. To travel downstream, as did Halbwachs's passenger, is an act of piloting. One moves with the stream of tradition into unknown waters, identifying new landmarks along the river's course as one passes them. But plotting the course at journey's end is an act of navigation. One studies the map of landmarks to determine the extent and shape of the river as a whole. The historians on whom Halbwachs relied are a bit like navigators. They survey the river of tradition in a detached way. The landmarks correlate with abstract points on a map, and they are interested in them for what they signify about the changing directions a tradition takes over the course of time. The historians' task is one of phenomenological description. They locate the salient places of memory that signify turns in the river of tradition as a basis for explaining the phenomenon of commemoration. But the pilgrims on whose work Halbwachs also relied are more like river pilots. They are actively engaged in present tasks along the river. They are looking at the landmarks as a guide to their destination. Theirs is a task of exegesis. They reckon by the landmarks so that they may maintain their course on the waters of tradition.

The question, however, is whether it is really possible for the navigating historian to get off the boat at journey's end, for today many historians would argue that history, like memory, is a moving vessel. Indeed, Halbwachs as historian of the construction of the Holy Land might be said to have his own navigators and pilots. Their writings intertwine to become his places of memory. The navigators provided him with his map of the terrain of Christian tradition. But the pilots helped him to visualize the sites of commemoration. It is, moreover, their living memories that originally elicited his curiosity and drew him into his historical research.

As for his navigators, Halbwachs relied on the best biblical scholarship of his day, and for the most part he accepted their findings.[67] One does note in his choice of sources an attempt to provide a balanced assessment by taking into account an enduring historiographical quarrel dating from the Reformation: the Catholic claims for the primacy of tradition as opposed to the Protestant ones for that of origins. His primary Catholic source was Hughes Vincent and Félix Abel, *Jérusalem: Recherches de topographie, d'archéologie et d'histoire* (1912–26). The authors were Catholic priests, and Halbwachs appreciated their work for its comprehensive approach to the elaboration of the entire tradition of the Holy Land.[68] But he felt more affinity, one might conclude, for the study by Gustave Dalman, *L'Itinéraire de Jésus* (1924). Dalman was a German Lutheran. In the manner of Luther before him, he wished to dig beneath medieval tradition to get close to the problem of the historical Jesus in the cultural and geographical environment in which he had actually lived. Dalman's interpretation of primitive Christianity betokened a deeper memory, for he stressed its links to an anterior Jewish religious tradition.[69]

But Halbwachs also valued his pilots, who helped him to imagine the places of Christian memory. He was particularly interested in the eyewitness accounts by the earliest pilgrims, which might be characterized as an ancient travel literature.[70] He devoted his longest chapter to the impressions of the first pilgrim whose writings have survived, the Bordeaux Pilgrim of 333.[71] The Holy Land as a cultural geography might be said to have been his invention. But what interested Halbwachs especially about the text was the way in which it revealed how little there was for the pilgrim to see. Halbwachs's point is that in the fourth century the Holy Land was still a largely barren landscape. The Bordeaux pilgrim's account is valuable not for what he discovered but rather for the way in which his observations established a base by which to measure later modifications and elaborations of the commemorative architecture. "No document is more precious," he commented. "It brings us as close as possible to the origins from which these traditions subsequently developed spontaneously on their own."[72] The Bordeaux pilgrim's memoir also provided important evidence for Halbwachs's argument that the Christian commemorative landscape had been prefigured in Jewish memory. All of the places that the pilgrim identified as Christian shrines had previously been venerated in Jewish tradition.[73]

For each succeeding pilgrim who bothered to write a memoir of his travels, the contours of the commemorative landscape of the Holy Land assumed more refined detail. Halbwachs alluded only briefly to the leading medieval pilgrims who provide testimony about further embellishment of the commemorative landscape, among them Saint Silvia (Aetheria) (383), Theodosius (530), Antoninus Placentinus (circa 570), Arculfe (circa 670), Eucher (early sixth century), and Bede (early eighth century).[74] The nineteenth-century biblical scholars sometimes doubled as pilgrims to the Holy Land. Such was the case of François de Chateaubriand, who as a young man left a detailed account of his travels, *Itinéraire de Paris à Jérusalem* (1800), as a preface to his famous homily on Christianity.[75] Another was Ernest Renan, who among all the historians was the one to whom Halbwachs felt closest in his sympathies. Renan's *Vie de Jésus* (1863) was imbued with his own admiration for the life mixed with doubts about the divine calling.[76] In his repertoire of nineteenth-century sources, the believer Chateaubriand provided a counterpoint to the skeptic Renan, just as the traditionalist Vincent counterbalanced the fundamentalist Dalman in his twentieth-century references.

The significance of pilgrimage for the historians, therefore, needs to be underscored, for the appeal of firsthand observation of the terrain of the Holy Land was too compelling for even the most detached of the modern historians to resist. To return to our analogy, all of these modern historians who marked out a navigational design also tried their hand at piloting. All were pilgrims to Palestine, including Halbwachs himself, who journeyed there at least twice during the 1930s.[77] This crossing between the analysis of texts and firsthand observations of the commemorative landscape suggests something of the interchange between history and memory that Halbwachs in his more theoretical writings was reluctant to concede. For the historians, after all, the textual representations of the past were their primary frame of reference. In approaching the actual places of Jesus' historical sojourn, Halbwachs doubted that one could go beyond the written descriptions left by these early pilgrims.

But for the pilgrims who have left us their accounts, what mattered most were not the memorials but the memories that they evoked of a tradition in which they still lived and to which they responded emotionally. The meaning of their faith was in the resurrection, and what they wanted was memory's magical capacity for a resurrecting in their own minds of images of the landscape that Jesus himself had once perceived. As Halbwachs remarked:

> One must recognize that there was not at Jerusalem or anywhere in Palestine any authentic vestige . . . that marked the passage of Jesus—any building that he might have entered, or on which he might have cast his eye, any wall

against which he might have reclined, any stone on which he might have set his foot. . . . Certainly there is that which does not change, or hardly changes—the shape of the mountains, the wonderful view of the Dead Sea and the country of Moab that one sees from the heights of the Mount of Olives. But all of that is too vast, too anonymous and impersonal. What one hoped to find, to see and touch, what the pilgrims sought for centuries, was a more specific material setting closer to the one the evangelists represented to us, objects and places on a measurable scale, where a man like us might have left something of himself, where one might sense his presence, and which would evoke that past, which was for him the present, in our presence.[78]

As a pilgrim, Halbwachs meditated on this resurrectionist frame of mind when he happened upon a ruin of a synagogue at Capharnaum that, he surmised, might actually have existed at the time of Jesus' ministry and with which Jesus too might have had physical contact.[79] He noted how Chateaubriand and even Renan in their visits to such places had permitted themselves to be transported into flights of romantic imaginings about the experiences of the living Jesus.[80] But as he scanned the landscape of the Holy Land, his sober conclusion was that the memorable past that the pilgrims sought to evoke was irretrievable. Its physical places had long since disappeared; its oral traditions, insofar as they remained alive, had been endlessly modified over the course of time. The times of Jesus lived no more. As for their memories, the historians' tasks were strictly archaeological. What might be described were only the imaginative representations projected on this landscape of commemoration from time to time in this living tradition for which the life of Jesus was the unseen inspiration.

This reaching out from history toward memory has many affinities with what is presently characterized by students of oral tradition as the orality/literacy problem.[81] The written word enshrines memory, whereas the spoken word enables it to remain fluid and dynamic. Halbwachs recognized that ultimately everything that we know about the historical Jesus is derived from such an oral tradition, the gospels included. They too were written long after the death of Jesus, at a time when the living memory of his life was beginning to fade. The places of memory of the Holy Land were based on a living tradition about Jesus carried continuously by Christian believers from Palestine to Europe and back again. The memory of Jesus was the lost source of this tradition of commemoration that the pilgrims were trying to resurrect. But the tradition, as embodied in its texts and its monuments, was all that remained. "In topography as in history," Halbwachs quoted Renan, "an imposing façade has succeeded in covering over the traces of the great founder."[82] The tradition, therefore, not the person it reverences, becomes the historians' point of departure.

Halbwachs's History as Model and as Inspiration for Contemporary Historiography

To conclude, we might say that Halbwachs provided modern historiography with a model for the history of tradition as it is revealed in its representations along the way. In his interest in the changing patterns of the imagery of collective memory over time, he identified a new way of looking at historical evidence. For him, the history of memory bore testimony of memory's unreliability. But for today's historians, it illuminates a number of problems in the history of collective mentalities: imaginative representation as a topic for the historian's scrutiny; the archaeological character of the history of memory; tradition as an index to the power of political or social groups; the long periods of time that must be scanned in order to grasp the otherwise imperceptible process by which traditions are modified; the broad range of evidentiary sources, once considered beyond the historian's ken, that can be brought together to illuminate an historical problem: among them, iconography, architecture, geography, archaeological artifacts, eyewitness accounts, and historiographical traditions.

Accordingly, Halbwachs's work has inspired a range of studies of commemoration, although with a turn that reflects the problems of our own culture. Today's historians are very sensitive to the manipulative aspect of commemoration. A traditional society might want only to preserve a sacred memory of its origins. But a modern one might prefer to refashion it in order to further some present political objective. In other words, there has been a shift of interest in recent years from the memorialists' representation of power to their power of representation. This is the approach of Eric Hobsbawm and Terence Ranger in their recent *The Invention of Tradition,* which emphasizes the contrived and often factitious commemorative representations and rituals staged by politicians of the late nineteenth century in order to enhance the power of the modern state.[83] It is this issue that has inspired so much of the historical writing on nineteenth-century commemoration, especially in France and the United States.[84]

The most direct and imposing contemporary application of Halbwachs's method, however, is the study of the representation of the French national memory, edited by Pierre Nora, *Les Lieux de mémoire.*[85] Acknowledging the significance of Halbwachs's work directly, Nora follows his method in working backward from the present—upstream if you will—to inventory the many traditions that have enshrined the French national memory. A more conventional historiography had been predisposed to seek a common origin, as in the founding of nations. But herein Nora shows how the river of tradition branches as historians seek its sources. Thus the search for the French national identity branched into republican, national, and cultural traditions, to name only the most salient. It is a timely work for a nation thinking hard about its identity on the bicentennial of the French Revolution and the eve of the economic integration of Europe. Nora's anthology, to which some forty-five of France's most eminent historians contributed, follows Halbwachs's model closely in its interest in the way in which memory of the past is central to identity in the present; in its focus on the alternative ways in which the past may be represented; its method of working back from the present into the past to disclose sometimes discordant traditions; its preoccupation with the politics of memory; its wide-ranging use of archaeological, geographical, iconographic, and historiographic sources; and its insistence on the way in which history is anchored in tradition.

One might mention, too, how modern historical discoveries have confirmed some of Halbwachs's speculations about primitive Christianity. I am thinking of the significance of the Nag Hammadi finds of the lost gnostic gospels in 1945 and the interesting book by Elaine Pagels, *The Gnostic Gospels,* which deals with the politics of early Christianity.[86] The unearthing of a host of gnostic texts reveals the significance of a forgotten tradition and confirms Halbwachs's suggestion that a creed cannot be sustained without the supporting structures of collective memory.[87] Here, too, the notion of Christianity as a culture of pristine simplicity vanishes once the conflicts among competing contemporaneous local traditions have been revealed. The formation of the early Church, Pagels argues, was the outcome of a political struggle in which an official memory of the meaning of the life of Christ was imposed by the Church. Without the support of an institutional structure to sustain their memory, alternative gnostic conceptions were easily suppressed. This is the topic into which Renan had early insight and that in turn set Halbwachs in search of the deep structure of Jewish memory underpinning Christianity. In this sense, the kind of extrapolation from the written record about contemporaneous oral traditions in which Halbwachs engaged raises new issues for the historians' consideration. The crossing from literacy into orality may stimulate new directions of research that, as in the case of this remarkable find, may eventually be confirmed.

This point, too, may suggest something of what Halbwachs himself was looking for in undertaking this study. It raises the poignant question of whether this project on which he labored through the 1930s was an apostrophe to his age. At the time that he was conducting his research, was not Nazi Germany seeking to colonize Europe, as Europe had once colonized Palestine? Halbwachs's history shows how Jewish memory was covered over by the Christian one that was superimposed. Was not Jewish identity in modern Europe being threatened in a similar, if far more pernicious, way? Halbwachs's intentions, too, lie hidden beneath the text that he has bequeathed to us.

Our contemporary age is one that stands in awe of the power of imagery. Halbwachs was among the first twentieth-century scholars to foresee the significance of the study of imaginative representations for what they reveal about the modifications of collective memory as it is borne forward in living tradition. At the very least, he has shown us how easily the images of memory are manipulated, a topic poignant for those of us who live in a culture in which such manipulation threatens to compromise the quality of democratic political life. On a loftier plane, he has taught us how historical inquiry remains deeply embedded in the traditions from which it proceeds. One may laud the historians' caution in insisting on certain knowledge of the past, provided one recognizes that the curiosity that inspires their quest issues in its deepest promptings from memorable traditions.

5

PHILIPPE ARIÈS
Between Tradition and History

The Manor House as Memory Palace: An Enchanted Memory of a Lost Heritage

In *L'Enfant et la vie familiale sous l'Ancien Régime* (1960), his celebrated history of childhood in Western culture, the French historian Philippe Ariès presents a tableau of the manor house of an aristocratic family in the seventeenth century.[1] He characterizes the house as a place of public concourse, where members of an extended family gather, servants come and go, and clients and retainers make impromptu visits. It is a house of many rooms, all of which are accessible and none of which has an exclusive purpose. In this open space of spontaneity and informality, the family lives its life on public display, united by an ideal of sociability. How different is the way of life of this family from that of its modern counterpart, a smaller, more intimate group that segregates its daily activities into specialized rooms apart and conceals them from the world at large with a wall of privacy. Ariès's portrayal of the manor house owes much to his historical research. But it also owes something to his encounter as a child with the traditions of his own family.[2] His tableau of the manor house was in effect his version of a mnemonist's memory palace, close enough to the way of life of his own family to be recognizable, remote enough to be strange and enchanting. It gave concrete expression to the deep tradition out of which his love of history was born. Ariès's history of the family spanned several centuries. But the image of the manor house was culled from memory and so marked the place where his fascination with history began.[3] The memory of one's own heritage, he believed, is the most enticing lure into historical inquiry. For this reason, memory and history in Ariès's work are always mutually involved.

Philippe Ariès (1914–84) is today regarded as one of the most important pioneers in the history of collective mentalities, the history of popular mores that has acquired such prominence in contemporary historiography.[4] He introduced historians to a field of inquiry beyond the political terrain that had long been their primary domain. He is known especially for his history of attitudes toward childhood and family in early modern France and subsequently for his history of attitudes toward death and dying in Western society since the Middle Ages. Both have inspired a plethora of specialized studies.[5] Yet it is not these topics alone that make his work so interesting. Underpinning all of his scholarly research is his deeper interest in the nature of tradition, a field of study previously left to students of folklore and anthropology. In the early critical assessments, Ariès's work was perceived to be a species of social history of the sort then in vogue within *Annales* scholarship.[6] But if his was a social history, it was one grounded more in psychological than in biological or material realities, for he was primarily interested in the traditions tacitly shared by social groups.[7] To study tradition, Ariès learned in the course of his apprenticeship as an historian, is to become familiar with the workings of collective memory, for traditions are sustained by habits of mind bequeathed from one generation to the next across vast expanses of time.

In following Ariès's lead, historians today are finding their way back to the problem of collective memory as the deep source of their interest in collective mentalities.[8] It is worth pointing out, however, that Ariès's inquiries proceeded in the reverse direction. It was his insight into the nature of collective memory that enabled him to make his way into the history of collective mentalities. That is why his first works, *Les Traditions sociales dans les pays de France* (1943), and especially his *Le Temps de l'histoire* (1954) are so important for an appreciation of the nature of his contribution to historical scholarship. In these studies, he addressed historiographical issues that have today become central to the scholars' consideration of the memory/history problem: the role that habits of mind play in sustaining tradition, the way in which such habits are modified, the patterns of change that traditions display, and the methods by which historians may gain a perspective on their workings.

It was Ariès's personal memory of the traditions of his family that first lured him into the study of history. Scion of a family steeped in France's royalist heritage, he was nurtured as a child on the immemorial legends of medieval French society.[9] He knew that by modern standards the vital role that such folklore still played in his family's conception of its heritage was unusual. But he also recognized that it gave him a perspective on a culture with which the vast majority of his contemporaries had lost contact. Hidden in the deep recesses of his family's tradition, he believed, lay a path to a lost history of popular culture. This tradition reached back from the genealogies of his immediate ancestors toward a more anonymous heritage of sociable noble households, popular religious practices, and heroic medieval kings. There was no telling where this tradition began. At its farthest remove it retreated into legend. Particular stories issuing from this mythological past may have been apocryphal. But if the events in such stories mixed fact with fiction, their depiction of social mores provided a treasure trove of information about the attitudes and values of an earlier age. By investigating the folklore of a traditionalist family such as his own, the historian might discover truths about its self-conceptions that the modern world had forgotten.[10]

Ariès portrayed traditions as if they were layered substrata of collective memory hidden beneath the topography of historical interpretation.[11] He knew how difficult a task it would be to acquire an historical perspective on such traditions, for changes in the habits of mind that sustain them are so gradual that they escape the notice of those caught up in them. The modification of collective memory, he recognized, proceeds at a pace too slow to be detected across the three generations that typically constitute the span of living memory.[12] Once modified, moreover, the sources of a tradition tend to be forgotten, the victim of memory's tendency to discard that which does not serve its present needs. Humans thus live with the illusion that their attitudes toward their everyday lives are timeless. It is only through the historical study of these mores over very long periods of time that the refashioning of collective memory can be perceived. Traditions are defined by their places of memory, which the historian must learn to uncover. Ariès's view of history, therefore, might be characterized as an art of memory, the art being the historian's capacity to unblock the memories that traditions contain. The vision of the past that he had acquired in his crossing from memory into history as a child became the basis of his quest as an adult to return across that divide.[13]

To appreciate Ariès's insights into the relationship between collective memory and historical understanding, one must return to his study of the history of historical writing in France, *Le Temps de l'histoire,* which he composed as a series of essays during the years immediately following the Second World War. Unlike his later studies of childhood and death, it received little critical attention when it first appeared, and it is today a largely forgotten work.[14] It is nonetheless an essential text for understanding the conceptions underpinning his mature historical writings. Blending autobiographical reminiscences with historiographical reconstruction, he drew parallels between his personal discovery of history and the beginnings of a French historiographical tradition. The work was inspired by his experiences of the war years, which were decisive in his formation as an historian. The war brought hardship and disillusionment. But it enabled him to move beyond the ingenuous enthusiasms of his youth to the more mature historical judgments of his middle age. As he remarked at the outset of his study, 1940 marked the turning point in his life, for it was then that he first encountered "History."[15]

By referring to History with a capital "H," Ariès had in mind a conception of the past that had affected him both personally and intellectually. On a personal plane, he sensed that anonymous historical forces were intruding into his private world, bringing to an abrupt end a sheltered way of life he had come to cherish. "Until the armistice of 1940," he remarked, "I lived in an oasis closed to the outside world."[16] The war with Germany threw his projects for life into confusion. Laying aside his studies at the Sorbonne, where he was preparing for a career in teaching, he enrolled in the French army as an officer candidate and was sent to boot camp in the fall 1939. Demobilized in August 1940 shortly after the armistice, he found himself suddenly cast adrift, with neither work nor a formal course of academic study nor the friends he had known in prewar Paris to sustain him.[17] Left to his own devices, he seques- tered himself for nearly a year in the Bibliothèque nationale, where his reading of the *Annales* historians Marc Bloch and Lucien Febvre opened his eyes to new approaches to social and cultural history.[18] Yet such study was of little help on his qualifying examination for the professoriat (the *agrégation*), which he failed for the second time in 1941, thus barring his way to a teaching career in the university.[19] Family troubles were another burden. The well-being of his mother was an ongoing concern, and he was deeply aggrieved by the death of his brother in combat shortly before the end of the war.[20] Despite oppor- tunities lost and privations suffered, he muddled through the war years. For his livelihood, he taught briefly in a Vichy-sponsored school, then in 1943 found a job in a French administrative bureau for overseas commerce that he would hold throughout his working life.[21] His encounter with History had permanently altered his life course and diminished his prospects for the future.

On an intellectual plane, however, the war years were a time of growth that enabled him to understand history in broader terms and, so, launched him on his particular path as an historian. In his autobiographical writings years later, he explained the nature of his maturation as a scholar.[22] Before the war, he noted, his social world had been limited to a tightly knit circle of university friends who shared his deep attachment to royalist tradition. During the 1930s, he had played at politics by joining the royalist *Action française*.[23] He admired Charles Maurras, that organization's ideological apologist, particu- larly for his reverence for the traditions of the Old Regime.[24] On the fall of the Third Republic, he may have wanted to believe that the Vichy regime would restore attachments to this traditionalist past.[25] The war dispelled such illusions, as he witnessed the travesty made of Old Regime traditions by Vi- chy's leaders in their futile efforts to appease Nazi Germany.[26]

By war's end, Ariès was able to see how parochial his attitudes and alle- giances of the 1930s had been. In that era, he explained in *Le Temps de l'histoire,* his conception of history had been close to his conception of tradition. He had held royalist historiography to be an emanation of Old Regime traditions, of value for its edifying lessons about how to live wisely in a world too easily taken in by the false promises of modern culture for the coming of an earthly salvation.[27] But in his historical assessment of his experiences of the war years, he acknowledged that his traditionalist conception of the past had ceased to provide a haven from History's imposing presence in the world at large.[28] For Ariès, the war signified the onslaught of the modern age, severing in an abrupt and dramatic way the attachments of his generation to particular traditions issuing from the past. In his awe before the power of these historical forces, he sought to widen his conceptual horizons to take cognizance of the ensemble of attitudes that had fostered the making of modern culture: the pervasive respect for science, especially in its positivist guise; the mechanistic view of culture promoted by the new industrial technologies; and the rising popular support for the wide-ranging responsibilities of the welfare state.[29] At the same time, he sought to reaffirm the enduring significance of the traditionalist perspective within this larger conception of history. The appreciation of traditional French society, he argued, need not be sacrificed in the shame of Vichy. The historian's task is to sort out the authentic from the factitious in the royalist heritage.

In devoting himself to this endeavor in *Le Temps de l'histoire,* Ariès repudiated much of what he had been taught by the royalist historians who had been his mentors in prewar days. From his postwar vantage point, the royalist historians of the early twentieth century had never approached an ethnographic understanding of traditional French culture because of their preoccupation with political history. Scholars such as Jacques Bainville and Pierre Gaxotte, anxious to preserve for royalism a place in modern political history, had trivialized the culture they professed to defend. In substituting a nostalgia that pleased the reading public for a realistic appreciation of the mores of traditional French society, they had lost sight of the deep sources of their own history.[30] Coming to terms with the modern world, Ariès contended, also meant coming to terms with the one that had been lost. To find a place for ancient traditions in contemporary historiography, therefore, became his vocation as an historian. What was needed, he argued, was an appreciation of that heritage, not an apology for it.[31] That is why his contributions to the history of mentalities in his mature years are so interesting and appealing, for he sought to explain to the modern world the nature of a traditional one from which there is still much to learn, even if it is one to which there can be no return.

The Memory of French History: Ariès as Historiographer

There is thus a profound ambiguity in Ariès's conception of history.[32] On the one hand, the term History served as his metaphor for the modern temper. History erodes tradition; it wrests collective memories from their particular settings and refashions them to serve more general interpretations within a larger public domain. This is the imperialist side of history for Ariès—history as it destroys the private attachments through which tradition flourishes, leaving the individual alone and rootless, vulnerable to the demands of society at large for public professions of faith.[33] On the other hand, he maintained the residual importance of the traditionalist conception of history in which he had received his early formation. This is the sustaining side of history—history as it illuminates the inertial power of tradition to resist demands for improvisation. For Ariès, one might say, there are two moments of history: one that universalizes and homogenizes the past within a single interpretative pattern; the other that diversifies the past into a myriad of particular traditions. Ariès conceded that in his own day History in the former sense threatened to take possession of history in the latter.[34] But faced with this encounter, he saw no reason why History itself could not be reconceived in a wider conceptual framework through which the particular traditions that it had absorbed might be identified and given prominence. Moving beyond the political history of the modern state, History might provide the means by which lost traditions could be retrieved, revealing in the process the pluralism of the past, the many "times" of history that exist apart from those favored by the present age.[35]

Le Temps de l'histoire, therefore, was a highly personal memoir, situated at the crossroads at which his appreciation of tradition encountered his commitment to historical inquiry. As historian, Ariès's gaze was always fixed on those places of memory where the critical understanding of history displaces the tacit understanding of tradition. He conceived of historical inquiry as the pursuit of the receding horizon of collective memory.[36] In the face of tradition, considered as the ensemble of human experience contained in living memory, historians wrote histories that were no more than forays into a past they could never hope to fathom. In pursuit of the horizon of memory, they might push their investigations into ever deeper recesses of the past. But the horizon itself would remain an unattainable goal, for tradition always beckons toward earlier antecedents. On the far side of the horizon, the past would always be enshrouded in memory's mystery, for collective memory is a milieu of habits of mind out of which history emerges.[37] In this sense, memory is the ground of history. It is the interior state of mind from which the exterior framework of history is drawn. For Ariès, the move from tradition into history signifies a move away from a past surveyed from the vantage point of living memory toward one appreciated from a critical distance with a chronological conception of time. In this respect, he conceived of the remembered past in terms of not one but several timelines. Historical chronologies are abstracted from mnemonic schemes, formed out of places of memory that had once been prominent in living traditions. Such schemes vary according to the traditions from which they are drawn. The political chronology privileged by modern historians might appear to provide the essential framework for the consideration of the past. But it is inadequate for plotting patterns of change in our everyday lives—be they personal relationship, life's passages, or religious piety—which are shaped by different milieux of memory.[38]

Le Temps de l'histoire also reflects Ariès's disillusionment with the pretensions of the professional historians of his own day. As he passed from the spontaneity of his precocious reading of the royalist histories that he found in his family's library as a child into the discipline of the formal study of history as a university student (first at Grenoble, then at the Sorbonne), he was put off by the abstractions of academic historical writing. This history came clothed in the mantle of science. But what passed for scientific history seemed to him to be uncomfortably close to the parochial conceptions of the past held by the politicians of the Third Republic. For all of their professed objectivity, learned studies in French history reinforced an arbitrary political perspective on the past, and he chided historians of the Right as of the Left for the inadequacy of their limited perspective. Debates among these historians, he claimed, typically turned on their ideological viewpoints. Hence they failed to see that all of their interpretations were lodged within a common conceptual framework, focused on the making of the modern state. From the end of the eighteenth century, he argued, historians had lost sight of the way in which this particular tradition of historiography had been elaborated.[39]

One purpose of *Le Temps de l'histoire,* therefore, was to show how modern historiography obscured particular traditions. The historians that had come to dominate the profession prided themselves on their scrupulous attention to objective facts. But they too were immersed in a subjective historiographical tradition of which they were largely unaware. Long before the memory/history problem had become a topic of lively scholarly interest, Ariès had begun to explore the way in which all historical writing is an extension of particular traditions of collective memory. Herein lies the originality of his study. Whereas the historians of his day continued to divorce the problem of politics from that of culture, Ariès sought to show how they were bound together by the sinews of memory. The persuasiveness of an historical viewpoint, he suggested, is tied to the political influence of the group for which it speaks. Social groups bend memory to conform to their conceptions. As an offspring of memory, historical interpretation retains the conceptual framework that such memory imposes. In sum, the culture of memory establishes the preconditions for the history of culture.[40]

The primacy of political history in the modern age, Ariès asserted, is closely tied to the needs of the nation-state. His point was that the idea of the nation-state is a modern abstraction. Heralded by the French Revolution at the end of the eighteenth century and fashioned by its apostles over the course of the nineteenth century, the idea of the nation-state in modern historiography came to dominate all earlier conceptions of community. Modern historians, in effect, commemorated its ascendancy. Just as nation-states colonized territories overseas, so their apologists colonized the past. The history of the Old Regime, which issued from a texture of social life that predated this modern conception of community, was redesigned by academic historians to fit their present framework. History became the story of the making of the modern state, one invariably told in a political idiom.[41]

Ariès contended that a historiography that considered the past according to such canons could not help but forget the significance of those small and intermediate-size communities that had dominated traditional European society.[42] The ties that bound such groups were based on personal loyalties rather than public definitions of the obligations of citizenship. The signature of modern historiography, however, was the arbitrary line it drew between public and private life. Such a distinction was part of the modern temper, which identifies privacy with individual autonomy. But such a conception, he argued, merely mimics contemporary political definitions. To understand the traditional world of the Old Regime, he contended, one had to appreciate its separate and distinct sensibilities. In that world, a line between public and private life had yet to be drawn.[43] Politics was the province not only of kings and estates, but of fraternal societies and powerful families. The notion of sovereignty was not yet concentrated within a single authority but was diffused amidst a welter of overlapping and often conflicting personal loyalties.[44] For Ariès, this pluralistic culture, lost on modern historians, nonetheless survived in collective memory as a resource on which future historians might draw. Even though the activities of smaller communities escaped the notice of professional historians, these groups continued to transmit their culture from generation to generation through oral tradition. This hidden history of the mores of everyday life was one that he wanted to expose.[45]

To explain how modern historical writing had become divorced from its sources in tradition, Ariès considered the history of French historiography. Just as he had retraced his formation as an historian to his childhood encounter with the traditions of his family, so he retraced modern French historiography to its immersion in a milieu of medieval traditions.[46] In the Middle Ages, he explained, histories were based on highly personal chronologies. Rarely did their time spans extend very far beyond living memory. Nor did they share any conception of a common temporal framework. The complex patterns of historiography corresponded to the complexities of the distribution of cultural power among political and ecclesiastical authorities. Monks as well as counts and kings recorded their versions of the past, and each group formed its conception in a different way. Only over several centuries were the diverse timelines with which they plotted the patterns of the past blended into a uniform chronology acknowledged as a common frame of reference. Until then, these competing schemes were like islands of historical time in a sea of collective memory. They constituted a congeries of incongruent timelines, as churchmen vied with kings to advance their competing formulae for punctuating the past.[47]

As the kings of France consolidated their power over the course of the seventeenth century, so they conflated these disparate traditions of historical writing into a single royalist historiography. The major historiographical event of seventeenth-century France, Ariès remarked, was the writing of the Grand Chronicle of France, a saga of the rise of the absolutist monarchy. From that time forward, historical writing about France built on this chronological prototype. In this way, politics became the backbone of modern historical writing. The Chronicle itself, of course, continued to bear the hallmarks of the royalist tradition out of which it had been born. The places of memory that its timeline highlighted were drawn from salient events in the lives of a lineage of kings. For this reason, the chronology of modern French history carried forward a framework that demarcated historical time according to the royal succession. Even as the Chronicle gave way in the nineteenth century to a conception of the past broadened to incorporate the French Revolution and its various traditions, the propensity to structure the French past according to the royal succession retained an inertial power well into the twentieth century.[48]

The construction of a universal chronology by the official historians of the absolutist kings of the seventeenth century may have signified a consolidation of historical understanding. But it was a triumph won at the price of crowding out alternative historiographical conceptions. As this royalist historiography became in the course of the eighteenth century the official memory of the rise of the modern French state, the paths into the past provided by local and regional histories were covered over and lost from view. Indeed, in the eighteenth century, it became the ambition of historians to reduce the totality of the past to a single chronology.[49] There was to be no time in the past that would not find its place in this framework. But in their zeal to fill the space on their timeline, these historians deleted that part of the pageant of the past that least served their purposes, even if it was the part that most affected the lives of ordinary people. In the process, an emerging modern historiography severed its ties with the collective memory carried forward in a variety of living, popular traditions.[50]

In the nineteenth century, Ariès continued, this historiographical reduction of the past to the history of the reigning political powers became even more pronounced. The nineteenth century discovered the significance of historical time. Historians wished as fervently as before to maintain the connections between past and present, but they were newly sensitive to the differences between them. Although aware of the irreversibility of changing historical realities, they were nonetheless optimistic about the promise the future held. In the name of progress, many were willing to leave the traditions of the past behind, unmindful of their tenacious inertial power to influence the present.[51] Thenceforth, historical bias was recast in ideological terms, so that even those who professed to be conservative historians accepted the premises of their intellectual adversaries about history's political foundations. For those with strong ideological commitments, history was often reconstructed in light of political expectations about what the future might hold, whereas those who professed more impartial views laid claim to scientific objectivity.[52] Either way, the political chronology of modern historiography became an absolute frame of reference. A past evoked by places of memory was displaced by one punctuated by events on an abstract timeline.[53]

Only in our own time, Ariès contended, has the interest in collective memory as a route into the past been revived. That such a route would resurface, he believed, was inevitable, for collective memory continued to animate the private worlds in which ordinary people lived and formed their values. For the vast majority, the public world of politics was never more than a secondary concern. Ironically, it was in the present age, as public authority threatened to intrude more deeply into the private worlds of familial, religious, and social life, that historians were prompted to search for the significance of these lost cultural traditions.[54] That is why 1940 was a year of such personal moment for Ariès in his formation as an historian. It marked the place in his own memory when he was called from the parochial tradition in which he had been happily ensconced since childhood to face the demand for a public accounting by a universalizing historiography.

From Memory to Mentalities: Ariès as Historian

It is in this context that Ariès defined his task as an historian. If History was to intrude into the private lives of ordinary people, the limitations of the political framework of modern scholarship ought no longer to be countenanced. It was time for the framework of historical writing to be broadened and diversified. He therefore made it his vocation to show his age something of the plurality of the past—times of history that proceeded according to different rhythms of change and that were strange and foreign to the modern temper. Obliged to come to terms with History, Ariès was determined to widen the scope of its considerations to include popular culture. Composing Le Temps de l'histoire in the late 1940s, he provided a preview of the research into this lost history that would come to occupy the center of historiographical interest by the 1970s. Just as his own disillusionment with politics during the Vichy years had prompted him to seek out the unexamined history of his own familial tradition, so he anticipated that many historians would seek to repair the severed connections with other forgotten traditions as the modern state encroached on more domains of private life.[55] In his view, the myth of progress through politics vaunted by the modern nation-state in the nineteenth century was by the mid-twentieth century in the process of being dispelled. The state, once viewed as an instrument of progress, was now recognized by many to be a threat to the integrity of private life. For Ariès, the isolation of the individual in the modern world, bound up in a highly individualized code of social discipline, could not help but incite a desire to rediscover that lost world of sociability left behind.[56]

Ariès labeled his approach "existential history" when he was drafting Le Temps de l'histoire.[57] But the conception of history that he presented therein, with its emphasis on the subjectivity of one's appreciation of the past, is not far removed from the one in our own day that is identified with the history of collective mentalities.[58] Such a history, he argued, would provide insight into the tenor of social life in a way that political history could not. The issue was not only the subject matter but the context in which it should be studied. To write a history of popular mores, he explained, historians would have to abandon the constraining framework of political history. Although long regarded as the backbone of history, its chronology was only one among many possible schemata, each of which would organize historical time in a different way. From the trend toward a common political frame of reference for the study of history, Ariès wished to turn toward a more pluralistic cultural framework reminiscent of that which had existed when history's interchange with its milieux of memory was more readily apparent. In this way, he believed, the sources of history in living memory would be revealed once more.[59]

To this end, Ariès outlined his perception of the pattern of change in the history of popular mores in the move out of traditional into modern European culture. Its dynamics had little to do with politics as ordinarily conceived. In the time between the late Middle Ages and the modern era, roughly the sixteenth and the nineteenth centuries, he argued, there was a slow transformation of the way in which humans expressed their feelings about social life. Its tenor in traditional European culture was based on an ideal of sociability, whereas that in modern culture was based on one of privacy.[60] Conventions of everyday life that once dispersed emotion through broad social networks were gradually displaced by others that intensified them in more intimate transactions. In the more precarious society of the Middle Ages, people thought in terms of survival through the stability of their social customs. By the nineteenth century they thought in terms of personal fulfillment through a code of conduct that favored and indeed fostered change. In the modern world, meaningful social relationships may be fewer, but they are more dependent on mutual affection.[61] The sociability so evident in the extended family of traditional European society had been miniaturized in the intimacy of the modern nuclear family. In light of this revolution in the organization of emotional life in Western culture, people growing up in the modern era acquired expectations different from those of their ancestors only a few centuries before.[62] With different expectations, moreover, they remembered growing up in a different way. The historical reshaping of emotional life in Western culture, Ariès suggested, has led to a refashioning of the uses of memory itself. The collective memory that sustained custom in traditional society has given way to the personal memory that fosters the modern search for identity.

What Ariès was tracing, of course, was a modification in habits of mind, not a succession of events. Not only was the pace of change slower for this kind of cultural history but it was also conceived in a different way. Ariès offered a synchronic conception of time. He was arguing, in effect, that old ways of thinking do not completely disappear but continue to coexist with new ones, if with ever-diminishing importance. Within tradition, the past past remains the ground of the past present. The time of tradition cannot be plotted as a succession of discrete states of mind in which new habits displace old ones. To plot changes in mentality the historian must take account of the ongoing, dynamic relationship between habit and improvisation. A habit of mind is modified within a larger structure of collective attitudes. Improvisation, therefore, alters the structure of memory in the process of being integrated into it. Within that structure, every modification of a habit represents a tension between the old and the new. Old and new ways of thinking are coordinates that coexist in roughly inverse proportion, if the structure of collective memory is considered over a long period of time. Only over the aeons will the oldest state of mind be totally lost from view. To measure the slow, often imperceptible pace of change in a tradition, therefore, historians must make quantum leaps in the moments of time that they choose to observe.[63]

Ariès was aware that his theory about history's grounding in memory was not without its antecedents. He found kindred sentiments among nineteenth-century historians with a romantic flair, such as Jules Michelet and Fustel de Coulanges.[64] Both sought to convey the mentality of the past through its imagery. Their work, however, remained impressionistic. Their imagery failed to reveal the structural dimensions of the culture they sought to epitomize. To convey the meaning of a history of mores adequately, Ariès believed, one would have to place images within larger cultural contexts. In effect, his prescription for a history of mentalities appropriated the technique of the ancient art of memory: it assigned the meaning of the past to images rather than events, and it located these within larger mental structures. Historical change was revealed through the way in which the structures were modified and the images reduced in size.[65] Ariès also acknowledged his considerable debt to *Annales* historians Bloch and Febvre. Lessons learned from Febvre's work particularly may have enabled him to formulate his notions about tradition from an historical perspective. Febvre had alluded frequently to the notion of habits of mind without inquiring deeply into their nature, and Ariès may be said to have followed up on this lead.[66]

Ariès's exploration of the relationship between memory and history is an essential background for appreciating the study of childhood and family for which he is famous. Not only does it show how traditions evolve, it also reveals how collective memory itself is reshaped in the process. Few critics have appreciated *L'Enfant et la vie familiale* in this way. Critical discussion of this pioneering study has turned on the "discovery of childhood" considered as a social problem.[67] Some of the critics have misinterpreted the proposition to mean that medieval people had no conception of childhood.[68] Rather Ariès's point was that they had no developmental conception of life through which childhood might be appreciated as a preparatory stage for adulthood.[69] *L'Enfant et la vie familiale* concerns the historical elaboration of the idea of the life cycle as a developmental pattern between the sixteenth and the twentieth centuries. The change was in expectations for psychological, not biological, growth. By the sixteenth century, he contended, parents in middle-class and aristocratic families were treating their children with an unprecedented measure of affection. The tenor of life had become less violent; diseases that had ravaged the European population for centuries had become less virulent. As child mortality rates declined and the conditions of life became marginally more predictable, parents, with the encouragement of religious educators, were increasingly disposed to plan for their children's future.[70] Childhood was thenceforth viewed as a special estate in life, different from but preparatory for adulthood.[71] Over the following centuries, the trend toward greater expectations for one's prospects in life quickened, and accordingly the conception of the developmental process became more refined. By the eighteenth century, youth was recognized as a separate stage of development between childhood and adulthood.[72] By the end of the nineteenth century, adolescence was interjected as a further delineation in this model of the developmental process.[73] Additional refinements extending into middle and old age were recognized by the late twentieth century, as the model of lifelong growth devised by the ego psychologist Erik Erikson revealed.[74] Ariès's point was that psychological growth, if it is in some measure a biological reality, has become for the modern age a compelling cultural ideal.

L'Enfant et la vie familiale, therefore, provides a case study of the propositions about memory set forth in *Le Temps de l'histoire.* The historical emergence of the developmental conception of the life cycle reshaped collective memory in that it effected the slow modification of expectations about life's possibilities. People in the modern age gradually acquired the habit of expecting developmental growth and planned their lives and those of their children accordingly. Such habits were transmitted from generation to generation in light of what was remembered collectively about growing up. Imperceptibly, the older conception of life as a cycle of passages, punctuated by rites of initiation but without developmental significance, yielded to one that anticipated developmental change. Conceptual schemes of the process of the sort devised by Erikson provide an architectonic framework for an appreciation of the process.[75] Erikson's model was, in effect, a mnemonic model to highlight transitions in a process of self-fashioning that had been elaborated historically over several centuries.

Changing expectations about the life cycle were reinforced and integrally related to changes in the conception of the family. Once focused on the social status of parents as bearers of a genealogical heritage, the meaning of family life correspondingly shifted to the preparation of children for adult responsibilities. A social unit whose identity had previously been conceived in light of the past was reconceived in light of hopes for the future. Focused on its children, the family gradually retreated from its role as a public community with policing powers.[76] In diminished form, the family became a refuge from the world at large, a place of privacy where personal relationships could develop. The diverse and largely superficial relationships of the extended family of traditional European society were displaced by the deeper and more intimate ones of the nuclear family in the modern age. The family became a unit of affection in which the relationship between parent and child took on an unprecedented emotional intensity. The ideal of sociability for the present thus yielded to one of social discipline with a view toward prospects for the future and thus contributed powerfully to a deepening of the need for individual identity and autonomy.[77] The synchronic relationship between the old and the new ideal of family life nonetheless remained intact. The mind of the child became the archive in which parents invested their family traditions, even as they fostered the expectations of their children for a more promising future.[78] In this way, an historical dimension was introduced into collective memory, contributing to the modern need to commemorate a past that is different from the present, and, when connections with that past have become tenuous, to search for it in forgotten memories of childhood.[79]

Ariès's following study of changing attitudes toward death and dying in Western civilization, *L'Homme devant la mort* (1977), reveals a similar preoccupation with the way in which collective memory has been historicized in the modern era.[80] Once again, Ariès described the historical elaboration of a succession of stages of attitudes, this time toward life's final passage. His most noteworthy contribution in this work was his discovery of how recent is the emergence of the need for the personal commemoration of ordinary people.[81] The lavish expression of grief about the loss of a loved one and the need to commemorate that life, he explained, came to the fore in Western culture only in the nineteenth century. Again, such mourning practices were tied to a long-range transformation of attitudes dating from the end of the Middle Ages. The individual tombstone, he noted, was a modern invention. Its prototype, a tiny commemorative plaque on the gravesite, dates from the sixteenth century; its most grandiose form was the burial monument of the nineteenth century. Personal commemoration reflected the need to express the feelings of affection fostered by life in the modern family. It suggested, too, a newfound awareness of the irreversibility of change and the uniqueness of each life, which in turn deepened the sense of loss.[82]

Just as there are parallels between Ariès's and Erikson's analysis of the stages of preparing for life, so there are corresponding ones between Ariès's and the American psychiatrist Elisabeth Kübler-Ross's interpretation of the stages of preparing to die. The five historical stages of such attitudes whose development Ariès plots across several centuries in his *L'Homme devant la mort* display striking affinities with the psychological stages identified by Kübler-Ross in her clinical studies of the individual's preparation for death in the contemporary Western world.[83] The models devised by Erikson and Kübler-Ross as psychological schemes recapitulate the historical stages of the evolution of such attitudes as they were depicted by Ariès. The comparison suggests that the collective memory of attitudes toward mourning was refashioned imperceptibly along the way, while bearing forward memory's illusion that feelings of bereavement have always been expressed in the same way. In the psychological interpretations offered by Erikson and Kübler-Ross, therefore, the collective memory of what was a long-range historical transformation of attitudes is presented in concentrated form.

Ariès's work on the relationship between historical understanding and collective memory has profound implications for historiography that are only beginning to be recognized. The memory of the culture bequeathed by the past, dismissed as irrelevant by the positivist political historians of the nineteenth century, has become an issue in historical interpretation once more, in some measure because of Ariès's pioneering investigations. In the course of his work, he revealed how vulnerable the memories underpinning tradition are to the requirements of political power in the present. Despite his traditionalism, he was the first historian to show how alternative traditions lie unexamined in the shadow of those identified with academic or political discourse. He was the first to raise the disturbing proposition that our ability to remember the past is dependent on those who presently define the official memory of our culture. For this reason, he anticipated the interests of those poststructuralist historians and philosophers who have stressed the dependence of knowledge on power. He himself often noted the affinities between his interpretations and those of Michel Foucault, the most celebrated of this coterie of scholars.[84] Ariès even employed the term "archaeology" of history long before Foucault made it fashionable.[85] Ariès was nonetheless cautious about the implications of Foucault's use of the term. For Foucault, archaeology excises living memory from its considerations. Focusing on the forms in which the past has been represented, this method brackets the remembered past with which one might identify and, so, consigns it to oblivion. But Ariès's reverence for the particular traditions in which he had been formed provides a counterpoint to this poststructuralist stance of studied detachment. His work affirms the importance of acknowledging the reality of the living memory of the past even if it fails to serve the needs of contemporary politicians. For Ariès, the problem of memory concerns more than its archaeological leavings. His commitment as an historian was to show that in the study of the past the power of forgotten memories cannot be denied, for they are at once the source of the curiosity and the enthusiasm that inspires historical inquiry.[86]

6

MICHEL FOUCAULT
History as Counter-Memory

The Foucault Phenomenon and Contemporary French Historiography

In *Histoire de la folie* (1961), the study that first won him international recognition, the French philosopher and historian Michel Foucault (1926–84) opens his narrative with a dramatic tableau of the ruins of the medieval lazar house, where those afflicted with leprosy were consigned in order to allay the fears of the public at large.[1] Highly contagious and terrifying in the physical symptoms it displayed, leprosy was a disease that ravaged the population of western Europe in the late Middle Ages. In the thirteenth century, Foucault notes, at least 2,000 such asylums were officially listed on the royal records for France alone. Over the following centuries, this dreaded disease beat a retreat from Europe, and by the seventeenth century it had all but disappeared. The lazar houses were thus emptied of their inmates. But the edifices themselves survived, and for a long time acted as reminders of the role they had formerly played as places of exclusion.

The waning fear of leprosy, Foucault points out, was nonetheless strangely tied to a waxing fear of insanity. In a civilization that by the eighteenth century prided itself on its "enlightened," rational ways, the crazed, the nonconformist, and the eccentric were less easily tolerated than they had been during the Middle Ages. Madmen, once identified in the popular imagination with divine possession, were gradually transformed into social outcasts and were treated as a problem for their unreasonable behavior. Foucault plots their historical journey in imaginary discourse in his own imaginative use of the Renaissance literary motif of the "ship of fools." Shipped down the rivers of Europe as unwanted burdens by public officials from the sixteenth century, the mad eventually landed in the "great houses of confinement" of the eighteenth century, which, having been emptied of lepers, were available for a different kind of pariah.[2]

If these modern-day insane asylums rarely occupied the same physical places as the medieval lazar houses, Foucault proposes, they would nonetheless come to occupy the same symbolic space in public discourse about places of exclusion. An old form of asylum, he contends, had been appropriated to house a new kind of outcast, one whose impairment was mental rather than physical. Madness in the popular mind had lost its oracular mystique, and the mad were pitied for having lost their reason and with it their claims to their humanity. To these places, therefore, public health officials and later physicians and therapists made "counter-pilgrimages" to aid the unreasonable in the recovery of the reason of which they had been dispossessed. In associating madness with unreason, though, they stripped the notion of its connotations of divine genius, and so privileged the social efficiency of conformist behavior, so dear to modern civilization, over the insight and creativity that sometimes comes with eccentric behavior.[3]

So far is the medieval lazar house from the modern insane asylum, Foucault argues, that the memory of the former was all but obliterated by the time that the latter had come into being. Only the archaeologist, he suggests, can see in this modern form the ancient ruin from which it is genealogically descended. But like the lazar house, the modern asylum is a monument to a social need to segregate the unwanted, an enduring symbolic space that marks the place of earlier exclusions.

For this reason, Foucault's tableau of the madhouse, too, might be characterized as a memory palace, one all the more imposing for the forgotten memories once contained within its walls. His description of this place of memory conveys a sense of awe in the face of its unremembered history, lost in the repeated creation and dismantling of the images in which the purposes of the space were over time represented. Like archaeologists who happen upon Druidic ruins whose purposes they are unable to decipher, Foucault excavates and describes the ruins that memorialize humankind's efforts to segregate its outcasts. He traces the route backward from the modern asylums to the eighteenth-century houses of confinement to the thirteenth-century lazar houses. But he intimates that the lineage of this imaginary house of exclusion could be traced back further still. The probe reaches into a past of which we have no memory.

In this way, Foucault the archaeologist of a commemorative space in which the idea of the asylum was located sets himself apart from the historian of the development of this institution. In devising an historiographical method that deals with the rhetorical forms with which institutionalization is justified rather than with the development of institutions themselves, Foucault has opened a new domain of historical research—one principally concerned with the history of discourse, or more broadly, of representation. That interest in the rhetoric of imaginary discourse has become the signature of postmodern historiography and, so, suggests why Foucault's work has become so important in our postmodern age.

Few scholars in our time have been so lionized. His scholarship early won him recognition in France, where he was elected to the Collège de France in 1970. His fame soon reached the United States, and by the mid-1970s he was making frequent speaking tours of American campuses, visits since enshrined in the scholarly record.[4] Interviews with him about the nature of his work began to appear in the learned journals, and he sometimes joined American scholars in joint publishing ventures that touched on his research interests.[5] A Foucault bibliography was published in 1982, so extensive had the writings by and about him by then become.[6] Since his death in 1984, comment on his work has proceeded apace, and compilations of his later writings and interviews continue to appear, one promising the "final Foucault."[7] But certainly we have not heard the last of him. He seems destined to become an icon of scholarship in our time.

Although much has been written about the meaning of Foucault's thought, little effort has been made to assess its practical importance for contemporary historical scholarship, the field in which he made his largest mark. My purpose in this chapter will be to consider that problem with respect to French historiography. Foucault did not think of himself particularly as a French historian. But most of his research for his several books on the history of asylums was drawn from French sources.[8] More important, he challenged the methodological assumptions of French historians, who had long prided themselves on their innovative historiography. I shall therefore seek to explain the significance of his work for historians, with special attention to his repudiation of historiographical traditions that have long served as frames of reference in French history. Then I wish to say something about his impact on the practice of historical writing today on topics of particular interest to French historians. Among scholars, historians were the last to warm to Foucault's ideas, but his significance for their work may in the end be the most substantial. The Foucault phenomenon well illustrates the turn from social to cultural history in French historiography since the early 1970s. An emblem of that shift, Foucault also contributed to its accomplishment.

Foucault came to history by way of philosophy, the discipline in which he had received his academic training. In the 1950s and 1960s he passed through a succession of teaching posts in France (Lille, Clermont-Ferrand, Nanterre), punctuated by stays in universities in Sweden, Poland, West Germany, and Tunisia. All the while, he pursued his own intellectual interests, and these eventually led him into the byways of cultural history. His interest in philosophy, however, first crossed over into psychology, a field whose practice he decided to observe firsthand.[9] He earned a *licence* in clinical psychology, and during the 1950s he pursued advanced work in psychopathology and interned for a time in a Parisian hospital. Such experiences became the basis of his first publication, *Maladie mentale et personnalité* (1954), a modest essay on philosophical issues raised by contemporary psychiatric practice, and one that reveals little of the provocative interpretation of the history of the asylum he would expound a few years later.[10]

The task of sorting out personal and intellectual influences in his formation presents a puzzle that is only beginning to be addressed.[11] He reveals little of himself in his formal writings, and his self-references in interviews tend to be elliptical. Among his teachers, Georges Canguilhem, a philosopher of science, whetted his interest in the historical problem of the conceptual foundations of the sciences. He also appears to have been influenced by the musings of Raymond Roussel, an exotic literary figure of prewar Paris, on the formative power of language.[12] Among his colleagues, Foucault particularly admired Gilles Deleuze, whose formulation of the philosophical problem of repetition and difference set him thinking about its applications in historical inquiry.[13] Foucault once speculated that posterity would remember ours as the Deleuzian century.[14] But in the end, Deleuze wrote a book about Foucault, holding him in conversation with Kant, Nietzsche, Bergson, and Heidegger in the great tradition of Western philosophy.[15] Characteristically, Foucault himself claimed no special mentors. A student of many, he was a disciple of none.

The nature of the intellectual milieu from which Foucault embarked on his journey is more easily discerned. He came of age during the heyday of existentialism, a movement whose emphasis on the radical subjectivity of the human condition acquired passion in the moral philosophy of Jean-Paul Sartre and intellectual rigor in the phenomenology of Maurice Merleau-Ponty.[16] By the late 1960s, existentialism had also led many French scholars back to the psychoanalytic theory of Sigmund Freud, which was at last making headway in French academic and scientific circles.[17] Foucault's instinct, however, was to react against these trends in French philosophy, which valued self-analysis as a means of uncovering the truth of the human condition. He found that he was less taken with the goal of this quest than he was with the strategies devised to accomplish it. His concern with the form as opposed to the content of intellectual inquiry became the distinguishing signature of his scholarship. Foucault's philosophy, therefore, might be said to be characterized by its radical objectivity.[18] That notion suggests as well the context of his deeper philosophical allegiances.

Although wary of all philosophical and ideological labels, Foucault did concede his sympathies for what he characterized as formalism. As Foucault used the term, formalists analyzed the way in which cognitive systems are constructed. For an interview in *Telos* in 1982, he reviewed how this mode of thought had rippled through the scholarly discourse of the twentieth century, generating successive waves of inquiry—from the linguistic theorizing of Ferdinand de Saussure, to the more widely publicized anthropological research of Claude Lévi-Strauss, to Jacques Lacan's structuralist reading of Freud's insights. Formalism, Foucault contended, was the most powerful intellectual current of the twentieth century, analogous in its influence to that of romanticism or positivism in the nineteenth.[19] In riding the formalist wave of the 1960s, Foucault identified himself loosely with the intellectual movement known as poststructuralism, conspicuous for its fascination with the properties of the written text and for its studied deconstruction of what were characterized as the canons of Western literature and philosophy.[20] As a contributor to the little magazines of the Parisian literary scene during that decade, he participated actively in topical discussions about theories of discourse with such luminaries as Roland Barthes and Jacques Derrida,[21] in which the affinities between Foucault's interests and those of the poststructuralists are easily observed. Like the others, he proposed to examine texts as objects on their own terms, not as expressions of subjective viewpoints. The referents for a text are other texts, the poststructuralists proposed, and so a new interest in intertextuality came to the fore in their philosophical discussions. What gave poststructuralist theory its raison d'être were the rhetorical strategies to which writers turned to articulate their viewpoints. Not the pursuit of truth but an inventory of ways of seeking the truth became the subject of inquiry. Not the vision of the author but the place of his writings in a larger framework of discourse became the locus of intellectual concern.[22]

Such an argument proved provocative because it rejected the sovereign imprint of authorship with which knowledge had been stamped since the eighteenth century. Poststructuralist analysis shifted the focus to the text, thereby setting the author's intentions aside. In this way, texts acquired an autonomy of their own, and their authors, extraneous to their future fate, were relegated to a less obtrusive role. Individual works might bear an author's signature, but they were more important for the way in which they helped to shape a larger discourse. In an illuminating observation on the historical preconditions of his own line of inquiry, Foucault pointed out that authorship conceived as the individual ownership of ideas was a nineteenth-century invention.[23] Texts of authors in that romantic age supposedly served as mirrors of their souls. But from a poststructuralist perspective, texts do not mirror but rather construct identity. To look into texts is not to look into the minds of authors but only at surfaces that contain their words. Far from revealing their identities, texts conceal them. The identity of a text is derived from its relationship to other texts.[24] Foucault, therefore, preferred to think of learning as a collective endeavor, in which knowledge is fashioned through colloquy, a view he believed had been favored from antiquity until the Classical Age. That is why he presented much of his own work in progress in the format of the seminar, especially in his later years.[25] Correspondingly, he liked the dialogical style of interviews, which in the end have become one of our most important sources for understanding his thought.

The History of Discursive Practice and the Repudiation of Tradition

What distinguished Foucault within the galaxy of poststructuralists was the importance he attached to historical inquiry. Among these scholars, he

displayed a surpassing interest in the process of historical change, and his work
would have the most far-reaching implications for historians.[26] His *L'Ordre du
discours,* delivered at his induction into the Collège de France in 1970, was a
manifesto for rewriting intellectual history on the basis of the analysis of discursive practices.[27] Foucault criticized the tendency of intellectual historians
to present the ideas of authors of an earlier age as mirrors of their present
concerns, that is, as frames of reference for self-validation. Between the author
in the past and the reader in the present Foucault interposed the text. He did
so to show that from an historical perspective the production of a text creates
an unprecedented reality, turning patterns of thought in new directions. He
pointed out that texts possess a historicity as singular as events or personalities
and hence provide primary evidence of the way in which our knowledge of
the past has been constituted. Discourse itself is an historical construct, and
no author's ideas can be presented for consideration save through the frameworks that such constructs define. This suggested the importance of the codes
of knowledge communicated through the web of intertextuality as data for
the historian's consideration. In Foucault's rendering, rhetoric became important to the history of ideas in an unprecedented way.[28]

Foucault had already blocked out this conception of history in considerable
detail in two preliminary theoretical studies: *Les Mots et les choses* (1966) and
L'Archéologie du savoir (1969). The former plotted changes in the linguistic conventions through which knowledge was reorganized between the Renaissance
of the sixteenth century and the Enlightenment of the late eighteenth.[29] The
latter explained his method in that investigation, which had placed the accent
on discursive practices rather than on the purposes of the authors who employed them.[30] In both studies he argued that knowledge is not only communicated but created through its mode of organization. A discourse about
knowledge is less important for the ideas it contains than for the new forms
of discourse that it generates.[31] Foucault was fascinated with the historically
specific forms through which knowledge is conveyed. He questioned why one
system of knowledge should be preferred to another, explaining that the way
in which we encode knowledge determines the way in which we understand
the world. Discourse molds knowledge and in the process crowds out alternative formulations. It therefore raises issues not only about the ideas it frames
but also about those it excludes.[32]

The problem of exclusion was for Foucault the reverse side of the problem
of tradition. His importance as a theorist of history turns on his repudiation
of tradition as the ground of historical inquiry. In appealing to tradition, he
contended, historians identify with particular conceptions of the past. This is
especially evident among historians of ideas, whose methods typically rely on
the recollection of precedent. One recalls the line of inquiry of an original
author, whose ideas have been modified in a causal chain advancing toward
our own age.[33] Such a view, he argued, ascribes transcendental power to the
subjective vision of a founding author and a commemorative value to the in-

tellectual tradition that bears it forward over time. But the notion of such an origin, Foucault charged, is a fiction, designed to use the past to hold sway over present thinking.[34] Interpretation in the history of ideas, therefore, is limited by the traditions it seeks to explicate. Tradition creates the illusion of unity and direction in the intellectual quest by reiterating and modifying a pre-existing intellectual frame of reference. Foucault, by contrast, sought to show how discourse about ideas incessantly creates new formulations and thereby moves beyond the horizons of the most elaborate working hypotheses. Discursive practice, he argued, proceeds through a dispersion and proliferation of modes of thought.[35]

Herein Foucault's argument resembles that of Friedrich Nietzsche, who a century before had warned of the perils of building present conceptions out of nostalgia for the past.[36] History should not be a commemorative exercise but rather a contributing element to a philosophy for fashioning the future. Rather than returning to some mythical beginning and working forward, the historian would do better to proceed from the present backward. Each event considered along the way may be appreciated for the unique new direction it signals, not for some general trend from the past it supposedly confirms. Such retrogressive historical analysis, mimicking recollection but detaching the historian from it, had been the basis of Nietzsche's notion of genealogy. Foucault turned it into a methodological principle. Discourse creates its own chains of intellectual descent apart from the authors' intentions.[37]

Like Nietzsche, Foucault was challenging the Hegelian notion that history unfolds logically from primordial beginnings.[38] Most historians practicing today would consider this an intellectual battle long since won. Few would place their faith in metahistorical designs. But Foucault's argument took the challenge a step further by charging that an historiographical tradition unwittingly perpetuates belief in such a design. Any approach to history that stresses continuity from formative beginnings superimposes on the past a pattern that, when deconstructed, contains a hidden agenda.[39] Few historians, he suggested, have emancipated themselves completely from such traditions. They honor them in their patriotism or their ideology. Traditions, for example, lay beneath the national histories written in the nineteenth century and around which the curriculum of historical study continues to be organized into our own times. More profoundly, historians tend to accept the conventions of the historiographical traditions within which they receive their training.[40]

Some historians view this predicament more sympathetically. They argue that writing within a tradition is a form of hermeneutical understanding. Historians integrate new ideas into frameworks of interpretation that serve inescapably as their points of departure.[41] Foucault's method, therefore, might be said to be anti-hermeneutical, for it challenged the notion that the historians' task is to widen the horizons of the intellectual traditions in which they find themselves.[42] Discourse, Foucault argued, creates a whole new order of understanding. Each discourse opens on a different intellectual vista, obscuring older ones in the process. From the hermeneutical interest in the collective memories through which traditions are perpetuated Foucault shifted attention to counter-memories: the discursive practices through which memories are perpetually revised.[43] The archive of history, he explained, is not a repository of facts underpinning intellectual traditions but rather an inventory of the countless discursive practices through which these traditions have been re-fashioned along the way.[44]

It would be inappropriate in so short an essay to canvass Foucault's excursions into that archive in any detail. Suffice it to say that he began with the asylum and ended with the self, an intellectual odyssey in which he remained faithful in practice to the historiographical method he had devised for plotting those moments when new discursive practices displace old ones.[45] In theory as in practice, Foucault emphasized the rhetorical strategies through which humans seek truth. Discourse, he explained, sets forth rules about what is appropriate to that quest. In this way, truth claims are reduced to truth games, formulated on the boundaries where rules of exclusion are generated.[46] That is why so much of Foucault's early historical inquiry examined discourses employed to justify the containment of errant behavior. The definition of reason, for example, acquired form in the process of elaborating a discourse about types of unreason.[47] Considered in its ensemble, his history of the asylum is actually a history of the discourse about the meaning and purpose of the segregation of deviancy, one that proliferated over time into a refined commentary on a widening array of places of confinement: madhouses, clinics, and prisons. Each generated a discourse of justification. Foucault's interest in the dispersion of techniques for controlling errant behavior, moreover, led logically to his reflections on the larger topic of the policing process, which linked the management of social behavior with the rising power of the modern state.[48] Disassembled, the discourse on the asylum was a discourse about power, a topic on which Foucault ruminated more frequently as his project matured. The old axiom of the Enlightenment, knowledge wields power, he reformulated as power produces knowledge. Power bends discourse to its needs and so revises our conceptions of the past.[49]

Foucault's detailed investigation of discursive practices sometimes led him into obscure recesses of the past. But his characterization of the relationship between knowledge and power shed brilliant light on a major preoccupation of present-day Western culture: namely, the power of publicity to determine which voices will be heard in the public forum. In his reformulation of the historian's method, Foucault was responding to the intellectual anxieties of an age that sensed that an earlier consensus about values had broken down, leaving arguments about ideas to the whims of cultural power brokers dealing in the remnants of fragmenting intellectual traditions. Foucault was providing the historiographical groundwork for confirming the popular sentiment, pervasive, yet ill-formulated, that the influence of an idea is relative to the cultural power of the tradition within which it is located. Other historians might have acknowledged that the nineteenth-century consensus about an historical vision of linear progress had broken down. But Foucault's argument was at once more provocative and consoling, given its contention that claims about intellectual consensus only reflect the dominant discursive practice of an age. By contrast, he sought to show how the process of differentiating ideas is integral to the production of discourse and accordingly suggested that intellectual discontinuity in fact marks every age. Laments about the demise of coherent traditions of literature or patterns of history invoke myths invented to serve the ends of those presently in power. The canons of literature, like the turning points of history, are objects of belief that lend structure to the traditions they are called on to affirm.

Foucault's turn to the history of sexuality followed logically from his earlier work. The link between his studies of asylums and of sexuality was forged in his consideration of discourses generated by the policing process.[50] As in his earlier work, he focused on rhetoric rather than behavior, a rhetoric that described, delimited, and ultimately policed sexual behavior. Foucault sought to show how the topic of human sexuality had entered the discourse of Western culture as a problem identified with the search for truth. Emphasized in Catholic confessional practices from the seventeenth century and confirmed in the medical and psychiatric discourses of the nineteenth and twentieth centuries, the problem of sexuality as a truth game was of relatively recent historical origin. The imperative to speak openly about sexuality as a means of finding out the truth about ourselves, he observed, is the true sexual revolution of our times.[51]

Foucault's study of discourses about sexuality, in turn, drew him into a consideration of those about the self, a turn of interest that deflected the course of his final intellectual journey. To talk about one's sexuality, he explained, is to become more reflective about oneself. His discussion about techniques by which humans try to understand themselves began to appear midway through his projected multivolume study of sexuality and led him to alter it in such a way that the themes became intertwined.[52] Like all objects of inquiry into truth, the self was constituted in the course of efforts to define it. The self was the most profound of human constructs, but like the others it was the product of a discourse about truth that justified a set of policing practices. Foucault traced its genealogical descent to antiquity. In the technologies of the self, however, the individual turns the policing process to his own advantage. The search for the self generates strategies for self-care in reply to the technologies of domination that shape so much of human behavior and aspiration.[53]

Although never openly presented as a challenge to Freud, Foucault's reduction of the search for the self to a series of discursive practices consigned the truth claims of psychoanalysis to an order of rhetoric. Foucault's final intellectual contest, therefore, was with Freud, who in Foucault's view had drawn together a number of ancient practices of self-care in order to construct an imposing medical discourse about the nature of the self.[54] In his culminating critique of psychoanalysis as a discursive practice, Foucault had returned by a different route to his initial interest in discourse about madness.

Freud's faith that all forgotten experiences are retrievable from a reservoir of repressed memories was a reassuring one for the modern age. If there is little coherence in our present philosophies of life, he contended, there is at least a unity of meaning to be discerned in the continuity of our life experience, stored in the archive of the unconscious psyche. When we consciously reconstruct that experience, we reconfirm who we are. Although Foucault would concede that Freud's psychoanalytic method discloses significant meanings about ourselves, he would contend that none of these can provide us with a definitive understanding. The search for the self is a journey into a mental labyrinth that takes random courses and ultimately ends at impasses. The memory fragments recovered along the way cannot provide us with a basis for interpreting the overall meaning of the journey. The meanings that we derive from our memories are only partial truths, and their value is ephemeral.

For Foucault, the psyche is not an archive but a mirror. To search the psyche for the truth about ourselves is a futile task because the psyche can only reflect the images that we have conjured up to describe ourselves. Looking into the psyche, therefore, is like looking into the mirror image of a mirror. One sees oneself in an image of infinite regress. Our gaze is led not toward the substance of our beginnings but rather into the meaninglessness of previously discarded images of the self. In the end, the meaning of the self for Foucault is less important than the methods we employ to understand it. It is in the techniques that we as humans have devised for the care of the self across the centuries that we find continuities. What we seek in psychoanalysis is less self-knowledge than a method for self-care.[55]

Had Foucault merely opened new roads of historical inquiry, his work would have been provocative enough. But it represented a frontal attack on the historiographical traditions in which most scholars worked, particularly those in social and intellectual history. By the mid-1970s, historians were pointing out the theoretical implications of his work.[56] Given his project of redirecting scholarly analysis from authorship to discourse, Foucault was understandably uncomfortable with this critical focus on his own role as an author. He could be thin-skinned about criticism of his methods by professional historians, as his angry reply to a review by Lawrence Stone in the pages of the *New York Review of Books* revealed.[57] But so daring a revaluation of the teachings of the Western intellectual tradition as a congeries of rhetorical strategies was bound to provoke efforts to place his work in context.

The early critics identified him as a structuralist.[58] He tolerated the appellation for a time, before pointedly rejecting it.[59] A smaller contingent focused on his relationship to Marxism.[60] About this label he was more coy. As a sacred discourse for many left-wing French academicians during the 1960s, Marxism was as much a posture as a philosophy.[61] Politically, Foucault sym-

pathized with the Left, and while hardly a Marxist ideologist, he had no wish
to condemn this tradition completely.[62] He won the affection of the students
of the University of Paris for openly supporting their uprising in May 1968
against governmental policies on higher education. He also professed admiration for Louis Althusser's reading of Marx, which was heavy on structuralist
conceptions.[63] But it is worth noting that Foucault's observations on Marxism
and on left-wing politics generally were usually elicited in interviews rather
than stated at his own initiative.[64] He acknowledged Marx (as he did Nietzsche
and Freud) for his intellectual contribution. But he was suspicious of a ha-
giography that characterized him as the founder of a tradition with which
present-day intellectuals ought to identify. The great thinkers of the past
should not serve as mirrors to validate current thinking.[65]

Foucault's work provoked a response from historians practicing a more
conventional historiography. Some set out to correct his conceptions by pointing to studies of greater nuance and discretion.[66] But even where they sought
to discredit Foucault's interpretative claims, these scholars testified to the theoretical point he wanted to make: discourse generates discourse, apart from
its subject matter. Thus studies of madness, prisons, and asylums multiplied
during the 1970s and 1980s, nearly all acknowledging the inspiration provided
by Foucault's heuristic initiatives.[67] Foucault's purpose, however, was more
subversive. He called for histories that subjected the discourse of history itself
to scrutiny. His method implied a reinvention of history in a new, rhetorical
mode. Not only new topics of historical inquiry, but events, personalities, and
ideas previously studied in depth for their intrinsic interest were now open to
reevaluation as rhetorical images at a more abstract level of cognition.[68]

Foucault's Impact on Contemporary French Historical Writing

In light of Foucault's repudiation of tradition, it might seem ironical to
speak of a Foucauldian tradition.[69] But that is precisely what he inaugurated
in his invitation to historians to inventory the discursive practices with which
Western culture had been elaborated. Just as Foucault aroused critics, so too
he acquired followers along the way. Some were devotees who analyzed and
even mimicked his vocabulary. But others saw beyond his particular studies
to the possibilities raised by his method for a new order of historical investigation. Events, personalities, and ideas once considered for their intrinsic
meaning might now be reinterpreted for their extrinsic forms. How wide the
net of Foucault's intellectual influence may be cast remains problematic. But
permit me to block out some areas of French historiography where his influence is already visible.

The world of French historiography into which Foucault entered in the
1960s had for several decades been dominated by the social history practiced

by scholars identified with the learned periodical *Les Annales*. Founded by Lucien Febvre and Marc Bloch in the late 1920s and given impressive credentials by Fernand Braudel and his students in the 1950s, the *Annales* school of historiography broadened the interests of French historians beyond politics to encompass material realities, social stratification, economic influences, and demographic trends, not just in France but throughout the world. Still bearing the imprint of nineteenth-century positivism, *Annales* scholars based their interpretations on prodigious quantities of research, by the 1960s more easily collated thanks to new techniques of statistical and computer-assisted research. Professing to advance the writing of "total history," they actually tended, with the exception of the greatest practitioners, toward minute specialization.[70]

Foucault's historiographical method signaled a reorientation of French historians from social topics examined through quantitative methods toward cultural ones interpreted through their rhetorical signatures. Not surprisingly, historians of collective mentalities, whose work flourished in the 1960s, were the first to express an interest in his scholarship.[71] The study of mentalities was an outgrowth of an interest in historical psychology pioneered by Febvre more than a half century before.[72] For those historians who returned to Febvre's project, Foucault's call for an inventory of the discursive practices of Western culture may have seemed reminiscent of Febvre's call for an inventory of the "mental equipment" of ages past. But Febvre also attached considerable significance to the inertial power of tradition, the historiographical preoccupation that Foucault wished to set aside.[73]

Foucault's collective memory/counter-memory distinction, therefore, intruded to divide them. The leading historians of mentalities—Philippe Ariès, Robert Mandrou, and Emmanuel Le Roy Ladurie, for example—shared Febvre's interest in tradition and even viewed it with a certain reverence. They culled traditions for their archaic values and their enduring sentimental attachments to the past. Foucault studied them to understand the cultural process of rhetorical construction that set a different course for the future.[74] The historians of mentalities sought to break down the boundaries between literacy and orality. Many of the major works—Mandrou's study of popular culture in sixteenth-century France, for example, or Le Roy Ladurie's story of popular religious belief in Montaillou, or Natalie Davis's account of self-fashioning in popular and elite culture in the world of Martin Guerre—use the written record to extrapolate about the mores of cultures still immersed in oral tradition.[75] By contrast, Foucault's work is almost exclusively devoted to the discursive practices of highly literate people, even in antiquity. Foucault viewed language as an instrument of exclusion and pointed out how language creates barriers that are difficult to cross. Conventions of language, he taught, set one cultural epoch apart from another, sealing off earlier conceptions of the past by redefining the framework in which they are considered. In this regard, Foucault's plotting of the reorganization of knowledge between the sixteenth and the eighteenth centuries, and the corresponding redefinition of the conventions of thought that this process implied, unwittingly deconstructs those modifications of rhetoric that accompanied the move from a literate culture still heavily influenced by orality toward a literate one intensified by the ever-more pervasive influence of printed texts.[76] Within the context of the history of mentalities, therefore, his influence is most visible among those historians who are describing a cultural world in which the imperial power of written discourse shapes social behavior.

Consider, for example, Jacques Donzelot's La Police des familles (1977). In his preface, Donzelot mentions that his work is carried out on the margins of the investigations by Foucault.[77] But the connection is more direct, because Donzelot adheres closely to Foucault's method in his historical analysis of discourses produced to justify the policing of modern domestic life.[78] He plots the elaboration and proliferation of rhetorical strategies employed by public and quasi-public authorities to manage child-rearing and family relations from the nineteenth century into our own day. He proceeds by describing a literature of memoirs, legal studies, and medical and psychiatric reports written to guide clergymen, social workers, and eventually psychologists and psychiatrists in the counsel they dispensed about what is appropriate to parenting, childhood development, and the dynamics of family life. Donzelot shows how the moralistic writings of clergymen and doctors on strategies of intervention in family affairs generated a discourse that, in the course of its elaboration and revision, eventually became a social and then a medical science for the policing of families. The discourse was initiated over specific problems on the boundaries of acceptable behavior—the foibles of wayward husbands or the truancies of delinquent children. But the scope of the discourse was eventually extended to encompass ordinary behavior as well. Through discourse about the family, personal relationships generally came to be treated as problems. Over the course of the century, the rhetoric of justification for intervention changed—from clerical moralizing to social assistance to psychiatric counseling. In the process, an older discourse about society conceived in terms of sociability was shunted aside by a new one that called for social discipline. The problem of society was recast as one of management. New practices of scrutinizing social behavior came into being, as did a host of new officials to carry them out. But the new institutions, like the new personnel, were integrally bound to an expanding discourse that shaped expectations about what was normal in family life.

Like Foucault, Donzelot traced the elaboration of a discourse that defined anticipated behavior, labeled and delineated delinquencies, and in the process subtly imposed a social discipline that eventually became pervasive throughout society.[79] Both authors point out the constancy of the policing process despite the changing faces of the managers (clergy, social workers, psychologists), who brought to their endeavor a succession of ideological justifications. In his depiction of the emergence of a proliferating discourse about the policing of families, Donzelot followed the historiographical method pursued by Foucault in his corresponding studies of asylums and sexuality.

Less explicit but equally compelling are the links between Foucault's method and the recent historiography of the French Revolution, enlivened by the call to celebrate its bicentennial. Since the late nineteenth century, the interpretation of the dynamics of the revolution has focused on the social conflicts between elite and popular classes. These studies, too, bore the imprint of positivism, if not of *Annales* scholarship, and they displayed a lingering sympathy for Marxism, at least as reconceived in a more humanistic, erudite way by such historians as Georges Lefebvre. In an historiographical tradition that runs from Jean Jaurès to Albert Soboul, these historians placed their emphasis on the motives and aspirations of participating social groups, especially the popular classes. They also engaged in a far-reaching study of the material realities confronting society as a basis for explaining the incentives for revolt against the Old Regime. Over time, this line of inquiry became a well-defined historiographical tradition, one tied to the sympathy of its practitioners for the more promising future the revolution augured.[80]

Since the 1970s, however, this approach has been countered by a line of argument not unlike that espoused by Foucault. The leading exponent of this revisionist approach is François Furet, who has written extensively about the revolution and its historiographical interpretation. In his best known study, *Penser la Révolution française* (1977), Furet, too, quarrels with the historian's recourse to tradition.[81] Indeed, he builds his argument around the three major points of interpretation on which Foucault had insisted: the repudiation of tradition, the spread of the policing process, and the emergence of new discursive practices. Furet dismisses the dominant, left-wing tradition of historiography as commemorative in nature. In an argument reminiscent of Foucault's critique of the history of ideas, Furet contends that this tradition of historiography seeks to confirm the emotional links between the revolution conceived as a founding event and the present-day causes of its historians. The tradition, he contends, has a hidden agenda in the continuities it seeks to confirm with the revolution itself.[82] With respect to the policing process, Furet reconsiders the revolution in light of the enormous power that the state acquired over its course despite changes in regimes, parties, leaders, and ideological positions. In arguing that the revolution was less significant for its social conflicts than for the enhancement of state power, he pursues a line of inquiry similar to Foucault's account of the ever-more pervasive influence of the managerial techniques of public authority in modern culture.[83] As for discursive practice, Furet contends that what left-wing historians present as a social revolution was in fact a revolution in rhetoric. Jacobinism was less powerful as a political party than as the mode of parlance that established the conventions of revolutionary discourse. Jacobin discourse was more than an ideology. It was a constituent mode of a new political culture.[84] In this reinterpretation of the meaning of the revolution in light of the production of a new linguistic code, Furet accomplished in the political realm what Foucault had in the cultural. Both confirmed the proposition that discourse is a primary element in the elaboration of a new historical reality.[85]

Mediated by Furet, the deconstructionist approach to the revolution would dominate its study by the time of the bicentennial. Whereas historians at its centennial had looked back to the revolution to confirm their heritage, historians at its bicentennial were more detached observers. Not surprisingly, their treatment of the revolution as a complex past reflected their present-day preoccupation with the complexities of rhetoric. No single interpretative study emerged to honor the event; no single historian was credited with having propounded a unified point of view. Rather multivolume anthologies appeared, with a heavy accent on the myriad discourses of the revolution. As collaborative ventures of the sort that Foucault had advocated, they strove to convey the intellectual syncretism of the political culture constructed in the name of the revolution.[86]

This focus on rhetoric in contemporary historical writing about the revolution may be better appreciated in light of the work of Pierre Nora, who has edited a history of the French national memory entitled *Les Lieux de mémoire* (1984).[87] Nora and his colleagues inventory the political and historiographical traditions through which the national memory has been elaborated. In the manner of Foucault (whose work he once edited), Nora presents his multivolume project as a genealogical deconstruction, beginning with recent discourse about the making of the republic, returning then to the French nation at the time of the revolution, proceeding finally (in a volume just published) to the deeper structures of French culture. Collectively they deconstruct the cultural edifice that shaped and contained the national memory through its endless revisions. For them, that memory is not a spirit to be resurrected, a mentality to be enlivened, or even mores that endure. Rather it is a rhetoric of commemoration whose diverse formulations over the ages may now be dispassionately described.

Nora's point is that French historiography has become more self-conscious about the traditions from which it emerged.[88] For this reason, Foucault's method of shifting the focus from memory to counter-memory appeals to French historians today and suggests why a plethora of historical studies of the political uses of commemoration has recently appeared.[89] Traditions once valued for the way in which they sustained the French national memory are now studied to ascertain how commemoration served political purposes. The rhetoric of historical writings, like the style of monuments and ceremonial rituals, is deciphered for what it reveals about the making of political culture. Herein Foucault's argument about the power/knowledge relationship becomes a working proposition.

If the study of the French Revolution remains focused on waning traditions of historiography, that of French women is preoccupied with a tradition in the making. The history of French women has become the most visible new historiographical discourse of our time. Not surprisingly, a certain literature about Foucault's relationship to feminist perspectives has already emerged, but as in other spheres of historical scholarship the accent has been on Foucault's sympathies rather than on the practical consequences of his way of thinking for historiographical practice.[90] One exception is Joan Wallach Scott's *Gender and the Politics of History* (1988),[91] in which she blends essays on women's role in the French labor movement in the nineteenth century with a more general consideration of the concept of gender as a basis for fashioning a new historiography. Scott, too, is casting about for an alternative to the historiographical traditions with which feminist historians sense themselves confronted. Scott finds equally unappealing approaches to the history of women that seek to assimilate the topic into extant frameworks or that claim to establish it as an autonomous field. The former permits the woman's voice to be heard, but within a context that views it as inherently inferior. The latter leads to a segregation that marginalizes the project, while leaving dominant traditions of historical writing unchallenged. The task is not to find a place for women's history but rather a role in a broader reconstruction of our understanding of the past.[92]

In propounding her argument, Scott distances her present work from a tradition of labor history to which she herself has contributed an admirable study.[93] In some ways this tradition, which may once have provided her with guidance in her introduction to the field, now seems disappointing in its consideration of the cause of oppressed women, despite good intentions. For example, she chides E. P. Thompson, who played such an influential role in the intellectual formation of labor historians who came of age during the 1960s, for a bias about gender implicit in his studies of nineteenth-century England. Thompson, Scott concedes, may have presented working women as one exploited and disaffected group among many. But his approach leaves intact the deeply ingrained notion of the inferiority of women's work and status. To seek a place for women's history within such an historiographical framework is self-defeating, no matter how accommodating it may be.[94] What must be acknowledged, Scott contends, is that our conception of history has been fashioned in the image of the middle-class white male of Western culture, posing as universal man.[95] The task, therefore, is not to broaden the existing framework to accommodate new issues but to deconstruct the rhetoric through which that framework has been elaborated as a prelude to its reconstruction in a different rhetorical vein. The writing of history is a political act, she maintains; it does not represent the past but rather molds it. We construct history through the language we use, just as we do the society in which we live.[96] Recent labor history, a discourse fashioned from a conception of class conflict, preaches equality while institutionalizing a hierarchy of discrimination. The concept of gender may not provide a global foundation for the rewriting of history any more than did that of class. But if we intend to construct a society in which gender differences are accepted within a more pluralistic milieu, we must acknowledge the degree to which our appreciation of those differences is shaped by our conception of the past.[97] The puzzle, she concedes, is how to reconcile differences with equality. But that is a present project for constructing the future in which a reconstruction of our understanding of the past can only sustain us.[98]

In all of this analysis, Scott draws deeply on Foucault's argument about the primacy of rhetoric in the writing of history.[99] He provided her with a new line of inquiry into the way cultural exclusion is hidden in the constructs of language. History, like the human imagination itself, is constructed through language, for language establishes the categories within which we apprehend the past. The issue is not just who has the power to speak but who shapes the structure of the discourse. Scott is particularly taken with Foucault's argument that meanings are created through discourse about exclusion and uses it to show how her-story has been domesticated by an historiographical framework constructed to present his-story. The distinguishing complaint of feminist protest, she points out, is less material need than cultural exclusion. Like Foucault, she wishes to show how the power of discourse operates and how present-day conceptions of the past are engendered by that power—a power to determine what is to be forgotten as well as what is to be remembered. It is therefore important, she contends, that we reexamine the most basic terms of our language: class, gender, equality, political theory, history itself. The way in which each term is used implies a particular understanding of underlying configurations of power.[100] Writing history today requires an acknowledgment of the politics that makes it possible and that shapes its design. In that way the writing of history may become an element in a broader struggle to end oppression.[101]

One might argue that all of these recent lines of inquiry within French historiography—mentalities, the revolution, women—can be explained without recourse to Foucault's writings. Postmodernism, after all, is a movement whose horizons extend far beyond his vision. While acknowledging his influence on their thinking, the authors I have cited might prefer to set sharper limits on the depth of its intrusion into the sphere of their obvious originality. But none would deny that Foucault epitomizes the style that French historiography is beginning to assume. Social history has yielded some of its ground to cultural history, signaling a disenchantment with the positivist method of the *Annales* school as the foundation of scholarly authority. For historians trained in that method, the aggregation of data was the primary task because they assumed that there was only one past to uncover. But Foucault has shown that the historical past is a rhetorical construct for the present. The style of the historian's inquiry, as well as the quantity of data assembled, determines the way it is rendered.

But the recent turn in French historiography is more than an emancipation from its enduring traditions, especially those associated with positivism. There also is a larger perspective on the rhetoric of the Foucault phenomenon.

It signifies a reckoning with the revolution in the technologies of communication in our time. The historical move from typographic to electronic modes of communication, from the world of texts to the world of multimedia has made us more reflective about the nature of the culture we are leaving behind.[102] The printed word, cracked free of the rock bed of textual authority in which it has been enshrined for two centuries, may now be perceived as an historical construct, more clearly defined but less imposing in its capacity to set the course of our thinking. It was Foucault who showed historians the way in which discourse receives its shape and how in turn that shape frames our understanding of the past. In sorting out differences among discourses, Foucault's deconstruction of discursive practice provides insight into the hidden workings of power.

The insight is not without its costs, for Foucault takes us to a level of abstraction beyond the plane where life experience is observed. Personalities, events, even social and economic trends retreat before the power of rhetoric to transform them into abstractions. The danger in this method lies in losing touch with collective memory as it carries forward ideas and values that we might still wish to honor. To privilege rhetoric is to diminish tradition. But the past elicits our sympathy as well as our scrutiny. In discarding the ties that tradition renders familiar, we weaken our appreciation of what is worth caring for in the past. It may be that tradition in its formative powers defies our efforts to transform our thinking through new rhetorical formulations, as some students of hermeneutics continue to claim.[103] Despite their sympathy for Foucault and his methods, the historians we have considered remain engaged with the traditions that prompted their inquiries. The issue, therefore, is how historians will reconcile their newfound interest in the puzzles of rhetoric with their ongoing need to address the substantive problems that have long served as the stuff of history.

7

THE ROLE OF MEMORY
IN THE HISTORIOGRAPHY OF THE
FRENCH REVOLUTION

The French Revolutionary Tradition and the History of the French Revolution

French historians were recently called upon to commemorate the French Revolution on the occasion of its bicentennial. But to commemorate the Revolution is not the same thing as to understand it historically. Since Herbert Butterfield offered his famous critique of Whig history some sixty years ago, historians have been particularly suspicious of historical writing that eulogizes the subjects it considers.[1] Butterfield condemned the Whig historians for ascribing to the historical actors of an earlier age their present bias about the meaning and direction of modern English history. The past, he advised, is better appreciated with a disinterested curiosity, and countless historians have since echoed his caution about an anachronistic reading of the historical record. But as the bicentennial of the French Revolution has revealed, anniversaries of memorable personalities or events continue to quicken the historian's interest, as even those who decry commemorative historical writing take advantage of the opportunity to state or restate their interpretations.[2] To offer an historical interpretation of a memorable event need not be a form of commemoration. Commemoration, after all, is grounded in tradition, toward which all historians will establish at least some critical distance.[3] But the notion that an historian's inquiry may be completely disinterested is equally problematic.[4] The issue is how the relationship between collective memory and historical understanding is established, for often it is tradition that carries the events of the past into the purview of the historian in the first place. The project of commemoration, therefore, prompts us to rethink the relationship between remembering the past and understanding it historically.

The historiography of the French Revolution provides us with such an opportunity. The Revolution was not just an event of the late eighteenth century.

Its memory inspired a revolutionary tradition that directly influenced French politics at least until the Paris Commune of 1871. The revolutions of 1830, 1848, and 1871, not to mention a number of abortive popular insurrections along the way, were perceived by many of their participants to be reenactments of the prototype of 1789. Even as the influence of the revolutionary tradition waned toward the end of the nineteenth century, politicians continued to memorialize it in a way that reinforced the authority of the Third Republic. Well into the twentieth century, it was difficult to discuss the French Revolution without adopting some stance toward the living tradition through which it was remembered.

The revolutionary tradition in modern France, of course, had several strands, and there were sharp antagonisms among them. There was a liberal strand that shaped the politics of Orleanism in the 1830s and the 1840s. Its influence remained strong in the parliamentary politics of the Third and Fourth Republics and in a respect for civil and political liberties that has endured to this day. There was also an authoritarian strand that contributed to the politics of Bonapartism in the 1850s and the 1860s.[5] Though viewed ambiguously by the French Left, it, too, has had reverberations into modern times by virtue of its association with Boulangism (1880s), Pétainism (1940s), and Gaullism (1960s). But the most memorable and ultimately most influential strand has been the republican one.[6] It was in republican imagery that the revolutionary tradition was enshrined in civic rituals in the late nineteenth century and through which the identity of modern France as a nation-state was formed. The commemoration of the storming of the Bastille on 14 July as the national holiday beginning in the late nineteenth century is the best known, but it was only the centerpiece of a host of commemorative gestures that sought to reaffirm the mnemonic connections between the political culture of modern France and its inspiring sources in the events of the late eighteenth century.[7] Even as references to the Revolution faded from political discourse, its leading events and personalities remained objects of veneration, places of memory in the deep conceptual structure through which the terms of French politics had been defined and would continue to be tacitly understood. The republican strand of the revolutionary tradition, moreover, continued to exercise the most profound influence on historical thinking about the French heritage throughout most of the twentieth century. For this reason, the commemoration of the French republic and the historiography of the French Revolution have been closely intertwined.

The Problem of Tradition Revisited

The French revolutionary tradition is particularly germane to our consideration of the memory/history problem, for it provides an opportunity to apply the theories that we have been discussing in earlier chapters to a practical

historiographical problem. How, we may ask, does the collective memory
identified with the revolutionary tradition influence the historian's interpretation of the meaning of the French Revolution? The question begs a preliminary one about the nature of tradition itself, whose consideration requires a
brief recapitulation and comparison of the theorists that we have studied thus
far. The teachings of Giambattista Vico provide us with our point of departure. Of all the students of memory that we have examined, he comes closest
to formulating a theory of the life cycle of memory. Vico was imbued with
the Enlightenment's faith that there is a universal pattern to the past that the
"new science" of history had enabled him to uncover.[8] Vico's new science of
history, as we have argued, was actually a theory of the dynamics of oral tradition. He had devised a theory of history's stages, beginning with an age of
poetic inspiration and running down, as in a process of entropy, toward a stage
of passionless reflection. For Vico, history moves according to a cycle of memory, issuing from an age of poetic and inspired imagination but devolving
toward one of prosaic and dispassionate abstraction. Having lost the memory
of the cycle's inspired beginnings, a society at the cycle's end is obliged to
envisage the world once more.[9] Vico's insight into the tendency of oral tradition to follow a cyclical pattern serves as the foundation for his theory of the
evolution of civilization, "an ideal eternal history traversed in time by the histories of all nations."[10] As an historian, he wanted to view traditions from
outside to see how they operate over the long run. But his capacity to do so
was based on his sensitivity to the way in which traditions are transformed
imperceptibly by those immersed within their living memories.[11]

There are two sides to Vico's explanation of the dynamics of tradition, or,
as he puts it, the "course the nations run": a course (corso) and a recourse
(ricorso). The direction of the course is reckoned from the vantage point of
recollection, which he characterizes as "wisdom."[12] His contention is that all
efforts to perpetuate tradition on the basis of guiding memories will over the
long run succumb to degeneration and eventually dissolution. Surveying the
course of tradition from this recollective perspective, he notes: the remodeling
of the memory of the real past into a commemorative legend; the abandonment
of commitment to its remembered ways as a tradition's original meaning
grows obscure; and finally, the inevitable fading of its memory altogether into
a collective amnesia.[13] What survives the death of the living memory of a
tradition are the archaeological remains of languages and institutions. Such
traditions cannot be reconstituted by putting new life into these old forms.
Memory, conceived as the ground of imagination, can nonetheless inspire a
recourse and so permits a repetition of the process by which traditions are
made.[14] The course, therefore, is matched by the recourse, the past viewed in
light of the regenerative process through which new traditions are born: the
reawakening of imagination in new representations of reality; the renewed
commitments that such imagination inspires; and the invention of the linguistic and institutional forms of remembrance through which a tradition of

living memory may be sustained.[15] There is a way of understanding the Vichian course and recourse as a sequence but another in which they are a simultaneous presence.[16] The former concerns the past considered from the standpoint of recollection; the latter from that of repetition. Either way, it is their interaction that provides the historian with insight into the pattern underpinning the "course the nations run."[17] In Vico's theory, the oral traditions of the ancient world appear to follow a life cycle because those who were immersed in them tended to think about the past in cyclical terms.

But what of the modern traditions that have been invested with historical thinking about past and future? Do they, too, follow a cyclical pattern? The French revolutionary tradition provides us with an opportunity to examine these questions, for it is one identified with the making of the modern world. What is striking about the French revolutionary tradition as an exemplar of modern ones generally is that it is oriented toward future prospects more than past accomplishments. In other words, the revolutionary tradition is imbued with historicist thinking, and the problem of assessing its meaning is bound up with the historicist notion that the direction of human intentions sets the course of historical change. The attitudes toward tradition in the contemporary age, moreover, evoke a wider range of perspectives. Their future-oriented expectations about the course of change notwithstanding, modern traditions continue to bear traits of the cycle of memory that Vico identified with oral tradition. Recent work on institutional memory within large organizations reveals the repetitive pattern with which the same solutions are proposed, then forgotten, only to be proposed once more after relatively short periods of time.[18] Moreover, modern traditions in our postmodern age are being subjected to the scrutiny of critics for whom both the traditionalist idea of repetition and the modern one of recollection are devalued. The postmodern perspective stresses memory's revision of the past in light of present prospects. Accordingly, the postmodern historian is interested in the deconstruction of the formal elements of tradition—the disassembling of the linguistic and institutional forms through which living memory was once channeled. It is a position intimately tied to the perception of many historians today that the French revolutionary tradition has run its course.

If Vico was our theoretical guide to the traditions of the ancient world, the three students of tradition that we have just considered, Halbwachs, Ariès, and Foucault, provide us with counterparts for examining the traditions of the modern and postmodern world. Their appreciations of the meaning of tradition may differ, but the problems they address are essentially the same: the intrusion of present needs into memory's musings, the longing for a reaffirmation of continuities with the past coupled with an understanding of the snares of nostalgia when interpreting its meaning, the hidden traditions that official memories may distort or obscure, and the social contexts through which the politics of collective memory operate. In considering the differences among their interpretations, we can see aspects of the way in which modern traditions function. They provide us with an exchange of ideas about the problem of tradition in the modern world and enable us to see links with its status in both an earlier (traditional) and a later (postmodern) age. For this reason, we might say that the historiography of the French Revolution serves, too, as a crossroads for understanding the memory/history problem.

We have stressed the significance of Maurice Halbwachs's pioneering work. The first modern scholar to focus on the problem of collective memory, he wrote to save historians from succumbing to its wiles. He therefore tended to consider memory's resources in a pejorative light, his profound insight into its workings notwithstanding. Halbwachs explored the implications of the paradox that tradition concerns the present even though it invokes the past. In tradition, he explained, the past is appreciated relative to present need, and the similarities rather than the differences between them are therefore emphasized. The events of a past that has grown distant and strange are thereby integrated into the more familiar surroundings of the present. In this eclipse of time, memory builds an emotional link to the past rather than a critical perspective on it. Even though traditions are continually being revised to serve present ends, he observed, they convey an illusion of timelessness. Through its incorporation into tradition, living memory is grounded within a larger continuum in which events from the distant past are rendered more immediately enticing. In extending the horizon of remembrance beyond personal recollection, tradition widens the sphere of timelessness to which personal memory has recourse. The time of tradition is time immemorial. From its vantage point, the past appears not to have aged at all.

Because it uses collective memory to the advantage of present projects, Halbwachs argued, tradition invariably becomes an issue of political contention. The way in which the past is recalled depends on the power of the group that frames its memory. Tradition reinforces present politics; indeed, it is a weapon in its arsenal of tactics. Halbwachs suggests that through its tradition a group colonizes time by locating significant dates within a commemorative chronology, just as it colonizes space through the commemorative architecture with which it reshapes its topography. The most powerful group takes possession of the past by crowding out the traditions of its competitors or by reshaping them to conform to its own conceptions.

Halbwachs's purpose was to show how unreliable tradition can be as a guide to the past. In the process, he provided the philosophical groundwork for the kind of critique Butterfield made of Whig history. Preoccupied with the way in which memory fosters an anachronistic reading of the past, Halbwachs emphasized the differences between an understanding of the past conveyed by tradition and one acquired in the course of historical research. Indeed, he presented them as antinomies. Memorialists look for similarities between past and present; historians for differences. Memorialists seek to rouse emotions by depicting the past in vivid images; historians prefer to interpret its events dispassionately in more abstract descriptions. Memorialists will revise the images with which they perceive the past to conform to their present conceptions; historians will revise their conceptions to conform to the evidence they have discovered. For memorialists, the past is reconstructed as a malleable tableau of aesthetic images, whereas for historians it is conceived as a durable explanation built on empirical facts.

Halbwachs sought to make historians aware of the distortions that memory interjects into the historical record and of the need to remedy them by off-setting memory's appeal to the interior life of tradition with history's recourse to the stable frameworks established by external evidence. But he was naive in assuming that historians proceed without a conceptual framework derived from an historiographical tradition of their own. His distinction between memory and history, therefore, is too sharply drawn, for it is often sympathy with a tradition that initially lures the historian into the investigation of a topic. Although it may convey distortions, the perspective of tradition ought not to be discounted, for it brings the living memories that sustain it into the historian's field of vision.

Herein lies the interest of Philippe Ariès's approach to the problem of history's relationship to memory. While Ariès offered insights into memory's workings that are similar to those of Halbwachs, he wrote from a tradition-alist perspective and accordingly provided guidance of a different sort. He, too, appreciated the politics of memory, particularly in its historiographical applications. He wanted to recall traditions forgotten by historians that he himself remembered fondly. He therefore listened to his own memory's promptings, even as he pursued careful historical research. For him, tradition can provide historians with a point of entry for their research, marking places in the past wherein the perspectives of memory and history cross and inter-mingle. So conceived, the relationship between memory and history becomes dialogical, not mutually exclusive.

Ariès's point is that collective memory provides a context for the events that historians encounter in the course of their investigations. Even as historians deepen their critical perspective upon the events of the past, they never com-pletely discard the traditions through which the memory of these events has been conveyed into the present age. Traditions may be modified, he believed, but they cannot be invented anew.[19] Even though memorialists are continually revising tradition in light of the changing needs of the present, tradition carries forward a framework for remembering the events and personalities of the past that it honors. The historian may learn from such a tradition without ac-cepting its underlying assumptions. Indeed, making sense of the way in which a tradition evolves may be an essential preliminary task for understanding the events it commemorates. But to do so, Ariès argued, the historian must scan a tradition over a long period of time, for the assumptions that it tacitly con-tains change at a glacial pace in comparison with that of the course of events it typically describes.

It is important to point out that Ariès in his defense of tradition as a route into historical understanding did not invoke the presence of the past. He was ready to concede that there is a "world that we have lost."[20] But he believed that even as the past fades from memory and loses its presence in our minds, it continues to influence us in unacknowledged ways, and it retains a potential power of appeal that must be recognized if we are to deepen our historical understanding. The need, he believed, is for historians to recover lost memories so that they may be able to see beyond the limits of their present horizons.

For Michel Foucault, by contrast, the interior life of the past that tradition claims to perpetuate as living memory in the present is in fact an obstacle to the historians' need to break free from the constraints of tradition-bound interpretations. Writing from a poststructuralist perspective, he is the kind of theorist one would expect to find in the midst of the dissolution of the traditions of the modern age. Like Halbwachs, he would unfasten the link between memory and history in the consideration of a tradition's workings. But he goes beyond Halbwachs in that his own position is oriented toward the future. Halbwachs bracketed the historical value of the living memories that traditions bear because he believed that they discourage the search for evidence of alternative traditions or those that lie deeper in the past. Foucault, by contrast, dismisses traditions altogether as irrelevant to our present needs. Whatever we value in the past, he contends, we cannot rely on it for guidance. History teaches us that we must fashion our own future.[21] Vis-à-vis the past, Foucault's interest is in the way in which the constraints of tradition's forms are overcome or how they are reused in later ages for unrelated purposes. History in his poststructuralist musings, therefore, becomes an archaeology. His interest is in the deconstruction of the linguistic and institutional forms the past has given us. It is these alone, he argues, not the values they once embodied, that may be appropriated for future use.

In this odyssey among theorists whose perspectives would seem to journey from positivism to traditionalism to poststructuralism, there may be no apparent course, but we do see the degree to which the scholars' perspectives on modern traditions may differ. These scholars reflected on the memory/ history problem in widely divergent contexts. But what of historians engaged with the same tradition? Is there a pattern to their consideration of the memory/history problem? To address these questions, I propose to examine the role of memory in the historical reflections of four well-remembered historians of the French Revolution, matching each with what have been the chosen intervals for its anniversary remembrance: the official commemorations sponsored every fifty years. I shall consider Jules Michelet, who wrote his history of the revolution shortly after the semicentennial; Alphonse Aulard, who offered his assessment for the centennial; Georges Lefebvre, whose most influential work, Quatre-vingt-neuf, was written in conjunction with the sesquicentennial; and François Furet, whose revisionist interpretation coincides with the bicentennial. Each raises the issue of memory's relationship to history but treats it in a different way. What varies is the distance that each establishes between the perspective on the past embodied in the revolutionary tradition and his own critical perspective on its nature and significance. Through this comparison what reemerges within this tradition of historiography is a pattern reminiscent of the Vichian cycle of memory.

Jules Michelet: Resurrecting the French Revolution

Jules Michelet (1798–1874) is the best loved of the historians of the Revolution. Historians today continue to pay homage to his accomplishment, though he is rarely consulted for a critical understanding of the Revolution's events. In recent years, his style of presentation has attracted a certain historiographical interest, especially among historians concerned with the rhetoric of history.[22] He was a poet of the revolutionary tradition as much as he was an historian of the Revolution. Michelet said that history should be a resurrection of the spirit of the past, and he continues to be admired for his capacity to make the Revolution come alive for the present generation.[23] For him, the memory of the Revolution was in some sense an evocation of the mind-set of its historical participants. Remembrance was not an act of mere recollection but rather one of repetition. Michelet prided himself on his knowledge of archival sources, but he was at the same time sensitive to the historical uses of oral tradition. For him, the Revolution was still within the ambit of living memory.

Michelet was born and raised in the Paris of the Napoleonic era. He came to know many of his parent's generation who had witnessed the events of the Revolution, and he frequented the places where its great events had transpired. As he reached maturity, moreover, he sensed that the memory of the Revolution lived on in the public's perceptions of current events. He was enthralled with the Revolution of 1830, which he characterized as a resurrection of the French Revolution's passions and a carrying forward of its traditions. He referred to the popular insurrection of July 1830 that had ushered it in as "that eternal July," as if the uprising of July 1789 had come alive once more.[24] Michelet's sensitivity to the importance of that memory gave added purpose to his plan to write the Revolution's history, for he wanted to sustain the living memory of a revolutionary tradition that might otherwise fade with the passing of the Revolution's participants. By the semicentennial of 1839, with most of the revolutionaries of 1789 dead, the revolutionary tradition stood literally at the edge of living memory. As he embarked on his research, therefore, he sought out and conversed with some of the few remaining witnesses.[25]

Endowed with intelligence as well as passion, Michelet advanced rapidly to academic prominence. He passed his *agrégation* at age twenty-three and taught both philosophy and history at the *Ecole normale supérieure* from 1827 to 1837. Early on, he was recognized as an historian of distinction. He was named chief of the historical section of the National Archives by the leaders of the new liberal monarchy in 1830, and he was awarded a chair at the *Collège de France* in 1838. Thenceforth his monumental projects in history rolled forth, notably his *Histoire de la Révolution française* (1847–53), and his *Histoire de France* (1833–69).[26] But his conceptions of history had already been formed by his early inquiries into philosophical issues about history's overall meaning and design. These were deeply influenced by Vico, to whose work he devoted an important essay in 1835.[27]

Michelet agreed with Vico's proposition about memory's inspiring powers. But he recast Vico's cyclical theory of history as an upward spiraling gyre. Michelet identified poetic inspiration with the coming of each successive historical stage. Each stage had its creative beginnings, and each was identified with a different part of the globe. These founding events became places of memory in the ascent of civilization toward the Revolution in France that had ushered in the present age.[28] From Vico, too, Michelet professed to have learned to see the pageant of the past as a collective saga. He portrayed the people as the chief actors in history, although one would search his pages in vain for a factual description of the term. Rather he uses it metaphorically to convey the passion borne by collective memory through tradition. The people are for him an image of collective memory's inspiring power.[29] In his history of the Revolution, Michelet has a tendency to portray its chief historical actors as incarnations of collective values deeply embedded in a national tradition whose full meaning became visible only with the coming of the Revolution. Philosophers, such as Rousseau and Voltaire, or popular tribunes, such as the abbé Sieyès and Danton, personify a variety of revolutionary virtues. Larger than life in Michelet's characterization of them, they function in his writings as emblems of human traits rather than as concrete historical personalities.[30] The festivals of the Revolution in Michelet's history play a complementary role. Entire chapters are devoted to the festivals of 1790 that commemorated the revolutionary *journées* of 1789. As essential reference points for understanding the collective consciousness of a people forging an identity through self-liberation, they became the anchors of the revolutionary tradition he sought to bring alive once more in his historical writings.[31] For Michelet, the festivals are moments of arrested time that permit meditation on the Revolution's most memorable accomplishments.[32]

Michelet's history of the Revolution reveals the degree to which it remained the central event of a living tradition in his own day. The Revolution evoked a milieu of living memory with which republicans of the early nineteenth century had not yet lost touch. It is important to point out that the revolutionary tradition in the first half of the nineteenth century was still largely an oral tradition. Many histories of the Revolution were being written, but none acquired authority as an official framework for its remembrance until later in the century. Conflicting perspectives on its meaning competed for recognition and public favor.[33] Much of what was known about the radical revolution that had ushered in the First Republic, moreover, was transmitted through the oral accounts of those committed to carrying forward its memory. It was such popular legends that often inspired the revolutionaries of the early nineteenth century. Through the Bourbon restoration and the Orleanist monarchy, the republican movement remained an intellectual underground, judged subversive by governmental leaders and harassed in its activities. Its work was often animated by secret societies, and many of its leaders became legends themselves.[34] Much of the appeal of Michelet's writings was derived then, as it is now, from his capacity to give poetical expression to this revolutionary tradition.[35] He is an historian whose conceptions of the past emanated directly from a living tradition, one from which he established comparatively little distance. Michelet's history remains immersed in memory. Even from our remote vantage point, the enduring interest of his historical writing is derived from his capacity to convey some understanding of the passion of a tradition of which he sensed himself to be a part.

Alphonse Aulard: Recollecting the French Revolution

If Michelet is the best loved of the historians of the Revolution, Alphonse Aulard (1849–1928) is among the most respected. He was a literary historian by training, and his first work in history was a study of the orators of the Revolution.[36] Appointed in 1886 to the first endowed chair at the University of Paris in the history of the Revolution, he was for all practical purposes its official historian for the Third Republic. Though he came late to historical research, he is often characterized as the first serious scholar of the radical dimension of the Revolution, for he analyzed extensive documentary evidence about it in a systematic way.[37] But the republic that for Michelet had been an unfulfilled ideal was for Aulard an accomplished reality. When he acceded to his post at the Sorbonne, the Third Republic was in the process of fashioning a new identity. Though the memory of the Revolution had not yet faded, it was nonetheless being turned to different ends. The republican ideal identified for so long with a revolutionary tradition was now being redesigned to conform to one that would instill pride in the nation-state. In Aulard's view, the insurrectionary origins of the Third Republic might be honored, but they were no longer central to that regime's self-conceptions, which turned on projects for the future. Apologists for the young republic saw the state as an agency of progress, bringing to its citizens the benefits of social services, public education, and economic prosperity.[38] The place of the Revolution in this new nationalist tradition was of lesser importance than it had been in the revolutionary one from which it had been appropriated.[39] The Revolution was not to be repeated but rather commemorated as a milestone along the way to the founding of the Third Republic. In this way, the memory of the Revolution was bent to conform to the aspirations of a new, state-sponsored nationalism.[40] As an historian, Aulard formulated a vision of the Revolution that his generation could appreciate in light of present-day political preoccupations. Through his lectures and his historical writings, the memory of the Revolution was revised to serve the interests of a regime that wished to see itself in a modern and progressive image.

As a prelude to this endeavor, Aulard paid homage to Michelet. "One might wish that Michelet's book would become part of the moral conscience of every French student," he remarked in his inaugural lecture at the Sorbonne in 1886.[41] But having said that, he dismissed Michelet from further consideration. For his own conception of history, Aulard turned to the early nineteenth-century French philosopher Auguste Comte, whose science of society contributed so powerfully to the outlook of the savants of the Third Republic.[42] Comte appealed to Aulard because he provided a conceptual framework for his own work in history. Like Vico, Comte formulated a theory of history's stages, and he understood them as places in a long-range movement from a culture based on imaginative speculation toward one based upon empirical description. In contrast with Vico, however, Comte characterized this process as progressive rather than degenerative, for he placed his faith in the positive knowledge that humans would acquire in the final stage of civilization's development. It was, moreover, a process that was irreversible. History for Comte moves not in cycles but along a timeline of linear ascent toward the present age.[43] For Aulard, interpreting the past within Comte's framework, the Revolution became a way station in the triumph of rational understanding and deliberate planning. The Revolution had contributed to the making of the modern state, even if it was no longer germane to its future goals.

Aulard's reading of Comte prepared the way for recasting the relationship between the memory and the history of the Revolution. A memory that had been for Michelet the resurrection of a tradition became for Aulard the confirmation of a direction of change and accomplishment. The Revolution might be remembered, but it could not be repeated. The historian's task was not to evoke the mind-set of the leaders of the Revolution, as Michelet had proposed but rather to commemorate their deeds and accomplishments. Not only would the past become clear and certain in its factual description. It would also acquire solemn moment as a record of events that had altered the course of history once and for all time. History was a monument to real and irreversible changes in the human condition.

Having learned from Comte that a past conveyed through legend is no better than a fiction, Aulard self-consciously distanced himself from the revolutionary tradition. He dismissed the "malevolent legends" with which the memory of the Revolution had become encrusted in the course of the nineteenth century, and he sought to displace these with well-documented facts.[44] In a comparison of Michelet and Aulard, one can see the distance traveled from a history infused with living memory to one that viewed memory as an obstacle to an authentic appreciation of the past. Both honored the same revolutionary leaders, and both were fascinated with the role of festival in a revolutionary community. Michelet's revolutionary leaders embodied virtues and vices and hence exhibited collective human traits. Aulard described the same leaders as individual personalities; they were more practical than virtuous and hence less imposing as memory images.[45] Aulard's evocations of collective action, moreover, turned on political ideologies, not collective mentalities. Michelet's global image of the mind-set of the people was reduced by Aulard to the more modest proportions of the program of a Jacobin party, whose meetings he was the first to study assiduously.[46] Correspondingly, the public festivals described by Michelet as resurrections of the living memory of the Revolution were for Aulard only commemorative markers of strategic political decisions made during the course of its progress. The festivals were consciously planned and served more pragmatic purposes; they rooted out the vestiges of the old culture while memorializing a new one.[47]

It is not surprising to learn that Aulard became actively involved in planning the centennial of the Revolution in 1889.[48] Given his sensitivity to the efficacy of the commemorative rituals of the First Republic, he knew that like ceremonies might have a corresponding success in enhancing the image of the Third. Indeed, one might argue that his historical writings about the Revolution are commemorative in much the same way. Aulard's studies served a mnemonic end: they were intended to throw into bold relief the positive changes the Revolution had worked. The more he tried to lend authority to his interpretation by fortifying it with a modern science of historical documentation, the more it resembled an ancient art of memory. The presupposition of his positivist historiography, like that of the state-sponsored commemoration to which he lent his intellectual prestige, was that a permanent conceptual framework might be imposed on the past. Just as the art of memory had been a technique for holding memory in stasis, so positivist historiography of the sort written by Aulard was a stratagem for imposing a definitive structure on a past too easily modified in the legends of the revolutionary tradition. Whatever the scholarly trappings of Aulard's presentation of the past, the memory of the Revolution he bequeathed to his students was designed to deepen a present-day allegiance. The revolutionary tradition was being absorbed into a nationalist one, for which Aulard's history would provide a commemorative grounding in the guise of science.[49] A tradition that had once sustained revolutionary ardor was being redeployed by those who wished only to remember it as a formative stage in their own development.

Georges Lefebvre: Remodeling the Memory of the French Revolution

Michelet sought to resurrect the memory of the French Revolution; Aulard to recollect it. Georges Lefebvre (1874–1959) succeeded in remodeling the memory by incorporating it into a broader conception of history. He gave the meaning of the Revolution a new turn by placing its memory within the context of the quest to realize a socialist ideal. With Lefebvre, the republican tradition of historiography received its most comprehensive expression.[50]

Lefebvre was the dominant figure in the historiography of the French Revolution in the mid-twentieth century. A descendent of cotton mill workers from Flanders, he made his way to academic prominence from modest beginnings. He was a product of the laic schools instituted by the educational reformers of the early Third Republic, and he pursued the curriculum in teacher training (*enseignement spécial*) through which its values were to be imparted. Intellectually gifted, he passed through the University of Lille on his way to the *agrégation,* but the educational path he had chosen precluded his admission to the prestigious *Ecole normale supérieure,* the traditional route to high academic attainment. Among the French academic elite, therefore, Lefebvre always sensed himself to be an outsider. Patiently, he pursued his research for his doctoral thesis, a study of peasant life in the *département* of the *Nord* during the Revolution, for which he earned enduring intellectual respect.[51] He was fifty years old before the *doctorat d'état* was bestowed upon him in 1924. All the while, he taught in *lycées* and provincial universities (Strasbourg among them, where he was a colleague of Halbwachs) before being called to the Sorbonne as a titular professor in 1935. Two years later he was appointed to the chair in the history of the French Revolution first awarded to Aulard some fifty years before. Upon the death of Albert Mathiez in 1932, he assumed the editorship of the learned journal he had founded, *les Annales historiques de la Révolution française,* a position he held until his own death in 1959. During his mature years, he coordinated, indeed one might say presided over, scholarly research on the Revolution.[52]

True to his origins in the turn of his scholarship, Lefebvre used his prodigious research to reveal the significance of a side of the revolution previously neglected by scholars—the popular revolution, or, as he himself characterized it, the "revolution from below." Through his long apprenticeship on specialized topics in local and regional history, he set the style, not to mention the professional standards, for the detailed monographic studies of the social and economic foundations of the Revolution toward which historiographical interest gravitated in the era after the Second World War. This might be characterized as the artisanal side of his formation as an historian. Yet he is remembered with admiration to this day for his capacity to generalize and synthesize. In effect, he devised a comprehensive paradigm of the Revolution, all the more impressive for its grounding in painstaking historical research. In that sense, he might be described as the artisan who went on to become the master craftsman of the historiography of the revolutionary tradition.

In one sense, Lefebvre operated within the positivist historiographical tradition of professional scholarship inaugurated by Aulard. Like his predecessor, Lefebvre was a diligent scholar, and he stressed the importance of documentation. Lefebvre admired erudition, and his own was worthy of that nineteenth-century savant. But in another, he reaffirmed the moral values of the revolutionary tradition as they had been proclaimed by Michelet. These three historians were united in their perception of the Revolution as a milestone in the pageant of human progress, one since identified with the republican cause. In this respect, Lefebvre may be said to have reconciled his research with his ideological commitments extraordinarily well, for he used his masterful histories to reclaim the memory of the Revolution for present causes. If Michelet had worked for and Aulard had witnessed the triumph of the republican movement in the nineteenth century, Lefebvre in the twentieth watched it placed in jeopardy by the Nazi assault on the fundamental values that it had aspired to institutionalize. He was therefore particularly conscious of the significance of the memory of the Revolution for France and the world in his own day. Therein lay the appeal of his argument to his contemporaries: in the dark days of the late 1930s, as Nazi threats grew more menacing and as the democratic opposition mounted by the Popular Front faltered, Lefebvre propounded a vision of the French Revolution that he hoped his countrymen would find worthy of remembrance. In *Quatre-vingt-neuf,* the commemorative volume he published on the eve of the war, he called on French youth to reread the Declaration of the Rights of Man and Citizen and to remain true to the values that it enshrined.[53] After the war, as he resumed scholarly publication, he reaffirmed the importance of these values for the postwar generation with no less urgency. "These values," he remarked in an essay he wrote in 1948 on the larger meaning of the Revolution, "provide testimony of the echoes of the French Revolution throughout the world, and of the enduring significance of its memory."[54]

Aulard had placed the Revolution in what might seem to have been the broadest of contexts—a republican tradition of politics that spanned nearly a century. But Lefebvre reconfigured the historiographical appreciation of that tradition so as to amalgamate it with a socialist one closer to the affections of the left-wing historians of his own age and, so, widened the horizons of meaning that might be drawn from its events. The direction of change the Revolution augured for Aulard had been liberal, leaning toward democratic. But that about which Lefebvre prophesied was more socially egalitarian, Jacobin in inspiration but with a certain debt to Marxist analysis. Certainly his interpretation of the Revolution emphasized the class struggle by which the bourgeoisie ascended to political power. But the narrative framework in which he placed the Revolution concerned a struggle for liberty that dated from an earlier age and whose realization had yet to be achieved. He thereby vastly extended the commemorative timeline on which the leading events of the Revolution were to be situated. No longer was the Revolution the founding event of the modern age, as it had been for Aulard. In Lefebvre's rendering, it was a way station on an historical path dating at least from the Renaissance. The memory of the Revolution in the making of the Jacobin republic was therefore absorbed into another of a more enduring struggle for liberty that was to be fulfilled in the realization of the socialist ideal. The reminiscence of the Revolution he would evoke for posterity was of a social republic that mirrored the attributes that in his own age were beginning to be identified with the welfare state.[55] As the harbinger of a social revolution to follow the political one that it had ushered in, Lefebvre contended, the French Revolution was significant not only for the future of France but also for that of the world.[56]

In the scope of this formulation, Lefebvre might be said to have returned to the panoramic perspective laid out by Michelet. There were in Lefebvre's interpretation many affinities with that of Michelet: both offered a grand design of world history in which the Revolution figured prominently; both were interested in the Revolution from below; both identified the ordinary people who participated in the Revolution with a high moral idealism. Such correspondences explain Lefebvre's admiration for Michelet.[57] But if Michelet was the gifted amateur; Lefebvre was the respected professional, and it was with a more rigorously researched scholarship that he preferred to identify. To distance himself from Michelet, however, was not to choose Aulard. Aulard may have inaugurated a tradition of scholarship that Lefebvre was willing to characterize as modern. He nonetheless had reservations about Aulard's historical studies. There is the suggestion that Aulard, a literary scholar by training, lacked the historian's formation. Aulard's concerns, which centered on the making of the laic republic, seemed to Lefebvre to be outdated, and his interests too focused on the "revolution from above."[58]

To relate the work of the Revolution to the coming of the social republic that he envisioned Lefebvre needed a different guide. In a personal reminiscence on his own early professional formation, he professed to have chosen Jean Jaurès as his mentor. "I saw and heard Jaurès only two times, lost in the crowd. . . . But no matter how carefully one searches for my master, I recognize no one but him."[59] Jaurès was the eloquent, highly respected tribune of the socialist party at the turn of the century. A teacher by formation, a politician by vocation, he formulated a vision of politics that blended the new socialism with the democratic legacy of the revolutionary tradition.[60] He wrote the first social history of the Revolution, a direction in scholarship that his successors, Albert Mathiez and Lefebvre, were to follow. Lefebvre's identification with Jaurès was genuine, but his debt to him may have been more sentimental than substantive. Personally, Jaurès may have inspired his socialist politics, and professionally he brought to completion one of Jaurès's most important scholarly ventures. He published his *Histoire de la Révolution française* (1930) as the final volume in a series inaugurated by Jaurès some thirty years before.[61] What appealed to Lefebvre in Jaurès's historical vision was his eclectic blend of the socialist and revolutionary traditions. But just as Aulard had once patronized Michelet with fulsome praise, so Lefebvre may have exaggerated his debt to Jaurès, to whom he alluded only in passing references. If Jaurès was the icon of his memory of the Revolution, Mathiez, who wrote from a more visibly Marxist perspective, may have had more influence on the way in which he devised his historical model.[62] Moreover, it was for the Marxist slant of Lefebvre's work, with its focus upon long-range economic trends, class struggle, and the "revolution from below," that he was to be remembered by his own students and admirers.[63]

Much of the appeal of Lefebvre's argument to professional historians and laymen alike lies in the skill with which he pulled apart the dense web of events of the Revolution and rewove its strands into a compellingly simple narrative, deepened by his explanations of their relationship to underlying social and economic processes. But Lefebvre, too, had his places of memory, which, if camouflaged more effectively than were those of Michelet, nonetheless sharply define the structure of his interpretation of the meaning of the Revolution. Lefebvre's history is based on a comprehensive mnemonic scheme that enabled him to display the coherence of vision for which he is so admired. In fashioning this paradigm, he was far from naive. In his study of modern historiography, he reveals himself to have been particularly sensitive to the role that memory plays in historical reconstruction. He was, for example, among the first historians to comment on the significance of Halbwachs's pioneering study, and he pointed out how selective is the process by which historians privilege certain lines of inquiry into the past while neglecting others.[64] From the standpoint of the memory/history problem, Lefebvre conceived of his task as one of recollecting the hidden history of the revolution from below, whose memory had been forgotten in the academic historiography of the nineteenth century. The memory that Lefebvre sought to retrieve was that of the popular revolution, made manifest in the insurrections of 1789 and culminating in what he characterized as the "second French Revolution," that of the rising of the people of Paris in August 1792 to found the French Republic.

Lefebvre developed his thesis across a series of volumes about the revolutionary era.[65] But so striking were the mnemonic keys to his argument that it was possible for him to summarize it in a short book, *Quatre-vingt-neuf,* and even to sketch its outlines in an article of less than ten pages.[66] Laid out as a mnemonic scheme, therefore, his thesis is easily recapitulated. His main point is that the French Revolution was in reality a confluence of five revolutionary currents (aristocratic, bourgeois, municipal [i.e., federalist], urban popular, and peasant), each with its own distinct motivating forces and each with a different agenda. He was the first to identify the nobility's politics of protest in the waning years of the Old Regime as an "aristocratic" revolution, and he showed how it was crucial to the formation of the political consciousness that made the "bourgeois" revolution of 1789 possible. That one, in turn, used to its advantage the grievances presented by the *sans culottes* of the cities and the peasants of the countryside. Without their intervention, he argued, the bourgeois revolution could never have been sustained. In the summer of 1789, the currents converged in a way that made the Revolution a truly national upheaval. By 1792, moreover, the agitation produced by the revolution from below turned the dynamic element of leadership within the bourgeois elite in a more radical, "Jacobin" direction. The principal places of Lefebvre's mnemonic scheme, therefore, were moments of conjuncture, in which social tensions erupted into open conflict. The personalities and events that had served Michelet and Aulard as places of memory were displaced by these revolutionary *journées,* reidentified by Lefebvre with antagonisms within the social structure.

There was also a temporal dimension to Lefebvre's mnemonic scheme, for he argued that the Revolution unfolded in two stages. There was a liberal revolution of 1789, identified especially with the aspirations of the bourgeoisie. But there was also a second revolution of August 1792 that set forth the Jacobin agenda for social democracy. Though leadership for this phase of the Revolution remained bourgeois, it was sustained by popular forces, in effect Michelet's "people," now defined with greater scholarly precision. The "people," of course, had been a poetic category of epic proportions for Michelet; for Aulard the image of the people was mnemonically recoded as one of the Jacobins, a more prosaic term to specify a more practical group of leaders operating through a network of clubs. Lefebvre reconceptualized the notion of the people as images of distinct social classes—peasants and *sans culottes*—and explained how different were their motives and objectives from those of the bourgeois leadership.[67] With the fall of the Jacobin leaders in 1794, popular enthusiasm for the Revolution began to wane and accordingly the creative phase of the Revolution, identified by Lefebvre as socially driven political change, came to a close.

The differences in the use of imagery by these three historians may be illustrated by extending the comparison of leading figures of the Revolution, such as Danton, about whom all three ventured profiles. Lefebvre acknowledged the difference a single individual could make in altering the course of historical events. But in the wider scheme in which he placed the Revolution, there were limits to what even the most able leaders might accomplish. In Lefebvre's scheme, they were obliged to settle for diminished stature. For Michelet, for example, Danton had been the avatar of Jacobinism; for Aulard, he had been the hero of the Jacobin cause. For Lefebvre, he was only the leader of a faction, albeit one with heavy responsibilities, but one who displayed a complex mix of strengths and weaknesses.[68] In the end, Lefebvre suggests, Danton was done in by his venality, and for this reason he is less worthy of remembrance than his "incorruptible" rival, Maximilien Robespierre, who, following his rehabilitation by Mathiez, was elevated by Lefebvre to the status of what Pierre Nora has since characterized as an *homme mémoire.*[69]

This comparison of mnemonic conceptions may be extended to revolutionary festivals. For Michelet, they had been epiphanies lifting the revolution to spiritual heights that transcended the specific pattern of events in which they were situated.[70] Aulard demythologized the festivals but nonetheless underscored their symbolic significance in the political strategies of Jacobin leaders. In considering the leading events of the popular revolution, Lefebvre may be said to have further reduced quasi-religious symbolism to secular psychology. What Michelet had thought of as commemorative revolutionary festivals were characterized by Lefebvre as activist revolutionary *journées*. Michelet's suspended moments in time were Lefebvre's turning points in history. The days of the popular revolution that Lefebvre recalls in *Quatre-vingt-neuf* are not Michelet's days of peaceful celebration, nor Aulard's of official commemoration, but rather the days of insurrectionary violence: 14–15 July, 4 August, and 5–6 October. These are the principal places of memory on the timeline of the history of the Revolution of 1789, dramatic moments that reveal the conjuncture of the social, economic, and political forces of the revolution from below.[71] Not that Lefebvre dealt with them in a romantic way. Far more than Michelet, he analyzed the complexity of the intentions of the participants, pointing out differences in attitudes within the same social classes. He looked for the rational motives that inspired the passions of the crowd, and he showed sensitivity to the mixed, often contradictory incentives for popular insurrection.[72]

Just as Aulard had played a key role in the centennial, so Lefebvre played a corresponding one in the sesquicentennial. The conditions of the commemoration, of course, were quite different. In 1889, republicans rallied to the celebration as a way of fending off the somewhat farcical challenge to the government posed by General Georges Boulanger. But the 150th anniversary was carried out under the shadow of a more menacing Nazi aggression. In the summer of 1939, Europe was on the brink of war, and within France itself, republican politicians were divided about how best to deal with the Nazi threat. The commemorative events of 1939, therefore, lacked the fanfare and exuberance of 1889, and certainly its trappings of republican solidarity.[73] The collaboration of historians and politicians in the making of the earlier commemoration had also disappeared. For the historians, the sesquicentennial was observed apart as an occasion for the exchange of professional research. Lefebvre was a key figure in the organization of the historical conference convened to mark the event. There he dedicated himself to overseeing the collation of further documentation concerning the Revolution.[74]

If 1939 lacked festiveness, however, it was significant as the occasion for which Lefebvre wrote his *Quatre-vingt-neuf,* perhaps the most famous and admired work of synthesis on the Revolution ever published. Lefebvre's book reflects the tenor of the times. Though it is a work that emphasizes the power of economic and social forces to shape history, it concludes with a paean to the Declaration of the Rights of Man and Citizen. His closing paragraph (excised from the American historian Robert R. Palmer's better known English translation) was a rallying cry to safeguard its legacy: "Youth of 1939!" he exhorted. "The Declaration is a tradition, and a glorious one. In reading it, listen for the voices of our ancestors speaking to you, those who fought at Valmy, at Jemappes, at Fleuris to the cry of 'long live the Nation!'"[75] In recollecting the struggle for liberty through the Revolution, Lefebvre delivered an apostrophe to his fellow citizens concerning the immediate threat to their own. As such it operated as a screen memory for the republican cause during the reactionary days of Vichy and explains why that regime sought to ban the book's distribution. Nor is it surprising that Lefebvre's book, renamed in translation by Palmer as *The Coming of the French Revolution* (1947), should have served as a place of memory for the coming of the Fourth Republic, for there was in its early days much discussion of the nature of French democracy by historians and politicians alike as they looked back upon a revolutionary heritage in charting a new course.[76]

In the end, Lefebvre himself became an *homme mémoire*, for his work guided a generation of historians to the memorable events of the French Revolution. His scholarship epitomizes an historiographical tradition that he helped to found and to which he lent scholarly respectability. Beloved by his students and colleagues for the deep humanism of his scholarly endeavor, he was presented with a collection of his major essays on the occasion of his eightieth birthday (1954), and the *Annales historiques* has since published issues commemorating his work on the first, tenth, twentieth, and twenty-fifth anniversaries of his death.[77] In recasting the framework in which the Revolution was remembered, Lefebvre's model of the dynamics of the French Revolution and of its reverberations throughout world history over the following century shaped not only the history but also the memory of that event. It set the stage for a consideration of its place in world history—both as a prototype for modern revolutions and as a source of values and political practices. With Jacques Godechot and Robert Palmer, the Revolution as an "Atlantic" phenomenon became a major topic of study.[78]

By the mid-1970s, however, attachments to the revolutionary tradition as a framework for French historiography were being thoroughly challenged. It is ironical that Lefebvre, who sought to retrieve the memory of the forgotten revolution from below, should himself in our own times be accused of sponsoring a commemorative approach to the study of the Revolution that needs to be set aside. The challenge was first raised in the early 1950s by the English historian Alfred Cobban, who questioned whether one could speak of the French Revolution as a unified series of events. He pointed out that the leaders of the Revolution were not easily distinguished from those of the Old Regime in terms of their social background. Social change may have been real, Cobban conceded, but it was more gradual and complex than Lefebvre implied in his claims about a dramatic social revolution in the late eighteenth century. In that sense, Cobban argued, the "idea that there was *a* French Revolution, which you can be for or against" was a myth.[79] Cobban's criticism forced Lefebvre to ponder his thesis in a way that highlights his position on the memory/history problem. In replying to Cobban, he reaffirmed the importance of social considerations in making sense of the event. But in the end, he agreed that the revolution was a myth—not a fiction as Cobban suggested, but a commemorative conception on which the moral convictions of revolutionary leaders were based. It was these convictions that posterity remembered as it tried to fulfill the ideals of the Revolution.[80]

Setting interpretative preferences aside, what the Cobban/Lefebvre debate signaled was the waning of the revolutionary tradition as a frame of reference for French historiography. The debate continued through the 1960s, with Palmer taking up Lefebvre's side.[81] But by the mid-1970s, the challenge to French revolutionary historiography as a commemorative tradition was being raised by French historians as well. Lefebvre and his followers (notably Palmer, George Rude, and Albert Soboul), therefore, may be considered the last generation of historians to conceive of themselves as in some sense bearers of the living memory of the revolutionary tradition. To the opponents of this "commemorative" approach to history, memory remained a visible, indeed a self-conscious, issue, even as they approached it from a critical stance.

François Furet: Deconstructing Revolutionary Discourse

François Furet (1927–   ) may not enjoy the adoration still bestowed on Michelet, the deference once given Aulard, or the homage until recently accorded Lefebvre, but he is today the historian whose interpretation invites the most comment.[82] For him, the historiography associated with the revolutionary tradition is neither a source of inspiration nor an object of commemorative respect. Rather it has become a burden. "We must try to break the vicious circle of that commemorative historiography," he complains.[83] Furet is especially known for his essay *Penser la Révolution française,* which first appeared in 1978. Michelet was immersed in the revolutionary tradition; Aulard still honored it, Lefebvre expanded on its significance; Furet, by contrast, would like to write its requiem. As a commemoration of the rising of the people, he declares, "the Revolution is over."[84]

Furet has enjoyed a distinguished academic career. A graduate of the Sorbonne, he has taught for more than thirty years at the *Ecole pratique des hautes études,* a center for research that has been associated with the innovative scholarship of *Annales* historiography. In 1966 he was appointed director of studies, and he served as president of that institution from 1977 to 1985. His association with the *Ecole* gave him a scholarly independence more difficult to exercise within the regular university system, and he has used it to advantage to open new paths of historical inquiry. Because of his international scholarly prestige, he has also held a professorship at the University of Chicago since 1985.[85] Much of Furet's reputation rests on his revisionist interpretation of the French Revolution. But he has also written important studies on the history of the rise of literacy in modern France, and his historiographical interests connect with the postmodern perspectives that we have identified with a number of scholars of the memory/history problem.[86]

Michelet looked to Vico for the key to the workings of history; Aulard looked to Comte; Lefebvre took Jaurès as his intellectual mentor. Furet's guide is Alexis de Tocqueville, pointedly portrayed as Michelet's rival in setting the course for the historiography of the Revolution.[87] In his *L'Ancien Régime et la Révolution* (1856), Tocqueville minimized the significance of the Revolution as a social upheaval and hence of the efficacy of its popular insurrections, the very factors highlighted by the nineteenth-century revolutionary tradition. Instead, he traced the long-range trends that contributed to the making of the modern state, notably the centralization of political power in the agencies of the monarchy and the corresponding decline in the countervailing authority of local notables. His thesis is that the changes that the French Revolution revealed had been accomplished before the event transpired. The popular uprisings of the Revolution, so stirring in their drama, were inconsequential in their effects. Considered in the broader view, he argued, the Revolution concerned the consolidation of the power of the modern state, not the making of a social revolution.[88]

By adopting Tocqueville's focus on state power rather than on popular insurrection, Furet was able to disassociate himself from the historiographical tradition launched by Michelet and given scholarly authority by Aulard and his successors. Tocqueville enabled him to place his own work within an alternative historiographical framework, one that valued the libertarian (Orleanist) rather than the republican (Jacobin) strand of the revolutionary tradition. But he was still obliged to explain why the memory of the rising of the people had contributed so powerfully to the historiography of the Revolution. He therefore complements his exegesis of Tocqueville with another of Augustin Cochin, a largely forgotten historian of the early twentieth century who analyzed the subversive effects of the rhetoric of the Jacobin societies. Cochin proposed that Jacobinism was a new way of talking about politics. It was, moreover, a rhetoric that filled the power vacuum left by a crumbling monarchy. The collapse of royal authority in 1789 permitted the emergence of an imaginary political discourse that had been created within the philosophical and literary societies that had sprouted and flourished since midcentury. Jacobinism's power to shape public opinion lay in its mode of parlance.[89]

This was a proposition well-suited to the deconstructionist tenor of Furet's argument, and it was in this sense that he described Jacobinism as one of the Revolution's most important legacies. What had been for Michelet a memory incarnate in the revolutionary tradition, or for Aulard the remembrance of a party's struggle to prepare the way for a new regime, became for Furet a vocabulary that encoded a moral agenda for the political discussions of the future. By bracketing the issue of the values and commitments that Jacobinism implied, Furet was able to put his emphasis on its rhetorical forms and so to deemphasize its moral authority as an ideology. The political imagination of Jacobinism, therefore, shaped the collective memory of the Revolution in the nineteenth century. That memory, in turn, established the foundations for republican historiography, laid out by Michelet and Aulard and perpetuated into the twentieth century in an expanded but only slightly altered form by such eminent historians as Mathiez, Lefebvre, and Albert Soboul.[90] In Furet's view, therefore, the Revolution was more important for the symbolic political language it invented than for the social transformation with which it is typically credited in the historiography identified with the revolutionary tradition. History for Michelet concerned the sustaining of tradition; for Aulard it meant consecrating its events; for Lefebvre it entailed mindfulness of its larger promise; for Furet, by contrast, it demanded the deconstruction of the commemorative forms in which the history of the Revolution had been enshrined by this republican historiography.[91] In severing his ties with a tradition of historiography that traced its lineage to Michelet, he likewise banished the enthusiasms that had animated it along the way.

Furet's *Penser la Révolution française* was meant to be provocative, and in the process he may have overstated his case. The logic of his argument, with its special attention to the power of an imaginary Jacobin discourse, was close to the one that led Foucault to repudiate tradition altogether. In 1983, with the bicentenary of the Revolution approaching, Maurice Agulhon queried Furet about the implications of his critique of commemorative historiography for historians who might wish to honor that event.[92] Far from repudiating the revolutionary tradition, Furet replied, he wanted only to separate consideration of its liberal from its Jacobin strand, a distinction all but obliterated in the official memory of the Revolution as an event unified by a moral ideal deeper than particular ideological allegiances. He pointed out how bizarre he found a situation in which an "imaginary discourse of power" had come to dominate contemporary historiographical thinking about the Revolution. The Jacobin values of groups that had been of peripheral importance in the revolutionary era itself had become the focus of scholarly research, whereas the liberal ideals of the group most central to the experience, the bourgeoisie, were largely ignored. For the bicentennial, Furet explained, he wanted only to widen the discussion of interpretive issues so that the nineteenth-century liberal tradition of historiography (Adolphe Thiers, Auguste Mignet, François Guizot, and Edgar Quinet), obscured by the dominant Jacobin one of the twentieth (Mathiez, Lefebvre, Soboul), might once again receive its due.[93]

Lefebvre, of course, had justified his interest in the "revolution from below" with the claim that the Jacobin tradition had been forgotten in nineteenth-century historiography. But Furet remembered it differently, or rather, he countered that the way in which the French Revolution is remembered depends on the way in which its imagination is represented. His main point was that Jacobinism, framed as an imaginary discourse about the meaning of the French Revolution, had taken exclusive possession of the historians' memory of the event. From an historiographical perspective, he argued, the memory of the French Revolution since Aulard had been remodeled in a way that marginalized its most concrete and enduring accomplishments.[94]

The politics of memory was obviously at the center of Furet's concerns. In his seminar at the *Ecole pratique des hautes études* during the 1980s, therefore, he pondered, discussed, and refined his ideas about the "imaginary discourse of power." It is significant, I think, that for the bicentennial itself, Furet (together with his colleague Mona Ozouf) produced a dictionary of the French Revolution, thereby becoming the intellectual broker for our age of the rhetoric that had attended the making of that event. More than a lexicon of terms, Furet's dictionary provided an intellectually sophisticated exploration of the historiographical imagination of the event, useful not only for understanding the rhetoric of the Revolution but also that of the traditions it has inspired.[95]

Poignant in this respect is his article on the "university history" of the Revolution, which, he contended, had made of revolutionary historiography a rather limited and sanctimonious affair. Philosophical issues of the sort that gifted generalists of the nineteenth century had raised about the interpretation of the meaning of the Revolution were set aside in favor of an official interpretation accepted by modern-day university professors, who consoled themselves with problems of specialized research. Ironically, he points out, the professionalization of the historiography of the Revolution eventually led to the canonization of the Jacobin interpretation, which, if viewed in the passage from Mathiez to Lefebvre to Soboul, was explicated in ever more schematic terms. Furet chided his colleagues for their lack of imagination in clinging to a paradigm that required the manipulation of recent demographic, cultural, and economic findings that just did not fit a framework that featured class struggle. Epitomized in Lefebvre's proposition that modern history is guided by a "direction of moral intention," the interpretation advanced by these historians failed to consider the alternative forces that had successfully worked at cross-purposes. The official memory of the Revolution, Furet argued, constrained the imaginative possibilities for alternative interpretations that the event offered.[96]

In identifying the imaginary discourse of power as the central historiographical problem of the Revolution for our time, Furet offered a more refined version of the problem of the myth of the Revolution raised by Cobban and briefly considered by Lefebvre. In his dictionary, he commented on how the historians that we have discussed represented the revolutionary imagination and, so, lent depth to his sometimes cursory judgments on them in *Penser la Révolution française*. Herein he expressed a sympathy for Michelet largely absent in that earlier study. If the debate about the meaning of the French Revolution is primarily about the "mental representations" that gave it unity, he observed, then no one expressed these better than did Michelet. It was he who blocked out the evocative images that have since adorned the places of memory associated with the Jacobin tradition of historiography.[97] He portrays Aulard, in turn, as a prodigious researcher, who set the style for the professionalization of historical writing about the Revolution. Aulard, he suggests, was obsessed with the search for original documents. Furet characterizes him as a textualist, noting that the primary reference points of his history are not insurrectionary events but political documents—the debates of the represe⟨ for example, or the constitutional decrees. The leaders of ⟨ have fallen short of their own ideals. But the ideals them official documents, survived to inspire posterity. Aul opened the way for the more schematic interpretation of the Kev⟨ sued by his successors. From Mathiez to Soboul via Lefebvre, the trend toward more exacting documentation proceeded in parallel track with the streamlining of interpretative design.[98]

But it is Lefebvre's memorable stature that Furet would most substantially reduce and revise. He admired Lefebvre's study of the peasantry for his solid research on and careful judgments about the complexity of its predicament. But the historian so lionized by his disciples for the grandeur of his larger scheme of the Revolution's place in history is portrayed by Furet as surprisingly narrow in his preoccupations. In Furet's eyes, Lefebvre had become the guardian of a memory of the Revolution so thoroughly remodeled to conform to Jacobin and subsequently communist expectations that it has little value today for understanding the nature of the event. When Lefebvre's mantle of official approbation is removed, Furet contends, he appears not as the grand interpreter of the Revolution but only as a specialist on a grand scale. His much-praised overview of the Revolution served a commemorative role that pleased his disciples but led him to ignore a range of interpretative questions begging for answers.[99]

Furet's interest in the power of imaginary discourse and the implications that he draws from that notion are wonderfully illustrative of the way in which a tradition meets its demise. Moreover, his work sheds light on the memory/ history problem from the postmodern perspective. In arguing that the "French Revolution is over," Furet was contending that the Jacobin tradition of French revolutionary historiography had run its course. But like nearly all of the students of historiographical traditions that we have encountered, Furet is loath to deny the value of tradition itself. In his reconsideration of the historiography of the French Revolution, he is looking for the hidden traditions that historians may have too hastily set aside. His is a plea for the imaginative interpretation of the data so obsessively gathered by academic historians. Historians must be reflective about issues, he suggests, and it is their familiarity with many traditions that makes intelligent reflection possible.

Pierre Nora: The Archaeology of the French National Memory

There is still one more historian I wish to consider, and from a theoretical perspective he is in some ways the most important of all. I am referring to Pierre Nora (1931–   ), the French scholar and publisher. An editor of Gallimard Press and of the magazine of commentary *Le Débat,* he is best known

...ay as the editor of *Les Lieux de mémoire* (1984–92), which might be characterized as a practical guide for probing the deep structures of the French national memory.[100] A professor at the *Ecole pratique des hautes études,* he conducted a seminar in the late 1970s dealing with the topic of collective memory.[101] One product of his endeavor was this multivolume anthology, to which some forty-five of France's most eminent historians have contributed. A contemporary of Furet, he draws the theoretical implications of Furet's argument and applies them to the contemporary historiographical scene. With Nora, the postmodern perspective on the memory/history problem comes more clearly into view.

Les Lieux was written at the bicentenary of the Revolution but not exactly for its bicentennial. Focused on the national memory in the largest sense, it displaces the Revolution from its privileged place in French historiography. At the bicentenary of the Revolution, Nora suggests, the French identity is not as securely grounded in the revolutionary tradition as it was even a generation before. The Revolution no longer resonates in the collective memory of the French in the way it once did, for it is no longer perceived to be the central event in the making of the contemporary French identity. The past on which the French might draw today opens on a broader prospect of both past and future. There are lost traditions to uncover if the full range of her past identity is to come to light. As the French look to the future, moreover, they may choose to reshape their national identity in ways that will invite an appreciation of their past in other contexts.[102]

How then is this national memory to be construed for the contemporary age? Nora and his colleagues set for themselves the task of locating the places of the French memory as they have been elaborated over the centuries. Nora borrows the term from Frances Yates but uses it in a somewhat different way.[103] He conceives of these places as sites that once did but no longer provide direct access to living traditions. Today they evoke only intimations of what these traditions may have been like. "One looks for places of memory because there are no longer milieux of memory," Nora comments.[104] As he explains in an apt metaphor, contemporary historiography "operates primarily by introducing doubt, by running a knife between the tree of memory and the bark of history" in an effort to figure out how the two were originally joined.[105] To that end, Nora and his colleagues inventory the formal outworks of the national memory—commemorative monuments and shrines, national histories, civics manuals and history textbooks, public archives and museums that have been produced in the name of a French identity since the Middle Ages. "It is no longer genesis that we seek," Nora comments, "but rather the deciphering of who we are in light of who we are no longer."[106]

Nora coordinates the project with essays of his own. His introductory essay, "Between Memory and History," deals with the larger theoretical issues raised by the project, and he adopts a meditative stance. What Nora seems to be marking is the death of the traditions that served as the inspiration for the writing of modern French history. Although modern history plotted a course of events that moved in new directions, it nonetheless strove to maintain empathetic connections with the traditions from which it issued. In modern history, he asserts, the bonds between the milieux of inwardly experienced values and the places of their external commemoration were solidly joined. Postmodern history, by contrast, proceeds from the recognition that these ties have been broken. The postmodern historian, therefore, has only the residues of memory left at these places as a basis for inquiring into the past. History ceases to be a mnemonic reconstruction and becomes instead an archaeological deconstruction. There is, accordingly, a poetic quality to Nora's prose, reminiscent of Michelet, but by contrast solemn and accepting. As a consequence, his essay displays a subtle nostalgia, not for a particular past but for a time of innocence when unreflective attachments to tradition were still possible. Where memory is concerned, he notes, "the true sadness is to suffer no longer from what one has suffered so much, and henceforth to understand only with the mind's reason, no longer with the unreason of the heart."[107] It is such sentiments that give his work a postmodern signature.

In this respect, Foucault's method is clearly more important than Yates's title for understanding the nature of Nora's project. Rather than historical reconstruction as it is ordinarily conceived, Nora engages in genealogical deconstruction of the sort that Foucault popularized. In his scheme for surveying the national memory, Nora effectively reverses Comte's model of history's advance through progressive stages toward positive (i.e., certain) knowledge. The representations of the past rather than its events provide his main interest. Images, not facts, serve as his historical currency. The genealogical tree of knowledge branches backward, not forward. Like Foucault, Nora and his colleagues proceed from the present into the past: from the places of memory significant in the making of the self-image of the Third Republic in the late nineteenth century (vol. 1), to the milieux of memory out of which the image of the nation was formed in the early modern period (vol. 2), toward the wider collective memory of the traditional French society of the Middle Ages (in a third volume just published).[108] In the process, the significance of the revolutionary tradition is diminished, for it is only one stratum among many in the national memory unearthed in this archaeological probe.

In his larger conceptualization of the memory/history problem, Nora would seem to be placing modern history on a continuum between oral tradition and postmodern historiography. His thesis is that modern history attempted to take possession of collective memory. In the process, memory was transformed but so too was history. What he describes as "true" memory, that is, memory as it was traditionally understood, concerns the habits, customs, and folk wisdom that were passed unreflectively from generation to generation. It is the memory of oral tradition. It was a self-renewing resource on which traditional French society continually drew. But as memory was incorporated into modern history, its inner voice grew weaker. In the guise of history, memory was seen rather than heard in the visible forms bequeathed to the present age. Nora's point is that in taking possession of memory history materialized it. This is evinced in nineteenth-century historiography, which made of the document, particularly the state paper, a privileged form of evidence. In consulting documents, modern historians thought of themselves as accumulating knowledge, whereas in fact they were only exploring contexts: the places of memory where connections with the past had been encoded in documentary form. In other words, documentation shaped the way the past was to be remembered. Comte's formula was reversed. One does not discover objective knowledge in data. Rather data cue particular reminiscences. Were it not for the vast documentation accumulated in public archives during the revolutionary era, Nora argues, the history of the Revolution invented by its nineteenth-century practitioners would have been impossible to produce. These historians were unwittingly memorialists, and the conservation, organization, and preservation of documents in the archives preconditioned the nature of the past they would recall.[109]

Herein we may better appreciate Nora's particular interest in Ernest Lavisse, the most influential writer of textbooks in French history in the nineteenth century. In contrast with the modern historians of the Revolution that we have considered (from Michelet to Lefebvre), Nora views his historiographical mentor not as a guide but as a target for critical analysis. He uses Lavisse as an example with which to expound on the nature of modern history from the postmodern perspective of memory. Nora presents Lavisse as the typical nineteenth-century positivist historian. He is a key figure in the distillation of the manuscript sources found in the archives into the readily accessible interpretations provided in printed texts. He is a well-remembered historian neither for his particular insights nor his style but rather for his contribution to the encoding of the national memory in the published accounts of the French past that shaped the memory of several generations of French citizens. Lavisse used his powers of patronage authoritatively. He gathered about him an entourage of loyal students who aided him in his research. For his eighteen-volume history of France, he enlisted the support of some nineteen eminent academicians, and he oversaw their research and writing with meticulous care.[110] Lavisse and his team of researchers thought that their work was grounded in science and that they were writing a history that would endure. But Nora shows how it was actually grounded in a particular memory of national origins that is fast losing its meaning for the contemporary age. These historians naively joined the scientific with the sentimental and, so, constructed a well-documented but nonetheless nostalgic view of the way in which France as a modern nation had been formed.[111]

The weight of memory today, Nora would contend, is not in its moral influences but in its material leavings. For him, the archive is the modern memory palace, a physical place where material records were from the eighteenth century piled up at an accelerating rate. The memory palace of oral tradition, it may be recalled, had been an imaginary construct in which the memorialist interiorized factual knowledge by attaching it to imagery. In the modern age, however, the memory palace that is the archive became a tangible presence in which historians externalized the past they wanted to remember. It was a repository not of mores, values, and dreams but of inert artifacts, a place where they entombed memories that rarely sustained them in real ways but which they felt impelled to stock anyway. It was, moreover, a proliferating enterprise. Nora points to the paradox that modern society, more future oriented and less dependent on the past for its identity, nonetheless felt obliged to materialize its memory in every possible way. As editor of *Les Lieux de mémoire,* he uses this proposition as the foundation of his project to expose the hidden material structure of the French national memory. He absorbs the problem of documentation into a broader inquiry into the nature of the memorabilia that have shaped modern historical thinking. The document was the quintessential form through which the modern historian remembered the past. But postmodern historians such as Nora place the document among the countless artifacts in which memory has been materialized. They shift the emphasis from documents themselves to the architectural places of memory in which they and other memorabilia are contained—in archives, museums, commemorative monuments. As historians today become more aware of memory's many forms, he suggests, history reappears as a vast dispersion of representations that lead into a postmodern domain.[112]

Nora points out, however, that this trend toward the exteriorization of memory in its formal representations has also called into being a deepening interiorization. He locates the emergence of this process about the turn of the century in the work of Henri Bergson and particularly Sigmund Freud. The exteriorization of collective memory in public institutions designed to store them is complemented by the deepening interiorization of individual memory. In an age in which the collective identities of traditional society, especially those of family, church, and nation, were disintegrating, the individual felt the need to search his own memory for some surer sense of personal identity.

Just as society materializes its memory, Nora argues, so the individual feels the need to interiorize it. As collective memory is exteriorized, there are fewer values that individuals sense to be shared in their inner lives. Hence interiorization becomes a more isolated, private affair. It is a means of protecting personal identity in a setting in which there are fewer social cues. Individual memories, Nora suggests, surface in the interstices of broken collective memories. Amidst the remnants of the collective memories of family, church, and nation, the individual forges his identity by historicizing his own memory. Nora's remarks confirm our earlier observations on the nature of autobiographical memory. The process of interiorization leads at once to the intensification of private memories and to the attenuation of public ones. This resulting self-consciousness colors the historians' perspective, despite their public calling. Everyone is his own historian because everyone cultivates his personal memories. Hence historians, once self-effacing as the spokesmen for an enterprise that was collectively understood, strive to assert their individual identities as witnesses to their age, as if their individual memory, unsustained by collective allegiances, must now serve as the basis for history.[113]

Thus the balance between the moments of memory—its repetitions and its recollections—is maintained even in the historical perspective of postmodern memory. In one sense, Nora's *Les Lieux de mémoire* would appear to be a work of deconstruction. He and his colleagues survey the deep structures of the past through an examination of cultural artifacts whose identification with living memory has all but disappeared. Places of memory are like "moments of history torn away from the movement of history, then returned. No longer quite alive, not yet dead, they are like seashells on the shore from which the sea of living memory has retreated," Nora remarks in a telling simile.[114] In another sense, however, his study underscores the recurrent power of memory's promptings, as if with the turning of the tide the sea comes rushing back to the shore. In descending into the past following Nora's guidelines, the reader encounters traditions that once carried living memory forward into the present. If we in a later age are no longer able to identify with the commitments of these traditions, we may still try to acquire a sympathetic understanding of the way in which they inspired the historians of an earlier age. Making sense of the content of tradition is an important part of historiographical assessment, an element neglected in the poststructuralist focus on tradition's forms.

In this respect, it is worth noting that Nora characterizes history as a crossroads between tradition and historiography.[115] The analogy is suggestive, for it provides a context for assessing the role of memory in the writings of the historians under discussion. Crossing forward from Michelet to Furet, the historiography of the Revolution appears to trace the long-range waning of enthusiasm for its events and personalities as these have shaped our commitments in the present. The values that Michelet openly extolled through an appeal to memory Aulard disguised by cloaking his commemorative history in the mantle of science.[116] Furet would remove the mantle, but only to expose the memory, not to embrace it. In his view, the interpretation of the twentieth-century historians Mathiez and Lefebvre proceeds from the same commemorative assumptions as did that of Aulard. The ideological connections that they would preserve with the revolutionary tradition, Furet would sever in his analysis of the way in which the rhetoric of the Revolution constitutes its history.

Such a reading may not dismiss the importance of memory's power, but it does focus on only one of its dimensions: that of recollection to the exclusion of that of repetition. In Furet's view, memory is important not for the way in which it inspires historians to engage in their enterprise but rather for the way in which it shapes their conceptions. The politics of memory, conceived as the power of habits of mind issuing from the past to influence the present, is ignored in favor of the politics of memory reconceived as a self-conscious strategy for projecting images of the past into projects for the future. In analyzing the historiography emanating from the revolutionary tradition in terms of its rhetoric, Furet discards consideration of the ideals that the Revolution bequeathed to posterity and so contributes to an amnesia about the meaning of the event. Forgetful of the commitments that impassioned its participants, the history of the Revolution becomes a congeries of rhetorical constructs, monuments to the political strategies of its historians, but remote from us in all save what we might learn about the realities of power in historiographical conceptualization.

Crossing back from Furet to Aulard to Michelet, however, the historiography of the Revolution appears to have been empowered by a tradition that carried the commitments of its participants out of the past into the historian's field of vision. In the genealogical return toward the places of memory of the Revolution, the dispassion of Furet yields to the sentimentality of Aulard, then builds toward the fervor of Michelet. As Vico suggested to Michelet in his discussion of the cycle of memory in the nations of antiquity, memory must be conceived in terms of its repetitions as well as its recollections. A nation that has lost contact with its past must return to its places of memory once more in search of its identity. Places of memory are sources of inspiration. They contain the secrets of the commitments of historical actors, not to mention those of the historians who have sought to describe them. These were the wellsprings that Michelet wished to tap, and his efforts to do so suggest the basis of the respect he still enjoys. Today's historians may not wish to commemorate the past. But a historiography that dismisses the significance of tradition for understanding the passions of the past is likely to lose its appeal to posterity. The influence of the revolutionary tradition may have waned, for historiography today as it did for politics a century ago. But the historical writings emanating from that tradition remain themselves places of the memory of the Revolution. To overlook their power to reveal the meaning that the Revolution held for its participants in order to underscore their power to shape the form of its commemoration would be to deprive the event itself of its enduring appeal.

8

HISTORY AT THE CROSSROADS
OF MEMORY

Places Where Thoughts about Memory Converge

In the opening passages of his *Stages on Life's Way* (1845), the Danish philosopher Søren Kierkegaard offered a meditation on one of his own favorite place of meditation, the Nook of Eight Paths, a secluded spot not far from Copenhagen.[1] His description of the spot is full of the paradoxes so characteristic of his existential philosophy. The Nook was an isolated spot, yet one where eight roads met. Though it was a place for concourse, little traffic passed that way, and one rarely encountered other people there. In Kierkegaard's mind it was better suited for the circulation of ideas, and it was to this place that he retreated to reflect on the crossing perspectives of the pseudonymous personae in which he had earlier masked the authorship of his various writings. At the Nook, he sorted out these perspectives as if they were places of memory that marked the stages on his own journey as a poet toward religious understanding. As a place for memory, the Nook served as the setting for one of his most beautiful meditations on the subject. In this passage, Kierkegaard contrasted two conceptions of memory, viewed from opposite ends of a lifetime: the child's memory and the old man's recollection. The former concerns the child's apprehension. It is imaginative in the sense of Vico's primordial poets: quick, spontaneous, unreflective, and happy. The latter concerns the old man's reminiscences. It is reflective in the sense of Wordsworth's autobiographical musings: slower, more deliberate, meditative, and sad. The child's memory is filled with the myriad possibilities of present imagination, but in the old man's reminiscences only a few significant events stand out. Memory inspires the child's play, whereas recollection commemorates the old man's most cherished accomplishments. The child's vision is short-sighted; its outlines are blurred in the abundance of its interests. But the old man's recollections are more far-sighted, sharply etched in their focus on a few salient images out of the distant past, now perceived as in a distorted mirror. These moments of memory drawn from opposite ends of life's perceptions sustain one another, Kierkegaard argued, like the crossing paths of the Nook. The characteristics of memory's polarities stand out when viewed from the vantage point of life's extremes. But in the prime of life they merge, enriching one's understanding of past and future.

The Nook of Eight Paths was Kierkegaard's place of memory, but it can easily serve as our own. As the mnemonists of old taught, such places may be filled with interchangeable images. In the course of this study, we have considered eight paths between memory and history: mnemonic (Frances Yates); rhetorical (Giambattista Vico); autobiographical (William Wordsworth); psychological (Sigmund Freud); sociological (Maurice Halbwachs); historical (Philippe Ariès); archaeological (Michel Foucault); and historiographical (the French Revolution). For each, we have explored the relationship between memory and history in terms of the antinomies that Kierkegaard described so poetically. For each, however, we have tried to show how the mix between the two moments of memory varies and how in the present age that relationship has become obscure. Kierkegaard's exploration of the antinomies of memory was philosophical, but it mirrors the conceptions of nineteenth-century historians about the complementary relationship between memory and history. In their elaboration of a modern historiography, memory and history were meant to converge.

Autobiography as a genre helps us to see the connection between memory and history in modern historiography because it is life history written from the perspective of recollection with a view to recapturing the sources of inspiration in earlier stages of our lives. Reconceived in the late eighteenth century by Jean-Jacques Rousseau and William Wordsworth as the adult's reflections on the process of his self-fashioning, it became an art form that drew history and memory together. It lured the adult back toward his beginnings by giving conscious expression to the imperatives for self-analysis to which the culture of the eighteenth century had in so many ways become attuned. In its modern guise, autobiographical soul-searching contributed to the rise of the notion of the developing self. Increasingly aware of the way in which their minds were being transformed through a process of personal, psychological growth, individuals became fascinated with the stages left behind along the way. To revisit the early stages of one's life, particularly childhood, was to renew the connections with the sources of one's personal identity. Autobiography employed introspective techniques but underscored the historical character of each individual's formation. That is the particular importance of *The Prelude* of William Wordsworth. His notion of spots of time highlights the way in which the two moments of memory interacted in the writing of his own life history. It reflects the newfound sense of history of the modern age, one that owes a considerable debt to an emerging notion of the developing self.

From the vantage point of the memory/history problem, therefore, the autobiographical writings of Wordsworth are not so far removed from the masterworks of nineteenth-century historiography.[2] Wordsworth's sense of the crossing perspectives of two moments of memory, imagination and rec-ollection, parallels that of modern historiography. Historicism was the term that philosophers coined to characterize the relationship between memory and history as they became more reflective about their interaction in historical understanding. As a theory of history, it entailed a rethinking of the memory/history relationship because it presented the historian's task as one of recre-ating the imagination of the past for a world that acknowledged that there could be no repetition of its events. It drew the implications of a dawning awareness in the eighteenth and nineteenth centuries of the historicity of the human condition—an awareness that the past is a separate reality, forever re-moved from the present in time. In traditional societies, the past was contin-ually being updated in living memory, and imagination and memory were perceived to be interchangeable. One lived continually in the presence of the past. Events in the present were perceived to mimic timeless archetypes. As the historian of religion Mircea Eliade has argued, history in the ancient world was conceived in cyclical terms, as actors in the present sought to pursue their lives as had their ancestors *in illo tempore*.[3] The move into modern historical understanding opened a divide between past and present and, so, between apprehension and recollection. In this modern historical perspective, every event is situated at a particular time and place, for an historical event happens but once and for all time. In light of this conception of the past, the interest of the historian shifted from an appreciation of the edifying lessons the past may teach to an understanding of the way by which we have come to be who we are in this present time and place. Historicism, therefore, was a conception of historical understanding that stressed the concrete nature of historical knowledge. The historian sought to understand specific events and their par-ticular sequence in an emerging temporal pattern. In this view, history was a special kind of science that enabled historians to extend their vision beyond living memory's horizons. Whereas the science of nature stressed the timeless properties of its data, the science of history stressed the timefulness of all human endeavor.

The nineteenth-century historians identified with the historicist perspec-tive, therefore, aspired to reconstruct a past that surpassed living memory, but at the same time to place their fondest memories in historical perspective. Indeed, they believed that their task as historians was to nurture them. Thereby they hoped to maintain the connection between accomplishments in a hollowed past and present needs, while acknowledging the distance between them. As Philippe Ariès has shown, the masterworks of nineteenth-century historiography were often constructed around the political history of the de-veloping nation-state, and the interpretations that they expressed were ulti-mately grounded in the need to recollect inspiring origins and monumental stages along the way.[4] Such historians debated how the return to the imagination of these sacred origins could be accomplished. As we have noted in our chapter on French revolutionary historiography, Jules Michelet was one among a few early-nineteenth-century historians who still believed that the past could be resurrected in some imaginative sense. But for the most part the stance of the historian was recollective in the manner of Alphonse Aulard. To make the spirit of the past actually live again might be impossible, most historicists agreed. But recollection still permitted access to the interior life of historical actors out of the past. One could reconstruct their thought processes, think as they must have thought. One could imagine their motives and intentions and, so, understand the way in which they had anticipated their future. But to do so adequately, one had to reconstruct their mental world so as to perceive their problems in the context in which they lived. This was the crux of the argument of R. G. Collingwood, the English historian and philosopher considered by many to be the last and the most intellectually sophisticated of the historicists. Collingwood argued that we may enter into the mind-set of the historical actors of the past because they thought as we do. It is these common cognitive faculties of all humankind across time that make it possible for us to bridge the temporal divide between past and present. All history, Collingwood therefore contended, is the history of thought.[5]

Hans-Georg Gadamer and the Hermeneutics of Modern Historiography

It is important to recognize that historicism as an approach to historical understanding was closely tied to the particular needs of modern historiography as it emerged in the nineteenth century. Historians were preoccupied with confirming the identity they shared with the topics they considered. In history as in autobiography, they looked to origins and turning points along the way as determinants of present identity. To understand the limitations of this approach from a twentieth-century perspective, one may find the work of the German philosopher Hans-Georg Gadamer to be helpful. Gadamer was a student of Martin Heidegger, and he was deeply influenced by his concept of being (*Dasein*), which proclaimed temporality as the existential ground of the human condition.[6] In his *Truth and Method* (1960), he adapts Heidegger's line of inquiry to the problems of historical understanding, and he builds his argument around a critique of nineteenth-century German historicism, as evinced in the writings of such historians as Johann Droysen, Leopold von Ranke, and especially Wilhelm Dilthey.[7] There was much in the historicists' argument with which Gadamer was sympathetic. He was particularly taken with Dilthey's notion of life experience (*Erlebnis*), which emphasized the temporal dimension of human understanding in the crossing perspectives of memory and anticipation. But Dilthey, Gadamer explains, also confirmed the bias of historicism in arguing that one can measure progress in the present against a stable and sustaining past. In this judgment, Gadamer contends, he, like his English counterpart Collingwood, relied too heavily on a theory of a timeless, unchanging human psychology as a foundation for elaborating an objective pattern of the past. Dilthey, he explained, would recreate the thoughts of the actor in the past without considering the impact of that re-creation on those of the historian in the present. It was a perspective in which the past is made to stand still—a unique and singular past that may be grasped objectively, once and for all time.[8]

Gadamer's argument helps us to understand the historiographical bias of historicism. Living within a tradition given to a linear conception of historical change, Dilthey and his historicist colleagues were in search of ways in which to confirm the receding past's ties to the advancing present. In relying on a psychological argument to overcome the distance between past and present, Gadamer suggests, they placed too much emphasis on the historical actors and not enough on the historians interpreting their endeavor. Gadamer's argument accords with the present sense of historians of collective mentalities who con-tend that humankind's uses of its psychological resources vary from age to age. Their research reveals the many historical reconfigurations of the human mind-set, even in the recent past. Habits of mind change, as do modes of speech, the display of emotions, the organization of sensory perception, and the uses of memory.[9] Whereas the historicists had sought to confirm ties to a past rendered more familiar by a common psychology underpinning all hu-man endeavor, the distinguishing feature of Gadamer's analysis of historical understanding is his interest in what is unfamiliar in the encounter between past and present by virtue of the differences between the traditions that operate in each. For the historicist perspective, therefore, Gadamer substitutes the hermeneutical—the perspective of historians seeking to familiarize themselves with a past that is in some measure alien and strange to their way of thinking.[10]

Hermeneutics, as it was originally conceived in the early nineteenth century by religious thinkers such as Friedrich Schleiermacher, had been a method of biblical criticism. The hermeneutical scholar tried to understand scripture by considering the meanings that had been drawn from it over the course of time. Understanding a text, therefore, involved circular movements of interpretation from present into the past and back again. One tried to understand its original meaning in relationship to the religious tradition into which it had unfolded over the course of time. One reached back to the early interpretations of the text but then returned to its more recent appreciations in order to grasp the range of meanings that might be elicited from the tradition considered as a whole. In that sense, every text subtends a tradition.[11] Gadamer refashioned and widened this concept to encompass historical understanding generally. The circular movements of interpretation in which historians engage, he ar-gued, not only deepen their understanding of the past but also transform their appreciation of their present circumstances. Like the god Hermes, historians have to venture forth from Mount Olympus into distant lands and there to familiarize themselves with strange customs. But for Gadamer, the flight back was perhaps more important, for in returning home historians discover themselves not only more knowledgeable but newly aware of the historical nature of their own endeavor. In this sense, historical knowledge is self-transforming. Through their journeys into the past, historians come to recognize that time itself is a precondition of understanding, not a distance to be overcome. It is the timefulness of our human condition, not merely our critical faculties, that makes understanding of the past possible. Temporality resides not merely in our thoughts but in our existential condition.[12]

Gadamer's argument casts the memory/history problem in a different light. Interpretation is always carried out from within the traditions in which we are immersed and confirms their authority. For this reason, there can be no escape from the bias that tradition bears. It is inherent in the life situations that we are given. The fact that we share the temporality of the existential condition with all humankind, however, does not enable us to transpose ourselves magically into past surroundings. The problem of memory from an historical perspective lies in the encounter with traditions that encircle our living memories. Therefore, Gadamer contends, we must let ourselves be addressed by tradition. "Our historical consciousness is always filled with a variety of voices in which the echo of the past is heard. Only in the multifariousness of such voices does it exist: this constitutes the nature of tradition in which we want to share and to have a part."[13] In the course of their inquiries, historians widen their horizons, but only by acknowledging that the past has horizons of its own. Tradition's authority lies in the context it provides for the historians' interpretation of that which is strange and alien in the past. Thereby it facilitates their search for deeper meanings. So conceived, historical understanding involves a "fusing of the horizons" of past and present, of the unfamiliar and the familiar, of tradition as it presents its conceptions for the historians' consideration and history as it integrates them into present understanding. This fusion of horizons itself effects a transformation of understanding, for it places the past within a different context. That is why the meaning of an event that has transpired, or a text that has been written, is always open to new interpretation. The past as it is embodied in tradition remains a resource for the present and as such retains a measure of autonomy. The relationship between past and present is dynamic and hence always provisional. As new realities present themselves in the present, the past is reintegrated into historical understanding in new ways. Gadamer would contend that history, like memory, always involves reciprocal relationships. As recollection is to habit, so history is to tradition.[14]

The key to Gadamer's argument, therefore, turns on his appreciation of tradition as the ground of historical understanding. It is as if tradition were a continuum that situates both memory and history. It is a context from which ideas and events cannot be separated, for tradition preserves and updates what is significant in the past over time. It is a milieu of collective memory, con-

ceived as the web of customs, habits of mind, conventions, and linguistic protocols that lends meaning to any historical situation. For historians in the
present, as for historical actors in the past, tradition is a sustaining presence.
Usually historians encounter tradition by considering memorable persons,
events or ideas. These places of memory serve as the points of entry for their
historical inquiries. Yet the meanings they find there depend on the traditions
to which they appeal, for each will present the past in a different way. Each
historian, Gadamer argues further, must recognize that he, too, is located
within an historiographical tradition.[15] That is why historiography has become so important in theoretical discussions of the nature of historical understanding today. Historians are more aware than ever before of the degree to
which the directions of their inquiries are set by the traditions within which
they operate.

Gadamer's argument is particularly appealing in our current situation because of the sense of so many historians that we in this postmodern age are
wandering from the shepherding influences of the political, religious, and
cultural traditions by which nineteenth-century historians felt so securely
tended.[16] Accordingly, he provides an important philosophical perspective on
our study of memory's relationship to historical understanding. He shows us
the deep sources of history in memory as it operates through the mediation
of tradition. He offers an insightful critique of nineteenth-century historiography, enabling us to understand more adequately why it tried to hold fast to
particular reminiscences about memorable personalities and events and why
it was unable to do so. He shows how the remembered past that we tend to
appreciate as a series of memorable events is sustained by a continuum of
collective memory in which such events are localized. As collective memories
are modified, so their places of memory will be rededicated to conform to
these changing conceptions. For all of these reasons, he takes us beyond the
nineteenth-century formulation of the paradox of memory and so prepares the
way for a reconsideration of the present scene. Gadamer's study signifies the
move of philosophers of history in the contemporary age away from problems
of history toward those of historiography. It supplies the theoretical foundations for our consideration of the memory/history problem today. This concerns the encounter between two historiographical traditions that, while far
removed from one another in their inquiries, nonetheless share an interest in
the memory/history problem.

The Divergence of Memory and History in the
Postmodern Age

Historiographical traditions would seem to have life cycles in their appeal,
much in the manner that Vico suggested, and the historians' perception of
their meaning changes over time. Our chapter on the role of memory in the

historiography of the French Revolution was intended to serve a
of the way in which the historians' perspective on a national trac
as their sense of immersion in it diminishes and as their attach
clines. Today we would also seem to be at the end of a cycle fc
tradition that still enjoyed favor only a half-century ago. What is most striking
about the current historiographical scene is the way in which the nineteenth-
century historicist connection between history and memory has been repudiated. The historians' present-day investigations of the memory/history
problem seem not unlike Kierkegaard's contrast between the memories of
childhood and old age: they proceed in opposite directions. One prominent
line of inquiry has been into the history of representation or, more particularly,
the history of the forms of commemoration. The other has been the history
of oral tradition. The former is identified with our closing perspective on the
archaeology of memory of Michel Foucault. The latter is that of our opening
perspective on oral tradition by Giambattista Vico. One purpose of this chapter is to bring these two avenues of inquiry into dialogue with one another,
for there are limits to what either can explain in isolation. We might say that
it is an attempt to get Foucault and Vico to talk to one another.

We may begin with the problem of memory as it is considered within current work on the history of commemoration. As an approach to the history
of memory, it is the one that commands most of the historiographical attention
today. It deals almost exclusively with memory in the guise of representation.
In other words, it puts the accent on the recollective moment of memory and
virtually ignores that of repetition, or habits of mind. Our theoretical understanding of that perspective was pioneered by Maurice Halbwachs and has
been furthered especially in our own time by Michel Foucault. Foucault sets
aside all discussion of tradition as a matrix of institutions and values confirmed
in habits' promptings in favor of a phenomenology of the rhetorical and iconographic forms in which each historical age signifies its understanding of the
world. That is why he characterizes history as a project in archaeology. He is
more interested in form than in content, in the signifier than the signified.
Bracketing the problem of what "words and things" may have meant to those
who invented them, he concentrates instead on their role as signs in the power
struggles of the past. Whatever these images may have signified about their
creators' intentions, what they reveal to the historian of commemorative forms
are the strategies with which political and social communities used these images to assert their authority. The icons and artifacts of the past, together with
the rhetorical images of discourse about them, are the stuff of that endeavor.
In Foucault's sense, history is the study of commemorative forms, and its
essential interest is the politics of memory.

Foucault's provocative method enabled historians to look at the past in a
totally different way. His work shifted the historian's attention from idea to
image. It is a perspective he conveyed so evocatively in the opening passage
of his *Histoire de la folie*. Therein, it will be recalled, he describes the ruins of

the medieval lazar house as an archaeological form appropriated and refashioned by the public authorities of a later age into the modern madhouse as part of their widening strategy for segregating society's undesired members.[17] In his historical analysis, Foucault manages to combine high drama with seemingly clinical detachment. He proceeds "genealogically" from present to past. His genealogical probe of the antecedent forms of the modern asylum reveals change and complexity, in contrast with the common beginnings and simple identities that the historicists sought to uncover. Repetition as a moment of memory is effectively crowded out of Foucault's considerations. For Foucault as he surveys the past, images of representation as they are enshrined in the archaeological leavings of ages past provide points of stasis. One may describe these textualized images with some certainty, whereas the ideas associated with tradition are dynamic, ever-changing, and more difficult to document. The "archaeologist" of representation can inventory images without passing judgment on them, whereas the historian of ideas must offer some valuation of the meanings they convey. In scanning the inventory of commemorative forms that the historian displays, moreover, readers can see how these forms are modified, discarded, reused, and invested with different contents over time. In the process, they may see the connections among the forms with which each age has represented reality but always as strategies for advancing present concerns. The meanings these forms originally embodied are permanently lost from view. The fate of today's living memory, in Foucault's scenario, is to recede into tomorrow's oblivion.[18]

Though Foucault never made the connection, his archaeological method of doing history bears some affinities with the positivist tradition of French historiography and suggests something of the nature of its appeal. Like the positivists, Foucault promises certain knowledge of the formal residues of the past while concealing his own commitments as its interpreter. His history of representation might be likened to a photographic perspective. It reconstructs the past as if it were a series of still shots.[19] These static representations lend history a stability that tradition can never achieve, for they are only portraying what was created in the past, not what historical actors believed they were creating. Intentions, and with them the values that traditions bear, are factored out of the historian's consideration. Foucault, therefore, denies the need to enter into the imagination of the past and hence ignores the problem of its grounding in tradition. Because he values no tradition as a point of departure for his studies, he professes to proceed backward from the present with an open-mindedness about what he may encounter. Yet his pursuit of the genealogy of forms has no end because there are no moments of memory to respond to his queries.[20] Consider his meditation on Velásquez' painting *Las Meninas* in his opening tableau to *The Order of Things* (1966). The painting draws the observer's eye to a mirror, which reflects a portrait being painted. Though reflected in the mirror, the portrait too is a mirror, and, as the mirror image of a mirror, its reflection leads the observer's gaze into an infinite re-

Hutton's criticism

gress.[21] Foucault's history without memory leads the historian into labyrinthine recesses that grow more complex at each turn because there is no tradition to whose meaning he wishes to respond and over which he wishes to linger. There are limits, then, to what Foucault's archaeology of the forms of representation can reveal, for as a method it professes an impossible detachment, one that denies the inspiration that living memory evokes. Even Foucault in an occasional apocalyptic moment came close to conceding this, and students of his work continue to search for clues to the meanings that he was seeking in the forms that he studied.[22]

The orality side of the historians' current interest in the history of memory, by contrast, puts its accent on memory's moment of repetition. This approach to the history of memory was pioneered by Giambattista Vico and may account in some measure for the renaissance of interest in his work since the 1960s.[23] Although overshadowed by the attention being given to the history of commemorative representation, the history of oral tradition has elicited considerable appeal because of its insights into a kind of memory that has largely disappeared. The revival of interest in the topic proceeds from the scholars' interest in the oral traditions of classical antiquity. Memory as the deep source of human imagination was known in ancient Greek mythology as Mnemosyne, mother of the muses of the arts and sciences. Memory was later identified by Plato, and again by the Neoplatonists of the Renaissance, as knowledge of archetypes, based on the correspondences between human imagination and the ideal forms of a transcendent cosmos. Intimations of this kind of memory find modern echoes in the poetry of William Wordsworth and the psychological speculations of Carl Gustav Jung.

Vico's genius was to show that the sources of this kind of memory can be located historically in a primordial past, whether or not they have any divine correspondences with the heavens. The search for transcendence, he argued, in fact requires a delving into the primordial origins of the civilizing process. The problem of memory as a governing imagination is historical.[24] Vico's route into the understanding of this imaginative memory followed the poetic logic of tropes. The gradient of abstraction that separates metaphor from irony, he argued, was an historical creation.[25] To descend the gradient, therefore, is to move backward in time, toward the metaphorical correspondences of images and ideas in the origins of civilization. The modern historian (Vico's philologist) seeks knowledge of the certain, that is, seeks recollective memory in which the images of the past are reconstructed with accuracy and precision. The ancient poet, however, sought to convey knowledge of the true, that is, sought to give expression to an imagination attuned to the voices of the life world in which he was immersed.

Vico's interest in the sources of memory in ancient oral tradition was tied to his study of the Roman legal tradition and especially to his investigations of the role of the Homeric rhapsode, a type of poet who still sings in remote communities ensconced in a traditional way of life. Modern students of the

Homeric epics, notably Milman Parry, Albert Lord, and Eric Havelock, have revisited the problem of Homer's place in oral tradition, first raised by Vico. Indeed, scholarly research on the Homeric epics as expressions of oral poetry served as the starting point for the recent scholarly interest in oral traditions generally. To enter that world of orality requires the kind of openness to lost traditions on which Gadamer remarked. The poetic traits of mind and memory displayed by people in such a culture are foreign to modern modes of thought. Vico pointed out how the philosophers of his own age believed that Homer was a "sage of matchless wisdom," and there are scholars who to this day cling to that view.[26] The notion of "Homer" may signify a genius for storytelling, but in a sense everyman in such a culture exhibited these qualities of mind and memory. As Vico suggested, Homer was a generic term for the rhapsode, and there must have been many who told these epic tales of their Mycenaean heritage. In a way, Vico suggests, the rhapsodes were wizards of the imagination. They gave expression to a memory that was archetypal in its imagery. Their sense of their tradition reflected the concrete imagination of people immersed in orality. Their metaphorical rendering of their society's challenges bespoke a more visceral appreciation of life and a capacity to evoke wondrous emotions through their depiction of the world in images that were larger than life. As bearers of the traditions of the Greek people, the rhapsodes celebrated a memory that was interchangeable with their imagination in that it bodied forth the perpetual presence of their heritage.

The rhapsodes were renowned for their prodigious memories, for they could recite the long and intricate Homeric epics spontaneously. But as students of oral tradition have shown, the rhapsodes used their memories in a practical way for the oral culture in which they lived.[27] What distinguished the rhapsodes' memory was less its retentiveness than its capacity for invention. They employed mnemonic technique naturally and to the best advantage. Drawing their episodes from a repertoire of folktales, they wove their stories into a grand saga, but never in exactly the same way. Their capacity for sustained storytelling was enhanced by recourse to poetical formulae and metaphorical imagery, vibrant in the emotions they could rouse and evocative in the tableaux they could conjure up. That such uses of memory strike us immediately as different from our own suggests the historical evolution of memory into a more abstract capacity. Although the imaginative memory of the poets of antiquity would seem to have survived only in a limited way in some modern forms of poetical expression, it probably remains a residual human capacity that would be quickly revived were our conditions of culture to revert to those of an oral tradition. In the modern world, this imaginative, poetical memory has been displaced by the recollective memory of historical time, with its tendency toward private, self-conscious reflection. As a residual capacity, poetical memory might be characterized as the force of habit that unconsciously prompts our behavior. One might say that habit, or repetition, is a moment of memory foreign to the historian because of its insistence on

repetition and constancy. Habit militates against the modern historical penchant for change. In contrast with the representational side of memory, that
of oral tradition is far more elusive and difficult for the historian to grasp. In
modern times, its nature is more frequently discussed by biologists. Samuel
Butler considered the nature of this collective memory in the nineteenth century.[28] In our own, Rupert Sheldrake has characterized it as the phenomenon
of morphic resonances.[29]

For all of its insight, Vico's study was limited by the framework in which
he operated. Vico may have interpreted written texts for what they reveal
about an anterior oral culture. But his studies were restricted to oral traditions
viewed from the vantage point of manuscript culture. Recent historical studies
of the relationship between orality and literacy have made it possible for us to
gain a perspective on memory in its imaginative mode. Indeed, the history
of this relationship today serves as the historiographical framework in which
the problem of oral tradition is primarily considered. This suggests the significance of Walter Ong's study of the historically changing relationship between orality and literacy as it advances into print culture. Ong tied the
problem to changing technologies of communication. Not only did his thesis
open a new perspective on the history of memory, it placed the current interest
in the history of representation in context. Ong showed how the invention of
new forms of communication transforms the conditions in which imagination
operates without diminishing its resources. The uses of memory may have
been transformed with the rise of literacy and the development of more complex and abstract forms of communication. In script, print, and electronic
media, our imaginations may find new forms of expression. But the significance of imagination for historical understanding is not eclipsed in the process, as some historians of representation would have us believe. For Ong,
orality remains the matrix from which all more abstract forms of literacy
proceed, for imagination ultimately resides there. In this view imagination
and recollection, tradition and archaeology, are not unrelated tangents, but
inversely related positions within a continuum of historical understanding.[30]

History as an Art of Memory in the Postmodern Age

One purpose of this study has been to consider the possibilities for a dialogue between historians who approach these moments of memory as discrete
historical entities. In this postmodern age, we have gravitated toward a consideration of the extremes of habit and recollection, pressing forward separately our fascination with the deep sources of repetition in oral tradition and
the forms of recollection in the archaeology of commemorative practice. One
way beyond the impasse is to reconsider the mediating role that the art of
memory might play in the historical inquiries of our time. The invention of
the art, after all, was situated historically between orality and literacy. It pro-

vided an artificial sense of place for a world that had lost touch with the relationship between the two. Its invention and appeal were closely tied to the
particular need of manuscript culture for an artificial memory. Mnemonics
was a form of paradigm-building that lent structure to fragile ways of remembering the world. From the oral traditions of the past, the classical art of
memory borrowed techniques for the accurate and ready retrieval of information for a world beginning to experiment with literacy and whose powers
of spontaneous recollection were beginning to decline. At the same time, it
showed a society accustomed to thinking of the past as time immemorial a
way to structure its heritage in terms of places of memory. As historical thinking emerged in the modern era, the spatial model identified with the art was
reconfigured as a timeline, punctuated by memorable events. These memory-
filled chronologies invested the past with a new sense of linear time and, so,
contributed to the emergence of modern historical thought.

The needs of the manuscript culture of the Renaissance, in which the art
of memory flourished, are not unlike our own. The distinguishing feature of
Western culture in our postmodern age is its syncretism. Today there is no
consensus about the value of topics, fields, or methods of approaching the
past.[31] Indeed, the present historiographical scene is marked by a certain con-
tentiousness. Today's historiography focuses on cultural discontinuities and
has itself become the focus for a contest of authority in which many traditions
vie for recognition. We might say that in our postmodern culture we no longer
have a strong sense of the places of our memory. To some extent, this state of
affairs reflects the waning appeal of particular traditions. In another, it reflects
the nature of memory in an electronic age in which elements of tradition are
continually broken up and reused in a kaleidoscope of reconfigurations by
television and other electronic media. The sociologist Joshua Meyrowitz argues that the electronic revolution has contributed to our loss of the sense of
place on which our ancestors relied for their identity and orientation.[32] The
ecologist Bill McKibben suggests that television has substituted image for
reality to such a degree that the boundary between the two has become
blurred.[33]

Such trends in contemporary culture have contributed to a sense of severed
connections with the past and have raised attendant fears about cultural amnesia.[34] They also point to a way in which historians may renew their vocation,
for the current historiographical interest in memory suggests the need. Historians may feel beleaguered by the variety of traditions that vie for their favor,
yet they are privileged in their capacity to survey the historiographical scene
as if it were a vast landscape of memory, whose topographical features highlight the many traditions that may be investigated. The popular consensus
about the nature of our culture may be gone. But the richness of the resources
of tradition are as profound as the depths of human experience. The end of a
consensus about what is worth remembering in our present situation para-
doxically has opened up to us once more history's hidden roots in tradition,

covered over in modern historiography in the name of positivist science. That awareness has given new prominence to historiography, for it reveals that the preliminary task of the historian is to sort out alternative traditions, not just alternative ideological viewpoints, as was their habit in the era of modern history.

Historians encounter traditions at different stages in their evolution. Some traditions may be vital at the edge of living memory, others time-worn, still others lost and awaiting recollection. The traditions we have examined closely as models are well-worn—notably that of the Western nation-state, with its attendant ideologies and expectations, or the historiographical tradition of historicism. But one can see other traditions in their early stages—that of Israeli nationalism, for example, or the new tradition of feminist historiography. Still others, long lost, such as gnosticism, have quickened our interest in long-standing historical problems (Christian origins). As Halbwachs pointed out, the individual in his recourse to memory is accustomed to drawing on many dissimilar, often unrelated traditions simultaneously. Until recently, most historians avoided dealing with the problem by resorting to specialization in one tradition alone. But today there seems more urgency to confront relationships among traditions often awkwardly juxtaposed and glaring in their incongruities. The more pressing task of the historian today is to look for connections among them. Gadamer's notion of the fusion of horizons would seem to operate on a plane of gathering complexity.

Indeed, this has become the most appealing project of postmodern historiography. The historians of the nineteenth century were intent on keeping alive a political tradition of progress through the agency of the nation-state. Today's historians prefer to explore lost cultural worlds. The historians who receive most of the attention today are not the ones that confirm conventional values but those who investigate forgotten traditions and alien viewpoints. If one thinks of the most widely acclaimed historical studies of recent years, they are those that have uncovered unsuspected traditions. Consider, for example, Carlo Ginzburg's *The Cheese and the Worms* (1976), a study of a popular atheistic humanism hidden in the oral traditions of rural Italy in the era of the Reformation; or Emmanuel Le Roy Ladurie's *Montaillou* (1975), which uncovered the cultural and religious attitudes of ordinary people in their everyday lives in a village in the medieval Languedoc; or Natalie Davis's *Return of Martin Guerre* (1983), which juxtaposed the resources, relationships, and expectations of high and popular culture in rural France in the sixteenth century; or Robert Darnton's *Great Cat Massacre* (1984), which explored the mores of a variety of forgotten social types in mid-eighteenth-century France.

The philosophers, poets, and historians that we have examined, moreover, prefigure this interest in hidden wisdom. Our emphasis throughout this book has been on theory, but the theorists that we have emphasized have also written histories that evince this perspective. All would reveal concealed memories. Vico showed us the sublime emotions and harsh realities endured by early civilizations hidden beneath modern-day interpretations of the texts they have bequeathed to us. Wordsworth unveiled the fears and forebodings of a child, which, from a biographical perspective, would appear to have grown up in an enchanted landscape. Freud culminated his career with an historical inquiry into the hidden history of parricide, masked by traditions of religious belief. Halbwachs unearthed the deep Jewish religious traditions covered over by the commemorative forms of primitive Christianity. Ariès revealed Old Regime traditions of family politics overshadowed by the facade of modernity. Foucault described discarded cultural forms adapted to new and unrelated purposes.

One might say that the present map of historiography is not unlike the mnemonist's memory palace. Each historiographical tradition possesses a different code. The historian must find the key to the code, for each one opens a different door to a different room of meaning.[35] This observation brings us back to Frances Yates. She was the first to show us the intellectual significance of the memory palace and the forgotten history of the art of memory. It was exemplary of her larger historical project to uncover traditions that are lost in the past. They reveal the fuller dimensions of the culture in which they developed and the ways in which they continue to serve as a resource for the present age. In this sense, her authorship in the 1960s was the prototype for the history of mentalities, and it inscribed at the beginning the problem that has invited historiographical reflection only as that tradition of historical writing has matured—the deep sources of memory underpinning history.

Even today there are some historians who believe that the project of writing history is nearing completion.[36] The grand outlines of its design have been laid, and all that remains for subsequent generations of historians to do is to fill in the details. The interjection of the memory problem into such considerations has reintroduced an element of doubt. As Ariès remarked, history deals with the horizon between the known and the unknown. It is memory that lures us to this horizon. Even the widest horizon of our knowledge is overwhelmed by the mysteries of what lies beyond. Humankind has walked this earth for millions of years, yet the reach of our history is only a few thousand. One need not return to the distant past to confirm this observation, for not all the mysteries reside there. They are interspersed throughout our everyday lives, today as in the past. Even the historical topics with which we are most familiar are often full of surprises that rouse our curiosity. So the ancients depicted Mnemosyne, the daughter of ignorance, the mother of wisdom.

NOTES

I
PLACING MEMORY IN CONTEMPORARY HISTORIOGRAPHY

1. Philippe Joutard, "Mémoire collective," in *Dictionnaire des sciences historiques,* ed. André Burguière (Paris, 1986), 447–49; Jacques Le Goff, *History and Memory,* trans. Steven Rendall and Elizabeth Clamen (New York, 1992). See also Michael Kammen, *Mystic Chords of Memory* (New York, 1991), as well as the special issue, "Memory and Counter-Memory," ed. Natalie Zemon Davis and Randolf Starn in *Representations* 26 (Spring 1989), and the section on collective memory and American history edited by David Thelen in the *Journal of American History* 75/4 (March 1989), 1117–1221. A journal devoted to the topic, *History and Memory,* edited by Gulie Arad, Dan Diner, and Saul Friedländer, is now in its fourth year.
2. Nathan Wachtel, "Memory and History: An Introduction," *History and Anthropology* 2 (1986), 210–11.
3. For an overview, see Robert Mandrou, "L'Histoire des mentalités," *Encyclopaedia universalis* 8 (1968 ed.), 436–38; Philippe Ariès, "L'Histoire des mentalités," in *La Nouvelle Histoire,* ed. Jacques Le Goff et al. (Paris, 1978), 402–23; Patrick H. Hutton, "The History of Mentalities: The New Map of Cultural History," *History and Theory* 20/3 (1981), 237–59.
4. The pioneering *Annales* scholar Lucien Febvre dealt with the problem of habits of mind but never related it directly to a discussion of collective memory or even the nature of tradition. His colleague Marc Bloch wrote a review essay of the work of Maurice Halbwachs on collective memory in the *Revue de synthèse historique* 40 (1925), 73–83, although it appears to have been his sole excursion into the topic.
5. Pierre Nora, "Mémoire collective," in *La Nouvelle Histoire,* 398.
6. Philippe Ariès, *L'Enfant et la vie familiale sous l'Ancien Régime* (Paris, 1960), trans. Robert Baldick as *Centuries of Childhood* (New York, 1962). For the reception and impact of this work, see the review essay by Richard T. Vann, "The Youth of *Centuries of Childhood,*" *History and Theory* 21 (1982), 279–97.
7. Trans. as *The Hour of Our Death* by Helen Weaver (New York, 1981).
8. Ibid., 449, 471–72, 476, 508–13, 518, 524–36, 541–43; see also his *Western Attitudes toward Death from the Middle Ages to the Present* (Baltimore, 1974), 55–74.
9. Ariès, *Western Attitudes,* 75–82.

10. Trans. Janet Lloyd as *Marianne into Battle: Republican Imagery and Symbolism in France, 1789–1880* (Cambridge, England, 1981).
11. Ibid., 5–6.
12. Ibid., 2, 189.
13. Ibid., 25, 27, 112–15, 186–87.
14. Agulhon argues that in fact the term may have been coined as early as the French Revolution, to be later appropriated by the secret societies. Ibid., 9.
15. Ibid., 105, 122–31.
16. Ibid., 31, 36, 168–88.
17. Ibid., 182–85.
18. Ibid., 3–6, 181–89.
19. Representative examples include William Cohen, "Symbols of Power: Statues in Nineteenth-Century Provincial France," *Comparative Studies in Society and History* 31 (1989), 491–513; Reinhart Koselleck, "Les Monuments aux morts: Contribution à l'étude d'une marque visuelle des temps modernes," in *Iconographie et histoire des mentalités,* ed. Michel Vovelle (Paris, 1979), 117–18; Charles Rearick, "Festivals in Modern France: The Experience of the Third Republic," *Journal of Contemporary History* 12 (1977), 435–60, and "Festivals and Politics: The Michelet Centennial of 1898," *Historians in Politics* 1 (1974), 59–78; Rosemonde Sanson, *Les 14 Juillet (1789–1975): Fête et conscience nationale* (Paris, 1976), 25–79; Alice Gérard, *La Réevolution française; mythes et interprétations (1789–1970)* (Paris, 1970), 66–72. George L. Mosse, *Fallen Soldiers* (Oxford, 1990), 35–41, makes references to French commemoration but is more thorough on the German experience.
20. Eric Hobsbawm and Terence Ranger, eds., *The Invention of Tradition* (Cambridge, England, 1983).
21. Eric Hobsbawm, "Mass-Producing Traditions: Europe, 1870–1914," in ibid., 263–307.
22. Eric Hobsbawm, "Introduction: Inventing Traditions," in ibid., 1–14.
23. Ibid., 7.
24. On the relationship between tradition and kitsch, see Matei Calinescu, *Five Faces of Modernity* (Durham, N.C., 1987), 229–62; Saul Friedländer, *Reflections of Nazism: An Essay on Kitsch and Death,* trans. Thomas Weyr (New York, 1982), 25–53; Alan Gowans, *Learning to See* (Bowling Green, Ohio, 1981), 260.
25. On Foucault as historian, see Hayden V. White, *The Content of the Form* (Baltimore, 1987), 104–41; Allan Megill, "Foucault, Structuralism, and the Ends of History," *Journal of Modern History* 51 (1979), 451–503.
26. Michel Foucault, *L'Archéologie du savoir* (1969), trans. A. M. Sheridan Smith as *The Archaeology of Knowledge* (New York, 1976), 3–17, 135–48.
27. Ibid., 124–25; "Nietzsche, Genealogy, History," in *Language, Counter-Memory, Practice: Selected Essays and Interviews,* ed. Donald F. Bouchard (Ithaca, 1977), 152–54, 160; "Two Lectures," in *Power/Knowledge: Selected Interviews and Other Writings, 1972–77,* ed. Colin Gordon (New York, 1980), 83–87.
28. Foucault, "Nietzsche, Genealogy, History," 151, 160.
29. Foucault, *Archaeology of Knowledge,* 7, 147.
30. Michel Foucault, *Les Mots et les choses* (1966), trans. Alan Sheridan as *The Order of Things: An Archaeology of the Human Sciences* (New York, 1970), xv–xxiv, 303–43.
31. See esp. Maurice Halbwachs, *Les Cadres sociaux de la mémoire* (1925; rpt. New York, 1975); *The Collective Memory,* trans. Francis J. Ditter, Jr., and Vida Yazdi Ditter (1950; rpt. New York, 1980).
32. Discussions of the significance of Halbwachs's theory of memory may be found in Wachtel, "Memory and History," 211–14; Paul Connerton, *How Societies Remember* (Cambridge, England, 1989), 36–38; Gérard Namer, "Affectivité et temporalité de

la mémoire," *L'Homme et la société* 90 (1988), 9–14; Roger Bastide, "Mémoire collective et sociologie du bricolage," *L'Année sociologique*, 3d ser., 21 (1970), 65–108; Barry Schwartz, "The Social Context of Commemoration: A Study in Collective Memory," *Social Forces* 61 (1982), 376–77; Yael Zerubavel, *Recovered Roots: Collective Memory and the Making of Israeli National Tradition* (forthcoming).

33. Halbwachs, *Cadres sociaux*, 143–45; *Collective Memory*, 22–30, 97.

34. *Collective Memory*, 35–49, 55–63, 124–27.

35. *Cadres sociaux*, 2, 5, 20, 98–108; *Collective Memory*, 63–68.

36. One will recognize the theoretical foundation of Agulhon's argument here. Halbwachs, *Cadres sociaux*, 9; *Collective Memory*, 71, 106–20.

37. *Cadres sociaux*, 273–96; *Collective Memory*, 120–27. See the interesting study by Mary Douglas, *How Institutions Think* (Syracuse, 1986), 69–80, who builds on Halbwachs's insights in her discussion of the dynamics of public memory.

38. Sigmund Freud, "The Aetiology of Hysteria (1896)," in *Early Psychoanalytic Writings*, ed. Philip Rieff, trans. Cecil M. Baines (New York, 1963), 175–203, and *The Interpretation of Dreams* (1900), trans. James Strachey (New York, 1965), 54.

39. Significantly, Halbwachs began his study with a critique of Freud's theory of dreams. *Cadres sociaux*, vi–viii, 1–39.

40. This was the basis of Halbwachs's case study of the commemoration of the Holy Land, *La Topographie légendaire des évangiles en Terre Sainte* (1941; Paris, 1971), esp. 1–7, 117–64.

41. Pierre Nora, ed. *Les Lieux de mémoire*, 3 vols. (Paris, 1984–92).

42. On nineteenth-century commemoration, see esp. the essays in *Lieux de mémoire* by Christian Amalvi, "Le 14-Juillet," I: 421–69; Avner Ben-Amos, "Les Funérailles de Victor Hugo," I: 473–521; Pascal Ory, "Le Centenaire de la Révolution française," I: 523–60; Antoine Prost, "Les Monuments aux morts," I: 195–225; Madeleine Rébérioux, "Le Mur des fédérés," I: 619–49.

43. Pierre Nora, "De la république à la nation," in ibid., I: 651–55.

44. Ibid., I: 655–59.

45. Pierre Nora, "Entre mémoire et histoire: La Problématique des lieux," in ibid., I: xxv.

46. Ibid., xvii.

47. Pierre Nora, "L'Histoire de France de Lavisse," in ibid., II: 317–75.

48. Nora, "Entre mémoire et histoire," in ibid., I: xli.

49. Ibid., xvii–xix.

50. Ibid., xxiii, xxxi.

51. Ibid., xxiv–xxv, xxxiv–xxxv.

52. Ibid., xxxiii, xli–xlii.

53. L. A. Post, "Ancient Memory Systems," *The Classical Weekly* 25/14 (1 Feb. 1932), 105–09; Richard Sorabji, *Aristotle on Memory* (Providence, 1972), 22–34.

54. Frances A. Yates, *The Art of Memory* (Chicago, 1966); see also the important study covering many of the same themes by Paolo Rossi, *Clavis universalis: Arti mnemoniche e logica combinatoria da Lullo a Leibniz* (Milan, 1960).

55. Frances A. Yates, "Autobiographical Fragments," in *Collected Essays of Frances Yates*, ed. J. N. Hillgarth and J. B. Trapp (London, 1984), 3: 278–322. On the Warburg Institute, see Fritz Saxl, "The History of Warburg's Library," in E. H. Gombrich, *Aby Warburg: An Intellectual Biography* (Chicago, 1986), 325–38.

56. Yates, *Art of Memory*, 129–59.

57. Ibid., 251–59; also Frances A. Yates, *Giordano Bruno and the Hermetic Tradition* (1964; rpt. Chicago, 1979), 191–99.

58. Yates, *Art of Memory*, 340–41.

59. As epitomized in the work of Francis Bacon, a scientist who nonetheless dabbled in the art. Yates, *Art of Memory*, 368–72.

60. For an early, comprehensive statement of his thesis, see Marshall McLuhan, *Understanding Media: The Extension of Man* (New York, 1964). For his observations on the link between the art of memory and manuscript culture, see his *The Gutenberg Galaxy: The Making of Typographic Man* (Toronto, 1962), 108–09, and his review of Frances Yates, *The Art of Memory* in "The Memory Theatre," *Encounter* 28 (1967), 61–66.

61. On McLuhan, see esp. Philip Marchand, *Marshall McLuhan: The Medium and the Messenger* (New York, 1989); Graeme Patterson, *History and Communications: Harold Innis, Marshall McLuhan, the Interpretation of History* (Toronto, 1990); and the eight articles in the *Journal of Communication* 31/3 (Summer 1981) on the theme of "The Living McLuhan."

62. Marshall McLuhan and Quentin Fiore, *The Medium Is the Message,* ed. Jerome Agel (New York, 1967), evokes this notion in its very design by discarding printing conventions in favor of improvised typesetting, evocative illustrations, and dramatic aphorisms that merge in a celebration of the coming of the electronic age.

63. McLuhan, *Gutenberg Galaxy,* 199–252.

64. Ibid., 54–133, 265–79.

65. Marchand, *Marshall McLuhan,* 59; see also McLuhan's correspondence with Ong in *Letters of Marshall McLuhan,* ed. Matie Molinaro et al. (Oxford, 1987), 162, 188, and Ong's memoir "McLuhan as Teacher: The Future Is a Thing of the Past," *Journal of Communication* 31/1 (Summer, 1981), 129–35.

66. Yates nonetheless devotes a chapter to Ramus in her *Art of Memory,* 231–42. Walter J. Ong, *Ramus: Method and the Decay of Dialogue* (Cambridge, Mass., 1958), 194–95.

67. Ong, *Ramus,* 9, 287, and *Orality and Literacy: The Technologizing of the Word* (London, 1982). See also his *Rhetoric, Romance, and Technology* (Ithaca, 1971), and *The Presence of the Word* (New Haven, 1967).

68. Ong, *Orality and Literacy,* 31–77; *The Presence of the Word,* 111–38.

69. Ong, *Orality and Literacy,* 41, 93–108.

70. Ibid., 108–16. See also Martin Elsky, *Authorizing Words: Speech, Writing, and Print in the English Renaissance* (Ithaca, 1989), 110–25.

71. Ong, *Orality and Literacy,* 117–23. See also Murray Cohen, *Sensible Words: Linguistic Practice in England, 1640–1785* (Baltimore, 1977), 10–20.

72. Ong, *Orality and Literacy,* 123–29. See also Robert Darnton, *The Great Cat Massacre and Other Episodes in French History* (New York, 1984), 191–213; André Leroi-Gourhan, *Le Geste et la parole* (Paris, 1965), II: 9–34; Alvin Kernan, *Printing Technology, Letters, and Samuel Johnson* (Princeton, 1987), 4–5, 48–55.

73. Ong, *Orality and Literacy,* 130–32; also Darnton, *The Great Cat Massacre,* 215–52.

74. See Charles Taylor, *Sources of the Self: The Making of Modern Identity* (Cambridge, Mass., 1989), 177–78, 185, 285–302, 368–90; David Lowenthal, *The Past Is a Foreign Country* (Cambridge, England, 1985), 198–99; Georges Gusdorf, *Mémoire et personne* (Paris, 1951), I: 212–19.

75. Ong, *Orality and Literacy,* 135–38.

76. Ibid., 139–70. See also Joshua Meyrowitz, *No Sense of Place: The Impact of Electronic Media on Social Behavior* (Oxford, 1985), 18–23; George Lipsitz, *Time Passages: Collective Memory and American Popular Culture* (Minneapolis, 1990), 39–75.

77. On the significance of Ong's work, see the special issue, "A Festschrift for Walter J. Ong," ed. by John Miles Foley, in *Oral Tradition* 2 (1987). It includes a biographical sketch and a bibliography by Randolph F. Lumpp.

78. See esp. Michael Warner, *The Letters of the Republic: Publication and the Public Sphere in Eighteenth-Century America* (Cambridge, Mass., 1990), 5–11; Jonathan Goldberg, *Writing Matter* (Stanford, 1990), 16–18, 21; Mark Poster, *The Mode of Information: Poststructuralism and the Social Context* (Chicago, 1990), 15, 45, 76.

79. For orientation in this field, see esp. Philippe Joutard, *Ces Voix qui nous viennent du passé* (Paris, 1983), 73, 102–03, 208–11; Eric A. Havelock, *The Muse Learns to Write* (New Haven, 1986), 24–29; Paul Thompson, *The Voices of the Past*, 2d ed. (Oxford, 1988), 23–100.

80. See Mary Douglas, *Edward Evans-Prichard* (New York, 1980), 75–90; Jack Goody, *The Interface between the Written and the Oral* (Cambridge, England, 1987).

81. Frederic C. Bartlett, *Remembering* (Cambridge, England, 1932); Alexander Luria, *Cognitive Development: Its Cultural and Social Foundations*, trans. Martin Lopez-Morillas et al. (Cambridge, Mass., 1976).

82. The findings about the dynamics of memory by students of oral tradition have been reinforced by neuropsychologists conducting research on the workings of the brain. See esp. Gerald Edelman, *Neural Darwinism: The Theory of Neuronal Group Selection* (New York, 1987), 1–42, 315–30, and *The Remembered Present: A Biological Theory of Consciousness* (New York, 1989), 37–57, 109–18. Edelman contends that remembering is a dynamic process of remapping or recategorizing the past. See also Israel Rosenfield, *The Invention of Memory* (New York, 1988), who traces the history of research on the brain for clues to the workings of memory.

83. This was the way in which the ancient Greeks understood the relationship. For the poet Hesiod, Mnemosyne, the goddess of memory, was also the mother of invention. Likewise, the term mimesis at once implied imitation and creativity. On the interconnections between memory and imagination in oral culture, see the early statement by Giambattisa Vico in *The New Science of Giambattista Vico* (3d ed; 1744), trans. and ed. Thomas G. Bergin and Max H. Fisch (Ithaca, 1968), paras. 211, 699, 819.

84. Jan Vansina, *Oral Tradition as History* (Madison, Wis., 1985), 160–62; Goody, *The Interface between the Written and the Oral*, 86–91.

85. Havelock, *Muse Learns to Write*, 63–78.

86. See J. G. A. Pocock, *Politics, Language and Time: Essays on Political Thought and History* (London, 1972), 237–38. The classic study by Mircea Eliade, *Cosmos and History* (New York, 1959), 37–48, is also still useful on this point.

87. Milman Parry, "Studies in the Epic Technique of Oral Verse-Making," in *The Making of Homeric Verse: The Collected Papers of Milman Parry*, ed. Adam Parry (Oxford, 1971), 325–61.

88. Albert Lord, *The Singer of Tales* (Cambridge, Mass., 1960), 124–38; Eric A. Havelock, *The Literate Revolution in Greece and Its Cultural Consequences* (Princeton, 1982), 20–25, 143–49; Jack Goody and Ian Watt, "The Consequences of Literacy," in *Literacy in Traditional Societies*, ed. Jack Goody (Cambridge, England, 1968), 44–49.

89. For recent scholarship on the relationship between manuscript culture and oral tradition, see Goldberg, *Writing Matter*, 162–63, 183–89, 263; Michel Beaujour, *Miroirs d'encre* (Paris, 1980), 82–88; M. T. Clanchy, *From Memory to Written Record* (Cambridge, Mass., 1979), 149–265; Eric A. Havelock, *Preface to Plato* (Cambridge, Mass., 1960), 100–03, 115–28; Brian Stock, *The Implications of Literacy* (Princeton, 1983), 18, 34, 62, 66–77, and *Listening for the Text* (Baltimore, 1990), 36–37.

90. Clanchy, *From Memory*, 11–12, 18–28; Stock, *Listening for the Text*, 36–37; Joseph M. Levine, *Humanism and History: Origins of Modern English Historiography* (Ithaca, 1987), 11–12, 19–26, 38–39, 51.

91. Arthur B. Ferguson, *Clio Unbound: Perception of the Social and Cultural Past in Renaissance England* (Durham, N.C., 1979), xi–xii, 3–5; Peter Burke, *The Renaissance Sense of the Past* (New York, 1969), 1–20.

92. Donald R. Kelley, *The Human Measure: Social Thought in the Western Legal Tradition* (Cambridge, Mass., 1990), 106–08, 172, 201.

93. Patrick H. Hutton, "The Art of Memory Reconceived: From Rhetoric to Psychoanalysis," *Journal of the History of Ideas* 48 (1987), 371–92. See also Christian Jouhaud,

"Printing the Event: From La Rochelle to Paris," in *The Culture of Print: Power and the Uses of Print in Early Modern Europe*, ed. Roger Chartier, trans. Lydia G. Cochrane (Princeton, 1989), 302.

94. But see the suggestive remarks by McLuhan, *Gutenberg Galaxy*, 199, 218–24, 235–38, on the links between the rise of print culture and of nationalism. See also Levine, *Humanism and History*, 16, 155–56, 185–89, 192.

95. John Kenyon, *The History Men: The Historical Profession in England since the Renaissance* (Pittsburgh, 1983), 85–97.

96. Benedict Anderson, *Imagined Communities: Reflections on the Origin and Spread of Nationalism* (London, 1983), 47–49. On the rise of literary history, see Kernan, *Printing Technology*, 267–73.

97. The classic statement is by Søren Kierkegaard, *Repetition*, ed. and trans. Howard V. Hong and Edna H. Hong (Princeton, 1983), esp. 131–76. See also his *Stages on Life's Way*, ed. and trans. Howard V. Hong and Edna H. Hong (Princeton, 1988), 9–19. See the commentary by Gusdorf, *Mémoire et personne*, II: 553–56; Michael Sprinker, "Fictions of the Self: The End of Autobiography," in *Autobiography: Essays Theoretical and Critical*, ed. James Olney (Princeton, 1980), 321–42; Stephen Kern, *The Culture of Time and Space, 1880–1918* (Cambridge, Mass., 1983), 38–64.

98. This was originally Vico's insight in his critique of the conceit of scholars, in which he distinguished memory from historical understanding. *New Science*, para. 44, 59, 125, 222, 738, 846, 1111. On the move toward a common chronology, see David Lowenthal, *The Past Is a Foreign Country*, 219–24; Donald J. Wilcox, *The Measure of Times Past* (Chicago, 1987), 187–89; George Huppert, *The Idea of Perfect History: Historical Erudition and Historical Philosophy in Renaissance France* (Urbana, 1970), 23–27; Anthony Grafton, *Defenders of the Text: The Traditions of Scholarship in an Age of Science, 1450–1800* (Cambridge, Mass., 1991), 120–44.

99. Lowenthal, *The Past is a Foreign Country*, 231–38; Reinhart Koselleck, *Futures Past: On the Semantics of Historical Time*, trans. Keith Tribe (Cambridge, Mass., 1985), 16–20, 27–38.

100. On historicism, see esp. Georg G. Iggers, *The German Conception of History*, rev. ed. (Middletown, Conn., 1983), 29–43; Maurice Mandelbaum, *History, Man, and Reason* (Baltimore, 1971), 41–49; Hans Meyerhoff, "Introduction: History and Philosophy," in *The Philosophy of History in Our Times*, ed. Hans Meyerhoff (Garden City, N.Y., 1959), 9–25; R. G. Collingwood, *The Idea of History* (Oxford, 1946), 282–320.

101. See, for example, A. Dwight Culler, *The Victorian Mirror of History* (New Haven, 1985), 279–84.

102. Eliade, *Cosmos and History*, 147–54; Iggers, *German Conception*, 124–27.

103. Iggers, *German Conception*, 41–43, 80–84, 95, 103–04, 130–33, 210–12; Anderson, *Imagined Communities*, 66–103.

104. Poster, *Mode of Information*, 86–98; Ana Maria Alonzo, "The Effects of Truth: Re-Presentation of the Past and the Imagining of Community," *Journal of Historical Sociology* 1 (1988), 33–37; Richard Terdiman, "Deconstructing Memory: On Representing the Past and Theorizing Culture in France since the Revolution," *Diacritics* 15/4 (Winter, 1985), 13–36; Anderson, *Imagined Communities*, 14–16; Allan Megill, *Prophets of Extremity* (Berkeley, 1985), 294–98.

105. Warner, *Letters of the Republic*, 63–67; Vincent B. Leitch, *Deconstructive Criticism: An Advanced Introduction* (New York, 1983), 102–08, 144–61.

106. Herbert Butterfield, *The Whig Interpretation of History* (1931; rpt. New York, 1965), 9–33.

107. François Furet, *Interpreting the French Revolution*, trans. Elborg Forster (Cambridge, England, 1981), 1–17.

108. Ibid., 49–61.

109. See the discerning essay by Ruth Finnegan, "Tradition, But What Tradition and for Whom?" *Oral Tradition* 6 (1991), 104–24.
110. See Paul Ricoeur, *The Reality of the Historical Past* (Milwaukee, 1984), 1–36.
111. One thinks straightaway of the rising prestige of the American literary critic Stephen Greenblatt's "new historicism." See his "Toward a Poetics of Culture," in *The New Historicism,* ed. H. Aram Veeser (New York, 1989), 1–14. On the renewed interest in historicism among literary scholars, see also Marjorie Levinson, "The New Historicism: Back to the Future," in *Rethinking Historicism,* ed. Marjorie Levinson et al. (Oxford, 1989), 18–63. On the limits of representation, see Saul Friedländer, "Introduction," in *Probing the Limits of Representation: Nazism and the "Final Solution,"* ed. Saul Friedländer (Cambridge, Mass., 1992), 4–9; "Trauma, Transference and 'Working Through,'" *History and Memory* 4 (1992), 39–59.
112. Hans-Georg Gadamer, *Truth and Method* (1960), 2d rev. ed., trans. Joel Weinsheimer and Donald G. Marshall (New York, 1989), 19–24, 173–242, 505–16.
113. Ibid., xxvii–xxxviii, 505–41.
114. Ibid., 277–85.
115. Ibid., 291–300.
116. Ibid., 300–07.
117. Ibid., 16.
118. Cf. Roger Chartier, "L'Amitié de l'histoire," preface to *Le Temps de l'histoire* by Philippe Ariès (Paris, 1986), 9–31.
119. Philippe Ariès, *Le Temps de l'histoire* (Monaco, 1954), 107–71.
120. Ibid., 29, 50–57, 235, 279–85.
121. Ibid., 9–24.
122. Philippe Ariès, *Histoire des populations françaises et de leurs attitudes devant la vie depuis le XVIIIᵉ siècle* (1948; rpt. Paris, 1976), 399–412.
123. Ariès, "L'Histoire des mentalités," 402–23, and *Un Historien du dimanche* (Paris, 1982), 185.
124. Ariès, *Le Temps,* 90–96, 102, 105, 291.
125. Ibid., 291–311.
126. Ariès, *Historien du dimanche,* 117, 185.
127. Ariès, *Le Temps,* 307–10.

2

THE ART OF MEMORY RECONCEIVED

1. For a good example of how the art of memory was applied, see Jonathan D. Spence, *The Memory Palace of Matteo Ricci* (New York, 1984), 1–23.
2. Frances A. Yates, *The Art of Memory* (Chicago, 1966), 1–2, 22. See also Herwig Blum, *Die antike Mnemotechnik* (Hildesheim, 1969), 41–46.
3. Alexander R. Luria, *The Mind of a Mnemonist,* trans. Lynn Solotaroff (Cambridge, Mass., 1968).
4. Ibid., 21–38. See also Alexander R. Luria, *The Making of Mind: A Personal Account of Soviet Psychology,* ed. Michael Cole and Sheila Cole (Cambridge, Mass., 1979), 179–87.
5. Luria, *Mind of a Mnemonist,* 66–73, 111–36, 149–60; cf. Michel Beaujour, *Miroirs d'encre* (Paris, 1980), 93–105.
6. See also the memoir by Jorge Luis Borges, "Funes the Memorious," *Labyrinths: Selected Stories and Other Writings,* ed. Donald A. Yates and James E. Irby (New York, 1964), 59–66.
7. The psychologists' disdain for mnemonics is discussed by B. Richard Bugelski, "Mne-

monics," in the *International Encyclopedia of Psychiatry, Psychology, Psychoanalysis, and Neurology,* ed. Benjamin B. Wolman (New York, 1977), 7: 245–50.

8. Paolo Rossi, *Clavis universalis: Arti mnemoniche e logica combinatoria da Lullo a Leibniz* (Milan, 1960).

9. Frances A. Yates, *Giordano Bruno and the Hermetic Tradition* (Chicago, 1964), and "The Hermetic Tradition in Renaissance Science," in *Art, Science and History in the Renaissance,* ed. Charles S. Singleton (Baltimore, 1967), 255–74.

10. Yates, *Art of Memory,* xi–xii, 145, 151.

11. Ibid., 2–26.

12. Ibid., 31–36, 230.

13. Ibid., 36–39.

14. Ibid., 129–59.

15. Ibid., 199–230, and Yates, *Collected Essays* (London, 1983), 2: 101–11.

16. Yates, *Art of Memory,* 251–60, 293–99, 339–41; cf. Robert S. Westman, "Magical Reform and Astronomical Reform: The Yates Thesis Reconsidered," in *Hermeticism and the Scientific Revolution,* ed. Robert S. Westman and J. E. McGuire (Los Angeles, 1977), 5–72, challenging Yates' thesis about the magical implications of Bruno's cosmological design.

17. Ibid., 370–73; and Yates, *Collected Essays,* 3: 60–66. See also Paolo Rossi, *Francis Bacon: From Magic to Science,* trans. Sacha Rabinovitch (London, 1968), 207–14.

18. Yates, *Art of Memory,* 368–69, 378–89.

19. Anachronistic applications of the art of memory nonetheless survived into the nineteenth and twentieth centuries. Representative approaches include: Gregor von Feinaigle, *The Art of Memory* (London, 1813); Aimé Paris, *Principes et applications diverses de la mnémonique,* 7th ed. (Paris, 1833); A. E. Middleton, *Memory Systems, Old and New,* 3d rev. ed. (New York, 1888); Laird S. Cermak, *Improving Your Memory* (New York, 1975); and Harry Lorayne, *Harry Lorayne's Page-a-Minute Memory Book* (New York, 1985).

20. For Vico's relationship to the classical tradition of rhetoric, see esp. Ernesto Grassi, *Rhetoric as Philosophy: The Humanist Tradition* (University Park, Pa., 1980); Michael Mooney, *Vico in the Tradition of Rhetoric* (Princeton, 1985); John D. Schaeffer, *Sensus Communis: Vico, Rhetoric, and the Limits of Relativism* (Durham, N.C., 1990).

21. On Vico's relationship to Renaissance Neoplatonic mnemonics, see Paolo Rossi, "Schede Vichiane," *La Rassegna della letteratura italiana* 62 (1958), 375–83, and *Francis Bacon,* 77–79, 133–34; Emile Namer, "G. B. Vico et Giordano Bruno," *Archives de philosophie* 40 (1977), 107–14; and Donald Phillip Verene, "L'Originalità filosofica di Vico," in *Vico oggi,* ed. Andrea Battistini (Rome, 1979), 114–17. On the roots of Vico's "tree of knowledge" in mnemonic imagery, see Giorgio Tagliacozzo, "General Education as Unity of Knowledge: A Theory Based on Vichian Principles," *Social Research* 43 (1976), 772, 774 n. 30.

22. *The New Science of Giambattista Vico* (3d ed.; 1744), trans. and ed. Thomas G. Bergin and Max H. Fisch (Ithaca, 1970), 331, 342, 349, 374–83, 391, 494, 846 (hereafter *NS*; all references are to numbered paragraphs).

23. *NS,* 201, 211, 699, 811, 819, 833, 855, 878, 896 contain Vico's principal references to memory.

24. *NS,* 221, 700, 814, 816, 819, 833, 933. On the role of memory in Vico's theory of mind, see Donald Phillip Verene, *Vico's Science of Imagination* (Ithaca, 1981), 96–126.

25. *NS,* 297–98, 699, 768. Cf. Yates, *Art of Memory,* 31.

26. *NS,* 236, 331, 404–11. See also Hayden V. White, "The Tropics of History: The Deep Structure of the *New Science,*" in *Giambattista Vico's Science of Humanity,* ed. Giorgio Tagliacozzo and Donald Phillip Verene (Baltimore, 1976), 65–85.

27. *NS,* 402.

28. *NS,* 331, 338, 846.
29. *NS,* 211, 217, 375–77, 381, 447, 520, 692, 849, 855, 878, 896. See also Patrick H. Hutton, "The *New Science* of Giambattista Vico: Historicism in Its Relation to Poetics," *Journal of Aesthetics and Art Criticism* 30 (1972), 362–64.
30. *NS,* 220, 429, 444, 518.
31. On Vico and hermeneutics, see Hans-Georg Gadamer, *Truth and Method,* 2d rev. ed., trans. Joel Weinsheimer and Donald G. Marshall (New York, 1989), 19–24.
32. *NS,* 122, 604–06, 713, 741.
33. Luria's study of the mind of the mnemonist Sherashevsky confirms Vico's explanation of the poetics of memory. When demonstrating his skill before audiences, Sherashevsky developed techniques to speed his commitment of facts to memory. When the facts were extremely difficult, he relied on detailed metaphorical associations. But to recall less complicated data, he intuitively turned to metonymic or synecdochic images. The easier the facts, the further he ascended the tropological gradient of abstraction in his search for images that might be incorporated more rapidly into his memory. Luria, *Mind of a Mnemonist,* 38–61.
34. Georges Gusdorf, "Conditions and Limits of Autobiography," in *Autobiography: Essays Theoretical and Critical,* ed. James Olney (Princeton, 1980), 32–33, 40.
35. *NS,* 1–30.
36. For background on the frontispiece, see Margherita Frankel, "The 'Dipintura' and the Structure of Vico's *New Science* as a Mirror of the World," in *Vico: Past and Present,* ed. Giorgio Tagliacozzo (Atlantic Highlands, N.J., 1981), 43–51; Donald Phillip Verene, "Vico's Frontispiece and the Tablet of Cebes," in *Man, God, and Nature in the Enlightenment,* ed. Donald C. Mell et al. (East Lansing, Mich., 1988), 3–11.
37. On Vico's chronology, see Paolo Rossi, *The Dark Abyss of Time,* trans. Lydia G. Cochrane (Chicago, 1984), 168–76.
38. On the impact of printing on European culture, see Robert Darnton, *The Business of the Enlightenment* (Cambridge, Mass., 1979), 428–34, and *The Literary Underground of the Old Regime* (Cambridge, Mass., 1982), 167–208; Elizabeth L. Eisenstein, *The Printing Press as an Agent of Change* (Cambridge, England, 1979), I: 3–159; Roger Chartier, ed., *The Culture of Print* (Princeton, 1989), 1–10.
39. Giambattista Vico, *On the Study Methods of Our Time* (1709), trans. Elio Gianturco (Ithaca, 1990), 14, 72–73. See also Alain Pons, "Introduction," in *Encyclopédie, ou dictionnaire raisonné des sciences des arts et des métiers,* ed. Denis Diderot (Paris, 1986), I: 27–29.
40. For overviews, see Joshua Meyrowitz, *No Sense of Place* (Oxford, 1985), 1–8, 74–81, 93–114; Mark Poster, *The Mode of Information* (Chicago, 1990), 42–46, 82–85.
41. Umberto Eco, "Mnemotechniche come semiotiche," *MondOperaio* 12 (1989), 110–14.
42. See, for example, Karl Löwith, *Meaning in History* (Chicago, 1949), 115–36; Isaiah Berlin, *Vico and Herder: Two Studies in the History of Ideas* (New York, 1976), 3–98.
43. Paul Thompson, *The Voice of the Past: Oral History,* 2d ed. (Oxford, 1988), 1–21; Fernand Braudel, "History and the Social Sciences," in *On History,* trans. Sarah Matthews (Chicago, 1980), 28–29.
44. See Patrick H. Hutton, "Vico's Significance for the New Cultural History," *New Vico Studies* 3 (1985), 73–84.
45. Andrea Battistini, "Vico in America," *Lettera internazionale* 5/20 (1989), 47–48.
46. Originally propounded in Giambattista Vico, *On the Most Ancient Wisdom of the Italians* (1710), trans. Lucia M. Palmer (Ithaca, 1988), 152–58. See also *NS,* 151–52, 240, 354, and *The Autobiography of Giambattista Vico,* ed. and trans. Max Harold Fisch and Thomas Goddard Bergin (Ithaca, 1944), 148–53, 167.
47. See, for example, Jean Starobinski, *Words upon Words,* trans. Olivia Emmet (New Ha-

ven, 1979), 3–6, 120–23, 129; Jack Goody, *The Interface between the Written and the Oral* (Cambridge, England, 1987), 3–8, 261–64, 299–300; Brian Stock, *Listening for the Text* (Baltimore, 1990), 5–15, 129, 141–48.

48. *NS*, 145, 162, 428–29, 431, 1045; Vico, *Autobiography*, 169.

49. *NS*, 541, 679.

50. *NS*, 225, 401, 429, 432, 434, 680–81, 928–31.

51. *NS*, 128, 384, 522, 666.

52. *NS*, 738, 811, 815. On the remodeling of memory, see Jan Vansina, *Oral Tradition as History* (Madison, Wisc, 1985), 160–61.

53. *NS*, 338, 738.

54. For our purposes, see his references in the *NS* to Cicero, Dionysius of Halicarnassus, Livy, Polybius, Ulpian, and Varro on Roman law: Horace, Josephus, and Longinus on the Homeric epics.

55. *NS*, 1027, 1037.

56. *NS*, 473, 904.

57. For my orientation on the topic, I am indebted to Max H. Fisch, "Vico on Roman Law," in *Essays in Political Theory Presented to George H. Sabine*, ed. Milton R. Konvitz et al. (Ithaca, 1948), 62–88. See also Elio Gianturco, "Vico's Significance in the History of Legal Thought," in *Giambattista Vico: An International Symposium*, ed. Giorgio Tagliacozzo et al. (Baltimore, 1969), 327–47.

58. *NS*, 310, 313, 329, 394, 493, 972.

59. *NS*, 598, 612; Vico, *Autobiography*, 172, 193. See also Bruce A. Haddock, *Vico's Political Thought* (Swansea, England), 72–112.

60. *NS*, 394, 493, 972–73, 978, 1009.

61. *NS*, 309–11.

62. To confirm his point, Vico cites Jean Bodin, who argued for the aristocratic character of ancient Roman law. *NS*, 663, 952, 1009. On the interest of sixteenth-century French scholars in the customary sources of Roman law, see J. G. A. Pocock, *The Ancient Constitution and the Feudal Law* (Cambridge, England, 1957), 8–29; Donald R. Kelley, "Vico's Road: From Philology to Jurisprudence and Back," in *Giambattista Vico's Science of Humanity*, ed. Giorgio Tagliacozzo et al. (Baltimore, 1976), 15–29.

63. For a discussion of its place in Roman law, see Wolfgang Kunkel, *An Introduction to Roman Legal and Constitutional History*, 2d ed., trans. J. M. Kelly (Oxford, 1973), 23–33; Alan Watson, *Rome of the Twelve Tables* (Princeton, 1975), 3–8.

64. For a modern critical edition, see *The Twelve Tables*, ed. P. R. Coleman-Norton, rev. ed. (Princeton, 1960), 1–30.

65. *NS*, 598, 600, 612, 987.

66. *NS*, 631, 663, 677, 984–85, 1001.

67. *NS*, 394, 987.

68. The Law of the Twelve Tables revealed some of these but continued to withhold others, leading to the plebeians' demand three years later for public recognition of their marriages (the Canulean Law). *NS*, 284, 422, 612, 953.

69. *NS*, 398.

70. *NS*, 640, 653.

71. *NS*, 112, 612.

72. *NS*, 952, 978.

73. Vico notes that Cicero as a schoolboy in the first century (B.C.) was still obliged to commit the Law to memory. *NS*, 469. See also Kelley, "Vico's Road," 22.

74. On the legend, see A. Arthur Schiller, *Roman Law: Mechanisms of Development* (The Hague, 1978), 153–57.

75. *NS*, 987. See also Fisch, "Vico on Roman Law," 66–71.

76. *NS*, 386, 523, 570, 952, 968, 1027, 1030–31.

77. *NS*, 112, 653, 953.
78. *NS*, 284–85, 612, 769, 992, 1031.
79. *NS*, 642.
80. *NS*, 1003.
81. *NS*, 662, 952, 984, 1045.
82. Gianturco, "Vico's Significance in the History of Legal Thought," 328.
83. Patrick H. Hutton, "The Print Revolution of the Eighteenth Century and the Drafting of Written Constitutions," *Vermont History* 56 (1988), 161.
84. Michael Steinberg, "The Twelve Tables and Their Origins: An Eighteenth-Century Debate," *Journal of the History of Ideas* 43 (1982), 379–96.
85. See esp. Donald R. Kelley, *Historians and the Law in Postrevolutionary France* (Princeton, 1984), 101–05, and *The Human Measure: Social Thought in the Western Legal Tradition* (Cambridge, Mass., 1990), 239–42.
86. Jules Michelet, *Histoire Romaine* (1833), in *Œuvres complètes,* ed. Paul Viallaneix (Paris, 1972), 2: 340–42.
87. Gianturco, "Vico's Significance in the History of Legal Thought," 330–42; Pocock, *Ancient Constitution,* 246, 248.
88. On recent work on the sources of law in custom, see Donald R. Kelley, " 'Second Nature': The Idea of Custom in European Law, Society, and Culture," in *The Transmission of Culture in Early Modern Europe,* ed. Anthony Grafton and Ann Blair (Philadelphia, 1990), 131–72.
89. *NS*, 6, 41, 873. Cf. Bruce A. Haddock, "Vico's Discovery of the True Homer: A Case Study in Historical Reconstruction," *Journal of the History of Ideas* 40 (1979), 583–602, and Isaiah Berlin, "Vico and the Ideal of the Enlightenment," *Social Research* 43 (1976), 645–51.
90. *NS*, 904. See also Fisch, "Vico on Roman Law," 70–71.
91. *NS*, 780, 867.
92. *NS*, 904.
93. *NS*, 787, 806, 808, 836, 825.
94. *NS*. 23, 66, 788, 819.
95. *NS*, 852, 869–72, 878.
96. *NS*, 819, 873.
97. *NS*, 862.
98. *NS*, 808, 849, 851, 856.
99. *NS*, 852.
100. *NS*, 802, 808, 814–15.
101. *NS*, 652, 789, 866, 868, 879–80.
102. Vico places Homer chronologically some 460 years after the Trojan War, "about the period of (the Roman king) Numa" in the mid-eighth century B.C., a date that corresponds closely to that proposed by scholars today. *NS*, 853.
103. On the historical emergence of a more pronounced sense of personal identity, see Roy F. Baumeister, *Identity: Cultural Change and the Struggle for Self* (Oxford, 1986), 63–65; David Lowenthal, *The Past Is a Foreign Country* (Cambridge, England, 1985), 198–99; on the increasingly possessive character of authorship, Michel Foucault, *The Order of Things: An Archaeology of the Human Sciences,* trans. anon. (New York, 1970), 294–300, and "What Is an Author?" in *Language, Counter-Memory, Practice: Selected Essays and Interviews by Michel Foucault,* ed. Donald F. Bouchard (Ithaca, 1977), 124–31.
104. See the review of nineteenth-century Homeric criticism by John L. Myres, *Homer and His Critics* (London, 1958), 86–93, 197–219.
105. Many of these scholars acknowledged that the Homeric epics had more than one author. Indeed, they divided into schools of Unitarians (one author) and Analysts (several) over the question. But even the Analysts tended to treat the epics as an

aggregation of text fragments contributed by individual authors. The proposition that oral poetry was a different kind of creative enterprise from the written one with which they were familiar escaped them. John Miles Foley, *The Theory of Oral Composition* (Bloomington, Ind., 1988), 2–10.

106. Milman Parry, "Cor Huso: A Study of Southslavic Song," in *The Making of Homeric Verse: The Collected Papers of Milman Parry,* ed. Adam Parry (Oxford, 1971), 439–64.

107. Milman Parry, "The Historical Method in Literary Criticism," in ibid., 408–13.

108. Milman Parry, "Studies in the Epic Technique of Oral Verse-Making. II. The Homeric Language as the Language of an Oral Poetry," in ibid., 325–61.

109. See Albert B. Lord, "Homer, Parry and Huso," in ibid., 465–78.

110. Albert B. Lord, *The Singer of Tales* (Cambridge, Mass., 1960), 124–38, and "Memory, Fixity, and Genre in Oral Traditional Poetries," in *Oral Traditional Literature: A Festschrift for Albert Bates Lord,* ed. John Miles Foley (Columbus, Ohio, 1981), 451–61.

111. *NS,* 331.

112. Eric A. Havelock, *Preface to Plato* (Cambridge, Mass.,, 1963), 41, 47–49, 134, 137.

113. Ibid., 3–15, 165, 266.

114. Ibid., 45, 88, 91, 138, 228–30.

115. Ibid., 137, 208, 218–19, 267.

116. To explain this transition from the poetic to the prosaic mind, both authors find a prominent place for the poet Hesiod, who, situated in the midst of the change, recounts the genealogy of this transition. Equally intriguing is the equation they both draw between law and poetry as indices of this collective mentality. Havelock, *Preface,* 115, 97–111; *NS,* 97, 699, 819, 856, 901.

117. Havelock, *Preface,* 20–25, 30, 45; *NS,* 215–18, 225–29.

118. *NS,* 204, 225–29, 348, 447, 565–66, 590, 1032.

119. *NS,* 201, 211, 699, 811, 819.

120. Havelock, *Preface,* 41–45, 101, 120–22, 140–42; *NS,* 699, 819.

121. *NS,* 7, 156, 904.

122. Havelock, *Preface,* 61–84, 115, 125.

123. *NS,* 125, 1111.

124. *NS,* 59.

125. In his critique of these present-minded notions of a past that is undifferentiated from the present, Vico anticipated the famous critique of Whig history offered by the English historian Herbert Butterfield in his *The Whig Interpretation of History* (London, 1931) only a generation ago. Butterfield noted the tendency of English historians to read into their nation's past their present notions about England's destiny. They read the past anachronistically in terms of what they wanted to remember about it and so distorted the meaning it held for those for whom it had been a living experience.

126. *NS,* 44, 222, 738, 846.

127. *NS,* 137.

128. *NS,* 139.

129. *NS,* 140.

130. *NS,* 321.

131. *NS,* 149, 150, 356.

132. *NS,* 401, 808, 814.

133. *NS,* 1036.

134. *NS,* 367; Paolo Rossi, "Schede Vichiane," *La Rassegna della letteratura italiana* 62 (1958), 380–82; Giorgio Tagliacozzo, *The Arbor Scientiae Reconceived and the History of Vico's Resurrection* (Atlantic Highlands, N.J., 1993).

135. *NS,* 1097–1112.

136. See esp. Eric A. Havelock, *The Muse Learns to Write* (New Haven, 1986), 1–126; Ruth

Finnegan, *Literacy and Orality: Studies in the Technology of Communication* (Oxford, 1988), 15–44, 139–74.
137. Walter J. Ong, *Orality and Literacy: The Technologizing of the Word* (London, 1982), 81–83, 93–103, 130–38, 152, 156–60, and *Rhetoric, Romance, and Technology* (Ithaca, 1971), 272–302.
138. Ong, *Orality and Literacy,* 117–23.
139. Ibid., 115–16.
140. For a discussion of affinities between Vico and Ong within the tradition of rhetoric, see Schaeffer, *Sensus Communis,* 6–11.
141. Ibid., 136–38; *NS,* 1046.
142. *NS,* 349, 1096.
143. On the differences between Vico and Derrida on the theory of language, see the discerning discussion by Schaeffer, *Sensus Communis,* 127–49. See also Terence Hawkes, *Structuralism and Semiotics* (Berkeley, 1977), 145–50.
144. *NS,* 822.
145. *NS,* 412.
146. *NS,* 1051, 1078–87.
147. *NS,* 218–19, 221, 241–42, 707, 916–18.
148. Eliade, too, relates the cyclical conception of history in preliterate societies to the dynamics of collective memory. *Cosmos and History: The Myth of the Eternal Return,* trans. Willard R. Trask (New York, 1959), 34–48. Cf. Donald Phillip Verene, "Eliade's Vichianism: The Regeneration of Time and the Terror of History," *New Vico Studies* 4 (1986), 115–21.
149. See Löwith, *Meaning in History,* 131–34; H. Stuart Hughes, "Vico and Contemporary Social Theory and Social History," in *Giambattista Vico: An International Symposium,* ed. Tagliacozzo, 319–21; Arnold J. Toynbee, *A Study of History: Reconsiderations* (London, 1961), 12: 584–87.
150. *NS,* 338.
151. *NS,* 331.

3

WILLIAM WORDSWORTH AND SIGMUND FREUD

1. William Wordsworth, *The Prelude* (1805), XI, vss. 344–88, ed. Jonathan Wordsworth, M. H. Abrams, and Stephen Gill (New York, 1979), 433–34. All subsequent references are to book and verse of the 1805 edition.
2. *The Prelude,* III, 189.
3. *The Autobiography of Giambattista Vico* (1731), trans. Max Harold Fisch and Thomas Goddard Bergin (Ithaca, 1944).
4. A great deal has recently been written about the role of memory in autobiography. Some of the best articles on the topic are reproduced in the anthology edited by James Olney, *Autobiography: Essays Theoretical and Critical* (Princeton, 1980). Indispensable on conceptions of memory in this context is the wide-ranging study by Georges Gusdorf, *Mémoire et personne,* 2 vols. (Paris, 1951). For the relationship between the classical art of memory and the rhetoric of autobiography, see Beaujour, *Miroirs d'encre* (Paris, 1980), esp. 81–112.
5. William L. Howarth, "Some Principles of Autobiography," and Michael Sprinker, "The End of Autobiography," in Olney (ed.), *Autobiography,* 113, 325–26.
6. Jean-Jacques Rousseau, *The Confessions* (1781), trans. J.M. Cohen (Baltimore, 1953), 17.
7. Jean Starobinski, "The Style of Autobiography," in Olney (ed.), *Autobiography,* 80–82; Samuel S.B. Taylor, "Rousseau's Romanticism," in *Reappraisals of Rousseau,* ed. Simon

Harvey et al. (Totowa, N.J., 1980), 16–17; Ann Hartle, *The Modern Self in Rousseau's Confessions* (Notre Dame, Ind., 1983), 115–17.

8. On this point, see the interesting discussion by Robert Darnton, *The Great Cat Massacre and Other Episodes in French History* (New York, 1984), 215–52.

9. For biographies of Wordsworth, see Stephen Gill, *William Wordsworth: A Life* (Oxford, 1989); Mary Moorman, *William Wordsworth: A Biography*, 2 vols. (Oxford, 1957–65).

10. *The Prelude*, X, 692–93.

11. On Wordsworth's autobiography as an exploration of his interior life, see also James A.W. Heffernan, *Wordsworth's Theory of Poetry: The Transforming Imagination* (Ithaca, 1969), 264–71.

12. *The Prelude*, II, 29–33.

13. On the problem of memory in Wordsworth, see Bennett Weaver, "Wordsworth's *Prelude*: The Poetic Function of Memory," *Studies in Philology* 34 (1937), 552–63, and "Wordsworth's *Prelude*: An Intimation of Certain Problems in Criticism," *Studies in Philology* 31 (1934), 534–40; Richard J. Onorato, *The Character of the Poet: Wordsworth in "The Prelude"* (Princeton, 1971), 164–219.

14. On the versions of *The Prelude*, see Jonathan Wordsworth et al. "The Texts: History and Presentation," in Jonathan Wordsworth (ed.), *The Prelude*, pp. 510–26.

15. *The Prelude*, XI, 257–78. See also Alan Richardson, "Wordsworth at the Crossroads: 'Spots of Time' in the 'Two-Part Prelude,'" *The Wordsworth Circle* 19 (1988), 15–20.

16. *The Prelude*, XI, 335.

17. Ibid., XI, 279–327.

18. Ibid., 428–81.

19. Ibid., XI, 344–88.

20. Ibid., 363–504.

21. On the design of *The Prelude*, see M. H. Abrams, *Natural Supernaturalism: Tradition and Revolution in Romantic Literature* (New York, 1971), 74–80, 278–92; Geoffrey H. Hartman, *Wordsworth's Poetry* (New Haven, 1964), 208–59.

22. In this respect, see also Wordsworth's most famous short poem, "Lines Composed a Few Miles above Tintern Abbey," in *William Wordsworth, Poems*, ed. John O. Hayden (Harmondsworth, England, 1977), I, 357–62.

23. *The Prelude*, I, 373–426; II, 48–76; V, 57; VIII, 576–77, 712–41. On Wordsworth's cave imagery, see also Herbert Lindenberger, *On Wordsworth's Prelude* (Princeton, 1963), 79–85.

24. Hartman, *Wordsworth's Poetry*, 108, 212–13.

25. *The Prelude*, I, 428–51, 572–662; V, 608–29; VII, 717–41; VIII, 428–97; X, 604–12; XII, 1–13, 220–312; XIII, 67–118.

26. Ibid., II, 365–71; III, 142–67; IV, 200–21; V, 473–81.

27. Ibid., VIII, 512–22, 583–623; XIII, 289–331. On the relationship between imagination and fancy in Wordsworth, see M. H. Abrams, *The Mirror and the Lamp: Romantic Theory and the Critical Tradition* (New York, 1953), 180–82.

28. *The Prelude*, I, 626.

29. Ibid., II, 334–38.

30. Ibid., III, 340; VIII, 222–311.

31. Ibid., X, 440–44.

32. Cf. Alan Liu, *Wordsworth: The Sense of History* (Stanford, Calif., 1989), 3–51.

33. *The Prelude*, XI, 259.

34. Ibid., X, 904–40; XI, 74–95.

35. Ibid., III, 11.

36. Ibid., III, 260.

37. Ibid., V, 167–92; VIII, 754–68; XI, 250–56.

38. Ibid., VIII, 222–311.

39. Ibid., X, 662–65.

40. Ibid., VI, 488–523.

41. Ibid., XI, 341–42.

42. Sigmund Freud, "A Disturbance of Memory on the Acropolis," in *The Standard Edition of the Complete Psychological Works of Sigmund Freud*, trans. James Strachey (London, 1964), 22: 239–48.

43. Carlo Ginzburg, "Clues: Morelli, Freud, and Sherlock Holmes," in *The Sign of the Three*, ed. Umberto Eco and Thomas A. Sebeok (Bloomington, Ind., 1983), 84–87.

44. See Beaujour, *Miroirs d'encre*, 210, 213–16.

45. Sigmund Freud, *A Phylogenetic Fantasy*, ed. Ilse Grubrich-Simitis, trans. Axel Hoffer and Peter T. Hoffer (Cambridge, Mass., 1987), 5–20.

46. *The New Science of Giambattista Vico* (3d ed., 1744), trans. and ed. Thomas G. Bergin and Max H. Frisch (Ithaca, 1970), 346, 717 (references are to numbered paragraphs). For the relationship between Vico's and Freud's theories of mind, see Silvano Arieti, "Vico and Modern Psychiatry," *Social Research* 43 (1976), 739–50.

47. On the romantic antecedents of Freud's thought, see Lancelot Law Whyte, *The Unconscious before Freud* (New York, 1960), 167–70, 177–90; Henri F. Ellenberger, *The Discovery of the Unconscious* (New York, 1970), 204–10, 222–23; Arthur K. Berliner, *Psychoanalysis and Society* (Washington, D.C., 1983), 21–25.

48. Sigmund Freud, *An Autobiographical Study* (1925), trans. James Strachey (New York, 1952).

49. Carl E. Schorske, *Fin-de-Siècle Vienna: Politics and Culture* (New York, 1980), 6–8, 185–89; Peter Gay, *Freud: A Life for Our Time* (New York, 1988), 16–19.

50. Sigmund Freud, *Civilization and Its Discontents* (1930), trans. James Strachey (New York, 1961), 23–30.

51. Sigmund Freud, *An Outline of Psychoanalysis* (1940), trans. James Strachey (New York, 1949), 29–39.

52. Ibid., 52–64; *Civilization and Its Discontents*, 21–32; *Five Lectures on Psycho-Analysis* (1910), trans. James Strachey (New York, 1977), 49–55.

53. Sigmund Freud, *The Ego and the Id* (1923), trans. Joan Riviere (New York, 1960), 9–49; *Outline of Psychoanalysis*, 1–21.

54. Sigmund Freud, *Introductory Lectures on Psychoanalysis* (1917), trans. James Strachey (New York, 1966), 367–68; *Five Lectures on Psycho-Analysis*, 22–39.

55. Sigmund Freud, *The Interpretation of Dreams* (1900), trans. James Strachey (New York, 1965), 54.

56. Sigmund Freud, *The Psychopathology of Everyday Life* (1901), trans. Alan Tyson (New York, 1965), 43–52.

57. Freud, *Outline of Psychoanalysis*, 29–39.

58. For the history of Freud's formulation of the technique of psychoanalysis, see William J. McGrath, *Freud's Discovery of Psychoanalysis* (Ithaca, 1986).

59. Sigmund Freud, "Further Recommendations in the Technique of Psycho-Analysis: Recollection, Repetition and Working Through" (1914), *The Collected Papers of Sigmund Freud*, trans. Joan Riviere (New York, 1959), 2: 366–76.

60. Freud also characterized psychoanalysis as an archaeology of the unconscious. In one of his first formulations of the psychoanalytic method, he likened the recovery of a patient's repressed memories to the excavation of the ruins of an ancient palace or treasure house. Sigmund Freud, "The Aetiology of Hysteria (1896)," in *Collected Papers of Freud*, 1: 184–85. See also Peter Gay, *Freud, Jews and Other Germans* (Oxford, 1978), 39–46.

61. Freud, "The Aetiology of Hysteria," 1: 188–97; "Further Recommendations on the Technique of Psychoanalysis," 2: 366–76.

62. Freud, "The Aetiology of Hysteria" 1: 188–97.

63. Ibid., 1: 207–08; "Further Recommendations in the Technique of Psycho-Analysis," 2: 374–75; *Introductory Lectures on Psychoanalysis,* 243–56.

64. Freud, "Further Recommendations in the Technique of Psycho-Analysis," 2: 368–71; "Repression" (1915), in *Collected Papers of Freud,* 4: 84–97; "Extracts from the Fliess Papers," in *Standard Edition of the Complete Works of Freud,* 1: 220–39; *Five Lectures on Psycho-Analysis,* 16–23.

65. Freud, "Repression," 4: 93; *Five Lectures on Psycho-Analysis,* 24–28.

66. On the ties between mnemonics and psychoanalysis, see Freud, "The Aetiology of Hysteria," 1: 184–85.

67. Freud, *The Interpretation of Dreams,* 647–48.

68. Ibid., 44–55.

69. Sigmund Freud, "Screen Memories" (1899), in *The Standard Edition of the Complete Works of Freud,* 3: 303–22, and *The Psychopathology of Everyday Life,* 43–52. See also Paul Ricoeur, *Freud and Philosophy,* trans. Denis Savage (New Haven, 1970), 91, 97, 105.

70. Freud, "Screen Memories," 307, and *Psychopathology of Everyday Life,* 43–45, 50.

71. "Screen Memories," 307.

72. *Psychopathology of Everyday Life,* 49 n.2.

73. "Screen Memories," 308–09.

74. Ibid., 322; *Psychopathology of Everyday Life,* 43, 45.

75. Sigmund Freud, *Leonardo da Vinci: A Study in Psychosexuality* (1910), trans. A. A. Brill (New York, 1947), esp. 33–49. See also Freud's analysis of a screen memory taken from the autobiography of Johann von Goethe in his "A Childhood Recollection from *Dichtung und Wahrheit*" (1917), in *Standard Edition of the Works of Freud,* 17: 147–56.

76. For the parallel between Wordsworth's spots of time and Freud's screen memories, see David Ellis, *Wordsworth, Freud and the Spots of Time* (Cambridge, England, 1985), 18–19, 63–67.

77. On Freud as historian, see Peter Gay, *Freud for Historians* (Oxford, 1985), esp. 181–212; Michael S. Roth, *Psycho-Analysis as History* (Ithaca, 1987), esp. 21–24, 128–33; Paul Roazen, *Encountering Freud: The Politics and Histories of Psychoanalysis* (New Brunswick, N.J., 1990), 261–81.

78. Freud, *Civilization and Its Discontents,* 86–89; *An Autobiographical Study,* 138; *Moses and Monotheism* (1937), trans. Katherine Jones (New York, 1967), 90–101, 125–29, 153.

79. Sigmund Freud, *Totem and Taboo,* (1913), trans. James Strachey (New York, 1950), 155; *Moses and Monotheism,* 101–02, 164–69.

80. *Totem and Taboo,* 142–53; *Civilization and Its Discontents,* 47–54; *Moses and Monotheism,* 102–08, 152–53; *New Introductory Lectures on Psychoanalysis* (1933), trans. James Strachey (New York, 1965), 160–71.

81. *Totem and Taboo,* 153–55; *Moses and Monotheism,* 108–14, 174–76.

82. *Totem and Taboo,* 157; *Civilization and its Discontents,* 79; *Moses and Monotheism,* 157–60, 170.

83. See the important recent study by Yosef Yerushalmi, *Freud's Moses: Judaism Terminable and Interminable* (New Haven, 1991).

84. Freud, *Moses and Monotheism,* 16–65. Cf. Yerushalmi, *Freud's Moses,* 4–5.

85. Freud, *Moses and Monotheism,* 170–71.

86. Ibid., 125–30. See also Freud, *A Phylogenetic Fantasy,* 5–20.

87. Freud, *Moses and Monotheism,* 166–67.

88. Ibid., 169–76.

89. On temporality in Freud's conception of memory, see the interesting essay by Peter Munz, "The Evocation of the Senses by Freud and Proust," in *"Sinnlichkeit in Bild*

und Klang"; Festschrift für Paul Hoffmann zum 70, ed. Hansgerd Delbruck (Stuttgart, 1987), 415–29.

90. On the challenge to the notion of the integral self in autobiography, see Sprinker, "Fictions of the Self," in Olney (ed.), *Autobiography,* 321–42.

91. Michel Foucault, "Nietzsche, Genealogy, History," in *Language, Counter-Memory, Practice: Selected Essays and Interviews,* ed. Donald F. Bouchard (Ithaca, 1977), 139–64.

92. Oliver Sacks, "The Lost Mariner," *The New York Review of Books* (16 February 1984), 18–19.

93. Saul Friedländer, "Introduction," in *Probing the Limits of Representation: Nazism and the "Final Solution,"* ed. Saul Friedländer (Cambridge, Mass., 1992), 4–9.

94. Saul Friedländer, *When Memory Comes,* trans. Helen R. Lane (New York, 1979).

95. Saul Friedländer, *History and Psychoanalysis: An Inquiry into the Possibilities and Limits of Psychohistory,* trans. Susan Suleiman (New York, 1978), 1–42.

96. Lawrence L. Langer, *Holocaust Testimonies: The Ruins of Memory* (New Haven, 1991), 1–38.

97. Saul Friedländer, "Trauma, Transference and 'Working Through' in Writing the History of the *Shoah,*" in *History and Memory* 4/1 (Spring/Summer 1992), 39–59.

4

MAURICE HALBWACHS AS HISTORIAN OF COLLECTIVE MEMORY

1. Maurice Halbwachs, *Les Cadres sociaux de la mémoire* (1925; rpt. Paris, 1971), 18.

2. For an overview of Halbwachs's work, see the doctoral thesis by Suzanne Vromen, "The Sociology of Maurice Halbwachs" (New York University, 1975). For Halbwachs's assessment of the work of Durkheim, see his essay "La Doctrine d'Emile Durkheim," *Revue philosophique de la France et de l'étranger* 85 (1918), 353–411.

3. Subsequently he taught at the Sorbonne (1935–1939), and in his last years he held an appointment at the Collège de France.

4. For their appreciations of Halbwachs's work, see Paul Connerton, *How Societies Remember* (Cambridge, England, 1989), 36–38; Barry Schwartz, "The Social Context of Commemoration: A Study in Collective Memory," *Social Forces* 61 (1982), 375; Roger Bastide, "Mémoire collective et sociologie de bricolage," *L'Année sociologique,* 3d series, 21 (1970), 65–108.

5. Mary Douglas, "Introduction: Maurice Halbwachs (1877–1945)," in *The Collective Memory* (1950), by Maurice Halbwachs, trans. Francis J. Ditter and Vida Yazdi Ditter (New York, 1980), 1–21.

6. Mary Douglas, *Edward Evans-Pritchard* (New York, 1980), 76–77. See also her study of institutional memory, *How Institutions Think* (Syracuse, 1986), 70, 80, in which she suggests the significance of Halbwachs's theory for understanding the problem of structural amnesia.

7. Frederic C. Bartlett, *Remembering: A Study in Experimental and Social Psychology* (Cambridge, England, 1932), 294–96. Curiously, Bartlett does not stress this parallel. Instead, he emphasizes the limitations of Halbwachs's theory because it deals with collective memory in, not of, groups.

8. Barry Schwartz, "The Reconstruction of Abraham Lincoln," in *Collective Remembering,* ed. David Middleton and Derek Edwards (London, 1990), 81–107; Yael Zerubavel, "The Politics of Interpretation: Tel Hai in Israel's Collective Memory," *Journal of the Association for Jewish Studies* 16 (1991), 133–59, "New Beginnings, Old Past: The Collective Memory of Pioneering Israeli Culture," in *New Perspecitves on Israeli History,* ed. Laurence J. Silberstein (New York, 1990), 193–215; Barry Schwartz, Yael

Zerubavel, and Bernice Barnett, "The Recovery of Masada: A Study in Collective Memory," *The Sociological Quarterly* 27 (1986), 147–64.

9. See the discussion of Halbwachs in relationship to the renewed interest in the sociology of collective memory by Lewis A. Coser, "Introduction: Maurice Halbwachs, 1877–1945," in *On Collective Memory*, by Maurice Halbwachs, ed. and trans. Lewis A. Coser (Chicago, 1992), 1–34.

10. Terry Nichols Clark, *Prophets and Patrons: The French University and the Emergence of the Social Sciences* (Cambridge, Mass., 1973), 189n.

11. Philippe Ariès, *Les Traditions sociales dans les pays de France* (Paris, 1943), 10–11. See Patrick H. Hutton, "Collective Memory and Collective Mentalities: The Halbwachs-Ariès Connection," *Historical Reflections/Réflexions historiques* 15 (1988), 313–22.

12. Recent appreciations include Henry Rousso, *The Vichy Syndrome: History and Memory in France since 1944*, trans. Arthur Goldhammer (Cambridge, Mass., 1991), 2; Natalie Zemon Davis and Randolph Starn, "Introduction: Memory and Counter-Memory," *Representations* 26 (Spring 1989), 2–4; Gérard Namer, *La Commémoration en France, 1944–82* (Paris, 1983), 5–6, and "Affectivité et temporalité de la mémoire," *L'Homme et la société* 90 (1988), 9–14; Françoise Zonabend, *The Enduring Memory: Time and History in a French Village*, trans. Anthony Forster (Manchester, 1984), 201; Pierre Nora, "Mémoire collective," in *La Nouvelle Histoire*, ed. Jacques Le Goff et al. (Paris, 1978), 398–401.

13. Nathan Wachtel, "Memory and History," *History and Anthropology* 2/2 (October 1986), 207–24. See also Freddy Raphaël, "Le Travail de la mémoire et les limites de l'histoire orale," *Les Annales: Economies, sociétés, civilisations* 35/1 (January–February 1980), 127–45; Paul Thompson, *The Voice of the Past*, 2d ed. (Oxford, 1988), 62; Philippe Joutard, "Mémoire collective," in *Dictionnaire des sciences historiques*, ed. André Burguière (Paris, 1986), 447–49.

14. For an overview of the politics of representation as a "postmodern" problem, see Steven Connor, *Postmodernist Culture* (London, 1989), 3–21, 224–29.

15. See, for example, Ann Rigney, *The Rhetoric of Historical Representation: Three Narrative Histories of the French Revolution* (Cambridge, England, 1990); Philippe Carrard, *Poetics of the New History: French Historical Discourse from Braudel to Chartier* (Baltimore, 1992).

16. Even though the work itself has an unfinished feel. See the comments on the problems of its organization and presentation by Fernand Dumont in his preface to *La Topographie légendaire des évangiles en Terre Sainte*, by Maurice Halbwachs (1941; rpt. Paris, 1971), v–vi.

17. See Bloch's review of Halbwachs's *Cadres sociaux* in his "Mémoire collective, tradition et coutume: A propos d'un livre récent," *Revue de synthèse* 40 (1925), 73–83. For Febvre's comment on Halbwachs's work, see his note in *Les Annales: Economies, Sociétés, Civilisations* 1 (1946), 289.

18. Peter Burke, *The French Historical Revolution: The Annales School, 1929–89* (Stanford, Calif., 1990), 16, 22, 24–25, 103.

19. Lucien Febvre, *A New Kind of History*, ed. Peter Burke (New York, 1973): "History and Psychology," 5–11; "A New Kind of History," 40–42.

20. On Halbwachs's relations with the historians and his place within French scholarship generally, see the informative articles by John E. Craig, "Maurice Halbwachs à Strasbourg," *Revue française de sociologie* 20 (1979), 273–92, and "Sociology and Related Disciplines between the Wars: Maurice Halbwachs and the Imperialism of the Durkheimians," in *The Sociological Domain: The Durkheimians and the Founding of French Sociology*, ed. Philippe Besnard (Cambridge, England, 1983), 263–89.

21. Halbwachs, *La Mémoire collective*, 78, 83–87, 105–06.

22. Ibid., 52.

23. Ibid., 79.
24. Halbwachs was much taken with the methods of the literary scholar Gustave Lanson, who attempted a scientific study of literary texts. He notes how religious scholars soon adopted Lanson's methods. *La Topographie*, 3–4.
25. On French historiography in the early twentieth century, see William R. Keylor, *Academy and Community: The Foundation of the French Historical Profession* (Cambridge, Mass., 1975), 163–207.
26. *Collective Memory*, 55.
27. Ibid., 79–87.
28. Ibid., 78, 106–07.
29. On this point, see Wachtel, "Memory and History," 207; Pierre Nora, "Entre histoire et mémoire," in *Les Lieux de mémoire*, ed. Pierre Nora (Paris, 1984), I: xx–xxiii; David Lowenthal, *The Past Is a Foreign Country* (Cambridge, England, 1985), 185–259.
30. Halbwachs, *Cadres sociaux*, 35, 38–39, 92, 114–45, 275, *Collective Memory*, 30–33, 59.
31. *Cadres sociaux*, 4–8, 17. On this point, he was critical of Bergson as well. See *Collective Memory*, 75.
32. Sigmund Freud, *The Interpretation of Dreams* (1900), trans. James Strachey (New York, 1965), 53–54, *The Psychopathology of Everyday Life* (1901), trans. Alan Tyson (New York, 43–48, "Screen Memories," (1899), in *Early Psychoanalytic Writings*, ed. Philip Rieff (New York, 1963), 229–50.
33. *Cadres sociaux*, vii–viii, 3, 21–27, 36, 40–60, 278. See also his essay, "Individual Psychology and Collective Psychology," *American Sociological Review* 3 (1938), 615–23.
34. *Cadres sociaux*, 34–35, 110, 143, 155, 203; *Collective Memory*, 44–49, 64, 69, 77–78.
35. Halbwachs borrowed this notion of an interplay between two moments of memory from his former teacher, Henri Bergson, who developed a theory of the antinomies of memory in his *Matter and Memory* (1908), trans. Nancy Margaret Paul and W. Scott Palmer (New York, 1988), 79–90. He was also influenced by the work of the English naturalist Samuel Butler, *Life and Habit* (1878; rpt. London, 1924). On Bergson, see *Cadres sociaux*, 98–103; on Butler, 96, n. 1, 99, n. 1, 174.
36. *Cadres sociaux*, 98–103, 138–40, 142, 281; *Collective Memory*, 70–71, 76–78, 140–41. Cf. Connerton, *How Societies Remember*, 37–38, who contends that Halbwachs does not deal adequately with the problem of memory as habit.
37. *Cadres sociaux*, 104, 199, 214–16, 282, 292, 296; *Collective Memory*, 124–27.
38. Halbwachs explores variations on a theme in his chapters on familial, religious, and social traditions. He shows how some traditions can raise major obstacles to modification, as in the case of religious dogma, while others are far more fluid and permit tradition to be reinvented, as in the transformation of the European nobility in early modern European culture. *Cadres sociaux*, 198–217, 236–41.
39. *Collective Memory*, 139, 154–57.
40. Ibid., 90–93, 98–101.
41. *Cadres sociaux*, 126. Cf. Eviatar Zerubavel, *The Seven Day Circle* (New York, 1985).
42. *La Topographie*, 124. On the art of memory, see Frances Yates, *The Art of Memory* (Chicago, 1966), 1–26.
43. Patrick H. Hutton, "The Art of Memory Reconceived: From Rhetoric to Psychoanalysis," *Journal of the History of Ideas* 48 (1987), 385–86.
44. *La Topographie*, 124.
45. Ibid., 125.
46. Ibid., 117–20, 134.
47. Ibid., 48–49, 69, 151, 156–62.
48. Ibid., 37, 128–29, 152–54; *Cadres sociaux*, 199, 201–07.
49. *La Topographie*, 92, 150.

50. Ibid., 150, 157–64.
51. Ibid., 21, 45, 103, 109, 136–37.
52. Ibid., 64, 66–68.
53. Ibid., 90–99.
54. Ibid., 33, 90, 102.
55. Ibid., 106.
56. Ibid., 30, 163.
57. Ibid., 137.
58. Ibid., 116.
59. Ibid., 121–24.
60. Ibid., 21, 22, 24, 25–26, 37–38, 40, 46–47, 63, 67, 100, 111, 114, 137–39, 144.
61. Ibid., 46, 51, 58, 63.
62. Ibid., 46, 65, 68.
63. Ibid., 77.
64. Ibid., 25, 140; *Les Cadres sociaux*, 185–87, 196–97. On bricolage, see Bastide, "Mémoire collective et sociologie de bricolage," 96–97.
65. *La Topographie*, 46, 58.
66. *Collective Memory*, 53.
67. Halbwachs was in no position to undertake the on-site archaeological research in which these biblical scholars engaged. "What purpose would it serve," he quipped somewhat apologetically, "to redo a labor accomplished by such fine craftsmen." *La Topographie*, 6.
68. Ibid., 4.
69. Ibid., 4–5. See also Gustave Dalman, *Les Itinéraires de Jésus: Topographie des évangiles*, rev. ed., trans. Jacques Marty (Paris, 1930). See also his *Jesus-Jeshua: Studies in the Gospels*, trans. Paul P. Levertoff (1929; rpt. New York, 1971).
70. *La Topographie*, 2–3. Cf. the recent study by E. D. Hunt, *Holy Land Pilgrimage in the Later Roman Empire*, A.D. *312–460* (Oxford, 1982).
71. *La Topographie*, 9–49. For an English translation of the text, see the Bordeaux Pilgrim, "Itinerary from Bordeaux to Jerusalem" (333), trans. Aubrey Stewart, in the *Library of the Palestine Pilgrims' Text Society*, ed. C. W. Wilson (1887; rpt. New York, 1971), I: 1–68.
72. *La Topographie*, 49.
73. Ibid., 14, 20–22, 24–25, 27, 33, 40–42, 45, 46–47.
74. Ibid., 9–11.
75. Ibid., 33, 83–89, 130–33. See François de Chateaubriand, *Itinéraire de Paris à Jérusalem*, 3d ed. (Paris, 1800).
76. *La Topographie*, 2, 44–46, 62–63, 101, 105, 107, 115, 130, 153. See Ernest Renan, *La Vie de Jésus* (1863; rpt. Paris, 1974); Prosper Alfaric, *Les Manuscrits de la "Vie de Jésus" d'Ernest Renan* (Paris, 1939).
77. *La Topographie*, 16, 79.
78. Ibid., 113.
79. Ibid., 112–13, 147.
80. Ibid., 130–33.
81. Ibid., 117, 134–35. See also Philippe Joutard, *Ces Voix qui nous viennent du passé* (Paris, 1983), 73, 102–03, 208–11; Walter J. Ong, *Orality and Literacy* (London, 1982), 7–9, 95, 110–12, 115–16, 119; Eric A. Havelock, *The Literate Revolution in Greece and Its Cultural Consequences* (Princeton, 1982), 143–46.
82. *La Topographie*, 116.
83. Eric Hobsbawm, "Introduction: Inventing Traditions," in *The Invention of Tradition*, ed. Eric Hobsbawm and Terence Ranger (Cambridge, England, 1983), 1–14.

84. For the United States, see the comprehensive study by Michael Kammen, *Mystic Chords of Memory* (New York, 1991).
85. Pierre Nora, ed., *Les Lieux de mémoire*, 3 vols. (Paris, 1984–92).
86. Elaine Pagels, *The Gnostic Gospels* (New York, 1981).
87. *La Topographie*, 152–54.

5

PHILIPPE ARIÈS: BETWEEN TRADITION AND HISTORY

1. Trans. by Robert Baldick as *Centuries of Childhood: A Social History of Family Life* (New York, 1962), 391–98.
2. Philippe Ariès, *Un Historien du dimanche* (Paris, 1982), 111; "Confessions d'un anarchiste de droite," *Contrepoint* 16 (1974), 90.
3. See Ariès's interview with André Burguière, "La Singulière Histoire de Philippe Ariès," *Le Nouvel Observateur*, 20 February 1978, 81.
4. See Patrick H. Hutton, "The History of Mentalities: The New Map of Cultural History," *History and Theory* 20 (1981), 244–47.
5. On the influence of *Centuries of Childhood*, see the review of reviews by Richard T. Vann, "The Youth of *Centuries of Childhood*," *History and Theory* 21 (1982), 279–97; on Ariès's work on death and dying, see Pierre Chaunu, *L'Historien en cet instant* (Paris, 1985), 224–42.
6. See the review by Jean-Louis Flandrin, "Enfance et société," *Les Annales: Economies, sociétés, civilisations* 19 (1964), 322–29.
7. Early in his career as an historian, Ariès wrote a work on historical demography, in which he demonstrated his knowledge of material realities and his skill in quantitative methods. Yet in his closing remarks he noted the limitations of such a study and expressed his desire to describe a psychological reality that could not be captured through statistical analysis. Philippe Ariès, *Histoire des populations françaises et de leurs attitudes devant la vie depuis le XVIIIe siècle* (1948; rpt. Paris, 1976), 399–412; see also his remarks in "La Singulière Histoire," 94.
8. Pierre Nora, "La Mémoire collective," in *La Nouvelle Histoire*, ed. Jacques Le Goff et al. (Paris, 1978), 398.
9. Philippe Ariès, *Le Temps de l'histoire* (Monaco, 1954), 9–12; *Historien du dimanche*, 16, 26, 41, 51, 84.
10. *Temps de l'histoire*, 12–21; "Confessions d'un anarchiste de droite," 89–90.
11. In this respect, Ariès's first work, *Les Traditions sociales dans les pays de France* (Paris, 1943), is an important survey of the variations in customs from one region to another. *Le Temps de l'histoire* was a more theoretical exploration of issues first raised there.
12. *Temps de l'histoire*, 45.
13. Ibid., 22–24.
14. This text, though, has recently been reissued (Paris, 1986) with a preface by Roger Chartier. Chartier inventories the reviews of the book for 1954 and 1955 (p. 252). See also Ariès's comments on the reception of this work in *Historien du dimanche*, 118–20.
15. *Temps de l'histoire*, 9–12, 33, 63–64, 315; see also *Historien du dimanche*, 77–78.
16. *Temps de l'histoire*, 10.
17. *Historien du dimanche*, 73–77.
18. Ibid., 78; *Temps de l'histoire*, 292–304, 308.
19. *Historien du dimanche*, 77–78. Ariès's failure on this exam is something of a puzzle. Intellectually gifted, he was nonetheless personally rebellious, and he may not have taken the examination seriously. See the obervations of one of his friends of that era,

François Léger, "Philippe Ariès: l'histoire d'un historien," *La Revue universelle des faits et des idées* 65 (September 1986), 65.

20. *Historien du dimanche,* 79, 92–98.

21. The school was an *école des cadres,* responsible for teaching students attending the Vichy youth camps. Ariès resigned in protest against the appointment of Pierre Laval as prime minister in 1942. Ibid., 79–80, 82.

22. Ibid., 73–74.

23. Ariès thought of his circle of friends as a vestigial expression of the secret society, an institution that had emerged in the eighteenth century as a stepping-stone between the personalism of the family, whose political authority was waning, and the impersonalism of the modern nation-state, whose influence was then only beginning to become extensive. Ibid., 57–71, 163; "Confessions d'un anarchiste de droite," 89.

24. Ibid., 41–42, 58, 63–64, 68, 74–76, 84, 87, 208–10; *Temps de l'histoire,* 317.

25. Ariès's *Les Traditions sociales dans les pays de France* (1943), which argues for the value of regional communities in opposition to the centralized state, may reflect his idealized vision of what a traditionalist regime might be. But in retrospect, he claimed that this study signified his first step away from his earlier political conceptions of history toward the history of mentalities that he would later write. See his comments in *Historien du dimanche,* 80–81, 84–86, 89.

26. *Historien du dimanche,* 81, 101. Ariès, however, was dismayed by public demands for a sorting out of ideological allegiances during the war. *Temps de l'histoire,* 62–87. On the attitudes of right-wing intellectuals toward Vichy after the war, see the interesting study by Henry Rousso, *The Vichy Syndrome: History and Memory in France since 1944,* trans. Arthur Goldhammer (Cambridge, Mass., 1991), 27–32.

27. *Temps de l'histoire,* 9–24, 49, 56–59; see also "Confessions d'un anarchiste de droite," 90, 92.

28. *Temps de l'histoire,* 16–18.

29. Ibid., 321–25.

30. Ibid., 26–33, 46–60, 313; *Historien du dimanche,* 97–98; "Confessions d'un anarchiste de droite," 92.

31. *Temps de l'histoire,* 45, 259, 315–18; *Historien du dimanche,* 83.

32. Ariès specifically acknowledges this in *Temps de l'histoire,* 313, 317–18.

33. Ibid., 35–39, 61–72, 321–25.

34. Confessions d'un anarchiste de droite," 94–95; *Historien du dimanche,* 109–10.

35. *Temps de l'histoire,* 57, 318–19.

36. This method of reaching backward from the present, as opposed to a search for formal beginnings, is not unlike the concept of "genealogy" more recently publicized by Michel Foucault. Cf. Michel Foucault, "Nietzsche, Genealogy, History," in *Language, Counter-Memory, Practice,* ed. Donald F. Bouchard (Ithaca, 1977), 139–64.

37. Burguière, "La Singulière Histoire de Philippe Ariès," 82. Cf. Pierre Nora's discussion of the way in which places of memory emerge out of milieux of memory, making possible the historians' appropriation of them as place markers on chronological time-lines, in his "Entre mémoire et histoire," in *Les Lieux de mémoire,* ed. Pierre Nora (Paris, 1984), I: xvii–xxv.

38. *Historien du dimanche,* 125; *Temps de l'histoire,* 22–24, 43–49, 286–87, 403–04.

39. *Temps de l'histoire,* 26–33, 50–59, 258–59; *Historien du dimanche,* 53–56, 97–98, 116–17. See also William R. Keylor, *Jacques Bainville and the Renaissance of Royalist Historiography in Twentieth-Century France* (Baton Rouge, La., 1979), 214–18.

40. Ariès's notions on this subject reflect the influence of Maurice Halbwachs. He notes the significance of Halbwachs's work in *Les Traditions sociales dans les pays de France,* 10–11. See also Patrick H. Hutton, "Collective Memory and Collective Mentalities: the Halbwachs-Ariès Connection," *Historical Reflections* 15 (1988), 311–22.

41. *Temps de l'histoire*, 269–70.
42. Ariès's first published historical study, *Les Traditions dans les pays de France*, considered the nature of these groups in traditional society in depth. See also *Historien du dimanche*, 59–60, 84–86, 89, 134, 163.
43. *Historien du dimanche*, 134, 163, 182; *Centuries of Childhood*, 341.
44. *Temps de l'histoire*, 102–53. Cf. Donald J. Wilcox, *The Measure of Times Past* (Chicago, 1987), 9, 153–86; George Huppert, *The Idea of Perfect History* (Urbana, 1970), 12–27, 170–82.
45. Ariès, *Histoire des populations françaises*, 399–412; *Historien du dimanche*, 112.
46. *Historien du dimanche*, 111.
47. *Temps de l'histoire*, 109, 121, 133, 209.
48. Ibid., 142–53, 160–78. Cf. Orest Ranum, *Artisans of Glory* (Chapel Hill, N.C., 1980), 3–25; François Furet, *In the Workshop of History*, trans. Jonathan Mandelbaum (Chicago, 1984), 77–98.
49. *Temps de l'histoire*, 259.
50. Ariès also offers interesting remarks on the role of collectors in inventorying and authenticating texts. In their attention to documentary evidence, they accomplished an important preliminary step toward modern historical scholarship. Ibid., 158, 194–201.
51. Ibid., 261–68.
52. Ibid., 268–90.
53. Ibid., 90; see also Ranum, *Artisans of Glory*, 17–21, on the use of *topoi* (commonplaces or places of memory) in seventeenth-century historical writing.
54. Ariès, "L'Histoire des mentalités," in *La Nouvelle Histoire*, ed. Le Goff, 409–12, 420–23; "Confessions d'un anarchiste de droite," 95–97.
55. *Temps de l'histoire*, 91–93, 259.
56. "Confessions d'un anarchiste de droite," 97–99; "L'Histoire des mentalités," 410–12.
57. *Temps de l'histoire*, 105.
58. *Historien du dimanche*, 111, 117; "Confessions d'un anarchiste de droite," 96–97; "L'Histoire des mentalités," 402–23.
59. *Temps de l'histoire*, 90–93, 106.
60. *Historien du dimanche*, 59–60, 134, 136–37, 163, 182; "Confessions d'un anarchiste de droite," 92–95; *Temps de l'histoire*, 259; *Centuries of Childhood*, 346–47, 375–77.
61. *Historien du dimanche*, 135–36.
62. *Centuries of Childhood*, 411–15.
63. *Temps de l'histoire*, 294–304. Cf. his reflections on this topic late in life in Philippe Ariès, "La Sensibilité au changement dans la problématique de l'historiographie contemporaine," in *Certitudes et incertitudes de l'histoire*, ed. Gilbert Gadoffre (Paris, 1987), 169–75. Ariès's discussion of the dynamics of tradition is not unlike that subsequently developed by J. G. A. Pocock in his essay "Time, Institutions and Action: An Essay on Traditions and Their Understanding," in his *Politics, Language and Time: Essays on Political Thought and History* (London, 1972), 233–72.
64. *Temps de l'histoire*, 263–64, 267.
65. Ibid., 304–11. See also Patrick H. Hutton, "The Art of Memory Reconceived: From Rhetoric to Psychoanalysis," *Journal of the History of Ideas* 48 (1987), 376, 385–86.
66. *Temps de l'histoire*, 292–301; "Confessions d'un anarchiste de droite," 92, 97; *Historien du dimanche*, 53, 78, 88. On the limitations of Febvre's notion of habits of mind, see Saul Friedländer, *History and Psychoanalysis*, trans. Susan Suleiman (New York, 1978), 1–2.
67. See esp. the reviews by Flandrin, "Enfance et société," 322–29; Irene Q. Brown, "Philippe Ariès on Education and Society in Seventeenth- and Eighteenth-Century

France," *History of Education Quarterly* 7 (1967), 357–68; Lawrence Stone, "The Massacre of the Innocents," *New York Review of Books*, 14 November 1974, 25–28.

68. See the hostile review by Adrian Wilson, "The Infancy of the History of Childhood: An Appraisal of Philippe Ariès," *History and Theory* 19 (1980), 132–53.

69. *Centuries of Childhood*, 9–10, 47, 57, 82, 128.

70. Ariès, *Histoire des populations françaises*, 322–98.

71. *Centuries of Childhood*, 43–44, 88–89, 99, 110–21, 131–33, 164, 171, 174, 187, 239–40.

72. Ibid., 30.

73. Ibid., 29–30, 32.

74. See the comparison of Ariès and Erikson offered by David Hunt, *Parents and Children in History: The Psychology of Family Life in Early Modern France* (New York, 1970), 11–51.

75. See Philip Pomper, *The Structure of Mind in History* (New York, 1985), 81–114.

76. Cf. Jacques Donzelot, *The Policing of Families*, trans. Robert Hurley (New York, 1979), xxv, 48–95.

77. *Centuries of Childhood*, 251–52, 261–64, 284–85, 333–36, 353–57, 365–75, 398–408.

78. Ibid., 71, 375, 390.

79. Cf. Reinhart Koselleck, *Futures Past: On the Semantics of Historical Time*, trans. Keith Tribe (Cambridge, Mass., 1985), 36–38, 276–88.

80. Trans. as *At the Hour of Our Death* by Helen Weaver (New York, 1981), 449, 471–72, 476, 508–13, 518, 524–36, 541, 543.

81. Ibid. See also *Temps de l'histoire*, 46; *Historien du dimanche*, 168.

82. See his summary of this long-range trend in his *Western Attitudes toward Death from the Middle Ages to the Present*, trans. Patricia M. Ranum (Baltimore, 1974), 46–50, 66–76.

83. Elisabeth Kübler-Ross, *On Death and Dying* (New York, 1969), 38–137.

84. *Historien du dimanche*, 136, 149, 208; Burguière, "La Singulière Histoire de Philippe Ariès," 81–82, 88.

85. *Temps de l'histoire*, 305.

86. Burguière, "La Singulière Histoire de Philippe Ariès," 82.

6

MICHEL FOUCAULT: HISTORY AS COUNTER-MEMORY

1. Trans. as *Madness and Civilization: A History of Insanity in the Age of Reason* by Richard Howard (New York, 1965), 3–7. On the reasons for the decline of leprosy in early modern Europe, see the study by William H. McNeill, *Plagues and Peoples* (New York, 1976), 154–57.

2. Foucault, *Madness and Civilization*, 7–37.

3. Ibid., 38–84.

4. On Foucault's intellectual biography, see Jacques Revel, "Foucault," in *Dictionnaire des sciences historiques*, ed. André Burguière (Paris, 1986), 290–92; David R. Shumway, *Michel Foucault* (Boston, 1989), 7–13; James Miller, *The Passion of Michel Foucault* (New York, 1993).

5. Among the most useful compendia are: Michel Foucault, *Language, Counter-Memory, Practice: Selected Essays and Interviews*, ed. Donald F. Bouchard (Ithaca, 1977) (hereafter cited as *LCP*), *Power/Knowledge: Selected Interviews and Other Writings, 1972–77*, ed. Colin Gordon (New York, 1980) (hereafter *P/K*), and *Politics, Philosophy, Culture: Interviews and Other Writings, 1977–1984*, ed. Lawrence D. Kritzman (New York, 1988) (hereafter *PPC*).

6. Michael Clark, *Michel Foucault, An Annotated Bibliography: Tool Kit for a New Age* (New York, 1983).

7. In addition to an interview and critical essays, James Bernauer and David Rasmussen, eds., *The Final Foucault* (Cambridge, Mass., 1988), is useful for its chronology of Foucault's life and bibliography of his writings.

8. Even his last projects on sex and self in classical antiquity were based on his study of texts once considered essential to the intellectual formation of the well-educated French scholar.

9. For Foucault's personal observations on these early years, see Stephen Riggins, "Michel Foucault: An Interview" (1983), in *PPC*, 3–16.

10. Michel Foucault, *Mental Illness and Psychology*, trans. Alan Sheridan (New York, 1976).

11. See the perceptive essays by Jerrold Seigel, "Avoiding the Subject: A Foucaultian Itinerary," *Journal of the History of Ideas* 51 (1990), 273–99, and by Alexander Nehamas, "The Examined Life of Michel Foucault," *The New Republic*, 15 February 1993, 27–36.

12. On the influence of Canguilhem, see Gary Gutting, *Michel Foucault's Archaeology of Scientific Reason* (Cambridge, England, 1989), 9–54; on Roussel, Charles Ruas, "An Interview with Michel Foucault," in *Death and the Labyrinth*, by Michel Foucault (New York, 1986), 169–86.

13. Michel Foucault, "Theatrum Philosophicum," in *LCP*, 165–96.

14. Ibid., 165.

15. Gilles Deleuze, *Foucault*, trans. Sean Hand (Minneapolis, 1988).

16. On Foucault's relationship to Sartre and to existentialism, see Mark Poster, *Existential Marxism in Postwar France* (Princeton, 1975), 334–40, and *Foucault, Marxism, and History* (London, 1984), 3–7, 23–28.

17. For a time during the 1960s, Foucault attended the seminars of Jacques Lacan, a key figure in the introduction of Freud's thought into French intellectual circles. Sherry Turkle, *Psychoanalytic Politics: Freud's French Revolution* (New York, 1978), 27–93.

18. Cf. Seigel, "Avoiding the Subject," 273–99, who makes a persuasive case for a hermetic reading of Foucault's authorship in light of its cryptic hints at his deep concerns and commitments.

19. Gérard Raulet, "Structuralism and Post-Structuralism: An Interview with Michel Foucault," *Telos* 55 (Spring 1983), 195–211.

20. See esp. Terence Hawkes, *Structuralism and Semiotics* (Berkeley, 1977), 145–60.

21. See especially Foucault's essays and reviews in the periodical *Critique*, as well as his lead essay "Distance, Aspect, Origine," in *Théorie d'ensemble*, ed. Philippe Sollers (Paris, 1968), 11–24. On Foucault's role among the poststructuralists during the 1960s, see Clare O'Farrell, *Foucault: Historian or Philosopher* (New York, 1989), 1–19; Mark Poster, *Critical Theory and Poststructuralism in Search of a Context* (Ithaca, 1989), 12–33.

22. For Foucault's place among the poststructuralists, see Vincent B. Leitch, *Deconstructive Criticism: An Advanced Introduction* (New York, 1983), 143–83.

23. Michel Foucault, "What Is an Author?" in *LCP*, 124–30.

24. See Foucault's analysis of the significance of the mirror in Velázquez' painting *Las Meninas* in his *The Order of Things: An Archaeology of the Human Sciences*, trans. Alan Sheridan (New York, 1970), 3–16, and his "Language to Infinity," in *LCP*, 55–66. See also Martin Jay, "In the Empire of the Gaze: Foucault and the Denigration of Vision in Twentieth-Century French Thought," in *Foucault: A Critical Reader*, ed. David Couzens Hoy (Oxford, 1986), 188–89.

25. See, for example, Luther H. Martin et al., eds., *Technologies of the Self: A Seminar with Michel Foucault* (Amherst, 1988), the proceedings of one in which I had the privilege of participating.

26. Jonathan Culler, *Framing the Sign: Criticism and Its Institutions* (Norman, Okla., 1988), 62–64.

27. Trans. as "The Discourse on Language" by Rupert Sawyer in *Social Science Information* 10 (1971), 7–30.

28. Michel Foucault, "Nietzsche, Genealogy, History," in *LCP,* 146; "Theatrum Philosophicum," in *LCP,* 173–76, 192.

29. Trans. as *The Order of Things: An Archaeology of the Human Sciences* by Alan Sheridan (New York, 1970).

30. Trans. as *The Archaeology of Knowledge* by A. M. Sheridan Smith (New York, 1976).

31. Foucault, *Order of Things,* 29–44, 295–300, 320–22, 338, 369, *Archaeology of Knowledge,* 48–49, 111, 117.

32. Foucault, *Order of Things,* xx–xxi, 236, 312–18, *Archaeology of Knowledge,* 46–63, 67, 101, 165.

33. Michel Foucault, "The Father's 'No,'" in *LCP,* 72–74, *Order of Things,* 328–35, *Archaeology of Knowledge,* 6–15, 21, 135–40.

34. Michel Foucault, "The History of Sexuality," in *P/K,* 193, *Archaeology of Knowledge,* 13, 25.

35. Foucault, *Order of Things,* 367–73, *Archaeology of Knowledge,* 135–77; "What is an Author?" in *LCP,* 132–36; "Revolutionary Action: 'Until Now,'" in *LCP,* 220.

36. On Nietzsche's influence on Foucault's conception of history, see Allan Megill, "Foucault, Structuralism, and the Ends of History," *Journal of Modern History* 51 (1979), 451–503. See also Foucault's remarks in his interview with Raulet, "Structuralism and Post-Structuralism," 203–04.

37. Michel Foucault, "Nietzsche, Genealogy, History," in *LCP,* 139–64; *Archaeology of Knowledge,* 95.

38. Ibid., 163; "Theatrum Philosophicum," 184–86.

39. "Nietzsche, Genealogy, History," 140, 154–55, 158, 160, 164. See also the interesting discussion of Foucault in relationship to "historiographic metafiction" by Linda Hutcheon, *A Poetics of Postmodernism: History, Theory, Fiction* (New York, 1988), 87–101.

40. "What Is an Author?" 131–36, "Nietzsche, Genealogy, History," 159; "Revolutionary Action: 'Until Now,'" 219–25. Cf. Ana Maria Alonso, "The Effects of Truth: Re-Presentations of the Past and the Imagining of Community," *Journal of Historical Sociology* 1 (1988), 33–37. Herein Foucault may have felt that he had an advantage in having been trained as a philosopher and hence was able to offer a perspective free of such constraints.

41. Hans-Georg Gadamer, *Truth and Method,* 2d rev. ed., rev. trans. Joel Weinsheimer and Donald G. Marshall (New York, 1989), 277–85; David Harlan, "Intellectual History and the Return of Literature," *American Historical Review* 94 (1989), 583–89.

42. Foucault, "Nietzsche, Genealogy, History," in *LCP,* 151–52; "Nietzsche, Freud, Marx," *Cahiers de Royaumont* 6 (1967), 183–92; *Archaeology of Knowledge,* 149–56. Cf. Hubert L. Dreyfus and Paul Rabinow, *Michel Foucault: Beyond Structuralism and Hermeneutics,* 2d ed. (Chicago, 1983), xxiii, 183.

43. Foucault, "Nietzsche, Genealogy, History," in *LCP,* 152–54, 160; "Two Lectures," in *P/K,* 83–87, *Archaeology of Knowledge,* 124–25.

44. Foucault, *Archaeology of Knowledge,* 128–31.

45. For overviews of Foucault's historical oeuvre, see Barry Smart, *Michel Foucault* (London, 1985); Edith Kurzweil, "The Neo-Structuralism of Michel Foucault," in *Cultural Analysis,* ed. Robert Wuthnow et al. (London, 1984), 133–78.

46. Foucault, "Theatrum Philosophicum," 168.

47. Foucault, *Madness and Civilization,* 24–37, 274.

48. Foucault, *P/K:* "Truth and Power," 124–25, "The Politics of Health in the Eighteenth

Century," 170–71; "The Political Technologies of Individuals," in *Technologies of the Self,* 156–62.

49. Foucault, *LCP*: "Nietzsche, Genealogy, History," 151; "Prison Talk," in *P/K,* 51–52, "Two Lectures," in *P/K,* 88–108; "Truth and Power," in *P/K,* 109–33. Foucault's discussion of the way in which collective memory reflects configurations of cultural power invites comparison with the pioneering work of Maurice Halbwachs on the subject in *La Topographie légendaire des évangiles en Terre Sainte* (1941; rpt. Paris, 1971), 117–64.

50. Foucault, "The History of Sexuality," in *P/K,* 183–87.

51. Michel Foucault, *The History of Sexuality: An Introduction,* trans. Robert Hurley (New York, 1978), I: 53–80; "The Confessions of the Flesh," in *P/K,* 213–19.

52. Foucault, *History of Sexuality,* I: 129–31, *The Use of Pleasure,* trans. Robert Hurley (New York, 1986), II: 3–13.

53. Michel Foucault, "Technologies of the Self," in *Technologies of the Self,* ed. Martin, 16–49. See also Raul Fornet-Betancourt et al., "The Ethic of Care for the Self as a Practice of Freedom: An Interview with Michel Foucault," *Philosophy and Social Criticism* 12 (1987), 112–31.

54. Foucault, *History of Sexuality,* I: 158–59; "Body/Power," in *P/K,* 60–61; "History of Sexuality," in *P/K,* 191–92. See also Patrick H. Hutton, "Foucault, Freud, and the Technologies of the Self," in *Technologies of the Self,* ed. Martin, 121–44.

55. Hutton, "Foucault, Freud, and the Technologies of the Self," 138–39.

56. See esp. Megill, "Foucault, Structuralism, and the Ends of History," 451–503; Hayden V. White, "Foucault Decoded: Notes from Underground," *History and Theory* 12 (1975), 23–54; Paul Veyne, *Comment on écrit l'histoire* (Paris, 1978).

57. "An Exchange with Michel Foucault," *New York Review of Books* 30/5 (31 March 1983), 42–43.

58. On Foucault in relationship to structuralism, see Edith Kurzweil, *The Age of Structuralism: Lévi-Strauss to Foucault* (New York, 1980), 8–9, 194–95.

59. Foucault, "Orders of Discourse," 27, "Truth and Power," in *P/K,* 114; *Archaeology of Knowledge,* 15, 199.

60. On Foucault in relationship to Marxism, see Poster, *Foucault, Marxism and History,* 70–93; Barry Smart, *Foucault, Marxism and Critique* (London, 1983); Frank Lentricchia, *Ariel and the Police: Michel Foucault, William James, Wallace Stevens* (Madison, Wis., 1988), 29–102.

61. George Lichtheim, *Marxism in Modern France* (New York, 1966), 64–65, 73–75, 89–111.

62. On Foucault's politics in relationship to his scholarly endeavor, see the discerning essay by Edward W. Said, "Michel Foucault, 1926–84," in *After Foucault: Historical Knowledge, Postmodern Challenges,* ed. Jonathan Arac (New Brunswick, N.J., 1988), 1–11.

63. Foucault, "Questions on Geography," in *P/K,* 70. See also Poster, *Foucault, Marxism, History,* 37–40.

64. John K. Simon, "A Conversation with Michel Foucault," *Partisan Review* 38 (1971), 192–201.

65. Foucault, "Nietzsche, Freud, Marx," 185–87; "Prison Talk," in *P/K,* 52–53, "Two Lectures," in *P/K,* 84–89; Raulet, "Structuralism and Post-Structuralism: An Interview with Michel Foucault," in *P/K,* 208–11.

66. For the critique of Foucault's work on asylums, see esp. David J. Rothman, *The Discovery of the Asylum: Social Order and Disorder in the New Republic* (Boston, 1971), xvii–xviii; H. C. Erik Midelfort, "Madness and Civilization in Early Modern Europe: A Reappraisal of Michel Foucault," in *After the Reformation: Essays in Honor of J. H. Hexter* (Philadelphia, 1980), 247–65; Peter Sedgwick, *Psycho Politics* (New York, 1982), 125–48.

67. For comment on the positive impact of Foucault on scholarship in this field, see esp. Patricia O'Brien, *The Promise of Punishment: Prisons in Nineteenth-Century France* (Princeton, 1982), xi–xii, 19 n. 9; Robert A. Nye, *Crime, Madness and Politics in Modern France* (Princeton, 1984), 11–15.

68. On Foucault in relationship to the problem of rhetoric, see Hayden V. White, "Michel Foucault," in *Structuralism and Since: From Lévi-Strauss to Derrida*, ed. John Sturrock (Oxford, 1979), 92–98, *The Content of the Form* (Baltimore, 1987), 104–41.

69. Culler, *Framing the Sign*, 66–67.

70. On the impact of *Annales* scholarship on French historiography, see Georg G. Iggers, *New Directions in European Historiography* (Middletown, Conn., 1975), 43–79; Traian Stoianovich, *French Historical Method: The "Annales" Paradigm* (Ithaca, 1976); *Annales: Economies, sociétés, civilisations* 34 (1979): André Burguière, "Histoire d'une histoire: Naissance des *Annales*," 1347–59, Jacques Revel, "Histoire et sciences sociales: Les Paradigmes des *Annales*," 1360–76.

71. André Burguière, "La Singulière Histoire de Philippe Ariès," *Le Nouvel Observateur,* 20 February 1978, 82; Philippe Ariès, "L'Histoire des mentalités," in *La Nouvelle Histoire,* ed. Jacques Le Goff et al. (Paris, 1978), 411–12.

72. André Burguière, "The Fate of the History of Mentalities in the *Annales*," *Comparative Studies in Society and History* 24 (1982), 424–37.

73. Lucien Febvre, "History and Psychology" (1938), "Sensibility and History" (1941), and "A New Kind of History" (1949), in *A New Kind of History and Other Essays: Lucien Febvre,* ed. Peter Burke (New York, 1973), 1–43.

74. Patrick H. Hutton, "The History of Mentalities: The New Map of Cultural History," *History and Theory* 20 (1981), 237–59.

75. Robert Mandrou, *An Introduction to Modern France,* trans. R. E. Hallmark (New York, 1975); Emmanuel Le Roy Ladurie, *Montaillou: The Promised Land of Error,* trans. Barbara Bray (New York, 1979); Natalie Zemon Davis, *The Return of Martin Guerre* (Cambridge, Mass., 1983).

76. Foucault, *Order of Things,* 201–08. See also Shumway, *Foucault,* 69–91; White, "Michel Foucault," 92–95.

77. Trans. as *The Policing of Families* by Robert Hurley (New York, 1979), 6.

78. On the Donzelot/Foucault connection, see Jeffrey Minson, *Genealogies of Morals: Nietzsche, Foucault, Donzelot and the Eccentricity of Ethics* (New York, 1985), 180–84.

79. See Foucault's reference to parallels between his own work and that of Donzelot in "History of Sexuality," in *P/K,* 188–89.

80. On the historiography of the French Revolution, see Alice Gérard, *La Révolution française: Mythes et interprétations, 1789–1970* (Paris, 1970); Jacques Solé, *Questions of the French Revolution: A Historical Overview,* trans. Shelley Temchin (New York, 1989).

81. Trans. as *Interpreting the French Revolution* by Elborg Forster (Cambridge, England, 1981).

82. Ibid., 4–10.

83. Ibid., 15–17, 22, 135, 139.

84. Ibid., 26–33, 48–52, 77.

85. Note Foucault's reference to the role of discourse in the making of the French Revolution in *Archaeology of Knowledge,* 177.

86. The most imposing is Keith Baker, Colin Lucas, François Furet, and Mona Ozouf, eds., *The French Revolution and the Creation of Modern Political Culture,* 3 vols. (Oxford, 1987–90), a compendium of some eighty-five articles by French, English, and American scholars. Note also Baker's quotation from and references to Foucault in "Memory and Practice: Politics and the Representation of the Past in Eighteenth-Century France," *Representations* 11 (Summer 1985), 134.

87. Pierre Nora, ed., *Les Lieux de mémoire,* 3 vols. (Paris, 1984–92).

88. See Nora's introductory essay, "Entre mémoire et histoire," in ibid., I: xvii–xlii.
89. In addition to the essays in *Les Lieux de mémoire,* leading studies include Lynn Hunt, *Politics, Culture, and Class in the French Revolution* (Berkeley, 1984)(note her comment on Foucault, p. 57 n. 9); Maurice Agulhon, *Marianne into Battle: Republican Imagery and Symbolism in France, 1789–1880,* trans. Janet Lloyd (New York, 1981); Eric Hobsbawm, "Mass-Producing Traditions: Europe, 1870–1914," in *The Invention of Tradition,* ed. Eric Hobsbawm and Terence Ranger (Cambridge, England, 1983), 263–307.
90. See Irene Diamond and Lee Quinby, eds., *Feminism and Foucault: Reflections on Resistance* (Boston, 1988).
91. (New York, 1988).
92. Ibid., 15–67.
93. Joan Wallach Scott, *The Glassworkers of Carmaux* (Cambridge, Mass., 1974).
94. Scott, *Gender and the Politics of History,* 68–90.
95. Ibid., 72, 183, 186, 197.
96. Ibid., 9–11, 25–26, 46–50.
97. Ibid., 41–50.
98. Ibid., 193–98.
99. Ibid., 2, 4, 23, 26, 36, 59.
100. Ibid., 196–97.
101. Ibid., 42–50.
102. Marshall McLuhan, *The Gutenberg Galaxy* (Toronto, 1962); Walter J. Ong, *Orality and Literacy: The Technologizing of the Word* (London, 1982), 135–38, 165–70.
103. Paul Ricoeur, *Time and Narrative,* trans. Kathleen McLaughlin and David Pellauer (Chicago, 1983), I: 221–25, II: 14–15, 163–64.

7

THE ROLE OF MEMORY IN THE HISTORIOGRAPHY OF THE FRENCH REVOLUTION

1. Herbert Butterfield, *The Whig Interpretation of History* (1931; rpt. New York, 1965), 9–33.
2. On commemorating the bicentennial, see the exchange among historians: "Que commémore-t-on?" *Le Nouvel Observateur* 1278 (4 to 10 May 1989), 8–9; for a summary of current controversies, Maurice Agulhon, "Débats actuels sur la Révolution en France," *Annales historiques de la Révolution française* 279 (January–March 1990), 1–13; among contributions for the bicentennial, see esp. *The French Revolution and the Creation of Modern Culture,* ed. Keith Baker, Colin Lucas, François Furet, and Mona Ozouf, 3 vols. (Oxford, 1987–90), an anthology of some eighty-five articles by French, English, and American scholars.
3. See J. G. A. Pocock, *Politics, Language, and Time: Essays on Political Thought and History* (London, 1972), 233–71; Edward Shils, "Tradition," *Comparative Studies in Society and History* 13/2 (April 1971), 122–59.
4. Butterfield, to his credit, never made so extreme a claim. But, as his analysis became a working proposition for later historians, some construed it in this sense. For a discussion of Butterfield's notion in the context of English historical writing, see William H. Dray, "J. H. Hexter, Neo-Whiggism and Early Stuart Historiography," *History and Theory* 26 (1987), 133–49.
5. The classic discussion is by David Thomson, *Democracy in France,* 5th ed. (Oxford, 1969), 9–38. For a recent perspective, see Christine Piette, "Réflexions historiques sur les traditions révolutionnaires à Paris au XIX^c siècle," *Historical Reflections/Réflexions historiques* 12 (1985), 403–18.

6. Albert Soboul, "Tradition et création dans le mouvement révolutionnaire français au XIX^c siècle," *Le Mouvement social* 79 (April–June 1972), 22–27; Georges Weill, *Histoire du parti républicain en France, 1814–1870* (Paris, 1928), 403–07; Jacques Rougerie, "Mil huit cent soixante et onze," in *Colloque universitaire pour la commémoration du centenaire de la Commune de 1871* (Paris, 1971), 49–77.

7. Christian Amalvi, "Le 14-Juillet," in *Les Lieux de mémoire,* ed. Pierre Nora (Paris, 1984), I: 430–38; Charles Rearick, "Festivals in Modern France: The Experience of the Third Republic," *Journal of Contemporary History* 12 (1977), 435–60.

8. See Isaiah Berlin, *The Crooked Timber of Humanity* (New York, 1991), 49–69, and "Vico and the Ideal of the Enlightenment," *Social Research* 43 (1976), 640–53.

9. *The New Science of Giambattista Vico* (3d ed.; 1744), trans. and ed. Thomas G. Bergin and Max H. Fisch (Ithaca, 1968), 311. (Hereafter *NS.* References are to numbered paragraphs rather than to pages.)

10. *NS,* 114, 349.

11. *NS,* 150, 221, 249, 356.

12. *NS,* 364–65.

13. *NS,* 201, 205, 221, 356, 814, 915–78.

14. *NS,* 211, 699, 819.

15. *NS,* 1046.

16. *NS,* 348–49, 393, 1048–96.

17. *NS,* 338–60.

18. See esp. Mary Douglas, *How Institutions Think* (Syracuse, 1986).

19. Cf. Eric Hobsbawm, "Introduction: Inventing Traditions," in *The Invention of Tradition,* ed. Eric Hobsbawm and Terence Ranger (Cambridge, England, 1983), 1–14.

20. Ariès was much taken with the poetical effect of this phrase, borrowed from the title of a book by the English social historian Peter Laslett, *The World We Have Lost* (New York, 1965).

21. Michel Foucault, "Nietzsche, Genealogy, History," in *Language, Counter-Memory, Practice,* ed. Donald F. Bouchard (Ithaca, 1977), 153–56, 160, 164. See also Patrick H. Hutton, "Foucault, Freud, and the Technologies of the Self," in *Technologies of the Self: A Seminar with Michel Foucault,* ed. Luther Martin et al. (Amherst, 1988), 121–44.

22. Hayden White, *Metahistory: The Historical Imagination in Nineteenth-Century Europe* (Baltimore, 1973), 135–62; Linda Orr, *Headless History: Nineteenth-Century French Historiography of the Revolution* (Ithaca, 1990), 37–89.

23. Jules Michelet, *Histoire de la Révolution française,* ed. Gérard Walter (1847; rpt. Paris, 1939), I: 1–2.

24. Jules Michelet, "1869 Preface" to the *Histoire de France,* in Edward K. Kaplan, *Michelet's Poetic Vision* (Amherst, Mass., 1977), 152.

25. On Michelet's use of oral evidence, see Paul Thompson, *The Voice of the Past,* 2d ed. (Oxford, 1988), 44–47; Philippe Joutard, *Ces Voix qui nous viennent du passé* (Paris, 1983), 54–56.

26. For Michelet's biography, see Paul Viallaneix, "Michelet," in *Dictionnaire des sciences historiques,* ed. André Burguière (Paris, 1986), 461–63; Oscar A. Haac, *Jules Michelet* (Boston, 1982); Arthur Mitzman, *Michelet, Historian* (New Haven, 1990).

27. Jules Michelet, "Discours sur le système et la vie de Vico" (1835), in *Œuvres complètes de Michelet,* ed. Paul Viallaneix (Paris, 1971), I: 283–301, and "Vico," in *Biographie universelle* 48 (1827), 362–73. See also Patrick H. Hutton, "Vico's Theory of History and the French Revolutionary Tradition," *Journal of the History of Ideas* 37 (1976), 241–56.

28. Jules Michelet, "Introduction à l'histoire universelle" (1831), in *Œuvres complètes de Michelet,* II: 230–53.

29. Michelet, *Histoire de la Révolution,* I: 7, and *Le Peuple* (Paris, 1846), esp. 5–43, 163–76.

For a critical discussion of Michelet's concept of the people, see Paul Viallaneix, *La Voie royale: Essai sur l'idée de peuple dans l'œuvre de Michelet* (Paris, 1971), 335–37. On metaphor as the key to Michelet's writing style, see White, *Metahistory*, 149–62.

30. Michelet, *Histoire de la Révolution*, I: 56–61, 103; II: 157–64.

31. Jules Michelet, *The People* (1846), trans. John P. McKay (Urbana, Ill., 1973), esp. 194–99.

32. Michelet, *Histoire de la Révolution*, I: 7–8, 395–424.

33. Alice Gérard, *La Révolution française: Mythes et interprétations, 1789–1970* (Paris, 1970), 29–47.

34. Patrick H. Hutton, *The Cult of the Revolutionary Tradition* (Berkeley, 1981), 1–20.

35. The residual influence of orality on the French revolutionary tradition has yet to be studied systematically, but see the suggestive remarks by Gérard, *La Révolution française*, 29–47, 54–60, 66–67; Rougerie, "Mil huit cent soixante et onze," 49–77; Pierre Sorlin, *La Société française* (Paris, 1969), I: 247–48; Maurice Agulhon, *The Republican Experiment, 1848–1852*, trans. Janet Lloyd (Cambridge, England, 1983), 2–21; Edward Berenson, *Populist Religion and Left-Wing Politics in France, 1830–1852* (Princeton, 1984), 74–96, 169–202.

36. Alphonse Aulard, *L'Eloquence parlementaire pendant la Révolution française*, 3 vols. (Paris, 1882–86).

37. Paul Farmer, *France Reviews Its Revolutionary Origins* (New York, 1963), 60–61; William R. Keylor, *Academy and Community: The Foundation of the French Historical Profession* (Cambridge, Mass., 1975), 68–69.

38. Jean-Marie Mayeur, *Les Débuts de la Troisième République, 1871–1898* (Paris, 1973), 108–24.

39. Eric Hobsbawm, "Mass-Producing Traditions: Europe, 1870–1914," in *The Invention of Tradition*, 270–73.

40. On this concept of mnemonic *bricolage*, see Roger Bastide, "Mémoire collective et sociologie du bricolage," *L'Année sociologique*, 3d ser., 21 (1970), 65–105.

41. Alphonse Aulard, "Leçon d'ouverture" (1886), *Etudes et leçons sur la Révolution française*, 1st ser., 5th ed. (Paris, 1909), 37.

42. Alphonse Aulard, "Auguste Comte et la Révolution française" (1892), *Etudes et leçons sur la Révolution française*, 2d ser., 3d ed. (Paris, 1906), 7–38.

43. Auguste Comte, *A General View of Positivism*, trans. J. H. Bridges (1851; rpt. New York, 1975), 64–139.

44. Aulard, "Leçon d'ouverture," 17.

45. Alphonse Aulard, *The French Revolution: A Political History*, trans. Bernard Miall (New York, 1910), I: 88–99, 157–60; III: 88–91.

46. Alphonse Aulard, *La Société des Jacobins: Recueil de documents pour l'histoire du club des Jacobins de Paris* (Paris, 1889–97), 6 vols.

47. Alphonse Aulard, *Le Culte de la raison et le culte de l'être suprême* (Paris, 1904), vii–viii, 16–17; *French Revolution*, I: 214–17.

48. Pascal Ory, "Le Centenaire de la Révolution française," in *Les Lieux de mémoire*, I: 529, 547.

49. See James Friguglietti, "Alphonse Aulard and the Politics of History," *Proceedings of the Annual Meeting of the Western Society for French History* 15 (1988), 379–87.

50. For overviews of the historiographical significance of Lefebvre's work, see Albert Soboul, "Georges Lefebvre (1874–1959): Historian of the French Revolution," *Understanding the French Revolution* (New York, 1988), 237–54; Gordon H. McNeil, "Georges Lefebvre (1874–1959)," in *Essays in Modern Historiography*, ed. S. William Halperin (Chicago, 1970), 160–74; Beatrice Hyslop, "George Lefebvre, Historian," *French Historical Studies* 1 (1960), 265–82.

51. Georges Lefebvre, *Les Paysans du Nord pendant la Révolution française*, 2 vols. (Paris, 1924).
52. For Lefebvre's biography, see esp. "Notices," *Annales historiques de la Révolution française* 18 (1946), 185–86 (hereafter *AHRF*); Georges Lefebvre, "Pro Domo," *AHRF* 19 (1947), 188–89; "Georges Lefebvre: Notice biographique," preface to *Etudes sur la Révolution française*, by Georges Lefebvre (Paris, 1954); R. R. Palmer, "Georges Lefebvre: the Peasants and the French Revolution," *Journal of Modern History* 31 (1959), 329–42, and, the best of all, the disarming portrait by Richard Cobb, "Georges Lefebvre," *A Second Identity: Essays on France and French History* (Oxford, 1969), 84–100.
53. Françoise Brunel and Olivier Guérin, "Sur Georges Lefebvre," *AHRF* 41 (1969), 569.
54. Lefebvre, "La Révolution française dans l'histoire du monde," *Etudes sur la Révolution française*, 324.
55. Here Lefebvre offers a vision of socialism somewhat different from that of Marx with which it is often identified. His interest in the social conceptions of peasants and *sans culottes* is not simply as precursors of those of the proletariat but as worthy of consideration for their intrinsic importance to the synthesis he was trying to draw.
56. Lefebvre, "La Révolution française dans l'histoire du monde," in *Etudes sur la Révolution française*, 323–26.
57. Georges Lefebvre, *La Naissance de l'historiographie moderne* (Paris, 1971), 192–204.
58. Georges Lefebvre, "Son Œuvre historique," in *Etudes sur la Révolution française*, 13–15.
59. Lefebvre, "Pro Domo," *AHRF* 19 (1947), 189. Soboul, *Understanding the French Revolution*, 239, stresses the Jaurès connection.
60. See the biography by Harvey Goldberg, *The Life of Jean Jaurès* (Madison, Wis., 1962), esp. 77–93, 112–15.
61. Ibid., 283–90; Jean Jaurès, ed., *L'Histoire socialiste (1789–1900)*, 13 vols. (Paris, 1901–08).
62. Lefebvre, "Hommage à Albert Mathiez," in *Etudes sur la Révolution française*, 9–21. It is true that in his note "Pro Domo," 188–89, Lefebvre emphasizes his differences with Mathiez, but his remarks focus on those in their formation rather than those in the substance of their interpretations. Cf. the more recent assessment by Jean-René Suratteau, "Georges Lefebvre, disciple de Jaurès?" *AHRF* 51 (1979), 374–98.
63. Ernest Labrousse, "Georges Lefebvre dans l'évolution de l'historiographie française," *AHRF* 41 (1969), 549–56.
64. Lefebvre, *Naissance de l'historiographie moderne*, 18–22.
65. The most noteworthy being *La Révolution française* (Paris, 1930); *Les Thermidoriens* (Paris, 1946); *Le Directoire* (Paris, 1946); *Napoléon* (Paris, 1935).
66. Lefebvre, "La Révolution française dans l'histoire du monde," (1948), in *Etudes sur la Révolution française*, 317–26.
67. See Marie-Claire Laval, "Georges Lefebvre, historien et le peuple," *AHRF* 51 (1979), 357–73.
68. Georges Lefebvre, "Sur Danton" (1932), in *Etudes sur la Révolution française*, 25–66.
69. Georges Lefebvre, "Sur la pensée politique de Robespierre," *Etudes sur la Révolution française*, 95–98.
70. See Lionel Gossman, "Michelet and the French Revolution," in *Representing the French Revolution*, ed. Heffernan, 81–87.
71. Trans. by R. R. Palmer as *The Coming of the French Revolution* (Princeton, 1947), 110–22, 162–68, 198–205.
72. Lefebvre, "Foules révolutionnaires," *Etudes sur la Révolution française*, 271–87. That is why some scholars remember Lefebvre as a pioneer in the history of collective mentalities. See Cobb, "Georges Lefebvre," 90, 93.

73. See Pierre Caron, "Le Cent-Cinquantenaire de la Révolution française," *AHRF* 18 (1946), 97–114.

74. See Lefebvre's sober account of the proceedings, "A propos d'un congrès," *AHRF* 17 (1940), 56–61. See also Gérard, *La Révolution française*, 87–90.

75. Lefebvre, *Quatre-Vingt-Neuf*, 246–47.

76. See also Lefebvre, "D'Elle," originally published in the liberation newspaper *L'Université libre*, 23 September 1944, and reproduced in the *AHRF* 41 (1969), 570–73. See also David Thomson, *Democracy in France since 1870* (Oxford, 1946), 9–38; Gordon Wright, *The Reshaping of French Democracy* (1948; rpt. Boston, 1970).

77. *AHRF*, 30 (1960); 41 (1969); 51 (1979); 56 (1984).

78. For an overview of this trend in the historiography of the Revolution, see R. R. Palmer, *The Age of the Democratic Revolution*, 2 vols. (Princeton, 1959–64); Jacques Godechot, *Les Révolutions (1770–1799)*, 2d ed. (Paris, 1965).

79. Alfred Cobban, "The Myth of the French Revolution" (1955), *Aspects of the French Revolution* (New York, 1968), 90–108.

80. Georges Lefebvre, "Le Mythe de la Révolution française," *AHRF* 28 (1956), 337–45.

81. Alfred Cobban, *The Social Interpretation of the French Revolution* (Cambridge, 1964), esp. 162–73; Gerald J. Cavanaugh, "The Present State of French Revolutionary Historiography: Alfred Cobban and Beyond," *French Historical Studies* 7 (1972), 587–606.

82. For Furet's place in contemporary historical writing about the Revolution, see Jack R. Censer, "The Coming of a New Interpretation of the French Revolution," *Journal of Social History* 21 (1987), 295–309; George C. Comninel, *Rethinking the French Revolution: Marxism and the Revisionist Challenge* (London, 1987), 5–25. For his relationship to recent theoretical work in rhetoric, see the review of his book by Lynn Hunt in *History and Theory* 20 (1981), 313–23.

83. François Furet, *Interpreting the French Revolution*, trans. Elborg Forster (London, 1981), 10.

84. Ibid., 1–6.

85. *Qui est qui en France: Dictionnaire biographique, 1991–92*, 23d ed. (Paris, 1991), 721.

86. François Furet, *L'Atelier de l'histoire* (Paris, 1982), and with Jacques Ozouf, *Lire et écrire: L'Alphabétisation des Français de Calvin à Jules Ferry* (Paris, 1977).

87. Ibid., 14–17, 133.

88. Ibid., 133–35; Alexis de Tocqueville, *L'Ancien Régime et la Révolution*, 7th ed. (Paris, 1866).

89. Furet, *Interpreting the French Revolution*, 28, 37, 52, 73, 164, 173–80, 191–95, 201–03. See also Augustin Cochin, *La Crise de l'histoire révolutionnaire: Taine et M. Aulard* (Paris, 1909), 41–42, 49–53, 74, 86–96, 99.

90. Ibid., 7–9, 23–28, 37–61; see also François Furet, "Jacobinisme," in *Dictionnaire critique de la Révolution française*, ed. François Furet and Mona Ozouf (Paris, 1988), 756.

91. Furet, *Interpreting the Revolution*, 169–71, 194–95.

92. Maurice Agulhon, "Faut-il avoir peur de 1989," *Le Débat* 30 (1984), 27–37.

93. François Furet, "Réponse à Maurice Agulhon," *Le Débat* 30 (1984), 38–43. See also the interview with Furet, "Faut-il célébrer le bicentenaire de la Révolution française?" *L'Histoire* 52 (1983), 71–77.

94. François Furet, "La Révolution dans l'imaginaire politique français," *Le Débat* 26 (1983), 173–81.

95. François Furet and Mona Ozouf, eds., *Dictionnaire critique de la Révolution française* (Paris, 1988).

96. François Furet, "Histoire universitaire de la Révolution," in ibid., 979–83.

97. François Furet, "Michelet," in ibid., 1035.

98. Furet, "Histoire universitaire," in ibid., 983–87.

99. Ibid., 992–97. Furet points to Cobb's portrait of Lefebvre as solitary, humorless, and narrow in his life interests and, so, dismissive of what lies beyond these.
100. Pierre Nora, *Les Lieux de mémoire*, 3 vols. (Paris, 1984–92). For Nora's biography, see *Qui est qui en France*, 1249.
101. Pierre Nora, "Présentation," in *Lieux de mémoire*, 1: vii.
102. Pierre Nora, "Présentation," 1: xii–xiii, and "De la République à la Nation," 1: 651–59, in ibid.; "La Mémoire collective," in *La Nouvelle Histoire*, ed. Le Goff et al. (Paris, 1978), 400–01.
103. See Nora's endnote to Marc Roudebush's English translation of his "Entre mémoire et histoire," in *Representations* 26 (Spring 1989), 25.
104. Nora, "Entre mémoire et histoire," 1: xxv.
105. Ibid., 1: xxi.
106. Ibid., 1: xxxiii.
107. Ibid., 1: xlii.
108. For Nora's explanation of the framework of his study, see his "Présentation," 1: viii–xii.
109. "Entre mémoire et histoire," 1: xxv–xxviii.
110. Lavisse's project was published in two series: the *Histoire de France*, 9 vols. (Paris, 1903–11), and the *Histoire de France contemporaine depuis la Révolution jusqu'à la paix de 1919*, 9 vols. (Paris, 1920–22). It is interesting to note that both Lavisse and Nora worked with teams of historians, though in ways that reflect the differences between modern and postmodern styles of editorial direction. Lavisse's supervised his project with patronal authority, whereas Nora coordinated his in a managerial way. For Nora's comments on Lavisse and the historians who participated in his project, see Nora, "*L'Histoire de France* de Lavisse," in *Lieux de mémoire*, 2: 317–75.
111. Ibid., 2: 327–32.
112. Ibid., 332–43; "Entre mémoire et histoire," 1: xxxiv–xlii.
113. Ibid., 1: xxviii–xxxi.
114. Ibid., 1: xxiv.
115. Ibid., I: xxiii.
116. On the "hidden hermeneutic" of nationalist historiography in general, see Ana Maria Alonso, "The Effects of Truth: Re-presentations of the Past and the Imagining of Community," *Journal of Historical Sociology* 1 (1988), 33–37.

8

HISTORY AT THE CROSSROADS OF MEMORY

1. Søren Kierkegaard, *Stages on Life's Way*, ed. and trans. Howard V. Hong and Edna H. Hong (Princeton, 1988), 9–19, 503, 511, 518–25.
2. On historical conceptions in Wordsworth's writings, see James A. W. Heffernan, "History and Autobiography: The French Revolution in Wordsworth's *Prelude*," in *Representing the French Revolution*, ed. James A.W. Heffernan (Hanover, N.H., 1992), 41–62; Alan Liu, *Wordsworth: The Sense of History* (Stanford, 1989), 3–51.
3. Mircea Eliade, *Cosmos and History: The Myth of the Eternal Return* (1949), trans. Willard R. Trask (New York, 1959), 34–48, 73–77, 95–130, 147–58.
4. Philippe Ariès, *Le Temps de l'histoire* (Monaco, 1954), 25–32, 259–72.
5. R. G. Collingwood, *The Idea of History* (Oxford, 1946), 231–49, 282–302.
6. Hans-Georg Gadamer, *Philosophical Apprenticeships*, trans. Robert R. Sullivan (Cambridge, Mass., 1985), 45–54, 177–93.
7. Hans-Georg Gadamer, *Truth and Method*, 2d rev. ed., rev. trans. Joel Weinsheimer and Donald G. Marshall (New York, 1989), 173–218, 254–64.
8. Ibid., 218–42, 370–72.

9. Robert Mandrou, "L'Histoire des mentalités," *Encyclopaedia universalis* 8 (1968 ed.), 436–38; Philippe Ariès, "L'Histoire des mentalités," in *La Nouvelle Histoire*, ed. Jacques Le Goff et al. (Paris, 1978), 402–23.

10. Gadamer, *Truth and Method*, 295.

11. Ibid., 173–97.

12. Ibid., 294–300.

13. Ibid., 284.

14. Ibid., 280–85, 299–307, 373–79.

15. Ibid., 277, 307–41.

16. See the discerning study by George Allan, *The Importances of the Past: A Meditation on the Authority of Tradition* (Albany, 1986), esp. 191–225.

17. Michel Foucault, *Madness and Civilization: A History of Insanity in the Age of Reason*, trans. Richard Howard (New York, 1965), 3–7.

18. Michel Foucault, *The Order of Things: An Archaeology of the Human Sciences*, trans. anon. (New York, 1970), 383–87; *The Archaeology of Knowledge*, trans. A. M. Sheridan Smith (New York, 1972), 3–17, 135–40.

19. On the problem of collective memory and static representation, see Barry Schwartz, "The Reconstruction of Abraham Lincoln," in *Collective Remembering*, ed. David Middleton and Derek Edwards (London, 1990), 103–04.

20. This is what Foucault means by the term "counter-memory"—the absence of memory in archaeological inquiry, not the consideration of alternative memories. Michel Foucault, "Nietzsche, Genealogy, History," in *Language, Counter-Memory, Practice*, ed. Donald F. Bouchard (Ithaca, 1977), 139–64.

21. Foucault, *The Order of Things*, 3–16.

22. See Foucault's remarks on madness and creativity in his closing passage of *Madness and Civilization*, 279–89. On Foucault's hidden purposes, see Jerrold Seigel, "Avoiding the Subject: A Foucaultian Itinerary," *Journal of the History of Ideas* 51 (1990), 273–99.

23. See esp. the serial essay by Giorgio Tagliacozzo, "Toward a History of Recent Anglo-American Vico Scholarship," *New Vico Studies* 1 (1983)–5 (1987).

24. *The New Science of Giambattista Vico* (3d ed.; 1744), trans. and ed. Thomas G. Bergin and Max H. Fisch (Ithaca, 1968), para. 331.

25. Ibid., paras. 400–11.

26. See the discussion by John Halverson, "Havelock on Greek Orality and Literacy," *Journal of the History of Ideas* 53 (1992), 152–53.

27. John Miles Foley, *The Theory of Oral Composition* (Bloomington, Ind., 1988), 1–35; Jan Vansina, *Oral Tradition as History* (Madison, Wis., 1985), 147–85.

28. Samuel Butler, *Life and Habit* (1878; rpt. London, 1924).

29. Rupert Sheldrake, *The Presence of the Past: Morphic Resonance and the Habits of Nature* (New York, 1988), esp. xx–xxii, 3–17, 39–56, 107–14, 159–73, 200–09, 308–24, and "Memory and Morphic Resonance," *ReVision* 10 (1987), 9–12. See also Philip Kuberski, *The Persistence of Memory* (Berkeley, 1992), 110–14.

30. Walter J. Ong, *Orality and Literacy: The Technologizing of the Word* (London, 1982), 78–138.

31. See Steven Connor, *Postmodernist Culture: An Introduction to Theories of the Contemporary* (Oxford, 1989), 3–23.

32. Joshua Meyrowitz, *No Sense of Place: The Impact of Electronic Media on Social Behavior* (Oxford, 1985), 307–29.

33. Bill McKibben, *The Age of Missing Information* (New York, 1992), 54–67. See also George Lipsitz, *Time Passages: Collective Memory and American Popular Culture* (Minneapolis, 1990), 21–96.

34. Robert E. Proctor, *Education's Great Amnesia: Reconsidering the Humanities from Petrarch to Freud* (Bloomington, Ind., 1988), 162–99.
35. On the relationship between mnemonics and contemporary semiotic theory, see Umberto Eco, "Mnemotecniche come semiotiche," *MondOperaio* 12 (1989), 110–14.
36. See the provocative study by Francis Fukuyama, *The End of History and the Last Man* (New York, 1992).

BIBLIOGRAPHY

Abrams, M. H. *The Mirror and the Lamp: Romantic Theory and the Critical Tradition.* New York: Norton, 1958.

———. *Natural Supernaturalism: Tradition and Revolution in Romantic Literature.* New York: Norton, 1971.

Agulhon, Maurice. "Débats actuels sur la Révolution en France." *Annales historiques de la Révolution française* 279 (1990), 1–13.

———. "Faut-il avoir peur de 1989?" *Le Débat* 30 (1984), 27–37.

———. *Marianne into Battle: Republican Imagery and Symbolism in France, 1879–1880.* Trans. Janet Lloyd. Cambridge: Cambridge University Press, 1981.

———. *The Republican Experiment, 1848–1852.* Trans. Janet Lloyd. Cambridge: Cambridge University Press, 1983.

———. "La 'Statuomanie' et l'histoire." *Ethnologie française* 8 (1978), 145–72.

Alfaric, Prosper. *Les Manuscrits de la "Vie de Jésus" d'Ernest Renan.* Paris: Belles-Lettres, 1939.

Allan, George. *The Importances of the Past: A Meditation on the Authority of Tradition.* Albany: State University of New York Press, 1986.

Alonzo, Ana Maria. "The Effects of Truth: Re-Presentation of the Past and the Imagining of Community." *Journal of Historical Sociology* 1 (1988), 33–57.

Anderson, Benedict R. *Imagined Communities: Reflections on the Origin and Spread of Nationalism.* London: Verso, 1983.

Arac, Jonathan, ed. *After Foucault: Historical Knowledge, Postmodern Challenges.* New Brunswick: Rutgers University Press, 1988.

Ariès, Philippe. *Centuries of Childhood.* Trans. Robert Baldick. New York: Random House, 1962.

———. "Confessions d'un anarchiste de droite." *Contrepoint* 16 (1974).

———. *Histoire des populations françaises et de leurs attitudes devant la vie depuis le XVIIIᵉ siècle.* 1948; Paris: Editions du Seuil, 1976.

———. *Un Historien du dimanche.* Paris: Editions du Seuil, 1982.

———. *The Hour of Our Death.* Trans. Helen Weaver. New York: Knopf, 1981.

———. *Le Temps de l'histoire.* Monaco: Editions du Rocher, 1954. Rpt. Editions du Seuil, 1986.

————. *Les Traditions sociales dans les pays de France.* Paris: Les Editions de la Nouvelle France, 1943.

————. *Western Attitudes toward Death.* Trans. Patricia Ranum. Baltimore: Johns Hopkins University Press, 1974.

Arieti, Silvano. "Vico and Modern Psychiatry." *Social Research* 43 (1976), 739–50.

Aulard, Alphonse. *Le Culte de la raison et le culte du l'être suprême (1793–1794).* Paris: Alcan, 1904.

————. *L'Eloquence parlementaire pendant la Révolution française.* 3 vols. Paris: Hachette, 1882–86.

————. *Etudes et leçons sur la Révolution française.* 1st series. 5th ed. Paris: Alcan, 1909.

————. *The French Revolution: A Political History* Trans. Bernard Miall. 4 vols. New York: Scribner, 1910.

————, ed. *La Société des Jacobins: Recueil de documents pour l'histoire du club des Jacobins de Paris.* 6 vols. Paris: Librairie L. Cerf, 1889–97.

Badano, Gigliola. "Storia della scienza." *Il Veltro: Rivista della civiltà* 35 (1991), 366–70.

Baker, Keith Michael. "Memory and Practice: Politics and the Representation of the Past in Eighteenth-Century France." *Representations* 11 (Summer 1985), 134–64.

Baker, Keith, Colin Lucas, François Furet, and Mona Ozouf, eds. *The French Revolution and the Creation of Modern Political Culture.* 3 vols. Oxford: Pergamon Press, 1987–90.

Baldwin, Peter, ed. *Reworking the Past: Hitler, the Holocaust, and the Historians' Debates.* Boston: Beacon Press, 1990.

Bartlett, Frederic C. *Remembering: A Study in Experimental and Social Psychology.* 1932; Cambridge: Cambridge University Press, 1967.

Bastide, Roger. "Mémoire collective et sociologie de bricolage." *L'Année sociologique* 3d ser. 21 (1970), 65–108.

Battistini, Andrea, ed. *Vico oggi.* Rome: Armando Armando Editore, 1979.

————. "Vico in America." *Lettera internazionale* 5/20 (1989).

Baumeister, Roy F. *Identity: Cultural Change and the Struggle for Self.* Oxford: Oxford University Press, 1986.

Beaujour, Michel. *Miroirs d'encre: Rhétorique de l'autoportrait* Paris: Editions du Seuil, 1980.

Berenson, Edward. *Populist Religion and Left-Wing Politics in France, 1830–1852.* Princeton: Princeton University Press, 1984.

Bergson, Henri. *Matter and Memory.* Trans. N. M. Paul and W. S. Palmer. 1908; New York: Zone Books, 1988.

Berlin, Isaiah. *The Crooked Timber of Humanity.* New York: Knopf, 1991.

————. *Vico and Herder: Two Studies in the History of Ideas.* New York: Random House, 1976.

————. "Vico and the Ideal of the Enlightenment." *Social Research* 43 (1976), 640–53.

Berliner, Arthur K. *Psychoanalysis and Society.* Washington, D.C.: University Press of America, 1983.

Bernauer, James, and David Rasmussen, eds. *The Final Foucault.* Cambridge: MIT Press, 1988.

Besnard, Philippe, ed. *The Sociological Domain: The Durkheimians and the Founding of French Sociology.* Cambridge: Cambridge University Press, 1983.

Bloch, Marc. "Mémoire collective, tradition et coutume: A propos d'un livre récent." *Revue de synthèse* 40 (1925), 73–83.

Blum, Herwig. *Die Antike Mnemotechnik*. Hildesheim: Olms, 1969.

Bousma, William James, and Barbara C. Malament, eds. *After the Reformation: Essays in Honor of J. H. Hexter*. Philadelphia: University of Pennsylvania Press, 1980.

Braudel, Fernand. *On History*. Trans. Sarah Matthews. Chicago: University of Chicago Press, 1980.

Brown, Irene Q. "Philippe Ariès on Education and Society in Seventeenth- and Eighteenth-Century France." *History of Education Quarterly* 7 (1967), 357–68.

Brunel, Françoise, and Olivier Guérin. "Sur Georges Lefebvre." *Annales historiques de la Révolution française* 41 (1969), 549–69.

Burguière, André, ed. *Dictionnaire des sciences historiques*. Paris: Presses Universitaires de France, 1986.

———. "The Fate of the History of Mentalities in the *Annales*." *Comparative Studies in Society and History* 24 (1982), 424–37.

———. "Histoire d'une histoire: Naissance des *Annales*." *Annales: Economies, Sociétés, Civilisations* 34 (1979), 1347–59.

———. "La Singulière Histoire de Philippe Ariès." *Le Nouvel Observateur*, 20 February 1978.

Burke, Peter. *The French Historical Revolution: The* Annales *School, 1929–89*. Stanford: Stanford University Press, 1990.

———. *The Renaissance Sense of the Past*. New York: St. Martin's, 1969.

Butler, Samuel. *Life and Habit*. 1878; London: Jonathan Cape, 1924

Butterfield, Herbert. *The Whig Interpretation of History*. 1931; New York: Norton, 1965.

Calinescu, Matei. *Five Faces of Modernity*. Durham, N.C.: Duke University Press, 1987.

Caron, Pierre. "Le Cent-Cinquantenaire de la Révolution française." *Annales historiques de la Révolution française* 18 (1946), 97–114.

Carrard, Philippe. *Poetics of the New History: French Historical Discourse from Braudel to Chartier*. Baltimore: Johns Hopkins University Press, 1992.

Casey, Edward S. *Remembering: A Phenomenological Study*. Bloomington: Indiana University Press, 1987.

Cavanaugh, Gerald J. "The Present State of French Revolutionary Historiography: Alfred Cobban and Beyond." *French Historical Studies* 7 (1972), 587–606.

Censer, Jack R. "The Coming of a New Interpretation of the French Revolution." *Journal of Social History* 21 (1987), 295–309.

Cermak, Laird S. *Improving Your Memory*. New York: Norton, 1975.

Certeau, Michel de. *The Writing of History*. Trans. Tom Conley. New York: Columbia University Press, 1988.

Chartier, Roger. "L'Amitié de l'histoire." Preface to *Le Temps de l'histoire* by Philippe Ariès. Paris: Editions du Seuil, 1986, 9–31.

———, ed. *The Culture of Print*. Princeton: Princeton University Press, 1989.

Chateaubriand, François-René, vicomte de. *Itinéraire de Paris à Jérusalem*. 3d ed. 2 vols. Paris: Calmann-Levy, 1800.

Chaunu, Pierre. *L'Historien en cet instant*. Paris: Hachette, 1985.

———. "Sur le chemin de Philippe Ariès, historien de la mort." *Histoire, économie et société* 3 (1984), 651–63.

Cheetham, Mark A., with Linda Hutcheon. *Remembering Postmodernism: Trends in Recent Canadian Art*. Toronto: Oxford University Press, 1991.

Clanchy, M. T. *From Memory to Written Record: England, 1066–1307*. Cambridge: Harvard University Press, 1979.

Clark, Michael. *Michel Foucault, An Annotated Bibliography: Tool Kit for a New Age*. New York: Garland, 1983.

Clark, Terry Nichols. *Prophets and Patrons: The French University and the Emergence of the Social Sciences*. Cambridge: Harvard University Press, 1973.

Cobb, Richard. *A Second Identity: Essays on France and French History*. Oxford: Oxford University Press, 1969.

Cobban, Alfred. *Aspects of the French Revolution*. New York: Braziller, 1968.

———. *The Social Interpretation of the French Revolution*. Cambridge: Cambridge University Press, 1964.

Cochin, Augustin. *La Crise de l'histoire révolutionnaire: Taine et M. Aulard*. Paris: Champion, 1909.

Cohen, Murray. *Sensible Words: Linguistic Practice in England, 1640–1785*. Baltimore: Johns Hopkins University Press, 1977.

Cohen, William. "Symbols of Power: Statues in Nineteenth-Century Provincial France." *Comparative Studies in Society and History* 31 (1989), 491–513.

Coleman-Norton, P. R. *The Twelve Tables*. Rev. ed. Princeton: Princeton University, Department of Classics, 1960.

Collingwood, R. G. *The Idea of History*. Oxford: Oxford University Press, 1946.

Comninel, George C. *Rethinking the French Revolution: Marxism and the Revisionist Challenge*. London: Verso, 1987.

Comte, Auguste. *A General View of Positivism*. Trans. J. H. Bridges. 1851; New York: Robert Speller & Sons, 1975.

Connerton, Paul. *How Societies Remember*. Cambridge: Cambridge University Press, 1989.

Connor, Steven. *Postmodernist Culture: An Introduction to Theories of the Contemporary*. Oxford: Blackwell, 1985.

Craig, John E. "Maurice Halbwachs à Strasbourg." *Revue française de sociologie* 20 (1979), 273–92.

Culler, Jonathan. *Framing the Sign: Criticism and Its Institutions*. Norman: University of Oklahoma Press, 1988.

Dalman, Gustave. *Les Itinéraires de Jésus: Topographie des évangiles*. Rev. ed. Trans. Jacques Marty. Paris: Payot, 1930.

———. *Jesus-Jeshua: Studies in the Gospels*. Trans. Paul P. Levertoff. 1929; New York: Ktav Publishing House, 1971.

Darnton, Robert. *The Business of the Enlightenment: A Publishing History of the Encyclopédie, 1775–1800*. Cambridge: Harvard University Press, 1979.

———. *The Great Cat Massacre and Other Episodes in French History*. New York: Basic Books, 1984.

———. *The Literary Underground of the Old Regime*. Cambridge: Harvard University Press, 1982.

Davis, Natalie Zemon, and Randolf Starn. "Introduction: Memory and Counter-Memory." *Representations* 26 (Spring 1989), 1–6.

Davis, Natalie Zemon. *The Return of Martin Guerre*. Cambridge: Harvard University Press, 1983.

Deleuze, Gilles. *Foucault.* Trans. Sean Hand. Minneapolis: University of Minnesota Press, 1988.

Dennett, Daniel Clement. *Consciousness Explained.* Boston: Little, Brown, 1991.

Diamond, Irene, and Lee Quinby, eds. *Feminism and Foucault: Reflections on Resistance.* Boston: Northeastern University Press, 1988.

Donzelot, Jacques. *The Policing of Families.* Trans. Robert Hurley. New York: Pantheon Books, 1979.

Douglas, Mary. *Edward Evans-Pritchard.* New York: Viking Press, 1980.

———. *How Institutions Think.* Syracuse: Syracuse University Press, 1986.

———. "Introduction: Maurice Halbwachs (1877–1945)." In *The Collective Memory* by Maurice Halbwachs. New York: Harper & Row, 1980.

Dray, William H. "J. H. Hexter, Neo-Whiggism and Early Stuart Historiography." *History and Theory* 26 (1987), 133–49.

Dreyfus, Hubert L., and Paul Rabinow, eds. *Michel Foucault: Beyond Structuralism and Hermeneutics.* 2d ed. Chicago: University of Chicago Press, 1983.

Eco, Umberto. "Mnemotechniche come semiotiche." *MondOperaio* 12 (1989), 110–14.

Edelman, Gerald M. *Neural Darwinism: The Theory of Neuronal Group Selection.* New York: Basic Books, 1987.

———. *The Remembered Present: A Biological Theory of Consciousness.* New York: Basic Books, 1989.

Eisenstein, Elizabeth L. *The Printing Press as an Agent of Change.* 2 vols. Cambridge: Cambridge University Press, 1979.

Eliade, Mircea. *Cosmos and History: The Myth of the Eternal Return.* Trans. Willard R. Trask. 1949; New York: Harper & Row, 1959.

Ellenberger, Henri F. *The Discovery of the Unconscious.* New York: Basic Books, 1970.

Ellis, David. *Wordsworth, Freud and the Spots of Time.* Cambridge: Cambridge University Press, 1985.

Elsky, Martin. *Authorizing Words: Speech, Writing, and Print in the English Renaissance.* Ithaca: Cornell University Press, 1989.

Farmer, Paul. *France Reviews Its Revolutionary Origins.* New York: Octagon Books, 1963.

Febvre, Lucien. *A New Kind of History.* Ed. Peter Burke. New York: Harper & Row, 1973.

Feinaigle, Gregor von. *The New Art of Memory.* London: Sherwood, Neely, and Jones, 1813.

Ferguson, Arthur B. *Clio Unbound: Perception of the Social and Cultural Past in Renaissance England.* Durham, N.C.: Duke University Press, 1979.

Finnegan, Ruth. *Literacy and Orality: Studies in the Technology of Communication.* Oxford: Blackwell, 1988.

———. "Tradition, But What Tradition and for Whom?" *Oral Tradition* 6 (1991), 104–24.

Flandrin, Jean-Louis. "Enfance et société." *Annales: Economies, sociétés, civilisations* 19 (1964), 322–29.

Foley, John Miles, ed. "A Festschrift for Walter J. Ong." *Oral Tradition* 2 (1987).

———, ed. *Oral Traditional Literature: A Festschrift for Albert Bates Lord.* Columbus, Ohio: Slavica Publishers, 1981.

———. *The Theory of Oral Composition.* Bloomington: Indiana University Press, 1988.

Fornet-Betancourt, Raul. "The Ethic of Care for the Self as a Practice of Freedom: An Interview with Michel Foucault." *Philosophy and Social Criticism* 12 (1987), 112–31.

Foucault, Michel. *The Archaeology of Knowledge.* Trans. A.M. Sheridan Smith. New York: Harper & Row, 1972.

———. *The Birth of the Clinic: An Archaeology of Medical Perception.* Trans. A. M. Sheridan Smith. New York: Random House, 1973.

———. *The Care of the Self.* Trans. Robert Hurley. New York: Random House, 1986.

———. *Death and the Labyrinth.* Trans. and ed. Charles Ruas. Garden City, N.Y.: Doubleday, 1986.

———. "The Discourse on Language." *Social Science Information* 10 (1971), 7–30.

———. *The History of Sexuality: An Introduction.* Trans. Robert Hurley. New York: Pantheon, 1878.

———. *Language, Counter-Memory, Practice: Selected Essays and Interviews.* Ed. Donald F. Bouchard. Trans. Donald F. Bouchard and Sherry Simon. Ithaca: Cornell University Press, 1977.

———. *Madness and Civilization: A History of Insanity in the Age of Reason.* Trans. Richard Howard. 1961; New York: Random House, 1973.

———. *Mental Illness and Psychology.* Trans. Alan Sheridan. 1954. New York: Harper & Row, 1976.

———. "Nietzsche, Freud, Marx." *Cahiers de Royaument* 6 (1967), 183–92.

———. *The Order of Things: An Archaeology of the Human Sciences.* Trans. Alan Sheridan. New York: Random House, 1970.

———. *Politics, Philosophy, Culture: Interviews and Other Writings, 1977–1984.* Ed. Lawrence D. Kritzman. Trans. Alan Sheridan et al. New York: Routledge, 1988.

———. *Power/Knowledge: Selected Interviews and Other Writings, 1972–77.* Ed. Colin Gordon. Trans. Colin Gordon et al. New York: Pantheon, 1980.

———. *This Is Not a Pipe.* Trans. James Harkness. Berkeley: University of California Press, 1982.

———. *The Use of Pleasure.* Trans. Robert Hurley. New York: Random House, 1985.

Freud, Sigmund. *An Autobiographical Study.* Trans. James Strachey. 1935; New York: Norton, 1963.

———. *Civilization and Its Discontents.* Trans. James Strachey. 1930; New York: Norton, 1961.

———. *The Collected Papers of Sigmund Freud.* Ed. Joan Riviere. 5 vols. New York: Basic Books, 1959.

———. *The Ego and the Id.* Trans. Joan Riviere. 1923; New York: Norton, 1962.

———. *Five Lectures on Psycho-Analysis.* Trans. James Strachey. 1910; New York: Norton, 1977.

———. *The Interpretation of Dreams.* Trans. James Strachey. 1900; New York: Avon Books, 1965.

———. *Introductory Lectures on Psychoanalysis.* Trans. James Strachey. 1917; New York: Norton, 1966.

———. *Leonardo da Vinci: A Study in Psychosexuality.* Trans. A. A. Brill. 1916; New York: Random House, 1947.

———. *Moses and Monotheism.* Trans. Katherine Jones. 1939; New York: Random House, 1967.

———. *New Introductory Lectures on Psychoanalysis.* Trans. James Strachey. 1933; New York: Norton, 1965.

———. *An Outline of Psychoanalysis.* Trans. James Strachey. 1940; New York: Norton, 1949.

———. *A Phylogenetic Fantasy.* Ed. Ilse Grubrich-Simitis. Trans. Axel Hoffer and Peter T. Hoffer. Cambridge: Harvard University Press, 1987.

———. *The Psychopathology of Everyday Life.* Trans. Alan Tyson. 1901; New York: Norton, 1965.

———. *The Standard Edition of the Complete Psychological Works of Sigmund Freud.* Ed. James Strachey. 24 vols. London: Hogarth Press, 1966–74.

———. *Totem and Taboo.* Trans. James Strachey. 1913; New York: Norton, 1950.

Friedländer, Saul. *History and Psychoanalysis.* Trans. Susan Suleiman. New York: Holmes & Meier, 1980.

———, ed. *Probing the Limits of Representation: Nazism and the "Final Solution."* Cambridge: Harvard University Press, 1992.

———. *Reflections of Nazism: An Essay on Kitsch and Death.* Trans. Thomas Weyr. New York: Harper & Row, 1982.

———. "Trauma, Transference and 'Working Through' in Writing the History of the *Shoah.*" *History and Memory* 4 (1992), 39–55.

———. *When Memory Comes.* Trans. Helen R. Lane. New York: Noonday Press, 1991.

Friguglietti, James. "Alphonse Aulard and the Politics of History." *Proceedings of the Annual Meeting of the Western Society for French History* 15 (1988), 379–87.

Fukuyama, Francis. *The End of History and the Last Man.* New York: Free Press, 1992.

Furet, François. "Faut-il célébrer le bicentenaire de la Révolution française?" *L'Histoire* 52 (1983), 71–77.

———. *Interpreting the French Revolution.* Trans. Elborg Forster. Cambridge: Cambridge University Press, 1981.

———. *In the Workshop of History.* Trans. Jonathan Mandelbaum. Chicago: University of Chicago Press, 1984.

———. "Réponse à Maurice Agulhon." *Le Débat* 30 (1984), 38–43.

———. "La Révolution dans l'imaginaire politique français." *Le Débat* 26 (1983), 173–81.

Furet, François, and Jacques Ozouf. *Reading and Writing: Literacy in France from Calvin to Jules Ferry.* Trans. anon. Cambridge: Cambridge University Press, 1982.

Furet, François, and Mona Ozouf, eds. *Dictionnaire critique de la Révolution française.* Paris: Flammarion, 1988.

Gadamer, Hans-Georg. *Philosophical Apprenticeships.* Trans. Robert R. Sullivan. Cambridge: MIT Press, 1985.

———. *Truth and Method.* 2d rev. ed. Trans. and ed. Joel Weinsheimer and Donald G. Marshall. New York: Crossroad Publishing, 1989.

Gadoffre, Gilbert, ed. *Certitudes et incertitudes de l'histoire.* Paris: Presses Universitaires de France, 1987.

Gay, Peter. *Freud: A Life for Our Times.* New York: Norton, 1988.

———. *Freud for Historians.* Oxford: Oxford University Press, 1985.

———. *Freud, Jews and Other Germans: Masters and Victims in Modernist Culture.* Oxford: Oxford University Press, 1978.

———. *A Godless Jew: Freud, Atheism, and the Making of Psychoanalysis.* New Haven: Yale University Press, 1987.

Gérard, Alice. *La Révolution française: mythes et interprétations (1789–1970)*. Paris: Flammarion, 1970.

Gill, Stephen. *William Wordsworth: A Life*. Oxford: Clarendon, 1989.

Ginzburg, Carlo. "Clues: Morelli, Freud, and Sherlock Holmes." In *The Sign of the Three*. Ed. Umberto Eco and Thomas A. Sebeok. Bloomington: Indiana University Press, 1983.

Godechot, Jacques. *Les Révolutions (1770–1799)*. 2d ed. Paris: Presses Universitaires de France, 1965.

Goldberg, Harvey. *The Life of Jean Jaurès*. Madison: University of Wisconsin Press, 1962.

Goldberg, Jonathan. *Writing Matter: From the Hands of the English Renaissance*. Stanford: Stanford University Press, 1990.

Gombrich, E.H. *Aby Warburg: An Intellectual Biography*. Chicago: University of Chicago Press, 1986.

Goody, Jack. *The Domestication of the Savage Mind*. Cambridge: Cambridge University Press, 1977.

———. *The Interface between the Written and the Oral*. Cambridge: Cambridge University Press, 1987.

———, ed. *Literacy in Traditional Societies*. Cambridge: Cambridge University Press, 1968.

Gowans, Alan. *Learning to See*. Bowling Green, Ohio: Bowling Green University Press, 1981.

Grafton, Anthony. *Defenders of the Text: The Traditions of Scholarship in an Age of Science, 1450–1800*. Cambridge: Harvard University Press, 1991.

Grafton, Anthony, and Ann Blair, eds. *The Transmission of Culture in Early Modern Europe*. Philadelphia: University of Pennsylvania Press, 1990.

Grassi, Ernesto. *Rhetoric as Philosophy: The Humanist Tradition*. University Park: Pennsylvania State University Press, 1980.

Gusdorf, Georges. *Mémoire et personne*. 2 vols. Paris: Presses Universitaires de France, 1951.

Gutting, Gary. *Michel Foucault's Archaeology of Scientific Reason*. Cambridge: Cambridge University Press, 1989.

Haac, Oscar A. *Jules Michelet*. Boston: Twayne, 1982.

Haddock, Bruce A. "Vico's Discovery of the True Homer: A Case Study in Historical Reconstruction." *Journal of the History of Ideas* 40 (1979), 583–602.

———. *Vico's Political Thought*. Swansea, U.K.: Mortlake Press, 1986.

Halbwachs, Maurice. *Les Cadres sociaux de la mémoire*. 1925; New York: Arno Press, 1975.

———. *The Collective Memory*. Trans. Francis J. Ditter and Vida Yazdi Ditter. 1950; New York: Harper & Row, 1980.

———. "La Doctrine d'Emile Durkheim." *Revue philosophique de la France et de l'étranger* 85 (1918), 353–411.

———. "Individual Psychology and Collective Psychology." *American Sociological Review* 3 (1938), 615–23.

———. *On Maurice Halbwachs*. Trans. and ed. Lewis A. Coser. Chicago: University of Chicago Press, 1992.

———. *The Psychology of Social Class*. Trans. Claire Delavenay. Ed. Georges Friedmann. Glencoe, Ill.: Free Press, 1958.

————. *La Topographie légendaire des évangiles en Terre Sainte.* Ed. Fernand Dumont. 1941; Paris: Presses Universitaires de France, 1971.

Halperin, S. William, ed. *Essays in Modern Historiography.* Chicago: University of Chicago Press, 1970.

Halverson, John. "Havelock on Greek Orality and Literacy." *Journal of the History of Ideas* 53 (1992), 148–63.

Harlan, David. "Intellectual History and the Return of Literature." *American Historical Review* 94 (1989), 581–609.

Hartle, Ann. *The Modern Self in Rousseau's Confessions.* Notre Dame, Ind.: University of Notre Dame Press, 1983.

Hartman, Geoffrey H. *Wordsworth's Poetry.* New Haven: Yale University Press, 1964.

Harvey, Simon, and R. A. Leigh, eds. *Reappraisals of Rousseau.* Totowa, N.J.: Barnes & Noble, 1980.

Havelock, Eric A. *The Literate Revolution in Greece and Its Cultural Consequences.* Princeton: Princeton University Press, 1982.

————. *The Muse Learns to Write.* New Haven: Yale University Press, 1986.

————. *Preface to Plato.* Cambridge: Harvard University Press, 1963.

Hawkes, Terence. "Is There Anything There Out There? Rev. of Umberto Eco, *The Limits of Interpretation.*" *Times Literary Supplement,* 1 February 1991.

————. *Structuralism and Semiotics.* Berkeley: University of California Press, 1977.

Heffernan, James A. W., ed. *Representing the French Revolution: Literature, Historiography, and Art.* Hanover: University Press of New England, 1992.

————. *Wordsworth's Theory of Poetry: The Transforming Imagination.* Ithaca: Cornell University Press, 1969.

Hesiod. *Theogony: Works and Days.* Trans. and ed. M. L. West. Oxford: Oxford University Press, 1988.

Hobsbawm, Eric, and Terence Ranger, eds. *The Invention of Tradition.* Cambridge: Cambridge University Press, 1983.

Hoy, David Couzens, ed. *Foucault: A Critical Reader.* Oxford: Blackwell, 1986.

Hunt, David. *Parents and Children in History: The Psychology of Family Life in Early Modern France.* New York: Harper & Row, 1970.

Hunt, E.D. *Holy Land Pilgrimage in the Later Roman Empire, AD 312–460.* Oxford: Clarendon, 1982.

Hunt, Lynn. *Politics, Culture, and Class in the French Revolution.* Berkeley: University of California Press, 1984.

Huppert, George. *The Idea of Perfect History: Historical Erudition and Historical Philosophy in Renaissance France.* Urbana: University of Illinois Press, 1970.

Hutcheon, Linda. *A Poetics of Postmodernism: History, Theory, Fiction.* New York: Routledge, 1988.

Hutton, Patrick H. "The Art of Memory Reconceived: From Rhetoric to Psychoanalysis." *Journal of the History of Ideas* 48 (1987), 371–92.

————. "Collective Memory and Collective Mentalities: The Halbwachs-Ariès Connection." *Historical Reflections/Réflexions historiques* 15 (1988), 313–22.

————. *The Cult of the Revolutionary Tradition: The Blanquists in French Politics, 1864–1893.* Berkeley: University of California Press, 1981.

————. "The Foucault Phenomenon and Contemporary French Historiography." *Historical Reflections* 17 (1991), 77–102.

————. "The History of Mentalities: The New Map of Cultural History." *History and Theory* 20 (1981), 237–59.

————. "The *New Science* of Giambattista Vico: Historicism in Its Relation to Poetics." *Journal of Aesthetics and Art Criticism* 30 (1972), 359–67.

————. "The Problem of Memory in the Historical Writings of Philippe Ariès." *History and Memory* 4 (1992), 95–122.

————. The Problem of Oral Tradition in Vico's Historical Scholarship." *Journal of the History of Ideas* 53 (1992), 3–23.

————. "The Role of Memory in the Historiography of the French Revolution." *History and Theory* 30 (1991), 56–69.

————. "Vico's Significance for the New Cultural History." *New Vico Studies* 3 (1985), 73–84.

————. "Vico's Theory of History and the French Revolutionary Tradition." *Journal of the History of Ideas* 37 (1976), 241–56.

Hyslop, Beatrice. "George Lefebvre, Historian." *French Historical Studies* 1 (1960), 265–82.

Iggers, Georg G. *The German Conception of History.* Rev. ed. Middletown, Conn.: Wesleyan University Press, 1983.

————. *New Directions in European Historiography.* Middletown, Conn.: Wesleyan University Press, 1984.

Jameson, Frederic. *Postmodernism: Or, The Cultural Logic of Late Capitalism.* Durham, N.C.: Duke University Press, 1991.

Jaurès, Jean, ed. *L'Histoire socialiste (1789–1900).* 13 vols. Paris: Jules Rouff, 1901–08.

Jouhard, Christian. "Printing the Event: From La Rochelle to Paris." In *The Culture of Print: Power and the Uses of Print in Early Modern Europe.* Ed. Roger Chartier. Trans. Lydia G. Cochrane. Princeton: Princeton University Press, 1989.

Joutard, Philippe. *Ces Voix qui nous viennent du passé.* Paris: Hachette, 1983.

Kammen, Michael. *Mystic Chords of Memory: The Transformation of Tradition in American Culture.* New York: Knopf, 1991.

Kaplan, Edward K. *Michelet's Poetic Vision.* Amherst: University of Massachusetts Press, 1977.

Kelley, Donald R. *Historians and the Law in Postrevolutionary France.* Princeton: Princeton University Press, 1984.

————. *The Human Measure: Social Thought in the Western Legal Tradition.* Cambridge: Harvard University Press, 1990.

Kenyon, John P. *The History Men: The Historical Profession in England since the Renaissance.* Pittsburgh: University of Pittsburgh Press, 1983.

Kern, Stephen. *The Culture of Time and Space, 1880–1918.* Cambridge: Harvard University Press, 1983.

Kernan, Alvin. *Printing Technology, Letters and Samuel Johnson.* Princeton: Princeton University Press, 1987.

Keylor, William R. *Academy and Community: The Foundation of the French Historical Profession.* Cambridge: Harvard University Press, 1975.

————. *Jacques Bainville and the Renaissance of Royalist Historiography in Twentieth-Century France.* Baton Rouge: Louisiana State University Press, 1979.

Kierkegaard, Søren. *Repetition.* Ed. and trans. Howard V. Hong and Edna H. Hong. Princeton: Princeton University Press, 1983.

——. *Stages on Life's Way.* Ed. and trans. Howard V. Hong and Edna H. Hong. Princeton: Princeton University Press, 1988.

Konvitz, Milton R., ed. *Essays in Political Theory Presented to George H. Sabine.* Ithaca: Cornell University Press, 1948.

Koselleck, Reinhart. *Futures Past: On the Semantics of Historical Time.* Trans. Keith Tribe. Cambridge: MIT Press, 1985.

——. "Les Monuments aux morts: Contribution à l'étude d'une marque visuelle des temps modernes." In *Iconographie et histoire des mentalités.* Ed. Michel Vovelle. Paris: Editions du Centre National de la Recherche Scientifique, 1979.

Kuberski, Philip. *The Persistence of Memory.* Berkeley: University of California Press, 1992.

Kübler-Ross, Elisabeth. *On Death and Dying.* New York: Macmillan, 1969.

Kunkel, Wolfgang. *An Introduction to Roman Legal and Constitutional History.* 2d ed. Trans. J.M. Kelly. Oxford: Clarendon, 1973.

Kurzweil, Edith. *The Age of Structuralism: Lévi-Strauss to Foucault.* New York: Columbia University Press, 1980.

Langer, Lawrence L. *Holocaust Testimonies: The Ruins of Memory.* New Haven: Yale University Press, 1991.

Laslett, Peter. *The World We Have Lost.* New York: Scribner, 1965.

Laval, Marie-Claire. "Georges Lefebvre, historien et le peuple." *Annales historiques de la Révolution française* 51 (1979), 357–73.

Lavisse, Ernest. *Histoire de France depuis les origines jusqu'à la Révolution.* 9 vols. Paris: Hachette, 1900–11.

——. *Histoire de France contemporaine depuis la Révolution jusqu'à la paix de 1919.* 9 vols. Paris: Hachette, 1920–22.

Le Goff, Jacques. *History and Memory.* Trans. Steven Rendall and Elizabeth Claman. New York: Columbia University Press, 1992.

Le Goff, Jacques, Roger Chartier, and Jacques Revel, eds. *La Nouvelle Histoire.* Paris: Retz-C.E.P.L., 1978.

Le Roy Ladurie, Emmanuel. *Montaillou: The Promised Land of Error.* Trans. Barbara Bray. New York: Random House, 1979.

Lefebvre, Georges. *The Coming of the French Revolution.* Trans. R. R. Palmer. Princeton: Princeton University Press, 1947.

——. *Le Directoire.* Paris: Colin, 1946.

——. "D'Elle." *Annales historiques de la Révolution française* 41 (1969), 570–73.

——. *Etudes sur la Révolution française.* Paris: Presses Universitaires de France, 1954.

——. "Le Mythe de la Révolution française." *Annales historiques de la Révolution française* 28 (1956), 337–45.

——. *La Naissance de l'historiographie moderne.* Paris: Flammarion, 1971.

——. *Napoléon.* Paris: Alcan, 1935.

——. *Les Paysans du Nord pendant la Révolution française.* 2 vols. Paris: F. Rieder, 1924.

——. "Pro Domo." *Annales historiques de la Révolution française* 19 (1947), 188–90.

——. "A propos d'un congrès." *Annales historiques de la Révolution française* 17 (1940), 56–61.

——. *La Révolution française.* Paris: Presses Universitaires de France, 1930.

——. *Les Thermidoriens.* 2d ed. Paris: Colin, 1946.

Léger, François, "Philippe Ariès: L'Histoire d'un historien." *La Revue universelle des faits et des idées* 65 (1986), 63–73.

Leitch, Vincent B. *Deconstructive Criticism: An Advanced Introduction.* New York: Columbia University Press, 1983.

Lentricchia, Frank. *Ariel and the Police: Michel Foucault, William James, Wallace Stevens.* Madison: University of Wisconsin Press, 1988.

Leroi-Gourhan, André. *Le Geste et la parole: La Mémoire et les rythmes.* 2 vols. Paris: Albin Michel, 1965.

Levine, Joseph M. *Humanism and History: Origins of Modern English Historiography.* Ithaca: Cornell University Press, 1987.

Levinson, Marjorie, ed. *Rethinking Historicism.* Oxford: Blackwell, 1989.

Lewis, Bernard. *History: Remembered, Recovered, Invented.* Princeton: Princeton University Press, 1975.

Lichtheim, George. *Marxism in Modern France.* New York: Columbia University Press, 1966.

Lipsitz, George. *Time Passages: Collective Memory and American Popular Culture.* Minneapolis: University of Minnesota Press, 1990.

Liu, Alan. *Wordsworth: The Sense of History.* Stanford: Stanford University Press, 1989.

Lorayne, Harry. *Harry Lorayne's Page-a-Minute Memory Book.* New York: Holt, Rinehart, and Winston, 1985.

Lord, Albert B. *The Singer of Tales.* Cambridge: Harvard University Press, 1960.

Lowenthal, David. *The Past Is a Foreign Country.* Cambridge: Cambridge University Press, 1985.

Löwith, Karl. *Meaning in History.* Chicago: University of Chicago Press, 1949.

Luria, Alexander R. *Cognitive Development: Its Cultural and Social Foundations.* Trans. Martin Lopez-Morillas and Lynn Solotaroff. Ed. Michael Cole. Cambridge: Harvard University Press, 1976.

———. *The Making of Mind: A Personal Account of Soviet Psychology.* Ed. Michael Cole and Sheila Cole. Cambridge: Harvard University Press, 1979.

———. *The Man with a Shattered World.* Trans. Lynn Solotaroff. Cambridge: Harvard University Press, 1972.

———. *The Mind of a Mnemonist.* Trans. Lynn Solotaroff. Cambridge: Harvard University Press, 1968.

Maier, Charles S. *The Unmasterable Past: History, Holocaust, and the German National Identity.* Cambridge: Harvard University Press, 1988.

Mandelbaum, Maurice. *History, Man, and Reason.* Baltimore: Johns Hopkins University Press, 1971.

Mandrou, Robert. "L'Histoire des mentalités." *Encyclopaedia universalis* 8 (1968 ed.), 436–38.

———. *An Introduction to Modern France.* Trans. R. E. Hallmark. New York: Harper & Row, 1975.

Marchand, Philip. *Marshall McLuhan: The Medium and the Messenger.* New York: Ticknor & Fields, 1989.

Martin, Luther H., Huck Gutman, and Patrick H. Hutton, eds. *Technologies of the Self: A Seminar with Michel Foucault.* Amherst: University of Massachusetts Press, 1988.

Mayeur, Jean-Marie. *Les Débuts de la Troisième République, 1871–1898.* Paris: Editions du Seuil, 1973.

McGrath, William J. *Freud's Discovery of Psychoanalysis: The Politics of Hysteria.* Ithaca: Cornell University Press, 1986.

McKibben, Bill. *The Age of Missing Information*. New York: Random House, 1992.

McLuhan, Marshall. *The Gutenberg Galaxy: The Making of Typographic Man*. Toronto: University of Toronto Press, 1962.

———. *Letters of Marshall McLuhan*. Ed. Matie Molinaro, Corine McLuhan, and William Toye. Toronto: Oxford University Press, 1987.

———. "The Memory Theatre." *Encounter* 28 (1967), 61–66.

———. *Understanding Media: The Extension of Man*. New York: McGraw-Hill, 1964.

McLuhan, Marshall, and Quentin Fiore. *The Medium Is the Message*. Ed. Jerome Agel. New York: Bantam Books, 1967.

McNeill, William H. *Plagues and Peoples*. Garden City, N.Y.: Anchor, 1976.

Megill, Allan. "Foucault, Structuralism, and the Ends of History." *Journal of Modern History* 51 (1979), 451–503.

———. *Prophets of Extremity*. Berkeley: University of California Press, 1985.

Mell, Donald C., Theodore E. D. Braun, and Lucia Palmer, eds. *Man, God, and Nature in the Enlightenment*. East Lansing, Mich.: Colleagues, 1988.

Meyerhoff, Hans, ed. *The Philosophy of History in Our Times*. Garden City, N.Y.: Doubleday, 1959.

Meyrowitz, Joshua. *No Sense of Place: The Impact of Electronic Media on Social Behavior*. Oxford: Oxford University Press, 1985.

Michelet, Jules. *Histoire de la Révolution française*. Ed. Gérard Walter. 2 vols. 1847; Paris: Nouvelle Revue Française, 1939.

———. *Œuvres complètes de Michelet*. Ed. Paul Viallaneix. Paris: Flammarion, 1971.

———. *The People*. Trans. John P. McKay. 1846; Urbana: University of Illinois Press, 1973.

———. "Vico." In *Biographie universelle* 48 (1827), 362–73.

Middleton, A. E. *Memory Systems, Old and New*. 3d rev. ed. New York: G. S. Fellows, 1888.

Middleton, David, and Derek Edwards, eds. *Collective Remembering*. London: Sage, 1990.

Miller, James. *The Passion of Michel Foucault*. New York: Simon & Schuster, 1993.

Minson, Jeffrey. *Genealogies of Morals: Nietzsche, Foucault, Donzelot and the Eccentricity of Ethics*. New York: St. Martin's Press, 1985.

Mitzman, Arthur. *Michelet, Historian*. New Haven: Yale University Press, 1990.

Mooney, Michael. *Vico in the Tradition of Rhetoric*. Princeton: Princeton University Press, 1985.

Moorman, Mary. *William Wordsworth: A Biography*. 2 vols. Oxford: Clarendon, 1957–65.

Mosse, George. *Fallen Soldiers: Reshaping the Memory of the World Wars*. Oxford: Oxford University Press, 1990.

Munz, Peter. "The Evocation of the Senses by Freud and Proust." In *"Sinnlichkeit in Bild und Klang": Festschrift für Paul Hoffmann zum 70*. Ed. Hansgerd Delbrück. Stuttgart: Hans-Dieter Heinz, 1987.

———. "The Rhetoric of Rhetoric." *Journal of the History of Ideas* 51 (1990), 121–42.

Myres, John L. *Homer and His Critics*. London: Routledge, 1958.

Namer, Emile. "G.B. Vico et Giordano Bruno." *Archives de philosophie* 40 (1977), 107–14.

Namer, Gérard. "Affectivité et temporalité de la mémoire." *L'Homme et la société* 90 (1988), 9–14.

————. *La Commémoration en France, 1944–82*. Paris: S.P.A.G./Papyrus, 1983.

Nehamas, Alexander. "The Examined Life of Michel Foucault." *The New Republic.* 15 February 1993, 27–36.

Nora, Pierre, ed. *Les Lieux de mémoire.* 3 vols. Paris: Gallimard, 1984–92.

Nye, Robert A. *Crime, Madness and Politics in Modern France.* Princeton: Princeton University Press, 1984.

O'Brien, Patricia. *The Promise of Punishment: Prisons in Nineteenth-Century France.* Princeton: Princeton University Press, 1982.

O'Farrell, Clare. *Foucault: Historian or Philosopher.* New York: St. Martin's Press, 1989.

Olney, James, ed. *Autobiography: Essays Theoretical and Critical.* Princeton: Princeton University Press, 1980.

————. *Metaphors of Self: The Meaning of Autobiography.* Princeton: Princeton University Press, 1972.

Ong, Walter J. "McLuhan as Teacher: The Future is a Thing of the Past." *Journal of Communication* 31 (1981), 129–35.

————. *Orality and Literacy: The Technologizing of the Word.* London: Methuen, 1982.

————. *The Presence of the Word.* New Haven: Yale University Press, 1967.

————. *Ramus: Method and the Decay of Dialogue.* Cambridge: Harvard University Press, 1958.

————. *Rhetoric, Romance, and Technology.* Ithaca: Cornell University Press, 1971.

Onorato, Richard J. *The Character of the Poet: Wordsworth in "The Prelude."* Princeton: Princeton University Press, 1971.

Orr, Linda. *Headless History: Nineteenth-Century French Historiography of the Revolution.* Ithaca: Cornell University Press, 1990.

Ozouf, Mona, Pierre Chaunu, and Régis Debray. "Que commémore-t-on?" *Le Nouvel Observateur* 1278 (4 to 10 May 1989).

Pagels, Elaine. *The Gnostic Gospels.* New York: Random House, 1981.

Palmer, R. R. *The Age of the Democratic Revolution.* 2 vols. Princeton: Princeton University Press, 1959–64.

————. "Georges Lefebvre: The Peasants and the French Revolution." *Journal of Modern History* 31 (1959), 329–42.

Paris, Aimé. *Principes et applications diverses de la mnémonique.* 7th ed. Paris: author, 1833.

Parry, Milman. *The Making of Homeric Verse: The Collected Papers of Milman Parry.* Ed. Adam Parry. Oxford: Clarendon, 1971.

Patterson, Graeme. *History and Communications: Harold Innis, Marshall McLuhan, the Intepretation of History.* Toronto: University of Toronto Press, 1990.

Peabody, Berkley. *The Winged Word.* Albany: State University of Albany Press, 1975.

Pertué, Michel. "La Révolution française: Est-elle terminée?" *Annales historiques de la Révolution française* 54 (1982), 329–48.

Piette, Christine. "Réflexions historiques sur les traditions révolutionnaires à Paris au XIXe siècle." *Historical Reflections* 12 (1985), 403–18.

Pocock, J. G. A. *The Ancient Constitution and the Feudal Law.* Cambridge: Cambridge University Press, 1957.

————. *Politics, Language and Time: Essays on Political Thought and History.* London: Methuen, 1972.

Pomper, Philip. *The Structure of Mind in History: Five Major Figures in Psychohistory.* New York: Columbia University Press, 1985.

Pons, Alain. "Introduction." In *Encyclopédie, ou dictionnaire raisonné des sciences des arts et des métiers*. Ed. Denis Diderot. Paris: Flammarion, 1986, 13–65.

Post, L. A. "Ancient Memory Systems." *The Classical Weekly* 25/14 (1 February 1932), 105–09.

Poster, Mark. *Critical Theory and Poststructuralism: In Search of a Context*. Ithaca: Cornell University Press, 1989.

———. *Existential Marxism in Postwar France*. Princeton: Princeton University Press, 1975.

———. *Foucault, Marxism, and History*. London: Polity Press, 1984.

———. *The Mode of Information: Poststructuralism and the Social Context*. Chicago: University of Chicago Press, 1990.

Proctor, Robert E. *Education's Great Amnesia: Reconsidering the Humanities from Petrarch to Freud*. Bloomington: Indiana University Press, 1988.

Ranum, Orest. *Artisans of Glory*. Chapel Hill: University of North Carolina Press, 1980.

Raphaël, Freddy. "Le Travail de la mémoire et les limites de l'histoire orale." *Annales: Economies, sociétés, civilisations* 35 (1980), 127–45.

Raulet, Gérard. "Structuralism and Post-Structuralism: An Interview with Michel Foucault." *Telos* 55 (1983), 195–211.

Rearick, Charles. "Festivals in Modern France: The Experience of the Third Republic." *Journal of Contemporary History* 12 (1977), 435–60.

———. "Festivals and Politics: The Michelet Centennial of 1898." *Historians in Politics* 1 (1974), 59–78.

Renan, Ernest. *La Vie de Jésus*. Paris: Gallimard, 1974.

Revel, Jacques. "Histoire et sciences sociales: Les Paradigmes des *Annales*." *Annales: Economies, Sociétés, Civilisations* 34 (1979), 1360–76.

Richardson, Alan. "Wordsworth at the Crossroads: 'Spots of Time' in the 'Two-Part Prelude.'" *The Wordsworth Circle* 19 (1988), 15–20.

Ricoeur, Paul. *Freud and Philosophy*. Trans. Denis Savage. New Haven: Yale University Press, 1970.

———. *The Reality of the Historical Past*. Milwaukee: Marquette University Press, 1984.

———. *Time and Narrative*. Trans. Kathleen McLaughlin and David Pellauer. 3 vols. Chicago: University of Chicago, 1983–85.

Rigney, Ann. *The Rhetoric of Historical Representation: Three Narrative Histories of the French Revolution*. Cambridge: Cambridge University Press, 1990.

Roazen, Paul. *Encountering Freud: The Politics and Histories of Psychoanalysis*. New Brunswick, N.J.: Transaction Publishers, 1990.

Rosenfield, Israel. *The Invention of Memory: A New View of the Brain*. New York: Basic Books, 1988.

Rossi, Paolo. *Clavis universalis: Arti mnemoniche e logica combinatoria da Lullo a Leibniz*. Milan: Ricciardi, 1960.

———. *The Dark Abyss of Time*. Trans. Lydia G. Cochrane. Chicago: University of Chicago Press, 1984.

———. *Frances Bacon: From Magic to Science*. Trans. Sacha Rabinovitch. Chicago: University of Chicago Press, 1968.

———. "Schede Vichiane." *La Rassegna della letteratura italiana* 62 (1958), 375–83.

Roth, Michael S. *Psycho-Analysis as History: Negation and Freedom in Freud*. Ithaca: Cornell University Press, 1987.

Rothman, David J. *The Discovery of the Asylum: Social Order and Disorder in the New Republic.* Boston: Little, Brown, 1971.

Rougerie, Jacques. "Mil huit cent soixante et onze." In *Colloque universitaire pour la commémoration du centenaire de la Commune de 1871.* Paris: Editions ouvrière, 1972, 49–77.

Rousseau, Jean-Jacques. *The Confessions.* Trans. J. M. Cohen. 1781; Baltimore: Penguin, 1953.

Rousso, Henry. *The Vichy Syndrome: History and Memory in France since 1944.* Trans. Arthur Goldhammer. Cambridge: Harvard University Press, 1991.

Sacks, Oliver. "The Lost Mariner." *The New York Review of Books,* 16 February 1984, 18–19.

———. "Neurology and the Soul." *New York Review of Books,* 22 November 1990.

Sanson, Rosemonde. *Les 14 Juillet (1789–1975): Fête et conscience nationale.* Paris: Flammarion, 1976.

Schaeffer, John D. *Sensus Communis: Vico, Rhetoric, and the Limits of Relativism.* Durham, N.C.: Duke University Press, 1990.

Schiller, A. Arthur. *Roman Law: Mechanisms of Development.* The Hague: Mouton, 1978.

Schorske, Carl E. *Fin-de-Siècle Vienna: Politics and Culture.* New York: Knopf, 1980.

Schwartz, Barry. "The Social Context of Commemoration: A Study in Collective Memory." *Social Forces* 61 (1982), 374–402.

Schwartz, Barry, Yael Zerubavel, and Bernice Barnett. "The Recovery of Masada: A Study in Collective Memory." *Sociological Quarterly* 27 (1986), 147–64.

Scott, Joan Wallach. *Gender and the Politics of History.* New York: Columbia University Press, 1988.

———. *The Glassworkers of Carmaux.* Cambridge: Harvard University Press, 1974.

Sedgwick, Peter. *Psycho Politics.* New York: Harper & Row, 1982.

Seigel, Jerrold. "Avoiding the Subject: A Foucaultian Itinerary." *Journal of the History of Ideas* 51 (1990), 273–99.

Sheldrake, Rupert. "Memory and Morphic Resonance." *ReVision* 10 (1987), 9–12.

———. *The Presence of the Past: Morphic Resonance and the Habits of Nature.* New York: Times Books, 1988.

Shumway, David. *Michel Foucault.* Boston: Twayne Publishers, 1989.

Silberstein, Laurence J., ed. *New Perspectives on Israeli History.* New York: New York University Press, 1990.

Simon, John K. "A Conversation with Michel Foucault." *Partisan Review* 38 (1971), 192–201.

Singleton, Charles, S., ed. *Art, Science and History in the Renaissance.* Baltimore: Johns Hopkins University Press, 1967.

Smart, Barry. *Foucault, Marxism and Critique.* London: Routledge, 1983.

———. *Michel Foucault.* London: Tavistock, 1985.

Soboul, Albert. "Tradition et création dans le mouvement révolutionnaire français au xixe siècle." *Le Mouvement social* 79 (1972), 15–31.

———. *Understanding the French Revolution.* Trans. April Anne Knutson. New York: International Publishers, 1988.

Solé, Jacques. *Questions of the French Revolution: An Historical Overview.* Trans. Shelley Temchin. New York: Pantheon, 1989.

Sollers, Philippe, ed. *Théorie d'ensemble.* Paris: 1968.

Sorabji, Richard. *Aristotle on Memory.* Providence: Brown University Press, 1972.

Sorlin, Pierre. *La Société française.* 2 vols. Paris: Arthaud, 1969.

Spence, Jonathan D. *The Memory Palace of Matteo Ricci.* New York: Viking, 1984.

Spiegel, Gabrielle. "History and Post-Modernism." *Past and Present* 135 (May 1992), 194–208.

———. "History, Historicism and the Social Logic of the Text in the Middle Ages." *Speculum* 65 (1990), 59–86.

Stannard, David E. *Shrinking History: On Freud and the Failure of Psychohistory.* Oxford: Oxford University Press, 1980.

Starobinski, Jean. *Words upon Words.* Trans. Olivia Emmet. New Haven: Yale University Press, 1979.

Steinberg, Michael. "The Twelve Tables and Their Origins: An Eighteenth-Century Debate." *Journal of the History of Ideas* 43 (1982), 379–96.

Stock, Brian. *The Implications of Literacy.* Princeton: Princeton University Press, 1983.

———. *Listening for the Text.* Baltimore: Johns Hopkins University Press, 1990.

Stoianovich, Traian. *French Historical Method: the "Annales" Paradigm.* Ithaca: Cornell University Press, 1976.

Stone, Lawrence, and Michel Foucault. "An Exchange with Michel Foucault." *New York Review of Books,* 31 March 1983.

———. "The Massacre of the Innocents." *New York Review of Books,* 14 November 1974.

Sturrock, John, ed. *Structuralism and Since: From Lévi-Strauss to Derrida.* Oxford: Oxford University Press, 1979.

Suratteau, Jean-René. "Georges Lefebvre, disciple de Jaurès?" *Annales historiques de la Révolution française* 51 (1979), 374–98.

Tagliacozzo, Giorgio. *The Arbor Scientiae Reconceived and the History of Vico's Resurrection.* Atlantic Highlands, N.J.: Humanities Press, 1993.

———. "General Education as Unity of Knowledge: A Theory Based on Vichian Principles." *Social Research* 43 (1976), 768–96.

———. "Toward a History of Recent Anglo-American Vico Scholarship." *New Vico Studies* 1 (1983)–5 (1987).

———, ed. *Vico: Past and Present.* Atlantic Highlands, N.J.: Humanities Press, 1981.

Tagliacozzo, Giorgio, and Donald Phillip Verene, eds. *Giambattista Vico's Science of Humanity.* Baltimore: Johns Hopkins University Press, 1976.

Tagliacozzo, Giorgio, and Hayden V. White, eds. *Giambattista Vico: An International Symposium.* Baltimore: Johns Hopkins University Press, 1969.

Taylor, Charles. *Sources of the Self: The Making of Modern Identity.* Cambridge: Harvard University Press, 1989.

Terdiman, Richard. "Deconstructing Memory: On Representing the Past and Theorizing Culture in France since the Revolution." *Diacritics* 15 (1985), 13–36.

Thompson, Paul. *The Voice of the Past.* 2d ed. Oxford: Oxford University Press, 1988.

Thomson, David. *Democracy in France since 1870.* 5th ed. Oxford: Oxford University Press, 1969.

Tocqueville, Alexis de. *L'Ancien Régime et la Révolution.* 7th ed. Paris: Lévy, 1866.

Toynbee, Arnold J. *A Study of History: Reconsiderations.* Vol. 12. Oxford: Oxford University Press, 1961.

Turkle, Sherry. *Psychoanalytic Politics: Freud's French Revolution.* New York: Basic Books, 1978.

Vann, Richard T. "The Youth of *Centuries of Childhood.*" *History and Theory* 21 (1982), 279–97.

Vansina, Jan. *Oral Tradition as History.* Madison: University of Wisconsin Press, 1985.

Veeser, H. Aram, ed. *The New Historicism.* New York: Routledge, 1989.

Verene, Donald Phillip. "Eliade's Vichianism: The Regeneration of Time and the Terror of History." *New Vico Studies* 4 (1986), 115–21.

———. *Vico's Science of Imagination.* Ithaca: Cornell University Press, 1981.

Veyne, Paul. *Comment on écrit l'histoire.* Paris: Editions du Seuil, 1971.

Viallaneix, Paul. *La Voie royale: Essai sur l'idée de peuple dans l'œuvre de Michelet.* Paris: Flammarion, 1971.

Vico, Giambattista. *The Autobiography of Giambattista Vico.* Trans. and ed. Max Harold Fisch and Thomas Goddard Bergin. Ithaca: Cornell University Press, 1944.

———. *The New Science of Giambattista Vico.* 3d ed. (1744). Trans. and ed. Thomas Goddard Bergin and Max Harold Fisch. Ithaca: Cornell University Press, 1968.

———. *On the Most Ancient Wisdom of the Italians.* Trans. Lucia M. Palmer. 1710; Ithaca: Cornell University Press, 1988.

———. *On the Study Methods of Our Time.* Trans. Elio Gianturco. Ed. Donald Phillip Verene. 1709; Ithaca: Cornell University Press, 1990.

Vromen, Suzanne. "The Sociology of Maurice Halbwachs." Ph.D. Diss., New York University, 1975.

Wachtel, Nathan. "Memory and History: An Introduction." *History and Anthropology* 2 (1986), 210–211.

Warner, Michael. *The Letters of the Republic: Publication and the Public Sphere in Eighteenth-Century America.* Cambridge: Harvard University Press, 1990.

Watson, Alan. *Rome of the Twelve Tables.* Princeton: Princeton University Press, 1975.

Weaver, Bennett. "On Wordsworth's *Prelude*: The Poetic Function of Memory." *Studies in Philology* 34 (1937), 552–63.

———. "Wordsworth's *Prelude*: An Intimation of Certain Problems in Criticism." *Studies in Philology* 31 (1934), 534–40.

Weill, Georges. *Histoire du parti républicain en France, 1814–1870.* Paris: Alcan, 1928.

Westman, Robert S., and J. E. McGuire, eds. *Hermeticism and the Scientific Revolution.* Los Angeles: William Andrews Clark Memorial Library, University of California, 1977.

White, Hayden V. *The Content of the Form.* Baltimore: Johns Hopkins University Press, 1987.

———. "Foucault Decoded: Notes from Underground." *History and Theory* 12 (1975), 23–54.

———. *Metahistory: The Historical Imagination in Nineteenth-Century Europe.* Baltimore: Johns Hopkins University Press, 1973.

Whyte, Lancelot Law. *The Unconscious before Freud.* New York: Basic Books, 1960.

Wilcox, Donald J. *The Measure of Times Past.* Chicago: University of Chicago Press, 1987.

Wilson, Adrian. "The Infancy of the History of Childhood: An Appraisal of Philippe Ariès." *History and Theory* 19 (1980), 132–53.

Wilson, C. W. *Library of the Palestine Pilgrims' Text Society.* Vol. 1. 1887; New York: AMS Press, 1971.

Wolman, Benjamin, ed. *International Encyclopedia of Psychiatry, Psychology, Psychoanalysis, and Neurology.* 12 vols. New York: Aesculapius Publishers, 1977.

Wordsworth, William. *The Prelude.* Ed. Jonathan Wordsworth, M. H. Abrams, and Stephen Gill. 1799, 1805, 1850; New York: Norton, 1979.

Wright, Gordon. *The Reshaping of French Democracy.* 1948; Boston: Fertig, 1970.

Wuthnow, Robert, ed. *Cultural Analysis.* London: Routledge, 1984.

Yates, Frances. *The Art of Memory.* Chicago: University of Chicago Press, 1966.

———. *Collected Essays of Frances Yates.* Ed. J. N. Hillgarth and J. B. Trapp. 3 vols. London: Routledge & Kegan Paul, 1984.

———. *Giordano Bruno and the Hermetic Tradition.* 1964; Chicago: University of Chicago Press, 1979.

Zagorin, Peter. "Historiography and Postmodernism: Reconsiderations." *History and Theory* 29 (1990), 263–74.

Zerubavel, Eviatar. *The Seven Day Circle.* New York: Free Press, 1985.

Zerubavel, Yael. "The Politics of Interpretation: Tel Hai in Israel's Collective Memory." *Journal of the Association of Jewish Studies* 16 (1991), 133–59.

———. *Recovered Roots: Collective Memory and the Making of the Israeli National Tradition.* (Forthcoming).

Zonabend, Françoise. *The Enduring Memory: Time and History in a French Village.* Trans. Anthony Forster. Manchester: Manchester University Press, 1984.

INDEX

Abel, Félix, 85
Agulhon, Maurice, 2–4, 21, 145
Archaeology as a memory problem, 21, 105,
107, 130, 161–63
Ariès, Philippe: his background and intellectual formation, 93–95; his conception of
history, 95–98, 168; his critique of modern
historiography, 96–97, 99; and historiography as a memory problem, 23–26, 92–93,
97–98, 130, 168; his history of childhood
and family, 91, 102–104; and the history of
collective mentalities, 91–92, 100–101; and
the history of commemoration, 2, 20; and
the history of death and dying, 2, 104; and
the history of French historiography, 24,
92, 98–100, 156; influenced by the *Annales*
historians, 94, 102; influenced by Halbwachs, 74; notes his affinities with Foucault, 105; *Le Temps de l'histoire*, 24, 92,
94–102; on tradition, 92–98, 100–102, 129–
30; World War II as a turning point in his
life, 93–95, 100
Aristotle: and the art of memory, 30–31
Augustine: his *Confessions*, 53
Aulard, Alphonse, 146–47, 152, 153; his
background, 133; his debt to Comte, 134;
and historicism, 157; his interpretation of
the French Revolution, 133–35; his role in
the centennial of the Revolution, 135; his
view of Michelet, 134–35
Autobiography: and the emergence of modern historical thinking, 52–53, 57, 155; as a
genre, 53; and introspection, 53, 58, 151–
52; and mnemonics, 56

Bacon, Francis: and mnemonics, 32
Bainville, Jacques, 95
Barthes, Roland, 110
Bartlett, Frederic, 17, 74

Battistini, Andrea, 37
Bergson, Henri, 74, 151
Bloch, Marc, 75, 94, 117
Braudel, Fernand, 117
Bruno, Giordano, 11, 31, 61
Butler, Samuel, 165
Butterfield, Herbert, 21, 124, 128

Camillo, Giulio, 11, 31
Canguilhem, Georges, 109
Cellini, Benvenuto: his *Autobiography*, 53
Chateaubriand, François de, 86–87
Chronology and memory. *See* Time: mne-
monic schemes; Memory, the art of: and
temporal frameworks
Cobban, Alfred: his critique of the historiog-
raphy of the French Revolution, 142–43
Cochin, Augustin, 144
Collingwood, Robin G., 157, 158
Commemoration: history of, 4–5, 8, 80–84;
mnemonics of, 79–80
Communication, changes in the technologies
of: impact on postmodern historiography,
122–23; and McLuhan's thesis, 13; and
Ong's thesis, 13–17; and Vico's new sci-
ence of history, 36–37. *See also* Orality/
literacy problem
Comte, Auguste, 76, 134, 149, 150
Custom. *See* Habits of mind; Tradition

Dalman, Gustave, 85
Danton, Georges-Jacques: as icon of the
French Revolution, 132, 140
Darnton, Robert, 167
Davis, Natalie, 167
Dee, John, 11
Deleuze, Gilles, 109
Derrida, Jacques, 50, 110
Dilthey, Wilhelm, 157, 158

UNIVERSITY PRESS OF NEW ENGLAND

publishes books under its own imprint and is the publisher for Brandeis University Press, Brown University Press, Clark University Press, University of Connecticut, Dartmouth College, Middlebury College Press, University of New Hampshire, University of Rhode Island, Tufts University, University of Vermont, and Wesleyan University Press.

LIBRARY OF CONGRESS CATALOGING-IN-PUBLICATION DATA

Hutton, Patrick H.

History as an art of memory / Patrick H. Hutton.

p.   cm.

Includes bibliographical references and index.

ISBN 0–87451–631–5. — ISBN 0–87451–637–4 (pbk.)

1. Historiography.   2. Memory.   3. History—Philosophy.

I. Title.

D13.H87   1993

907'.2—dc20   93-17246